G000241795

RESTORING THE KINGDOM

Restoring the Kingdom

The Radical Christianity
of the House Church Movement

Andrew Walker

eagle

Guildford, Surrey

Copyright © 1998 Dr Andrew Walker

The right of Andrew Walker to be identified as author of this work has been asserted by him in accordance with the Copyright, Design and Patents Act 1988.

British Library Cataloguing in Publication Data. A catalogue record for this book is available from the British Library.

Published by Eagle, an imprint of Inter Publishing Service (IPS) Ltd, St Nicholas House, 14 The Mount, Guildford, Surrey GU2 5HN.

All rights reserved. No part of this publication may be reproduced or transmitted in any form or by any means, electronic or mechanical, including photocopying, recording or any information storage and retrieval system, without either prior permission in writing from the publisher or a licence permitting restricted copying. In the United Kingdom such licences are issued by the Publishers Licensing Society Ltd, 90 Tottenham Court Road, London W1P 9HE.

Scripture quotations used in this book are noted as folows:

NEB, *The New English Bible*, (copyright:
NIV, *The Holy Bible, New International Version* (copyright: 1973, 1978, 1984 by International Bible Society. Used by permission of Hodder & Stoughton, a Division of Hodder Headline.
NKJ, *New King James* (copyright:

Typeset by Eagle Publishing, Guildford
Printed by Cox & Wyman, Reading
ISBN No: 0 86347 160 9

Dedication

For my mother and to the memory of my father,
Rev Victor John Lacey-Walker.

CONTENTS

Preface   13
Introduction   17
Prologue   27

Part One The Establishment of the Kingdom
            A History to 1985

1. House Churches? Never Heard of Them!   33
2. The Origins of Restoration   51
3. The Restored Kingdom Emerges   66
4. The Kingdom Established in Division   87
5. Extending the Kingdom   110

Part Two The Radical Kingdom
            An Evaluation until 1985

6. The Radical Principles of Restorationism
                              (Part One)   129
7. The Radical Principles of Restorationism
                              (Part Two)   151
8. The Structure and Shape of Kingdom Life   172
9. A Kingdom Tour   197
10 Is the Restoration Movement a Denomination? 212
11. Catholic Apostolics and Christian Brethren   228
12. Classical Pentecostalism and Restorationism   249
13. The Kingdom Under Attack   268

**Part Three The Breakdown of the Kingdom
            1985–90**

14. The Beginnings of Restorationist Decline   301
15. The Changing Character of R1   318
16. Drifting Apart and Breaking Away: Life in R2   341
Conclusion The End of an Era   368

Epilogue The Great Yorkshire Showground
            August 1989   373

Appendix 1 The Final Word   377
Appendix 2 Money, Sex and Power   379

Notes   383

ACKNOWLEDGEMENTS

For the initial preparation for the 1985 edition, I was particularly helped in 1982/1983, when working for the BBC, by interviews with Joyce Thurman, Arthur Wallis, Keri Jones, Terry Virgo, Dick Simms, Martyn Dunsford and David Matthew. The press officer for the Dales Bible Week in 1982, Richard White, was especially helpful.

Special gratitude is also due to David Matthew in 1984 for his in-depth interview and subsequent meetings, phone calls, and material sent. I enjoyed my frank interviews with Bryn Jones and Goos Vedder. A special thank you to Bryn Jones and Roger Day for subsequent information and further in-depth interviews in 1989. Timothy Larsen's help was invaluable in explaining the development of Covenant Ministries from the mid 1980s to the present day.

This new edition is indebted to correspondence with Terry Virgo and an in-depth interview in 1989.

Gerald Coates and John Noble gave me invaluable interviews in 1984 and 1987. Gerald also sent useful information on Pioneer and arranged an interview in 1989 and early 1997.

Special mention must be made of Dave and Pat Tomlinson who, since the early 1980s at Middlesbrough to the present day, have been my friends as well as reliable informants. Help and friendship have also come over the years from Vivien Culver, and Peter and Rita Fenwick at Sheffield, as well as Brian and Irene Howell at Gateshead. Mention must be made of the contributions of Rodney Kingston, Tony Morton, John MacLauchlan, David Mansell, Philip Mohabir, David Matthews, Peter Lyne, members of Team Work, Team Spirit and Pioneer.

I remember with special thanks and admiration Ted Rotherham and John Race, who were prepared to share their stories with me. A special debt is owed to Maurice Smith, who was as helpful as a research assistant, and to George Tarleton, who spent literally hours talking to me on the phone. I subsequently interviewed him and Maurice at his home in 1989.

Deep appreciation also for all those hundreds of Restorationists I have briefly talked to, and those whom I interviewed but who asked not to be named.

I would like also to thank Tom Smail, Michael Harper and Douglas MacBain for their help in relating the Renewal to the house churches. Thanks also for the (all too brief) conversations with Roger Forster.

The Rev Stephen Quicke, Dr David Russell, the Rev Bernard Green, and Dr Nigel Wright helped me to see things from the perspective of the Baptist Union. Since I first met him at the Lytham fellowship in Lancashire in the 1980s, Nigel has become a friend, colleague and valued confidant.

My historical chapters on the precursors to Restorationism were greatly helped by the late John Boyes and John Baigent of the Open Brethren. Work on Irving and the Catholic Apostolic Church were aided by trustees of the CAC and Dr Gordon Strachan. The Rev Desmond Cartwright was most helpful in my study of Elim; thanks also to Rev John Lancaster and Rev Brian Long. A thank you to G.W. Robson and Norman Cliff for putting me right on Watchman Nee.

My sociological approaches were helped over the years by conversations with Bryan Wilson and David Martin, and feedback from postgraduate students from All Souls, Oxford, the London School of Economics, and my own doctoral students at King's College, London.

I thank the BBC for permission to use material from the programme *Front Room Gospel*, and for the support of the producer David Coomes and the presenter Rosemary Hartill.

Lastly, although it was some years ago now, I would like to thank my wife who did all she could to keep our three young children quiet and amused while I ate up the long hours typing in the front room. Without her selfless support, I could not have finished this book.

Andrew Walker, 1997

PREFACE TO THE FOURTH EDITION

I have often been asked why I have never written a sequel to *Restoring the Kingdom*. The short answer is that I have been busy with other projects. Now, however, as charismatic events have unfolded in the 1990s, I realize that being busy is not the only reason. Restorationism has become engulfed in a whole stream of new events of such plurality and complexity that I doubt whether – even if I had had the time – I could have controlled the material in a satisfactory way.

Nevertheless, a revised and expanded edition of the original book would seem to be useful. Clive Calver, the former General Secretary of the Evangelical Alliance, at a conference on postmodernity at London Bible College in January 1996, publicly suggested that a new edition would be helpful to an historical understanding of what today are often called 'new churches'. For many younger charismatics, not to mention students of religion, the Restorationist story is largely unknown. Others have forgotten it or choose not to remember it.

Written in 1985, *Restoring the Kingdom* was my first book. With hindsight, I would have employed a more conventional academic apparatus if I were writing it again. I would also adopt the usual literary convention of using surnames instead of calling everyone by their Christian names; such a usage gives a false sense of familiarity, even if it is normal practice in house church circles.

Using sociological methods and concepts, but writing in a style best described as academic journalism, I attempted a book that would both tell the story and offer some analysis. Except for the historical sections, research was done on the hoof, and the writing was hurried and somewhat breathless. I did not expect that the book would become definitive (if only by default, as no other major work has yet been written on the movement), and as chapter 1 of this edition clearly states, I did not intend it to be so.

The new Introduction and Part Three of this edition contain substantial unpublished material and some content from the short-lived second edition. Otherwise, much of the text is taken from the original book, with some corrections of factual errors and conceptual weaknesses. I was faced, however, with a logistical problem in writing this expanded and revised edition. Research for *Restoring the Kingdom*, which was originally carried out in 1982–85, had to be updated with fieldwork conducted in 1986–90, and subsequent interviews in 1996–97. In 1985, except for the historical material, Parts One and Two of this book were written primarily in the present tense. By the time I wrote up my later field research, several years had passed since I had conducted it, and over twelve years had elapsed since the publication of the first edition. In the event, I opted to write Part Three of this new edition in the past tense, as writing in the present tense would not only be artificial, but would also fail to reflect the fact that the new chapters were written with hindsight. Conversely, readers will appreciate that Parts One and Two were written with foresight, so that my initial assessments of Restorationist Christianity were hit and miss.

Readers may also be interested to know that out of the original 'Fort Lauderdale Five', only Charles Simpson, Bob Mumford and Derek Prince are still alive. Sadly, as this book records, Arthur Wallis has also died. John Noble has retired as an apostle of his Romford churches, which are no longer operational as a recognizable Restorationist network. He now lives with his wife in the Leatherhead area, and is the senior statesman without portfolio of the charismatic movement. David Tomlinson is neither an apostle nor a house church leader: he was ordained as a priest of the Church of England in June 1997. Peter Fenwick, if not quite a cessationist, has come out against all things charismatic in its 'Toronto Blessing' guise.

Juan Carlos Ortiz, whom many consider the founder of 'shepherding' theology and practice, is now associated with the television ministry of Robert Schuller, and has completely abandoned the tenets of his earlier position.

Sadly as this book went to press in November 1997 we heard of the untimely death of John Wimber.

INTRODUCTION TO THE FOURTH EDITION

BEYOND THE KINGDOM

'A week,' Harold Wilson once famously said, 'is a long time in politics.' What, we might wonder, is a long time in religion? Typically, in the past, we would think of time measured in units of half centuries or longer, but these days whole movements can rise and fall in a decade.

> Everything in society is speeded up. This is because in a world with access to a million ideologies via the mass media and international travel, almost nothing stays still: new input in the form of different revelations or improved methods of business and organisational management is always threatening to break into (and break up) established structures. Mutation, sudden change, and often rapid decay or collapse, become the hallmarks of many religious organisations.[1]

Perhaps these words bring to mind the many new religious movements scattered across the western hemisphere since the 1960s, from the Moonies to Hare Krishna. But rapid religious change is now also a hallmark of Christian formations – especially those of a revivalist nature.

The End of the House Church Movement?

Who would have thought, for example, that the fastest growing Christian movement in Britain of the 1980s – the house church movement – has now slowed down almost to a snail's pace? Nigel Wright, former lecturer in systematic theology at Spurgeon's was, as early as 1989, talking of its demise:

> I think the changes have been marked and radical, and that basically the whole thing has fallen apart. The original rhetoric was, 'this is the last chapter of the Church,

17

and we are all together in a covenant relationship' – but clearly, what has emerged is that they are not. They are no more together in a covenant relationship than the rest of us in the Church, and they are subject to the same problems – what Brunner calls the 'earthly' side of the Church: competition, ambition and the rest of it.[2]

Nigel Wright's words may seem strange in light of the fact that Terry Virgo and New Frontiers remain alive and well in the south-east of England (with an outpost as far away as the north-east, and over 20,000 people visiting the Stoneleigh Bible Week).[3] Furthermore, Bryn Jones and Covenant Ministries are firmly ensconced – complete with Bible College – in the Midlands with no sign at present that they are about to roll over and give up the ghost.[4] Indeed, Nigel's sentiments might seem even more misplaced given the national profile of Restoration's most successful son, Gerald Coates, and his Pioneer Network.[5]

Carried away by a new wave – There is a profound sense, however, in which Nigel is right. When I wrote the first edition of *Restoring the Kingdom* in 1985, the Restorationists (as I call the house church movement in this book) had already peaked. By 1989, the date of my third edition, the movement was fragmenting and fading. In the 1990s, pockets of Restorationism have survived, but many of the apostolic networks have either been disbanded or become less doctrinaire. We could usefully say that in so far as Restorationist churches are still in the news, they have become part of a different story.

This story is not a sequel to the house church movement, but an altogether more complex affair in which, over the last few years, we have witnessed evangelistic endeavour, new alignments, strange prophetic stirrings and sensational charismatic phenomena. The early 1990s saw the charismatic movement responding to the decade of evangelism. Perhaps we remember JIM (Jesus In Me), the somewhat enigmatic advertising campaign spearheaded

18

by Wyn Lewis of Elim. Or maybe we received a copy of Reinhard Bonnke's gospel booklet, *From Minus to Plus*, through our letterbox in 1993. If we missed these events, no doubt we participated in, heard of, or read about, the marching on the city streets of throngs of people shouting, 'Make way for King Jesus'. This initiative was instigated by Ichthus leaders Roger Forster and Graham Kendrick, who combined with Gerald Coates of Pioneer and Lynn Green of YWAM (Youth With A Mission).[6]

John Wimber, as he had done since his 'Third Wave' conference in Westminster Central Hall in 1984, continued to influence Anglican churches in the 1990s. Indeed, from the late 1980s, his close friendship with Terry Virgo both altered the spiritual atmosphere of New Frontiers (although not diluting its Restorationism) and opened the way to his influence in house churches, which were increasingly being called 'new churches'. It was Gerald Coates who championed the new church concept in the 1990s – not as a Restorationist enclave, but as any new charismatic and evangelical church outside the existing denominational structures. New churches are now legion in Great Britain, though their numbers are impossible to ascertain, and they do not constitute a denomination or a common ideology, nor even a single network (although to adopt charismatic argot, some still think of themselves as a 'stream').

Meanwhile, the classical Pentecostal churches, Elim and the Assemblies of God, have recovered from the forays on their fellowships by Restorationists in the 1980s. This recovery has led to a new-found confidence and greater inter-denominational co-operation with other evangelical churches. Kensington City Temple of Elim has moved into the forefront of charismatic activity in recent years, and under its dynamic leader, Colin Dye, has become probably the largest church (numerically) in Great Britain, with some 5,000 members.[7]

But the two most significant events in the charismatic calendar as we count down to the millennium have both been connected with Wimber, one directly, the other indirectly. The direct connection was Wimber's unexpected involvement with a group of men known as the Kansas City Prophets, of whom the most well known is Paul Cain.[8] A throwback to earlier Pentecostal Holiness movements and the healing ministry of William Branham in the 1940s and 1950s, Cain was a sensation when he first arrived in Britain in the early 1990s. More in the tradition of a seer than an Old Testament prophet, Cain made specific predictions concerning people and events, and was not averse to calling out names at public meetings. Many thought that he had predicted a worldwide revival beginning in Wales in 1992.

In the event, despite the eager anticipation, there was no world revival and Wimber disentangled the Vineyard churches from Cain and the Kansas circle. He also later distanced himself from John Arnott, the pastor of the Toronto Vineyard Church, after the so-called Toronto Blessing in 1994 – with its spectacular 'slayings in the spirit', animal noises, jerks and uncontrollable laughter. In many ways, however, the Toronto Blessing, although on a grander scale than anything Wimber had orchestrated, bore all the hallmarks of Vineyard spirituality, albeit in an intense and frenetic form.

From the moment that Cain spoke out at the Docklands arena in 1992, to the full flush of the Toronto Blessing in 1995, we can note with interest that many of the Restorationist leaders, from Gerald Coates to Terry Virgo, were in the thick of the new happenings. Even Bryn Jones, the most independent of the house church leaders, came out in favour of what many were still calling 'Toronto', but he preferred to call 'a move of God'.[9]

In no sense, however, can we see this support for the new enthusiasm as a revival of Restorationism, but rather we must see it as Restorationists carried along on the crest of a new revival wave. Perhaps as Arthur Wallis foresaw (see Appendix 1), there was a bigger wave coming than Restoration, and he anticipated that all house church leaders would want to be immersed in the flood as it thundered towards that final shore.

Loss of momentum rather than extinction – This highly selective and shorthand account of charismatic activity in the last few years might be thought sufficient explanation as to why Restorationism was swept along by the revival tide. We might even be tempted to say that Restorationism, as a movement, was simply overwhelmed by events and ceased to exist. I think we should resist this temptation because it is misleading on two fronts.

In the first place, Restorationism may have lost its momentum in the late 1980s, but it did not drown in the 'revivals' of the 1990s. Not only (as we have briefly seen above) can it be said that Bryn Jones in the Midlands and Terry Virgo in the south-east have remained Restorationist, but many of the other networks have survived in altered form – from Gerald Coates, in the west and south of London, to Tony Morton in Southampton and Hampshire.[10] These groups and many of the house church leaders, as we have seen, have been deeply involved in recent charismatic activity. Some of them may have abandoned some Restorationist tenets such as 'discipling',[11] or even the insistence on the restored apostolic ministry of Ephesians chapter 4, but they have not given up on revival. Overtaken by the bigger wave, they went with the flow.

Secondly, it was not the new events of the 1990s that stopped Restorationism in its tracks, but rather external and internal changes from the mid to late 1980s. It is the contention of Part Three of this new edition of *Restoring the Kingdom* that the combination of these changes meant in effect that by 1990 the kingdom had, in Nigel Wright's language, 'fallen apart'.

To say, however, that Restoration has fallen apart is clearly hyperbole, and if we are going to use the phrase we cannot let it pass without qualification. An interesting perspective is that of David Lillie who, along with Arthur Wallis, is really the theological architect of modern

Restorationist ecclesiology. Lillie believes that the restoration of the Church is still very much on God's agenda, but he feels that the Restorationist movement restricted and distorted the theological vision through a false institutional understanding of the role of the apostle. He claims that the 'new breed' of apostles confused the foundational role of apostles, which belongs to the twelve disciples of Jesus, with what he calls the 'foundation laying' role of the post-Pentecostal apostles.[12] Lillie does not doubt that Restorationist apostles are men of God, but he does believe that they have mistakenly claimed for themselves New Testament warrant for the power and control that they enjoy. In short, Lillie fears that Restorationist apostles emerged as, ' "the hub of the wheel", the indispensable focal-point within . . . yes, within "a denominative" network'.[13]

Lillie's critique is really an indictment that the Restorationist movement did not follow the New Testament pattern of apostolic churches, but instead fell into the trap of denominationalism. David Tomlinson, on the other hand, an apostle in the movement until a few years back, is scathing about the very possibility of a restoration of apostolic churches. He feels that the Restoration movement has to be seen as a failure:

> It was such a ridiculously optimistic vision of restoring New Testament Christianity and the New Testament Church, which is what Restorationism is about. That could never be. It's an absurd vision really – the whole idea that we can recover something which is based on a mistaken idea of what the early Church was really like. Also the idea that this was a movement that was going to grow and grow, and become influential in terms of evangelism and bringing the kingdom of God to society, and this sort of thing. Yes, of course it failed.[14]

Tomlinson also believes that the failure of the movement amounted to a great deal of lost potential:

I still feel a great deal of sympathy for the initial impetus. I think the emphasis on fellowship and community was very important, but again as time went on all that became very institutionalized through the kind of emphasis on structure and commitment, apostleship, and all the rest of it.[15]

Lillie's critique might be described as disappointed and Tomlinson's as disillusioned, but it is important to register the fact that even those leaders who have remained within the Restorationist orbit have come to terms with the relative failure of their earlier vision. In this respect, Terry Virgo, Bryn Jones and Gerald Coates are quite well aware of the loss of momentum of early Restorationism, and none of them are blind to the fact that the restoration of the kingdom of God still has a long way to go.

Speaking for myself, I believe that the Restorationist movement lost its earlier radical vision of the alternative society, with its emphasis on community, co-operative Christian enterprises, and committed relationships. Such a vision went against the flow of cultural diversity and the hedonistic individualism of late modernity, not to mention the ideological dominance of Thatcherism in the 1980s. Gradually, Restorationists adapted to the larger cultural milieu and were domesticated by it. They did not merely slow down: they settled down to a regular church life and a principled charismatic evangelicalism.

What cannot be said, however, is that the loss of the Restorationist momentum in the late 1980s, when it can be said that it 'fell apart' as a coherent movement, amounted to a complete failure. If Restorationism as a movement floundered, very often house churches in the very act of settling down were able to make a significant contribution to their locality and region. Rodney Kingston, for example, of Worthing, Sussex, feels that his Broadwater fellowship may be part of a larger network, but it is primarily a service agency for Worthing.[16] It is a fellowship that lays less stress on the kingdom and more, he hopes, on the King. One that 'meets people at the point of their real need, rather than hit them with Bible verses or stick tracts in their hands'.[17]

Indeed, when house churches have become less overtly Restorationist, they have often opened up to the larger society in such a way that they have been able to make a major contribution both to social work and to ecumenical affairs. Nowhere is this more true than at Gateshead, where Brian Howell, the leader of Kelvin Grove Christian Fellowship, has encouraged co-operation with a whole host of Church, voluntary, and state welfare agencies. His fellowship is involved in a family centre, care for the elderly, and community business projects. Brian himself is not only the chairman of the Durham Churches Relations Group, but he also chairs both care review panels of Gateshead and South Tyne Health Authority, and many other inter-agency groups.[18]

Such examples demonstrate that relative decline and domestication does not mean the end of a useful life as far as the local church is concerned. Neither should we assume that domesticity means that Restorationist theology no longer has any influence. On the contrary, Restorationist ecclesiology, and its post-millennial eschatology, has found a voice in the British evangelical scene, even if it is only one voice among many.[19] In this respect, Restorationists, in the long term, will have to accept a more modest role in the evangelical world than being the apotheosis of radical Christianity. Their future – and they do have a future – would seem either to become part of the Christian denominational scene, or to operate as external denominational mission agencies. In time, of course, even missioners may settle down and pitch their tents with the other tribes. This would already seem to be the case with Terry Virgo's network of churches, 'New Frontiers'.

Bryn Jones, on the other hand, seems more concerned with influencing others than taking over and running vast networks of churches, although he is anxious for Covenant

Ministries to act as a beacon for Restorationist idealism. This needs to be said, because of all the Restorationist groups left in existence, Bryn's network seems the least likely to capitulate to a more domesticated Christianity. As the official historian of his churches put it: 'I think Bryn has wanted to model a lot of principles that are important to him. He would see that the influence of Restoration teaching has gone much wider than his own network, although he wanted to build something that was pure on the ground.'[20] This, I believe, offers a real recipe for Restorationist survival as a distinctive ideology, but not for church growth.

As for Gerald Coates, having championed the concept of the 'new church', he may in time find that new churches simply become old ones by virtue of age and the process of atrophy.[21] Whatever the case, new churches have gone beyond the kingdom of Restorationist ideology and in so doing include not only a second generation of Restorationists, but an altogether looser and wider federation of fellowships, both in terms of theological precepts and organizational control.[22]

What follows in this book is less speculation about Restorationism's future, and more concentration on recapitulating its history.

Recommended Reading

Gerald Coates, *An Intelligent Fire* (Eastbourne: Kingsway, 1991).

Barney Coombs, *Apostles Today: Christ's Love-Gift to the Church* (Chichester: Sovereign World, 1996).

Harvey Cox, *Fire from Heaven* (London: Cassell, 1996).

Ian Cotton, *The Hallelujah Revolution: The Rise of the New Christians* (London: Little Brown Company, 1995).

David Lillie, *Restoration: Is this Still on God's Programme?*

(Private publication, Kyrtonia Press, 1994).

John and Christine Noble, *Everyman's Guide to the Holy Spirit, the End of the World and You* (Eastbourne: Kingsway, 1991).

Tom Smail, Andrew Walker and Nigel Wright, *Charismatic Renewal: the Search for a Theology* (London: SPCK, new edition, 1995).

Restore: a Voice of Radical Christianity, Issue 4, Spring 1997.

Terry Virgo, *A People Prepared* (Eastbourne: Kingsway, 1996).

Andrew Walker, 'Sectarian Reactions: Pluralism and the Privatization of Religion', *2020 Visions: The Future of Christianity,* H. Willmer, Ed., (London: SPCK, 1992) pp 46–64.

PROLOGUE

THE GREAT YORKSHIRE SHOWGROUND, AUGUST 1982

It was the 6th of August 1982. I was at the Dales Bible Week in Yorkshire preparing a report for the BBC's Radio 4 programme, *Sunday*.[1] As I walked round the hundreds of tents and caravans housing some 8,000 people, it was impossible not to feel the excitement and enjoyment that people were experiencing. Everywhere I went, people were only too eager to tell me how they had been healed, delivered from demons, or simply blessed.

Going into a large tent that morning, I found hundreds of children laughing and clapping at the antics of a clown who was combining slapstick humour with stories from the Bible. Entering another tent, I saw a hundred or so teenagers – with hands lifted and eyes far away – singing in tongues and praising God.

Later in the day, while some were playing a version of *It's a Knockout*, I came across a group of people being baptized by immersion in an outside pool. Quite a few of them appeared to be Anglicans! Little knots of people praying, singing with a guitar or locked in passionate discussion were commonplace. There seemed to be a great deal of talk about 'the kingdom' – 'rule', 'reign', 'majesty', 'glory' were words I kept hearing everywhere.

In the evening, a huge wave of some 5,000 (maybe even 7,000) people surged into the giant hall of the Great Yorkshire Showground. The rousing songs and choruses reflected the language of majesty and kingship that I had been hearing throughout the day. 'All Hail, King Jesus' was one song I remember. Another was 'Jesus, we enthrone you, we proclaim you our king . . .'

This language of sovereignty and glory was matched by a corresponding sense of being kingdom people: soldiers of the King.

Gird up your armour ye sons of Zion
Gird up your armour, let's go to war.
We'll win the battle with great rejoicing
And so we'll praise him more and more.

I hear the sound of the army of the Lord,
I hear the sound of the army of the Lord,
It's the sound of praise, it's the sound of war.
The army of the Lord,
The army of the Lord,
The army of the Lord is marching on.[2]

The praise in the showground was joyful and loud. Much of it was accompanied by leaping, dancing, clapping, and even some high kicks. These mainly young people were geared up for war – rattling their spiritual shields, they were defying the devil himself. The whole scene, though in a Christianized form, resembled some massive tribal war dance in preparation for an imminent battle.

And, of course, that is exactly what it was. When the preacher for the evening, Bryn Jones, strode to the microphone, he described the reality of the demonic powers that controlled our cities. His sermon contrasted the kingdom of God with the principality of Satan. He left us in no doubt that we were in a state of war.

After the service, as I made my way out by the back of the rostrum, there was a sudden commotion. 'Don't, don't,' someone screamed. A number of men gathered round a young man on the ground. They were commanding evil spirits to leave him in the name of Jesus. 'I won't go,' boomed an angry voice. The leaders ignored me as I stood there. These leaders-turned-exorcists were too busy holding down the young man whose limbs were twitching and jerking involuntarily. The exorcism became wilder and more intense; I decided to move on.

Outside, in the growing dark, the crowds weaving their way through the caravans were singing and humming songs of the kingdom (and I noticed that I was singing too). The sound was harmonious, and with the torchlights bobbing and twinkling it made a dramatic contrast to the discordant cry of the demons.

'The church of God is moving, the church of God is moving . . .' sang the crowd. Everybody was relaxed yet triumphant. More music struck up a little further off:

We're singing and dancing and shouting and marching
As we execute the justice and rule of our God.
We'll take the nations for Jesus as Satan's kingdom falls.
Righteousness and truth will prevail through our God.[3]

That night, looking back, was the night I abandoned my investigation into house church movements and decided to concentrate on the kingdom people.

Part One

The Establishment of the Kingdom
A History to 1985

1

'HOUSE CHURCHES? NEVER HEARD OF THEM!'[1]

In the event, my decision to concentrate on what I call the 'kingdom people' was the right decision, both practically and tactically. When I first became interested in the so-called house churches in 1979,[2] I had no idea that there were so many different brands. By 1982, it was clear to me that the term 'house church movement' did not index a specific phenomenon. It is an inappropriate label, a misnomer that I think we should drop.

'House Church Movement' as an Inappropriate Label

The phrase 'house church movement' has become one of those convenient labels that we stick onto a variety of churches because they seem to be outside typical Christian experience. Certainly, as we shall see, these house churches typically do belong outside the mainline denominations. Unfortunately, convenient labels are difficult to remove once they become attached to anything; they become sanctioned by usage, even if they are misleading in fact. There are four reasons, it seems to me, why we should make the effort to abandon the house church label.

First, the label 'house church movement' masks the fact that there are quite different fellowships and organizations that come under this rubric. There is, for example, the Ichthus Christian Fellowship.[3] There are also the fellowships founded by Pastor G. W. North. The groups linked to Chard in Somerset have been around for a long time. More recently we have seen the establishment of the so-called base-line churches. In addition to these movements, there

are the 'apostolic' churches under the direction of Bryn
Jones and his colleagues, and the less structured churches
affiliated to John Noble, Gerald Coates, David Tomlinson
and their associates. There are the thriving Basingstoke
communities, The Invisible Church, Union Life, and a host
of independent groups who are not attached to anybody.

Secondly, the members of the various groups who
make up this extra-denominational phenomenon do not
like to be identified by the blanket term 'house church
movement'. (Unfortunately, for those of us who are out-
siders, neither do many of them like to be called by any
name that clearly identifies them.)

Thirdly, although it is true that many of these groups
started in homes, most of them have now grown into full-
blown churches with house groups attached. The church at
Bradford, under Bryn Jones's leadership, for example, has
over 600 members, and in Hove, Terry Virgo's church can
boast far in excess of 500 members. Many other churches
now have a membership exceeding 100 and even 300
members.[4] All these churches do have some things in common: they exist outside the mainline denominations of
Great Britain; many are evangelicals, and most of them are
Pentecostals. However, they are different in style and
organization. Furthermore, and perhaps most importantly,
these different movements have virtually nothing to do
with each other.

The fourth and final reason why the notion of a house
church movement is not very useful is because it confuses
extra-denominational churches with house churches
inside the denominations. There are scores, if not hundreds, of these churches within the Protestant and Catholic
ambits. Many of these churches are neither charismatic nor
evangelistic. Some of them do claim to be radical. It is certainly difficult to think of a more non-conformist church in
a house than Canon Ivor Smith-Cameron's at The Chase,
South London.

He once described his church to me as a sort of spiritual cafeteria: people – regardless of religious affiliation – can

come in and help themselves to whatever they fancy. On offer might be Eastern style prayer, Church of England Eucharist, discussions on politics and racism, or experiments in interfaith worship. If this sounds like a recipe for anarchic or syncretistic religion, it is based on Canon Smith-Cameron's conviction that you should not force inquiring people to have to eat the traditional three-course meal of Anglicanism; they may only want a quick snack, or to share in human fellowship.

What the Canon's house church shares with most of the denominational versions of house churches, is not only that they are primarily extensions of the denominations (or at least recognized by them), but that they are one-offs: in no sense do they belong to a movement of any kind. Indeed, in Canon Smith-Cameron's case, he sees his work at The Chase as essentially parochial in the sense of reaching out to those who live in his locality, regardless of their religion or church ties.

In no sense am I suggesting that denominational house churches are insignificant. But they are a separate phenomenon from the house churches outside the denominations, and they are not a subject that I shall be discussing in this book.

I have used the phrase 'house church movement' in the sub-title of this book, because it is a term already in usage. But I wish to orient readers to a religious movement outside the recognized denominations. This creates an immediate problem: what shall we call them? In order to help facilitate the identification of the phenomenon under study, I have invented a terminology that I think fits the facts and is not offensive to the members of the churches with which we shall be dealing.

That I have decided to concentrate on what I have called the 'kingdom people' allows us to go right to the heart of the new movements. To try to deal with all the movements' designated house churches would be virtually an impossible study. Not only are there simply too many to make this practically possible, but also there would be no conceptual warrant for such a study. What we would end up with would be a collection of disparate phenomena, a rag-bag, not something that hangs together.

Enter the Kingdom

My major justification for concentrating on kingdom people is not because they cohere together as a movement (which they do), but because they are the largest and most significant Christian formation to emerge in Great Britain for over a half a century. Not since the Pentecostal movements of Elim and the Assemblies of God were established in the late 1920s has such a distinctive and indigenous Christian grouping arrived on the religious scene.[5]

Furthermore, like all new groups, they have arrived in clouds of controversy. Nearly all the mythologies, criticisms and accusations levelled at so-called house churches, turn out on investigation to be aimed at people of the kingdom.

'House churches steal Christians from the established churches.'
'All the money goes into the leaders' pockets.'
'They operate a system of authoritarian control.'
'They are a new brain-washing cult.'
'It's a pyramid structure.'
'House churches are part of the international "shepherding" movement with its headquarters in North America.'

All these statements, and many similar ones, are the sort of things I hear people saying in evangelical circles.

In other religious groups, very little is known about kingdom people. Many Anglicans and Roman Catholics, for example, have never come across any. Until recently, the national press has taken little notice of the emerging phenomenon. However, things are changing. During the writing of this book, I know of one major Sunday newspaper that was threatening an exposé of the Bradford Community Church, and Bryn Jones's apostolic team. Many rumours were circulating: 'Did you know that Bryn Jones has a £40,000 Mercedes car?' 'His house in Yorkshire cost well over £150,000!' I mention these two, because I happen to know that they have no foundation in fact.[6]

Increasingly, too, the religious trade press is carrying major articles on the new groups. Both radio and television have now completed several programmes.[7] In short, kingdom people are becoming newsworthy. Because interest in them is growing, and as their churches become larger, doctrinally distinct, and more radical than their rivals, it is obviously timely as well as logical that we should look at them rather than the many other house church structures.

I have decided, on careful consideration, to reject a number of names which people have kindly suggested to me as possible titles for the new churches. Some names are simply too parochial. Bryn Jones and his churches are sometimes called 'Harvestime', after the name of the commercial organization which handles many of their products. Such a name excludes the two apostolic teams of Tony Morton and Terry Virgo, who are closely linked with Bryn Jones. At the other extreme, a number of people suggested the term 'shepherding movement'. This is much better, because it is the case that a great many loosely-knit churches, which differ in other respects, hold to similar doctrines of radical discipleship or 'shepherding'. However, I decided to resist this title for three reasons.

First, the term 'shepherding movement' is usually seen as something with its origins in America. I do not think that the movement that I have been investigating has its origins in America (although there are undoubtedly direct influences). Secondly, kingdom people would object to the term, because they understand what they are doing as far more than incorporating discipleship doctrines into their churches. Thirdly, kingdom people are essentially involved in trying to fulfil an eschatological vision: that vision is to replace denominations with the kingdom of

God that will fill the whole earth before the Second Coming of Christ. To talk of shepherding principles is totally to miss this eschatological dimension.

Perhaps, with the great deal of talk about kingship and kingdom, it would have been possible to talk about 'kingdom' as a proper noun and title? However, there are also three problems with this terminology. First, the movement of the kingdom people is in fact two movements that were once one; so we would have to have two kingdoms. Secondly, Gerald Coates once tried calling his fellowships at Cobham, 'Kingdom Life'. He found that people tended to confuse this with the Jehovah's Witnesses. I feel that we would have the same trouble if we used the term on a less parochial basis. Thirdly, while I am happy to use the concept of 'kingdom' as a metaphor (which I shall do constantly throughout this book), I do not wish to confuse 'kingdom' as a spiritual and theological concept with 'kingdom' as an organizational construct.

It is not my intention to deny that the kingdom of God is to be found in this new religious movement, but I do insist that we should not see the two as synonymous or interchangeable. Leaders of the new movements, such as Bryn Jones and David Tomlinson, for example, would agree with me that the kingdom of God is too big to be exclusively identified with a particular segment of the Christian Church.

Restorationism[8]

I have decided to adopt the term 'Restorationism' to index the two interrelated movements that I see as incorporating the people of the kingdom. The first thing to understand about this label is that it is not the proper name of a denomination, nor a religious movement. There is no church in existence, to my knowledge, called Restoration. Secondly, to talk sociologically of Restoration is primarily to understand the movements we are investigating as approximating an ideal type.[9]

A sociological ideal type is a rational construction based on the essential characteristics of the phenomenon under investigation. The model that emerges, therefore, is to be understood more in terms of a pure or ideal construction than a description of empirical reality. The actual churches we will be looking at therefore will be like the pure Restorationist type in many respects, but not all respects. As we will see, one of the two movements we will be looking at is a closer approximation to the ideal type than the other one. I propose to call the 'purer' of the two movements Restoration One (R1 for short), and the 'less pure' movement, Restoration Two, (R2 for short). The words 'pure' and 'less pure' are scientific analogies, not moral ones; there is no suggestion that R1 is better than R2 because it is purer – simply that it is closer to the ideal type.

A simpler way of looking at R1 and R2 is to realize that R1 is the more conservative movement (most like the ideal type) and R2 the more liberal movement (less like the ideal type, but still more Restorationist than not). If we are looking for an historical analogue to help our understanding of Restorationism, then we might say that R1 and R2 are, in some respects, a charismatic equivalent to the Exclusive and Open Brethren movements of the nineteenth century. Both Restoration and the Brethren stemmed from a generic movement; both split into different factions; and although the family resemblance has remained unmistakable, both movements diverged over time. But enough of analogues and algebraic rubrics: it is time to move on and identify R1 and R2 in terms of real groups and personalities. Only one theoretical task remains – to outline the essential features of Restorationism as an ideal type.

Restorationism as an ideal type – The term 'Restorationism' denotes a qualitative understanding of (so members believe) the work of the Holy Spirit. Leaders of the new movements insist that denominations are not in the plan of God. Restorationists wish to restore or return to the New

Testament pattern (as they see it) of the Early Church. The restoring of the Church as it was in its pristine form is to restore a charismatically-ordained church, and one in which Christians are seen as living in a kingdom run according to God's order and rules.

The nature of kingdom life is itself one of the distinguishing features of Restorationism. To see God's kingdom established (or re-established) is understood eschatologically. The 'end-time', which Restorationists believe is now, will be characterized not so much by world chaos and 'wars and rumours of wars', but by an outpouring of God's Spirit, culminating in the establishment of the kingdom that is ready and fit for the return of the King. (This is analogous to the Church as the Bride of Christ 'without blemish', who alone is worthy of full intimacy with the Bridegroom.)

Restorationists see themselves as evangelicals and Pentecostals, but in a new, radical mould. The crucible for this new shape is the doctrine of Church order stemming from the ecclesiology of Ephesians 4:8–12. The key verses are as follows:

It was he who gave some to be apostles, some to be prophets, some to be evangelists, and some to be pastors and teachers, to prepare God's people for works of service, so that the body of Christ may be built up until we all reach unity in the faith and in the knowledge of the Son of God and become mature, attaining to the whole measure of the fullness of Christ. (NIV)

From this, Restorationists believe that the Church should be run by divinely-appointed apostles, prophets and elders. Furthermore, they hold to a doctrine of 'discipleship', or 'shepherding', whereby church members submit themselves to those deemed to be their overseers and spiritual counsellors. Restorationists eschew notions that they are a new denomination or sect, preferring to see themselves as part of a potential worldwide Church where brethren will meet to 'break bread' and follow the apostles' teaching.[10]

Restorationism, as an ideal type then, refers to a recognizable cluster of doctrines and practices adhered to by a considerable number of churches which nevertheless prefer to see themselves as non-denominational. To turn from the ideal representation of Restorationism to its empirical embodiments is to recognize, as we have indicated, that there are two movements on the ground.

The character of R1 and R2 – Until 1985, Restoration One (R1) is clearly identifiable around a core of recognized leadership – Bryn Jones, Tony Morton, and Terry Virgo.[11] This leadership can be said to consist of inter-related apostolic teams, each with their own spheres of influence, churches and personnel. However, the apostolic leaders share platforms together (at the Dales Bible Week, for example) and are editorial associates of the magazine *Restoration*. R1, as the more conservative faction of Restorationism, can also be said to include fellow travellers, independent of the core leadership, such as Barney Coombs and the Basingstoke fellowships.

Many of the people in R1 refer to themselves as 'in the Restoration', and both apostles and elders prefer the term 'Restoration' to any other attempt to classify or pigeonhole them. Terry Virgo, the apostolic leader of a team based in Hove, West Sussex, is as adamant as the other apostles that he dislikes labels being attached to their work, but he does admit that if they have to be called something in order to help facilitate identification, then 'Restoration' would be the best term to use.[12] Certainly, the other Restorationist formation (R2) have no difficulty in seeing R1 as an organized movement; they usually refer to it by my generic term, 'Restoration'.

If we can apply that designation, with some confidence, to R1 as a proper noun, it is more difficult to do so to the second group without causing offence. This is not due to any major doctrinal differences between R1 and R2: it is more a question of style and history. Many of the people who belong to R2 are either refugees from R1, or they belonged at an earlier stage to a nascent Restorationism that had not yet hardened into the different factions of R1 and R2 – which emerged out of a split in the movement in 1976. Members of R2, in short, are not enthusiastic about the Restorationist label, because they do not wish to be seen as being too closely identified with R1.[13]

Nevertheless, I have decided to stick to the term R2. This is partly a pragmatic decision: in the absence of a more formal title, we have to call this clearly identifiable movement something which is applicable.[14] More conceptually, however, the use of the term R2 designates what is clearly a different (and more mixed) variety of Restorationism than R1. Despite R2's amorphous nature, there are a large number of independent yet affiliated churches which make up this Restorationist constituency. This sense of affiliation is evidence that R2 is not purely a random collection of Restored churches. They come together at such organized events as the 'Festival' celebrations where several thousands attend. Their common ideological beliefs and similar liturgical practices are further evidence that R2 is more than a bundle of disconnected pieces that just happen to bear close resemblance to each other.

After the 1976 schism, R2 coheres around the core apostolic ministries of John Noble and Gerald Coates – augmented in 1983 by David Tomlinson's defection from R1. However, R2, as a looser Restoration formation than R1, can be said to include many fellow travellers from Peter Fenwick at Sheffield, Peter Lyne in Bristol, Graham Perrins in South Wales and even, for a while, John MacLauchlan from Somerset.[15]

The South Chard and Pastor North Groups

Having decided not to concentrate on house churches within the mainstream denominations, and to concentrate on R1 and R2 as our central phenomena, I cannot dismiss all other house church movements without comment. The Chard and North fellowships, for example, both precede Restorationism, and are important in its historical development. Indeed, most Restorationists pay tribute to South Chard and the North fellowships as the forerunners of the house church system within their own movement. It would not be inaccurate to say that in the 1960s, the house church movement was Chard and North.

South Chard – The origins of South Chard prefigure much that has happened in the house church movement. It was founded by 'Uncle' Sid Purse as early as the 1940s. Sidney Purse was a member of the Open Brethren, and when he began to speak in tongues this caused friction with the rest of the Brethren in his local church. He and his wife, who also claimed the Pentecostal experience, began to hold meetings in their aptly-named Manor House. By 1956, a church was opened which was built adjacent to the Manor House. Influenced by a very small Pentecostal sect with the unlikely name of 'Henry's Revival', South Chard built up a 'praise and preaching ministry'. By the 1960s, South Chard began to reach out to many areas both nationally and abroad with this ministry.

Chard associates would train and encourage others to set up house churches, but with little evidence of empire building. This became clear during the 'heyday' of the Charismatic Renewal movement from the late 1960s to the mid-1970s. Chard teachings, methods and personnel could be found inside Pentecostal denominations, the historic churches, and the extra-denominational house churches. Many people now in Restoration, and some in Charismatic Renewal circles, first encountered both Pentecostalism and house churches through the Chard work.

However, Chard charismatics became provocateurs in a controversy that has existed since the inception of Pentecostalism at the beginning of this century. They adopted a baptismal formula whereby they baptized in the name of Jesus only. Bryn and Keri Jones – soon to become apostles in R1 – were to find themselves involved in this controversy during a 'mini-revival' in Cornwall at the end of the 1960s. South Chard leaders were declaring that those baptized in the name of the Holy Trinity were receiving an invalid baptism. Ill feeling was caused in the area, and rather than become embroiled, or take sides, the Jones brothers left the West Country. Shortly afterwards, in 1969, Bryn Jones moved to Bradford, which was to see the commencement of the Restoration movement in Yorkshire.

This doctrinal controversy highlights (I do not say it was a cause) the beginning of Chard's decline. In a way, the charismatic movement stole much of Chard's fire in the mid-1970s. It could be argued, of course, that Chard helped the Renewal on its way. Without doubt it became interrelated with it in many areas of Great Britain. After the 'discipleship' issue raised its head from 1975 onwards, the Chard movement, with its emphasis on praise rather than discipline and kingdom authority, began to lose out against the new, rising Restoration groups.[16] Today, South Chard is a shadow of its former self. Its historical moment may have passed, but there is little doubt that it was the pace-setter in the house church movement(s).[17]

The North fellowships – Pastor G. W. (Wally) North's fellowships also have their roots outside the classical Pentecostal denominations and before the Charismatic Renewal movement. Pastor North is a truly charismatic figure, and this can be seen in the way in which his character and doctrines are treated as out of the ordinary by his followers. The North fellowships are throwbacks to the Holiness movements of the nineteenth century and the perfectionist teaching of John Wesley. Wally North established his reputation at an independent Holiness church in Bradford, where he was pastor from 1952 to 1965.

In 1965, he moved to Liverpool, where he became chaplain to the Longcroft (a sort of spiritual rehabilitation centre in the Wirral) and founder of a number of fellowships in the city. The trustees of the Longcroft released North from his position as chaplain in 1968 to allow him to pursue a full-time itinerant ministry. This he did with considerable success, and to this day he travels to all parts of the world.

Pastor North has always insisted that he is not the founder of a denomination, but it would not be unfair to say that all the fellowships he has encouraged or overseen bear the imprint of his personality and teachings. It is these teachings, rather than his personality, that have ensured that the North approach would never become a recipe for large organizations. His doctrines, by evangelical and Pentecostal standards, contain elements of heresy. For instance, to be 'born again' is not for North the 'being saved' of evangelicalism or the initial forgiveness of sins. 'New birth' is to enter the fullness of the Holy Spirit. This not only means the collapse of the 'second blessing' of Pentecostalism to one experience of spiritual initiation, it also implies a 'walking in the Spirit' that is synonymous with sinlessness.

From a sociological viewpoint, the North fellowships failed to appeal to the full range of social class membership that Restoration has done so successfully. Furthermore, their emphasis on personal holiness rather than 'kingdom living' meant that they failed to develop a communitarian and organizational ethos. Consequently, the North house churches tend to be inward-looking, small in numbers, and appear to have no influence outside their own circles.

Since the 1970s, when Pastor North moved to Scotland, his work seems to have dwindled in the southern part of Great Britain. New churches are still being formed, but not in great numbers. It would be honest to admit that nobody seems to know how large Pastor North's operation really is. Joyce Thurman is of the opinion that Pastor North's own view is rather optimistic.[18] Most leaders in R1 and R2 that I talked to believe that the North fellowships have diminished as a result of their own appeal.

Wally North certainly provided a number of personnel

for the new Restoration movement. David Tomlinson, formerly an apostle with R1 (and now in R2), was in the North movement and, like most ex-members, holds the pastor in great regard. Furthermore, and with some irony, it was Bryn Jones, fresh from the squabbles of Cornwall, who appeared in Bradford in 1969 to become the temporary pastor of the New Covenant Church, which was the same church which Pastor North had built up until he left Bradford in 1965. According to Joyce Thurman, Pastor North sent a permanent pastor to Bradford, but in a short while Bryn Jones's influence held sway, and the North connection was broken.[19]

Neither the Chard movement nor the North fellowships had the aggressive discipline of the new Restoration churches. South Chard really could not offer anything that the Pentecostal churches and the Renewal movement between them were not offering by the mid-1970s. And clearly, by that time they were not matching the radicality of Restorationism. It is only speculation, but it is difficult to envisage the perfectionist teaching of Pastor North having much success without his personal charisma. He has expressed the view himself that the vision dies with the man.[20] It would seem that by the 1980s, even if the vision is still alive, fewer and fewer people are sharing it.

Other Movements

However much I may extend my rubric of R1 and R2, it is not possible, without excessive Procrusteanism, to force everybody to fit it. To try to do so would be no better than retaining the original misnomer of 'house church movement' with which we started. This being so, it is worth recapitulating that my schema is intended to inform us of a particular brand of extra-denominationalism. There are many other independent Pentecostal fellowships that look very similar on the surface, but they would not recognize themselves as belonging to my rubric. I am not sure whether the Ewell Fellowship in Surrey fits, for example.

There is also the recent importation from North America, 'Union Life', which certainly holds to no discipleship doctrines.[21]

Perhaps the most significant house church organization that lies outside my categories is the Ichthus movement. Headed by Roger Forster (who has one of the finest minds in the evangelical constituency that I have ever encountered), this organization with its headquarters in Forest Hill is essentially a mission group. Its ethos is Open Brethren (though its origins are the Honor Oak Fellowship) and Renewalist Pentecostalism. Strongly attached to the work of the Evangelical Alliance, the movement also supports evangelism wherever it may be found. While remaining a committed evangelical, Forster is open to Catholic and Orthodox insights. His work is welcome in R2, and admired in R1. Ichthus, however, does not subscribe to the discipleship teachings of R1 and R2. Neither do they have so narrow a definition of 'women's ministry' as that found in nearly all Restorationist churches (not to mention many Brethren assemblies).[22]

Having introduced enough caveats to avoid over-simplification, I would like to end this introductory chapter with a note on methodology and moral problems.

Methods and Morals

I have not used any form of covert investigation, believing it to be immoral and sometimes distressing to religious groups. My model here is Dr Bryan Wilson of All Souls, Oxford. His reputation for fairness and gentlemanly conduct is as great among the religious groups he has investigated as it is among sociologists of religion.

My methodology has simply been to read journals, letters and propaganda sheets, attend meetings, talk to members and conduct in-depth interviews with some of the leaders.[23] Many of the interviews were in the context of discussion and dialogue; friendships have emerged that I trust will survive a critical look at kingdom life.

In no sense have I attempted a definitive study. Such an approach would involve a standard of scholarship and a commitment of time beyond that which I have attempted here. Furthermore, I do not believe that such an approach could be attempted right now. The new movements are still in a period of flux, and they may grow rapidly or fade away just as quickly.

Although I am a committed Christian, I have primarily taken the role of an outsider, using the tools of sociological, historical and theological analysis, rather than providing a series of spiritual comments and moral asides throughout the text. However, I am also a human being, not merely a cypher of knowledge or an impassive recorder of events. Someone who has no opinions or prejudices at all, it seems to me, is an odd kind of investigator into human affairs. Part One of this book is really an interpretive narrative. I have often had to rely on my own judgment in the absence of firm or convincing data. The evidence has often been conflicting, and nobody I met seemed to have an overall or clear picture of all the historical events.

Part One is also more personal and revealing (in an eavesdropping sense) than I originally intended. The major reason for this is the nature of the material given me in conversation. But there is also another reason. Bryn Jones said to me, during an interview, that he hoped I would not make it all analysis. He hoped that the people I presented would have some life and character to them. I think that his instincts were basically right. Consequently, I have tried to balance analysis with personal pen-sketches, and objective accounting is interspersed with subjective impressions.

The research was conducted under some strain and pressure. I discovered that Restorationism is extremely factional: there was ill-feeling and bitterness as well as health and life in the kingdom. There was also considerable anger and anxiety among many denominational groups. More than a few Christian opponents of

Restorationism hoped that I would write a damning report of the movement. 'Make sure you show them up for what they are', was one comment. One father remarked: 'If you don't get Bryn Jones, I will.' This sort of atmosphere was not helped by the imminent threat of a Sunday newspaper exposure, nor the discovery on my part that some scandals did exist.[24]

However, this was compensated for in many ways by an openness to investigation that I found everywhere. When I did stumble upon some unpleasant facts (or, more typically, upon alleged unpleasantries), nobody made any attempt to stop me or curtail my activities. I am by nature a nosy person, and I saw no attempts at a cover-up.

As I am a member of the Russian Orthodox Church, I was obviously not the kind of observer that Restorationists are used to meeting. On the whole this was an advantage. The closer you are to division, the more you view it with dismay. Roman Catholics and Orthodox do not even know of Restorationism. It is the Baptists, Open Brethren, classical and neo-Pentecostals, who view the new dissenters with concern. Restorationist liturgy is not to my taste, but I do not find kingdom people in any way alien.

In the first place, I have been a professional investigator of charismatic groups since 1970. Secondly, my experience is by no means purely academic. I was brought up in a Pentecostal denomination (although I left it in 1960). In recent years, I have represented the British Council of Churches at the World Council's consultation on Charismatic Renewal in 1980, and I regularly speak in Pentecostal churches.

Quoting Herbert Spencer's dictum not to have contempt for the people prior to investigation, Arthur Wallis in an editorial of *Restoration* magazine makes the following comment:

> We do not ask our critics to take our word that we are not authoritarian or dictatorial, but that we seek to 'rule in the fear of God', as those who must give account. We

invite them, if they are motivated with a genuine desire to know the truth, to come and see for themselves . . .[25]

I do not see myself as a critic, but I have tried openly to discover what Restoration really stands for. My approach is primarily (though not exclusively) rationalistic and investigative. It does not pretend, therefore, to tell the whole truth. I do not believe that the reality of the Holy Spirit can be encapsulated by these methods, and I concede that a more theological and spiritual approach would not only proceed in a different way, but come up with a different level of findings.

2

THE ORIGINS OF RESTORATION 1958–70

Restoration has twin theological roots, I believe, in two nineteenth-century religious movements: the Irvingites (or Catholic Apostolic Church) and the Brethren movement. In the twentieth century, the immediate precursors of Restorationism were the classical Pentecostal movements of the Apostolic Church, and Elim and Assemblies of God. A look at these movements throws a great deal of light on the doctrines and developments of Restoration. However, before attempting to show these linkages in later chapters, I think it important that we first identify the immediate sources of this kingdom Christianity, and then trace its rise and early development.

This is vitally important, because a major misunderstanding concerning not only R1 and R2, but most house church movements, is that they are an outgrowth of the Charismatic Renewal within the mainstream churches. Seeing them in this way is to regard them as part of neo-Pentecostalism, whereas both theologically and sociologically they are as much akin to classical Pentecostalism. To be more accurate, Restorationism does not spring from the old Pentecostal denominationalism (although it could end up there); neither is it a 'spiritual deviation that sprang from the authentic charismatic movement'.[1] It is a hybrid strand of Pentecostalism that began to emerge in the 1950s.

The Early Years

While Restoration was not planned or orchestrated by any one person in particular, there is no doubt that Arthur Wallis can claim not only the early vision but also considerable influence in the way that vision unfolded. (Restorationists, of course, see God, and not Arthur Wallis, as the architect of his restored kingdom.)

Arthur Wallis – Arthur was the son of a famous preacher, Captain Reginald Wallis. Starting off with the Open Brethren, Captain Wallis later became an itinerant evangelist. Finding the Brethren too sectarian for his tastes, he left the movement while maintaining contacts with Brethren assemblies. Arthur Wallis was greatly influenced by his father, and as a young man he was very much brought up with an Open Brethren dislike of denominationalism. Despite his high-profile charismatic history, Arthur Wallis reminds one of a Christian 'brother'.

It was in 1951 that Arthur Wallis was 'baptized in the Holy Spirit'. Like his father before him, he had already abandoned the Brethren, and now he made two significant decisions which marked him off from many who receive the 'baptism of fire'. Firstly, he never aligned himself with the existing Pentecostal denominations. Secondly, although he became passionately committed to world revival, he had no time for denominational empire-building. He saw, in the 1950s, that praying for revival usually meant praying for Methodist, Baptist or Pentecostal revival.

In 1956, he wrote a book that was to give him an international reputation. This book, *In the Day of Thy Power: the Scriptural Principles of Revival*,[2] contained a similar vision to the earlier hopes of Principal George Jeffreys (Elim) and Smith-Wigglesworth (Assemblies of God) in the late 1920s. They had dreamed of a worldwide 'latter rain' that would herald the return of Christ to the world. This revival would see the demise of denominations and the rise of the universal and Spirit-endowed Church.

While Arthur Wallis had this 'burden' for world revival, he had come across other men, who like himself were looking towards a 'mighty outpouring of the Holy Spirit'. Chief among these was David Lillie, who was also a former member of a Brethren assembly. David Lillie had a major interest in Church structures based on New Testament principles. Both Arthur Wallis and David Lillie were Pentecostal by experience, but dissatisfied with the purely Pentecostal emphasis given by other groups that they were beginning to meet. Wallis was always wary of extreme emotionalism, and the 'glory meetings' of early Chard and other small independent Pentecostal fellowships were not really to his taste. Nevertheless, he had become convinced of the authenticity of tongues and prophecy. He was influenced here by two former members of the Apostolic Church, Cecil Cousen and Edgar Parkyns. Wallis himself admitted that by 1958, it was David Lillie who was the main protagonist of restoring a New Testament pattern of Church life.[3]

In 1958, the first conference organized specifically to discuss the ordering of God's Church and kingdom took place. The conference, which lasted three days, was entitled 'The Church of Jesus Christ – Its Purity, Power, Pattern and Programme in the Context of Today'. A young student named Graham Perrins was there; he became one of the earliest apostles in the Restoration movement in the 1970s, and also edited R2's magazine, *Fulness* (he was also a former member of the Brethren).

Two more early conferences developed this theme. There were some forty leaders at Okehampton in 1961, and eighty leaders at Mamhead Park near Exeter in 1962. Many were 'baptized in the Holy Spirit', and prophecies and interpretations of tongues were heard. A young Welsh evangelist, formerly connected to the Assemblies of God, was present. His name was Bryn Jones and he had caused 'a bit of a stir' in Cornwall by his powerful preaching and healing ministry. (By the late 1970s, this man was to emerge as the most powerful and charismatic leader of the British Restoration movement.)

Campbell McAlpine and New Zealand – At the beginning of the 1960s, two more former Brethren members had emerged as leaders in what was still a no-man's-land between the sectarian life of classical Pentecostalism and the renewalism of the charismatics in the mainstream churches that was to start a few years later. These men were Denis Clarke and Campbell McAlpine. Essentially, like Arthur Wallis, these men – no doubt due to their Brethren background – were wary not only of the traditional Pentecostals, but also of all denominational structures. Nevertheless, as itinerant preachers, they had considerable influence on Brethren, Baptists, and even some Anglicans.

I recall from those days that many Church leaders (including Pentecostalists) were suspicious of these itinerants. Denis was not always liked. His sermons tended to be menacing, and his public personality was somewhat abrasive. Both he and his wife, Beth, were extremely kind, however, and neither were really sectarian in outlook. Campbell was already by this time a moving speaker and was seen very much as a godly man. He is highly respected to this day, and has a reputation as a 'confessor' and confidant that would not be out of place in a Catholic or Orthodox setting. However, although no doubt it was unwitting, there is a sense in which Campbell plays an important part in the early Restoration story. And it takes place not in England, but in New Zealand.

Campbell arrived in New Zealand in 1959. Throughout that year and the next, he made a considerable impact on evangelicals in general and Brethren assemblies in particular. The Brethren, however, were not aware that the evangelist in their midst was a secret Pentecostal. Soon, the secret got out, and McAlpine was placed in a difficult position. The traditional Brethren approach to the gifts of the Spirit is a dispensationalist one: that the gifts belong to the era of the New Testament canon. McAlpine was so respected by the New Zealand Brethren, that some of the leaders begged him to stay, yet keep his Pentecostalism to himself. Through personal contacts and numerous 'cottage meetings', however, McAlpine had considerable influence on

Brethren evangelists and full-time workers.[4] By 1961, when he returned to England, Campbell had aroused great interest in the 'baptism of the Holy Spirit' and seen Christian leaders experience the 'second blessing'. He also left behind him a Brethren movement deeply divided against itself.

Before the Brethren had time to lick their wounds, Arthur Wallis arrived in 1963 at the invitation of the committee of an Easter camp. He was only allowed into a few Brethren assemblies, but in the twenty-one months he stayed in New Zealand he held many cottage meetings, and attempted to bring together those people of Pentecostal experience who were not in Pentecostal denominations.[5] As he had done with the new charismatics in England, he encouraged them to find their own identity outside the Pentecostal churches.

In 1964, a conference was held in New Zealand for the newly 'Spirit-filled Christians'. All speakers but one were former members of Open Brethren assemblies. This conference is evidence that Wallis had decided to attempt to put into practice not merely a Pentecostalist programme, but to establish a charismatically ordained church on New Testament lines (as he saw it). 'The time has come,' said a conference circular,[6] 'for a larger coming together to share the great vision that the Spirit of God is unfolding ... the Holy Spirit of God is wanting to work in apostolic power through a fully functioning body, fed and led and governed by spiritual elders, amongst them those with special gifts and callings.' Wallis believed that the conference was prophetic, pointing to what God would do. He said: 'We would not presume to raise a little finger to precipitate anything.'[7]

However, as McAlpine had returned for this conference, many Brethren leaders looked upon this as interference in the internal religious affairs of New Zealand. There is no doubt that Brethrenism in this part of the Antipodes had become bitterly divided – a division that exists to this day. If McAlpine and Wallis could be seen as divisive or even sectarian, then it must be said in their defence that international Brethren opinion considered the New Zealand Brethren to be extremely heavy-handed in their treatment of the new Pentecostals. In the event, after Wallis left New Zealand in 1964, the charismatic issue calmed down in Brethren assemblies. No new 'restored' church emerged. However, house churches began to appear, largely stocked by disaffected Brethren. Twenty years later, when Gerald Coates (an apostle of R2) returned to England after a visit to New Zealand, he told me: 'You're certainly right about Brethren influence on house churches – over there they're all Brethren.'[8]

The New Zealand episode can be seen as an aborted Restorationism (although it is alive there now), but it does demonstrate that the movement is not the 'Johnny come lately' that some have claimed it to be. Back in Great Britain, Campbell and Arthur found many Open Brethren were now closed to them. They were soon to become caught up in the Charismatic Renewal, but in the spring of 1965, David Lillie, Campbell McAlpine and Arthur Wallis called the third and final of their leaders' conferences. In a sense, this conference is really the beginning of the Restoration story proper; that it is difficult to see it in this way is due to the fact that the Renewal movement pushed the embryonic Restorationism to one side. At the very least, the 1965 conference is a link between the 1958 conference and the emergence of R1 and R2 in the 1970s.

The theme of the conference was the 'Apostolic Commission'. G. W. North was there. So too were Hugh Thompson (now a leader with Bryn Jones's team in Bradford) and Barney Coombs (the founder of the flourishing Basingstoke fellowships). At this time, Wallis's vision was Restorationist, but without the discipleship doctrines that were to become such a hallmark of the mature movement. Nevertheless, that vision, with its emphasis on New Testament structures and principles, was certainly more radical than renewalist ideology. Ironically, the outbreak of the Renewal prevented the radicality from having any effect.

Early Charismatic Renewal and Restorationism

The Charismatic Renewal was such a major religious phenomenon in certain church circles in Great Britain in the late 1960s and 1970s, that the rise of this neo-Pentecostalism simply carried Restorationism along with it. From about 1964 onwards, Arthur Wallis, Denis Clarke, Campbell McAlpine and David Lillie were caught up in this new revivalism. At first, I think that most of them saw the Renewal as both an answer to prayer and proof that the Pentecostal experience could transcend denominational barriers. Both McAlpine and Wallis were closely connected with the Fountain Trust, which was set up in 1964 to promote the Renewal. This organization until its demise in 1980 was non-denominational and very influential in both Anglican and Catholic churches.

Throughout the 1960s, Wallis, McAlpine and Clarke maintained their independent and itinerant status. They maintained links with South Chard, small independent groups, American organizations and mainstream charismatics. There was a great deal of Pentecostal 'jet-setting'; Campbell became one of those rare creatures who are acceptable wherever they go. His gracious manner and genuine openness to new things endeared him to people of widely differing theological opinions.

And yet none of these men became the leaders of the Renewal in Great Britain, precisely because they were outside the traditional denominational structures. British leaders, like their American and European counterparts, were primarily from the historic churches. The thrust of their message was that the existing churches could be spiritually renewed; they had no desire to establish either a new denomination, or create a sort of supra, transnational church.

The images one remembers from early Renewal are not angry young men, nor a Puritan call to re-establish the purity of unsullied Christianity. We remember Catholics dancing in the aisles and new liturgies (unconsciously adopted and adapted from classical Pentecostalism) married uneasily to the old. Hearing Anglicans saying, 'Praise the Lord' and 'Thank you Jesus' became as commonplace as Catholics speaking and singing in tongues. But tongues seemed to make nuns click their rosaries more vociferously, and shouting in extempore fashion only appeared to make Anglicans religiously attend the eucharist. In short, the Renewal created tension and disagreement between the charismatics and their leaders, but for many ordinary Christians it also led to a renewal of their traditional faiths. Perhaps, after all, some sociologists were beginning to say, Pentecostalism does not always lead to schism.[9]

At the very moment when leaders such as Michael Harper, Colin Urquhart, Tom Smail, Peter Hocken, Emmanuel Sullivan and David Watson were demonstrating that revival could be mainstream, other Pentecostalists were beginning to have their doubts. Cardinal Suenens of Belgium, by virtue of being a Catholic hierarch, alienated many Protestants who felt rooted in the Reformation. The fact that the Renewal could later boast at least one Anglican suffragan bishop, in Richard Hare, was proof for some that Charismatic Renewal was Establishment. Certainly, the classical Pentecostals were uneasy from the start.

It could be argued, of course, that the Renewal undercut their rationale; no doubt, sour grapes did play some part. However, Richards spoke for many of the older Pentecostals when he pointed out that renewalist Pentecostalism seemed to be able to hold truck with modernism, heresy, and papal practices at variance with the Word of God.[10] Quoting Scripture, he claimed that the Holy Spirit was not 'the author of confusion', and yet the charismatics seemed not to give up their errors. Perhaps, after all, the movement was demonic?

Increasingly, classical Pentecostals have become more sympathetic to renewal – or at least less antagonistic. They have taken up a position that I believe Arthur Wallis was already taking in the 1960s. He saw the Renewal as a movement of the Spirit of God, but he also saw its short-comings. To have the Pentecostal experience without discipline and authority, he thought, was to have power without responsibility. Furthermore, like so many of his fellow travellers who were former Plymouth Brethren, he was a man brought up to believe in 'sound' doctrine. A major weakness of classical Pentecostalism has been its poor theological understanding of its own experience. In so many Pentecostal circles, testimonies of personal salvation and healing have substituted for the more systematic and doctrinal approach that is the hallmark of many Brethren assemblies. In some respects, however, Wallis was quite happy to be at one with the older style Pentecostals; he was never neutral on doctrinal issues, and he was never at ease with those Anglicans and Catholic charismatics who seemed quite happy with infant baptism.

However, Wallis was hardly a voice being listened to in the 1960s. The stage was taken by the Renewalists, and the emphasis was on co-operation, ecumenism and being one in the Spirit while accepting differences in doctrine. But while everyone's eyes were up front watching the performance of the big denominations, slowly but surely house churches began to appear throughout the country. The members of these churches were primarily from sectarian backgrounds. They were suspicious of the mainstream success, yet at the same time they benefited from it. These new dissenters from Brethren, classical Pentecostal, Evangelical Free Baptists, Salvation Army, and various non-aligned churches, were hidden from close scrutiny by church leaders because they became identified with the Renewal. They did not deliberately hide under the skirts of the charismatic movement – the house churches were neither secret nor subversive – it was just that nobody noticed them until after the Renewal began to slow down from about 1980 onwards. Suddenly, they seemed to be everywhere.

One of the reasons they remained unnoticed was their music and ritual. Many house churches 'plugged into' the

Renewal, borrowing its songs and liturgical mannerisms; conversely, the Renewal picked up the new songs of Restoration. By the end of the 1970s, for example, the R2 'Bind us Together, Lord' could be found in every type of the British charismatic movement. Furthermore, many house church members joined in Renewalist jamborees, and Renewalists attended Downs Week and the Dales Bible Week. R1 and R2 were separate strands of Pentecostalism, but they did, for a while, become interwoven with the Charismatic Renewal *per se*.

Michael Harper and I have a disagreement concerning the decline of Charismatic Renewal. I believe that it slowed down after 1980, while Michael believes that it has still been quietly growing.[11] However, we both agree that the closure of the Fountain Trust in 1980 left the Renewal without a clear focus. Some of the charismatics eager to go 'where the action is' found that it was happening in house churches and, in particular, in R1. The Dales Bible Week at the Great Yorkshire showground provided a new focus and attracted many disaffected charismatics from the mainstream churches. Undoubtedly the Renewal had a profound spiritual effect on thousands of people's lives, but the denominations were left essentially unchanged.

Michael Harper does agree with me, with hindsight, that the Renewal provided the fuel for a new Pentecostalism outside the churches. I offer it as no more than a tentative hypothesis, but could it be that the historical role of Charismatic Renewal has been not to renew the Church, but to aid (albeit unwittingly) the rise of a new sectarianism?[12]

Nascent Restoration in the 1960s

John Noble – The heyday of the charismatic movement was in fact the 1970s, not the 1960s. But from about 1966 onwards it began to accelerate. During this time, throughout Britain, house churches began to appear. John Noble (the senior apostle in R2) started a house church in his front room at Ilford in 1967. He was 'baptized in the Spirit' in 1961 and knew Michael Harper when he was a curate at All Souls, Langham Place, London. During the early days of the charismatic movement, he attended meetings of the Fountain Trust. He recalls that Arthur Wallis was an adviser to the Fountain Trust, and that it was Campbell McAlpine who came up with the idea of the 'fountain gate' that led to the adoption of the title 'Fountain Trust'.

John Noble's background was Salvation Army, and although he was enamoured with the Renewal, he had little in common with establishment Christianity. Influenced by Watchman Nee's book, *Concerning Our Missions* – Nee was himself influenced by Brethren missionaries in China – he decided to start his own mission to homes. Soon, he lost all contact with his former charismatic friends in the Fountain Trust.

Gerald Coates and Cobham – About this time in Cobham, Surrey, a young Brethren member, Gerald Coates, and a few others formed a splinter group from their local assembly. These 'come-outers' met for the next three years in the local youth centre. During this time, they were visited by a number of itinerants, who were former members of Honor Oak (a neo-Brethren community). The group at the youth centre was not initially charismatic. Indeed, when Gerald Coates went to a retreat at Westwatch, West Sussex, in 1967 (organized by Maurice Smith), he thought they were all mad.

Meanwhile, back in Cobham, the splinter group began to have second thoughts about their separateness. 'You can't have two "tables" in the same town', goes the old Brethren adage concerning communion fellowship. So, many of the splinter group decided to return to the local assembly. Gerald Coates, his wife and three friends began to meet in his front room; this was the beginning of the now 400-strong Cobham Christian Fellowship. Gerald's own Pentecostal experience began as he found himself speaking in tongues while riding his bicycle. In those very early days, as others joined them and became 'baptized in the Spirit', the Cobham group had no idea that they were only one of scores of new charismatic house groups outside the mainstream denominations. As Gerald put it: 'We were insecure, green as green could be, and felt that we were probably the only people in Britain who really loved the Lord Jesus but didn't actually go to church on Sunday . . .'[13]

What characterized the Cobham group – and many others – during the late 1960s was above all a sense of freedom. They felt released from the dead formalism (as they saw it) of traditional Christianity. No more 'spiritual sandwiches' of prayer, hymn and preaching for them. Sometimes they would sing in tongues for hours, or dance and cry. There was prophecy and interpreting the glossolalia. The new freedom was also experienced as breaking through to 'real' relationships and commitment to each other. None of these groups really knew where they were going during this anarchic and exciting Pentecostalism – the emphasis was on experience, relationships and freewheeling liturgies. There was no overt leadership, and those who did minister were known by their first names.

And yet, as the 1967 Westwatch retreat demonstrates, there were conferences going on where Arthur Wallis's earlier vision was still alive although in dormant form. Maurice Smith believes that the 1967 conference (and the earlier one in 1965 organized by Arthur Wallis) was a vital stepping stone to the emergent Restorationism of the 1970s. His own story is worth telling[14] not only because it is interesting in itself, but also because it leads us into the first co-ordinating efforts of early Restorationism.

Maurice Smith – Maurice was converted in 1955. Then an Anglican, he soon became disillusioned with all types of denominations. By 1956, he was determined to remain Christian but without a church. He remembers praying by the side of his bed: 'Lord, I think your Son is wonderful, and your church is horrible. And I don't want any more to do with it. People in pubs are more friendly than in the churches.'

He eventually joined Honor Oak Fellowship which was a breakaway group from Honor Oak Baptist Church. This organization is an interesting link between the older-style evangelicalism and the modern house church movements. Some sixty years ago, it was dominated by the personality of T. Austin Sparks, who influenced Watchman Nee's writings. Honor Oak Fellowship was against emotionalism and mass evangelism. It put great stress on self-denial and the corporate life of the Christian community. Maurice Smith became an elder in the community, and remained in the movement for ten years. By 1966 he was desperate to get out. He felt that the community was committed to law rather than grace, and he felt that there was neither great love nor spiritual power. Honor Oak, like most orthodox Brethren assemblies at that time, were totally against any kind of Pentecostalism. Smith kept hearing of nothing else in the country, so it seemed to him, except 'baptism of the Holy Spirit, baptism of the Holy Spirit . . .'

At that time, he came under the influence of a Methodist called Edgar Trout. Smith was thinking of leaving Honor Oak as a result of Trout's influence, when, driving home to Canterbury through Sussex, 'My car was suddenly filled with light, supernatural light. I was not frightened. I knew that God had separated me to do his work.'

He gave up his job as a sales executive, and in February 1967 came out of Honor Oak with another community member, Ted Crick. Under their leadership, 'Canterbury became a little bit of a centre', and Maurice and Ted began to travel around the country. As they did so, they realized that charismatics and house groups were everywhere. Often without leadership, these groups were looking for fellowship with others like themselves. Ted and Maurice also discovered the by now quite well-developed work of Harry Greenwood and Sid Purse at Chard, and the fellowships of Wally North. Not being from the major denominations themselves, they had little in common with the Anglicans and Catholics (although Michael Harper later became a friend). They began to bump into other itinerants – many of whom had been present at David Lillie's and Arthur Wallis's conferences in 1962 and 1965. Such men as Denis Clarke, Campbell McAlpine, Cecil Cousen and Edgar Trout were ministering to people in the denominations and the new house groups.

The leaders who were invited to Westwatch in 1967, which Maurice organized, were really self-selecting. They were those who had either started house churches, or acted as itinerant ministers to new fellowships. Roger Forster (the founder of Ichthus) was there, as were Graham Perrins and Hugh Thompson (both former Brethren). Peter Lyne was also present, but his denominational background was Baptist of a 'vaguely liberal kind'. Arthur Wallis was in the thick of it all; perhaps by now he saw that the cottage meetings of New Zealand had a greater counterpart in Great Britain.

New leaders began to appear, such as Terry Virgo (now an apostle in R1), Ian McCullogh (now an independent leader but of R2 stripe), and Barney Coombs, whom we have already met at the 1965 conference. By 1970, leaders were meeting more frequently, house churches (on an *ad hoc* basis) were continuing to grow, and as the Charismatic Renewal entered its most successful decade, clusters of these new churches began to come together for common worship.

Recommended Reading

David Lillie, *Restoration: Is This Still on God's Programme?* (private publication, The Kyrtonia Express, 1995) chapters 1 and 2.

Jonathan Wallis, *Arthur Wallis: Radical Christian* (Eastbourne: Kingsway, 1991).

Arthur Wallis, 'Springs of Restoration', Part 1, *Restoration* (Harvestime Publications, July/August 1980).

Michael Harper, *None Can Guess* (London: Hodder & Stoughton, 1971).

Emmanuel Sullivan, S.A., 'Can the Pentecostal Movement Renew the Churches?' booklet (BCC, 1971).

Peter Hocken, *Streams of Renewal: Origins and Early Development of the Charismatic Movement in Great Britain* (Carlisle: Paternoster Press, 1986).

3

THE RESTORED KINGDOM EMERGES 1970–75

The coming together of scattered house churches was in no sense orchestrated within a predetermined ideological framework. While it was possible by 1975 to look back and see the events that led up to the establishment of Restorationism, it was not the case that house church leaders in 1970 knew either who exactly they were, or where they were going.

The years 1970–74 were heady days of great excitement and discovery: a discovery of meeting groups all over the country with similar beginnings and common aspirations. Those aspirations, on the whole, were related to 'walking with God' in such a way that the experiential and supernatural became a living grace that seemed to have done away with religious legalism once and for all. The legalism of clericalism, Church order, standardized liturgies, denominational certainties and dogmatic doctrines were seen to be swept aside by the coming of the Spirit. Certainly, people like Maurice Smith, John Noble, Gerald Coates and George Tarleton (who became an apostle in R2) experienced those early days as freedom from the old religious order; how this new freedom would develop (that is, what they would become free to do) was simply not known.

So unstructured were those days in the early 1970s that the leading participants find it difficult to recall the events in any logical or chronological way.[1] What does emerge clearly enough is this: from the end of the 1960s to 1974, London became a major focus of the emerging Restorationism. As we shall see, the Capel Bible Week in

West Sussex played a part in bringing Bryn Jones into the foreground, but he was already beginning to establish himself and his team in the north of England.

'The London Brothers' and the 'Festival of Light'

We can take up the story again with Maurice Smith. By the end of the 1960s he had left Canterbury and moved to a fellowship in Turner's Hall, Chigwell, North London. There, he met up with David Mansell. Mansell, whose 'prophetic' insights and controversial private life have been both sources of wonder and bewilderment for many Restoration followers, is a key figure in the movement. A major leader in the early days, he later became identified with R1 under the apostleship of Bryn Jones. By 1970, he and Maurice were 'into' community. (I recall that this was a major theme in Catholic charismatic circles at that time.) Maurice is always 'into' something, and usually ahead of the crowd.

The formation of leadership – By 1969, Maurice had, in his own words, 'a burden for London come upon me'. He wrote to eighteen leaders from different house church movements that included Chard and Wally North. Apparently, Wally North never came, and Lance Lambert of Halford House, Richmond (another small house church that predates the 1960s), came once, did not like what he saw, and never came again. This first meeting – which Maurice Smith thinks was in 1970, or possibly 1969 – was held in the Leprosy Mission Hall. Soon, these meetings became regular, and numbers rapidly increased. By this time, John Noble was a major figure by virtue of his strong personality and his success at Ilford and later Romford. Gerald Coates, Terry Virgo, George Tarleton, David Mansell and Maurice Smith began to be seen – with John Noble – as the core of what became known as the 'London Brothers'.

Chard's influence was strong in the early gatherings,

which were very similar to the 'Glory Meetings'. Sid Purse, however, according to Maurice Smith, saw the thing negatively as an attempt to organize unity. Chard influence petered out, as the London Brothers began to 'do their own thing'. It was the music and worship that marked those early meetings at the Leprosy Mission. Nobody formally led, but instead, free expression was the norm, and the sense of freedom itself generated a strong sense of unity. These Leprosy Mission Hall meetings were mainly for the emerging leadership, not the rank and file. The fact that there was little formality and a great deal of shouting, praising, leaping and dancing could not mask the fact that leadership was being formed.

Soon, the Leprosy Mission began to attract 100 or more people; not all, of course, were leaders. The Mission Hall organizers asked the charismatic enthusiasts to leave, because the noise and threatened structural damage to the floorboards were becoming cause for concern! The emerging leadership continued to meet on an informal basis. Strong personal relationships were formed, and no pecking order had yet arisen. Indeed, in 1970, hierarchical concepts of leadership went against the egalitarian spirit of the London Brothers.

The Festival of Light – 1971 saw the London Brotherhood moving into a different phase. A 'one off' meeting was held at All Souls, Langham Place, but by now house group leaders, itinerant evangelists, and rank and file members were too great in number to get in. It was agreed to start meeting at the London School of Economics.

That year, Peter Hill, who was himself in a house group, organized what Malcolm Muggeridge came to call the 'Festival of Light'. This demonstration against the 'permissive society' began on 25th September with a massive rally in Trafalgar Square. It was attended by thousands of Catholics, evangelicals, charismatics and some right-wing organizations and Establishment religious figures. Members of the London and south-east house churches came in droves. It must be remembered that although members thought they were 'under grace' and in freedom, most of them came to their new churches with well-conditioned Puritan consciences. The Festival of Light was a battle cry against the 'kingdom of this world' and its prince, Satan. God's kingdom, they realized, had to be ordered on biblical principles.

The Festival of Light was a 'call to seriousness' in the evangelical tradition of the nineteenth century.[2] Even in the 'glory days' of the Leprosy Mission Hall, much emphasis had been put on 'kingdom living', the imminent return of Jesus Christ, and discovering the significance of the revival they were all experiencing. On one occasion, some Argentinians who were distant associates of Juan Carlos Ortiz had come to tell the brethren of the need for discipleship and order. The Festival of Light was seen as an attack upon the disorder of a secular world. The fact that the new house groups responded to the call for moral purity in a way that many mainstream charismatics did not, is not very surprising. Many of the latter, being liberal by disposition, were sceptical of the political motivations behind the Festival; they did not share the Puritanism and evangelical traditions that characterized most house church members.

But if the Festival of Light was a moral crusade and evoked a moral response from house church members, it also had an unintended consequence. Singing and speaking in tongues, free-wheeling worship, fingers pointing high to the Jesus who is king, and cries of 'hallelujah' and 'amen' became a feature of the mass demonstrations. Charismatics were soon able to seek each other out as the Pentecostal signals were self-evident for all to see. And now house church groups found, perhaps for the first time, just how many of them there were. Group leaders had been telling them of an emerging movement of the Spirit, but now they could see for themselves. The Festival of Light did not give birth to Restoration, but it did confirm for many that something was emerging.

That something was still essentially an anarchic animal. The London School of Economics meetings swelled to some 500 people, with leaders bringing their wives and friends. Worship was still free and easy, and no formal leadership existed. John Noble was just plain John to everybody, and 'Gerald', 'Maurice', 'David' and 'George' was the order of the day. Everybody I have talked to about those early days agrees that the 'blessing' was related to friendliness and openness to new things of God.

All sorts of charismatic and non-charismatic things were tried. There was 'deliverance ministry', where sickness and sin were rebuked as evidence of demonic possession or oppression. Rebuking was done in the name of Jesus – the usual phrase being 'I command you', or 'I rebuke you, in the name of Jesus to come out'. Sometimes praying for the sick would be a 'laying on of hands ministry', with as many people doing the hand-laying as could reach the sick person. Even in those anarchic days, I can find no one who remembers seeing women laying on hands.[3] Demons, miracles and the exercise of spiritual gifts (such as speaking in tongues, the interpretation of tongues, prophecy, giving 'words of wisdom and knowledge') were an experienced reality within the context of an overwhelming conviction that Christ was about to return to claim his Church.

This strong eschatological thrust was one of the major reasons why early Restorationists began to ask themselves: what should be the nature of this Church for whom God is coming? What should we, as redeemed and Spirit-filled Christians be doing to hasten the coming? What does it mean that God is coming to establish his kingdom? What is the kingdom? Anarchic Pentecostalism has no answers to such questions. On the whole, mainstream Charismatic Renewal, which was now really taking off in Great Britain, was not concerned with such issues. House church leaders were asking such questions, but even so, many of them were still content to bask in the new-found light and warmth of discovered friendships. Finding friends with similar beliefs and practices to yourself is an essential pre-requisite to forming organizational structures.

Experimentalism was the hallmark of the LSE meetings. There was the curious practice of leg-lengthening: apparently, you stuck out both legs and invariably found one leg longer than the other one. It was believed that lengthening the short leg could improve all sorts of physical ailments. A kind of chiropractice seemed to be the method; massage would be used, sometimes with prayer and sometimes without. George Tarleton was really keen on this – 'the odder things were the better George liked them'[4] – but John Noble remained sceptical.

Two themes – By the end of 1971, John Noble in particular, but also George Tarleton, David Mansell, Gerald Coates, Terry Virgo, Hugh Thompson, Maurice Smith and Ted Crick were *de facto* leaders in the south-east. Graham Perrins and Peter Lyne, who were in association with them, were flying the flag of the nascent Restorationism in the west and south-west of the country. A magazine had appeared in 1970 called *Fulness*. The early editions were not particularly professional in presentation, neither were they dated,[5] but they do reveal that a line was already beginning to emerge amongst the leaders.

The first editions, from 1970 into 1971, were held together by that old duo Maurice Smith and Ted Crick, under the editorial direction of Graham Perrins. Guest writers were David Lillie and Hugh Thompson. Discipleship doctrines did not appear there, but there was already interest in apostleship (with reference to Ephesians 4). Two strong themes emerged. The first was the call to unity in the Spirit. St John's Gospel, chapter 17, was much in evidence. John Noble remembers that the desire to belong simply to the Church and not a new organization dominated those early days.[6] This call to unity was seen against the sin of denominationalism. A little book of John Noble from 1971 was entitled *Forgive Us Our Denominations*. In it, he wrote of denominationalism as dis-

unity, and thus sinfulness (a view also held by liberal ecu-
menists). The call to unity was understood not as building
a new superchurch, in the sense of a transdenominational
Church, but a call to repentance and the restoring of New
Testament spiritual gifts. Prophetically, John Noble
warned of forming a new 'non-sectarian sect' (which in
many ways, in my opinion, R2 has become).

This leads us to the second theme, for Ted Crick introduced the notion of the remnant Church (a theme much
loved by Brethren and Pentecostals over the years). This
was the true Church awaiting God's return; the false
Church being the apostate Church of nominal Christians,
under the direction of liberal and modernist leaders. There
was much talk of 'restoring' the Church or kingdom in the
power of the Holy Spirit. The belief that God was restoring
his Church – and that they were in it – was itself seen as a
sign or witness that the world ('this present age') was coming to an end.

The London Brothers, and the emerging southern leadership, continued to have influence for the next few years,
but in order to see how Bryn Jones and Bradford come into
the picture, I suggest we turn to his work and influence in
a new group of leaders. It is this group that takes
Restorationism out of its anarchic phase, and turns it into
the radical Christianity that it has become today.

The Rise of Bryn Jones and Covenanted Relationships

In Arthur Wallis's article, 'Springs of Restoration',[7] he
seeks to trace the origins of R1 in various 'tributaries' or
'streams' which eventually become the rushing torrent of
Restoration. Such imagery is popular in R1 and R2. 'The
streams make glad' of Psalm 46 is an ever-popular image
used to describe the various strands of the house churches.
Like all images, however, they can be misleading. I doubt
whether it is strictly accurate to describe early Restoration
as having two streams (in the sense of separate ideologies

or major differences). However, I think the imagery is helpful if we think not of separateness, but of a different geographical location and focus. While the London Brothers were pioneering the south-east and debating the tenets that were eventually to form the basic teaching of Restoration, Bryn Jones began to establish a well-organized community church in Bradford from 1969.

Since Arthur Wallis first met him in 1962, Bryn Jones had experienced a rather chequered career. He left Cornwall and went to France, and later Germany, where he worked for three months with the interdenominational evangelistic organization, Operation Mobilisation. He met his wife, Edna, at the Bible College of Wales. Having married her in 1964, they set off as missionaries to Guyana (then British Guiana). Bryn demonstrated the true evangelistic pioneering spirit in the three years he was there. Working with a West Indian leader, Philip Mohabir, he helped establish sixteen churches; there are now eighty-four.

He returned to Cornwall, the scene of his earlier success, but after the doctrinal squabbles with Chard and others, he moved on to Bradford. By 1970, Bryn was virtually unknown in the south, but his work began to flourish in the north. His brother Keri joined him and their pioneering work began. Bryn Jones would not wish it to be thought that the spectacular rise of the Bradford community church (after 1975) and the later establishment of an apostolic team under his direction was simply his doing. He would point to the fact that what I call R1 has other apostolic teams, and that the success of all the teams is primarily due to the Holy Spirit. It would be eccentric, however, to assume that the rise of R1 had nothing to do with the personality and style of Bryn Jones. He is no slouch when it comes to positive action. It is easy to believe that he would have been successful as a trade union leader or as the director of a large business corporation.

He has two strengths as a leader, in addition to his powerful preaching. Not only does he possess vision, but he has the ruthless determination to bring that vision to a reality. Somebody once described him to me as a 'bruiser under anointing'! His critics in R2 and elsewhere would say that he is an operator or a manipulator; they see him as an opportunist who knows a good thing when he sees it, and who grabs the main chance. I think that he is also an idealist. The idea that he must either be a saint or a rogue is, I believe, stretching it too far. There is a Russian Orthodox saying that I think might help us in trying to evaluate this interesting man and avoid having to see him as either the greatest saint of all time, or as a man 'on the make'. The saying is that 'great virtues cast long shadows'.[8]

Friends and critics alike admit that he is a born leader. In 1970, with almost no money or organization, he set up a summer camp at Pendine, South Wales. 'Two marquees, one for meetings, the other for eating, a team of three volunteer cooks and a set of tents for hire to would-be campers were the total equipment.'[9] These camps were later to become the summer camps at the Lakes, and from 1976 the Dales Bible Week at the Great Yorkshire Showground outside Harrogate. From the outset, they were designed as an interdenominational gathering. Initially, they concentrated on Bible teaching and Pentecostal ministry. It was not until after 1976 that they emerged as a shop-window for Restoration, and developed a distinctive and highly successful style of worship and song.

During 1970, Bryn developed relationships with American evangelists and religious leaders. He had already developed American connections, however, on his way back from Guyana when he stayed in North America for a while. From the start, the Bradford movement was different in kind from the London and southern fellowships. Biblical and family authority were stressed more than in the south. Members were noticeably more working class than the southerners. Understandably, therefore, leadership was more authoritarian, and followers more conservative than their southern counterparts.

Originally, Bryn Jones's Assemblies of God background showed: the doctrine and the worship were little different from classical Pentecostalism. The first few editions of *Restoration* magazine in 1975/76 have a traditional Pentecostal flavour to them, with a little added spice of Renewalism. There was a great expectancy, however, that God was beginning a great work. Bryn was (and still is) an outstanding and clever preacher. He can be folksy Welsh in the best *hwyl* tradition, an inspired expositor of Scripture, and a very funny and witty performer. Added to this talent, he is clearly intelligent and thoughtful. He has a reputation for prophetic insight and miraculous happenings have always been part of his ministry. This obviously looks, in religious terms, like a recipe for charismatic leadership that is hard to beat. As one of the former leaders of R2 said to me recently: 'If it was just a question of being on the winning side, I'd stick with Bryn Jones.'[10]

The 'magnificent seven' – Clearly, Arthur Wallis had not forgotten the youthful Jones of 1962. He knew of his outstanding talents and leadership potential, and in 1971 he called together a group of leaders to discuss not Restoration as such, nor even apostleship structures, but eschatology. By now Arthur, who had worked hard behind the scenes of Charismatic Renewal, was hankering after a more radical vision: a vision that he had glimpsed in New Zealand years before. What was now fanning the fires of this vision was his eschatological conviction that not only was Christ soon returning to earth to reign, but that he wanted to establish the foundations of his kingdom before he arrived. Wallis wanted to share with other leaders the possibility that the end-time was not to be characterized by total disaster, but the restoration of a glorious Church that was itself to signal the 'restoration of all things'.

In a way, Arthur's group got out of hand. What started as a series of meetings to discuss prophecy turned into a workshop to hammer out the principles of the restored kingdom. There was no law or line, and no overt leadership during these early meetings, but there soon emerged the conviction that God had separated the group to be leaders and apostles in his end-time Church. The first meeting included six people, and they met in February 1972. The Festival of Light was understood prophetically as a symbol – an outward sign of kingdom Christianity. The leadership meetings were the inner or spiritual heart of the kingdom, where the rules and order of God's Church would be revealed by the Word (*logos*) of God, and the word (*rhema*) of prophecy. The original six leaders were Arthur Wallis, Peter Lyne, Bryn Jones, David Mansell, Graham Perrins and Hugh Thompson. After Bryn Jones prophesied: 'Seven shall be your number, and thrice you shall meet', it was decided to add John Noble. Apparently, there was considerable discussion as to whether John Noble was suitable.

The group, who later jokingly called themselves the 'magnificent seven', did meet three times – indeed, John Noble thinks they met more than that. It was then decided to open out the leadership to a broader brotherhood. This has always been a point of controversy. Bryn Jones was away when this decision was taken and felt that it was premature. Years later, Arthur Wallis felt that the split of 1976 was caused by not heeding God's advice to limit the number to seven.[11] John Noble does not recall any such advice. In the event, the augmented 'magnificent seven' became known as the 'fabulous fourteen'.

In the first meetings of the seven, what began to emerge as they prayed and fasted together was a strong sense of mutual destiny. As they looked around and saw each other and recognized the work that they had already achieved, they became convinced – under numerous promptings of personal prophecies – that they were already exercising apostolic and prophetic functions. Their recognition of function became the way leadership emerged. So, for example, Graham Perrins could be seen as a prophet and an apostle because he had both the inspired word and had pioneered house churches in Wales (before any of the others, incidentally). Or again, David Mansell was seen as a prophet because of his insights and pronouncements, but he could not be seen as an apostle because he had not established churches. This establishment of churches certainly made Bryn an apostle, but he clearly had gifts of evangelism and prophecy too. John Noble was undoubtedly an apostle because of his 'laying of the foundations' of God's work in the south-east.

These functions were not simply recognized by the word of prophecy alone. They were thought to be confirmed by the Word of God. In particular, they were convinced that the words of Ephesians 4:8–12 were not meant merely for the New Testament dispensation, but were the divine principles on which the Church should have been ordered throughout history. To recapitulate, the key verses 11 and 12 state:

It was he who gave some to be apostles, some to be prophets, some to be evangelists, and some to be pastors and teachers, to prepare God's people for works of service, so that the body of Christ may be built up. (NIV)

As these men grappled with this startling vision that they now realized was applicable to them personally, they began to think also of what this meant in terms of personal commitment to each other. From this emerged a belief that they should form a covenant together, a belief that was extended to the full fourteen. At one meeting Graham Perrins failed to turn up; the others took this very personally, seeing in it a failure of commitment. The new seven that augmented the original group to the full 'fabulous fourteen' were George Tarleton, Gerald Coates, Barney Coombs, Maurice Smith, Ian McCullogh, John MacLauchlan, and Campbell McAlpine. There had been talk of including Denis Clarke, but this nomination did not meet with full approval (what Denis thought of his exclusion I cannot say, as sadly he died in 1981).

George Tarleton, who believes he was the most liberal character in the group, is now amazed that he could have turned his back on the freedom and grace which he saw as the hallmarks of the London Brothers. However, the workshops were so exciting, and there was such a feeling of God's purposes being worked out in their lives, that he failed to see that they were beginning what he now feels was the beginning of denominationalism. There is no doubt that the 'fabulous fourteen' did take a radical change in direction. Anarchic Pentecostalism was not yet entirely conquered among the London Brothers (as we shall see), but from 1974 onwards, a firm leadership began to be established both in the south and north.

House church fellowships did not seem to want to resist this leadership. On the contrary, scores of independent groups now began to align themselves with the emerging apostles. They wanted to be 'in' on the new thing that God was doing. The discipling and submission doctrines were couched in the language of biblical imagery such as 'shepherding' or 'covering'. To be under authority was seen to be in 'relatedness' to apostles and their appointed elders. Both the emerging leadership and the rank and file thought in terms of being 'bound by cords of love', and being released from the bondage of wilful independence. The apostolic doctrines were in no sense worked out at this time, and Bryn Jones and Arthur Wallis were more careful in their statements than a number of the London Brothers.

Nevertheless, by 1974, the self-selection (or God's election) of the 'fabulous fourteen' led to the establishment of a charismatically ordained leadership. This leadership was legitimated by an appeal to members to recognize the *de facto* leadership that had already emerged. Bryn Jones, for example, is an apostle, so the argument went, because he acts like an apostle. Furthermore, house church members were told, the Holy Spirit who had separated Barnabas and Saul in the Acts of the Apostles, was the same Spirit who had separated the fourteen to be leaders of the restored kingdom. This truth was confirmed for the leaders by the inner testimony of personal conviction and the outward seal of prophetic utterance. In a sense, the 'fabulous fourteen' had ordained each other not in any formal ceremony, but by mutual recognition of ministry, prophecy and the laying on of hands. In no sense, however, did these men have the delusions of grandeur that led them to believe that they were the only apostles in the world, and that they alone constituted the only true leadership in God's restored Church.

Establishing the Restorationist movement – The years 1972–74 were not merely the years that saw the gradual establishment of a new leadership structure. They were also the years in which the nascent Restoration movement gave way to a quite different ideological orientation. Now it was held that God's Spirit speaks in a special way through his ordained servants: the vertical relationship with God was now augmented (perhaps even superseded) by horizontal relationships with God via his apostles, prophets and elders.

I think that such an interpretation would be going too far for the majority of R1 and R2 leaders today. Nevertheless, it was an understanding that some house churches developed. This is particularly true of those groups who stressed the primacy of the prophet. Graham Perrins and John MacLauchlan were to fall out with the rest of the R2 leaders over this matter. In 1974/75, however, the radicality of this change in direction was not fully recognized or understood by many house groups, and the full implications were not even fully realized by some of the 'fabulous fourteen'.

It would seem to me to be unwise to break up our narrative with an analysis of this change of direction. Perhaps, however, we might pause for a parable. Some time ago, I was sent a duplicated letter in which the author had an amusing yet thoughtful insight into the adoption of apostolic and discipleship doctrines by the house churches. I include the piece, which is called 'Chiefs and Indians', in full:

In the not far distant past, the great spirit began to speak to the Indians in the north, in the western coastlands and on the eastern flats. Little bands began to meet in their tepees to rediscover their common life in the great spirit and to make deep friendship. They held pow-wows, spoke wisdom and smoked the pipe of peace. Each group was a band of equal brothers freely serving and sharing gifts with each other.

After a while, each band began to recognize a warrior who seemed to have a deeper knowledge of the great spirit, to whom they would listen with respect, go to for advice and look to for organization. They gave him a feather to wear and he was soon known as One Feather. After three moons, One Feather ceased to hunt and fish. The others brought him gifts. He told them great spirit's words, how to plan their lives, how to bring up their children. Some Indians found it more difficult to hear the great spirit for themselves, finding it easier to listen to One Feather.

It was not long before a One Feather with a larger band than most, was given a pony by his people and began to travel. He met with other bands and eventually called a meeting of One Feathers. 'We need to get more organized,' he told them. 'The present situation is a woolly mess.'

'Didn't the great spirit himself bring it about?' asked one brave.

'Of course,' replied the pony rider. 'But he has told me that things must change.'

So the One Feathers decided, as leaders, that they themselves should have a leader. So it was that pony rider became Little Chief Two Feathers with an appropriate headdress and a special tepee. He would not have much time to share with the 'no-feathers' now, but would instruct the One Feathers who would pass his teaching down. Some One Feathers now found it more difficult to hear the great spirit for themselves and found it easier to listen to Little Chief Two Feathers.

Some moons later, Two Feathers, who now had a horse and travelled more widely, holding many gatherings for One Feathers, came across others like himself. They met together in solemn conclave and decided that they too must be 'covered' (this curious term arose from an ancient writing, when a squaw was covered by a famous chief's blanket). After some fuss and a lot of pow-wow, Big Chief Many Feathers emerged. He was given a many-horsed chariot and a team of Two Feathers to travel the country giving input and guidance. Some Two Feathers now found it more difficult to hear the great spirit for themselves and found it easier to listen to Big Chief Many Feathers.

Meantime, the great spirit began to speak to many no-feathers in the north and in the coastlands and on the eastern flats. Little bands began to gather in their tepees to share their common life in the great spirit and to enter into deep friendship . . .[12]

This parable, while pertinent to the new movement, should not be interpreted literally as far as Restorationism is concerned. Indeed, what emerged from the meetings of the fourteen were not only differences of emphasis, but competing leadership. Bryn Jones, John Noble and Graham Perrins emerged as the strong personalities. Ironically, Arthur Wallis, who had originally called the seven together, was neither recognized as a prophet nor as an apostle. He had to be content to watch other people fulfil his vision while he was left in the honorary position of elder statesman. His formal role, until his untimely death in 1988, was to be a member of Tony Morton's apostolic team, with an itinerant role as the prophetic teacher of Restoration.

By 1974, I believe the Restorationist movement had

become tentatively established, with distinctive doctrines, leadership and liturgical practices. However, there was no formal organization, and no single leader. John Noble became the leading apostle in the South, and Bryn Jones dominated the North. Graham Perrins was strong in the West, but never established such a strong and wide circle as Jones and Noble (although Graham's 'covering' was accepted outside his Welsh stronghold – in Petersfield in Hampshire, for example).

The primary reason why we can see the years 1973–76 as the years when the 'restored kingdom' (although it did not have this name) had arrived, was the mutual recognition of leadership and ministry amongst the 'fabulous fourteen'. These men saw themselves in covenanted relationship and their work as the fruit of the Holy Spirit. Their vision, at that time, was for a worldwide Church founded on the lines revealed to them in their deliberations together. However, even during these years, the 'kingdom' was in no sense a uniform structure. The evidence seems to suggest that it was the London Brothers and their associates who first developed a strong interest in discipleship and apostleship.

Conversely, while it seems to be the case that Bryn Jones and his colleagues were a year or two behind in fully developing the apostolic/discipling structure, they were certainly ahead when it came to organizing successful and rational financial structures. Furthermore, although Bryn Jones and John Noble, for example, were in covenanted relationship in these years, they worked quite separately. Bryn Jones saw the work he was doing as never really a part of what I have called R2.[13] This is not an historical fact: it is a spiritual judgment of hindsight on his part. In the early 1970s, the 'fabulous fourteen' all thought that they were involved in the same work of restoring the kingdom.[14]

The London Brothers Go International and Capel Bible Week

When the 'fabulous fourteen' came together, the London Brothers had already gone up-market from the London School of Economics and had begun to hold regular meetings at the Bonnington Hotel (hotels seemed to be popular among the Restoration leaders). These meetings became a focal point for many of the ideas that were to be worked out by the fourteen leaders. The fourteen were later to become twenty-eight, but this larger number never had the same prestige as the smaller groups. Significantly, many of the ideas discussed at the Bonnington came from America and many of the guests were neither classical Pentecostals nor leaders from the mainstream Charismatic Renewal.

Dennis Bennet, author of a best-selling book, *Nine O'Clock in the Morning*, came to talk. A little later, Ern Baxter, who was a member of a group known as the 'Fort Lauderdale Five', made a major impact. These men were involved in similar movements to the English Restorationists, but their vision at that time was more fully worked out, and their commitment to 'church growth ministries' much greater. The London Brothers, with their grassroots fellowships, were somewhat overawed by the idealistic and grandiose plans of these American charismatics. Individual brothers began to make their own contacts with American counterparts. Graham Perrins linked up with a man from Minnesota called Charles Schmitt, and John MacLauchlan later related to a man from Arizona with the unlikely name of Wayne Drain.

But probably it was Orvil Swindoll, and other one-time associates of the Argentinian Juan Carlos Ortiz, who made the first major impact upon the Bonnington Hotel meetings. Ortiz can claim to be the father of discipling and shepherding doctrines in their modern Protestant form. Indeed, it was Ern Baxter and friends who took Ortiz's teachings and established them in North America. I can imagine some readers leaping to the conclusion that this whole Restoration thing is American – however, it is important that we distinguish between genesis and form. John Noble and Gerald Coates, for example, were already thinking along discipling lines when Swindoll came into the picture. Of course, unconsciously they may have picked it up from the earlier days at the Leprosy Mission Hall when they first met Argentinians there.

Bryn Jones insists too that the apostolic doctrines of Baxter were not the origins of his thinking. Bryn, anyhow, had been influenced in his youth by men of the Apostolic Church in Wales, which had been ordering its affairs according to Ephesians chapter 4 since the First World War.[15] Former members of that Church had already influenced nascent Restoration since David Lillie and Arthur Wallis had started their conferences back in 1958. What I believe Swindoll and later Baxter did do for the London Brothers (and R1, too) was to show them how to conceptualize and think through not only the principles of 'covering', but also the principles that were constitutive of the kingdom of God. The Americans helped shape the formation of Restoration, but the major influence was not on the London Brothers, but on the successful emergence of R1 as the major Restorationist movement in Great Britain. This influence was primarily felt at the Dales Bible Week in 1976, and at the Lakes Week the preceding year.

But we are looking ahead, because Bryn Jones's involvement with Ern Baxter commenced at an earlier Bible week. Some of the London Brothers had become involved in this Bible week at Capel, which was the home of the Elim Bible College[16] – not that Elim had much to do with the whole enterprise. Capel Bible Week was the successor to the Abinger Bible Week of Fred Pride. The Capel Week was run by a committee which was quite independent of Elim. This committee included such names as Harold Owen, Mike Pusey, George Tarleton – and later Gerald Coates and Barney Coombs. These men, while sympathetic to the flourishing Renewal movement, were not anxious to turn Capel into a Renewalist shop window.

Most of the committee, with their sectarian backgrounds, were more sympathetic to the revivalism of classical Pentecostalism and the radicalism of the newer independent groups, both in Great Britain and America. In particular, they wanted Capel to be involved with men who could 'preach and teach' in a style that belonged to the Holiness, Pentecostal, and evangelical traditions. People like Michael Harper did not really fit the bill, while Ortiz and Baxter did.

They also invited Bryn Jones in 1973. He was such a success that he was invited back in 1974, where he shared the platform with Ern Baxter. Arthur Wallis sees the Capel Bible Week as a significant 'spring' of Restoration.[17] I think this is far more true for the emergence of R1 than R2. Capel gave Bryn a southern platform. It introduced him to the freer styles of worship and praise pioneered by the London Brothers and other fellow travellers. He saw the potential of Capel-style conventions for providing a focus for the end-time message of God restoring his Church and establishing his reign and rule in his kingdom. There was no need for Bryn to do so, but he asked the committee if they would mind if he started a northern equivalent to Capel Bible Week. This became the Lakes Bible Week, and for sheer verve and professionalism it soon knocked the spots off Capel Bible Week. The success of the Lakes, and later the Dales, was a major factor in the decline of Capel Bible Week, which soon closed down altogether.

In the south, various new jamborees emerged in time, but the London Brothers were never able to set up a rival Restoration week. This was a conscious decision on their part; it was not an inability to get anything off the ground. Later in the 1970s, R1 started Downs Week under Terry Virgo, with input by Bryn Jones and his associates. Gerald Coates became involved with Royal Week in Cornwall. Don Double, an independent Pentecostalist, and Peter Lyne, of the 'magnificent seven', were involved in this. The mixture there was eclectic: a bit of old-style revivalism, house church, and Renewalism.

Meanwhile, before these southern replacements for Capel became established, the London Brothers continued to be successful in the capital itself. They could fill the Westminster Central Hall and the Albert Hall, even without international speakers. In 1974, 1,500 turned up at the Friends' Meeting House. That meeting and subsequent meetings at Westminster Central Hall demonstrated that the London Brothers had not yet completely abandoned anarchic Pentecostalism. In 1975, when 9,000 people came to the Royal Albert Hall, they found no big names, no overt leadership and no formal programme. At the start, David Mansell stood up and said: 'We've taken the Albert Hall tonight because we couldn't get you all into our front room.'[18]

The fun and frivolity of that night, and the spiritual blessing that many felt that they had received, were soon to give way to distress and bitterness in a formal split between R1 and R2.[19] Almost before relations between the northern and southern halves of the kingdom had been cemented, Restoration divided.

Recommended Reading

Arthur Wallis, 'Springs of Restoration', Part 2, *Restoration* (Harvestime Publications, Sept/Oct 1980).

John Noble, *Forgive Us Our Denominations* (private publication: 57 The Drive, Collier Row, Romford, Essex, 1971).

John Noble, *First Apostle, Last Apostle* (private publication: 57 The Drive, Collier Row, Romford, Essex, 1973), private publication.

Joyce V. Thurman, *New Wineskins: A Study of the House Church Movement,* chapter 2.

George Tarleton, *Birth of a Christian Anarchist* (private publication: Pendragon Press, 1993).

Fulness, Vols. 1-4 (Cairprint Ltd., Keighley, Yorks, undated).

4

THE KINGDOM ESTABLISHED IN DIVISION
1974–76

I do not think that one could honestly say that Restorationism became firmly established, and then soon after it divided into separate entities. It would be more accurate to observe that the Restoration kingdoms became firmly established during and after the formal split of 1976. Firm establishment, in short, took place in division. Furthermore, too much can be made of the formal breakdown between the northern and southern territories of Restoration. Most official dates of divisions and schisms in Church history come some time after *de facto* divisions. Thus, for example, although the formal schism between the Eastern and Western Catholic Churches took place in 1054, real cultural, linguistic and theological differences had existed for centuries. In many ways, the Eastern and Western halves of Christendom were never a natural organism.

Similarly, Restoration was never simply a single cell that separated into two organic structures. R1 and R2 were in embryonic form right from the start. Since the formal split, these forms have matured and developed separate existences. The seeds of disunity can be found in the uneasy alliance between, on the one hand, the London Brothers, Graham Perrins and Peter Lyne in the west, and on the other hand, Bryn Jones, Arthur Wallis and possibly Campbell McAlpine.

The Uneasy Peace

To be strictly chronological, it would be true to say that R2 preceded R1. It was the coming together of the 'magnificent seven' and the 'fabulous fourteen' that melded together the two factions into a single movement. This fusion can only be said to have lasted for three or four years. On the positive side, there was the feeling held by most of the members that they were engaged together in God's work and formed part of a covenanted brotherhood. As Gerald Coates puts it: 'We felt we had seen the nature of the Church . . . we all belong to the same brotherhood, we are all eating at the same altar, we are all sharing the same faith, we all talk to the same Father when we get up in the morning.'[1]

John Noble is quite clear that the brothers in the fourteen were primarily bound together not by doctrines but by the common breaking of bread and personal commitment to each other. Eucharistic fellowship is not exactly an evangelical phrase, but if you strip it of its Catholic connotations, it conveys the centrality of Communion to a Christian brotherhood. This concentration on the Lord's Table as the table of fellowship echoes, as we shall later see, the understanding of Church as held by the early Brethren movement in the first half of the nineteenth century. It was not that the fourteen could not share the Lord's table with all God's people, but it was the case that they saw a special significance in the Restoration leaders sharing the sacrament. This covenanting was taken seriously by the leaders. As John Noble understands it: 'If I'm working with somebody and committing myself to a Work, I also want to have a particular relationship with someone. That is what binds us together.'[2]

A clash of personalities – The binding together, however, never hid the clash of styles and personalities that always made for an uneasy peace. The older style Puritanism of Wallis and Jones was in marked contrast to the wit and acid remarks of Hugh Thompson, and the insightful yet seemingly irreverent manner of Mansell. John Noble, with that curious mixture of the authoritarian personality and a generous nature, was inevitably going to lock horns with Jones, whose powerful but bull-like approach tended to suggest that he would either win you over or knock you over. From an entirely different angle, Jones and Noble were the odd ones out of the seven: all the others (excepting Peter Lyne) were former Open Brethren. Nevertheless, the seven were a tighter and more controlled group than the extended 'fabulous fourteen'.

I am obviously in no position to say whether extending the original group to fourteen was in God's plan or not. However, from an organizational point of view, I do think that five or seven is probably the optimum number you want for a successful oligarchy. If you have a group that has to take executive-style decisions, then fourteen is really too large. Furthermore, as the seven operated on personal commitment rather than company lines, extending your covenant to fourteen is inevitably going to cause strain and create a greater possibility of division. There is no doubt that the 'fabulous fourteen' highlighted personality and ideological divisions more clearly than the original group.

There is a joke about Maurice Smith that he is so sold on teachings of 'grace' that as far as he is concerned, teachings on 'law' can go to hell. Smith himself believes that Arthur Wallis and Bryn Jones always saw him as a danger man and a person of instability, a man whose over-emphasis on grace would lead to unbridled licence. I think it not unfair to say that the London Brothers, in particular, were more liberal in their lifestyle and attitudes than some of the others. In many ways, for example, George Tarleton was always the odd man out. He did not come from recent sectarian movements, but was a former minister in the Congregational Church. His politics and theology were anarchic, and his general views more liberal than his colleagues. He welcomed women in the ministry, for example, which was enough to give some of the former Brethren apoplexy. He insisted on Christ alone being designated the *Logos*, and on this count refused to call the Scriptures the 'Word of God'.

What with that other strong character, Graham Perrins, insisting on the supremacy of the prophetic ministry over all others (a view shared by John MacLauchlan), Hugh Thompson's jokes 'often close to the knuckle', and Mansell's informality – 'let's chat a prophecy' – the four-teen were never dull but not always clear as to what they were doing. After a hard day's prophecy and prayer, sometimes held at Fairmile Court in Surrey, many of the group would go off to the pub for continued fellowship. George Tarleton saw it as 'all of a piece – part of being in the Lord'. Campbell McAlpine, who, like Arthur, was from an older generation of charismatics, found this hard to take. While he no doubt felt privileged to be in on the early workshops, his heart never seemed to be in it. George Tarleton recalls that he did not approve of mixing Spirit with spirit. In fact, Campbell soon quietly withdrew from the fourteen, and played no further direct part in the British Restoration story. Proof of his low profile and lack of participation is the fact that a good number of the 'fab-ulous fourteen' could not remember that he was one of their number.

Perhaps the most enigmatic aspect of the division between R1 and R2 is that when it took place, there was not a straight north–south divide, nor a split on personali-ty lines. When the schism came, it was between those who were with Arthur Wallis and Bryn Jones, and those who were not. From the south, Terry Virgo, Hugh Thompson and David Mansell entered R1. The rest of the leadership in R1 – such as Tony Morton, David Tomlinson, Keri Jones and Tony Ling – were never members of the fourteen.

A clash of styles – Apostleship and discipling emerged more firmly in the south at first. Gerald Coates recalls that Bryn and his colleagues admonished them for overemphasizing these doctrines in 1974/75. Looking through the early numbers of *Restoration* magazine in 1976, when Bryn Jones was editor, there is virtually no emphasis on apostleship at all. However, if the London Brothers were quick off the mark with the new teaching, they were fairly haphazard in their methods. Discipling was never established with a crack of the whip or in any formal and legalistic way. House groups increasingly – through their self-elected elders – related to John Noble or Graham Perrins, and later Gerald Coates.

Many of the groups that joined R2 and R1, were already established autonomous churches when they asked for 'covering' by the new apostles. Later, apostles would choose their own elders or approve those elders already established in leadership on the local level. Nick Butterworth, George Tarleton, John MacLauchlan, Peter Lyne and others continued to be seen as leaders. Whether they saw themselves directly as apostles in 1975 seems unlikely; moving towards apostleship, or taking on apostolic functions might be a better way of understanding their roles at that time.

By as early as 1974, Maurice Smith was prophet to John Noble's apostleship. This teamship, which was to last ten years, was an interesting and fruitful partnership of opposites. John Noble was very much the 'father in God'. He was strong (sometimes 'heavy') and he was always concerned, while Maurice was all quicksilver and effervescence. If Maurice led John a merry dance, they managed to keep in step for a remarkably long time.

By 1975, R1 was not really firmly set on the path of Restoration in its fully doctrinal sense, but it was already organizing itself into a powerful movement. You may call him opportunistic if you will, but Bryn Jones understood the importance of the organizational structure, sound management and financial security that is necessary to putting a big outfit on the road. The London Brothers never doubted this. They felt at the time that Bryn Jones, with his Assemblies of God background, was an institutional creature. For their tastes, he was too conservative and denominational in outlook; too bound by structures and rules. Judging from his reaction in 1976, Bryn Jones saw the Brothers and their associates as too frivolous and woolly-minded. If he was thought to question nothing by some of the Brothers, they also felt that Bryn was convinced that they questioned and doubted too much. I do not think it true that Bryn Jones does not have doubts and uncertainties, but he does not allow them to impede his course of action which he believes is right.[3] He seems to me to be essentially a man of action, not a man of reflection.

Given these tensions, personality clashes and differing styles of working, it is not surprising that 1975 and 1976 saw the emergence of public differences and a series of quarrels that was to end in bitterness and division. The specific issues involved in the split were the publication of *Restoration* magazine in 1975; the debate over law and grace that centred around the practice of masturbation;[4] the David Mansell problem; and the 'spirit of deception' letter that came from Arthur Wallis and Bryn Jones to the southern and western leaders of the 'fabulous fourteen'. While these are separate issues, there are connecting factors, in particular the nature of grace and holiness. In order to enter the complicated controversies that led to the division of the 'kingdom' almost before it was established, I think we could do worse than start with the powerful influence of an American, Ern Baxter.

The American Connection

As we noted in the last chapter, Bryn Jones and Ern Baxter met at the Capel Bible Week in 1974. Both men were attracted to each other's ministries. Ern Baxter is a much softer personality than Bryn Jones; a number of people have told me that he is also an insecure personality.[5] He certainly does not appear insecure, however, and his public performances are masterful and inspiring.

An older man, Ern Baxter has a long track-record of

charismatic activities that go back to the days after the Second World War when he was a Bible teacher with possibly the most controversial and interesting of all America's Pentecostal preachers, William Branham. I remember as a boy listening to Branham's raucous southern voice and hearing his amazing diagnostic talents when he claimed that he could see colours (or auras) that helped him correctly to diagnose illnesses. Professor Walter Hollenweger, who is not given to exaggeration, believes that while Branham's claims to healing were sometimes questionable, his ability correctly to diagnose illness was phenomenal.[6]

Ern Baxter and the 'Fort Lauderdale Five' – Baxter was the elder statesman of the group known as the 'Fort Lauderdale Five'. Their basic teachings were taken from Ortiz of Argentina, and they were responsible for establishing in North America chains of followers who submitted to their apostolic authority. They had been in existence since the early 1960s.

Baxter and Mumford were probably the most liked of the five: their personalities were attractive and their manner gracious. Derek Prince was an intellectual and a former fellow of King's College, Cambridge. Despite his erudition and obvious scholarship, he had a predilection for extreme biblical interpretations. In more recent years, he has become associated with a passionate Zionism, and Israel seems to dominate his interests. Basham was well known in America for deliverance ministry. A leading British charismatic told me that he was 'dead keen on demons and dead against masturbation: he thought the former were responsible for the latter'. Charles Simpson seems to have been the least liked of the five because of his aggressive personality and what many people saw as bullying tactics concerning submission and discipling doctrines. An indication of his personality can be picked up by the comment of a former London Brother: 'Charles Simpson makes Bryn Jones seem like a "wet".'

All of the five were intelligent men. In the American religious context they were somewhat of an enigma. They were conservative in their theology and politics, and yet they were not typical 'Bible-belters'. They were not exclusivists, and numbered among their friends and associates Roman Catholics from within the Charismatic Renewal. They had attempted to introduce their doctrines and 'covering power' inside and outside the traditional denominational structures. Their discipling doctrines, which flourished in some of the Catholic covenanted communities as well as Protestant churches, split the American Renewal movement down the middle at the very time that Restoration was springing up in Great Britain. Indeed, when Baxter was in England in 1975 and 1976, the American charismatic movement was attempting to heal its wounds over this matter.[7] Unlike Britain, therefore, the American experience of the 'shepherding movement' had been far more mainstream. Many Anglican and Catholic charismatics in England had never even heard of, or at least experienced, these controversies.

Clearly, we can see from an international perspective that the British Restoration movement was part of a much larger phenomenon. Admittedly, there was no international organization, and many of the groups had nothing to do with each other (indeed, they were sometimes opposed to each other), but they all adhered to a kingdom/apostleship/discipleship nexus. Like so many apparently indigenous religious movements in Britain, we are able to note firstly the international dimension, and secondly the domination of this internationalism by North American Pentecostals. Noting this is not only to recognize the importance of the American connection, but also to realize that the tale of British Restorationism is only one chapter in a much larger story. Bryn Jones has never claimed to be the leader of the Restoration movement *per se*. It was he who pointed out to me that similar work to his own was going on in South Africa, North and South America, Africa and Europe.[8]

As I mentioned in the previous chapter, I do not think that Ern Baxter introduced Restorationism to Britain; nor did he first outline the doctrines of discipleship and shepherding. What he did do, however, was to mould the thinking of the 'fabulous fourteen', and even help R1 on its way.

Although Bryn Jones made great use of Ern Baxter in the years 1975 and 1976, R2 was also involved with its new-found American friends. Members visited Florida, as did Bryn Jones, and talked with the Fort Lauderdale Five and their friends in their homes. But it was at the Lakes Week in 1975 that Baxter first made a real impact. David Tomlinson, who was an apostle in R1 at that time, recalls that Baxter's influence was sensational; the audiences went wild every time he appeared.[9] As a result of his teaching on the need for 'covered' relationships, many groups attending the Bible week joined themselves to Bryn and his fellow apostles. During the first Bible week at the Great Yorkshire Showground in 1976, Baxter was the great attraction and, as in the previous year, excitement was at fever pitch.

Interestingly, Ern Baxter's preaching style is not in the American Pentecostal tradition at all. There is no ranting, no table-thumping, very little overt emotionalism and no shouting. He relies heavily on notes, and in small gatherings favours the blackboard and other visual aids. His methodology is to build up strong arguments by means of biblical exposition and original hermeneutics. Like most of the five, he makes elaborate use of typology and Old Testament incidents, which are then read into the New Testament and the present day. The most effective typology that was used in those years was to compare the kingship of Saul and David with the state of leadership in the Church. It was pointed out that Saul was not ordained by God but chosen by the people. Democratic methods were compared unfavourably with the theocratic arrangements of God. The Lord, for example, chose David as the anointed of Israel. Today, he is anointing with his Spirit men who

are charismatically chosen to be the apostles of the kingdom.

The American solution – Ern Baxter may have helped R1
on its way, but he and the rest of the American group had
already become aware of the tensions within the British
Restoration movement. They were concerned at the lack of
real unity, and were convinced that the covering situation
was failing at the top. It is difficult to resist using Old
Testament typology in helping us to explain their understanding of the situation. Israel, as we know, was bound
together by the tribal structure, which itself can be seen as
a form of covenanted brotherhood. However, the nation
was divided into the ten tribes of the northern kingdom,
and Judah and Benjamin in the south. During Solomon's
reign, his power and kingship held the kingdom together,
but after his death the old tribal conflicts reasserted themselves: the kingdom was divided between Jeroboam in the
north and Rehoboam in the south.

In bringing the 'magnificent seven' together, Arthur
Wallis was also potentially healing a north–south divide.
The fourteen might have been bound together by covenant
like some ancient tribal system, but the kingdom that
emerged under their tutelage never found its king: no
Solomon or David was chosen. Given the hierarchical or
theocratic nature of Restoration ideology, the system of
relationships that developed demanded headship. Even
apostolic collegiality requires a 'first amongst equals'. The
American five felt that the problem lay in the personality
clash between John Noble and Bryn Jones. Their solution
to the problem was to ask both Bryn Jones and John Noble
to submit to Arthur Wallis.[10] He, in turn, would be covered
by an American apostle. I do not think that one need be too
cynical to realize that this was also a method of bringing
the English operation under their control. If that was their
intention, then they picked the wrong men in John Noble
and Bryn Jones.

Initially, Bryn Jones accepted this solution, but John

Noble refused it. John's view was simply that Arthur was not a strong enough personality for the job, nor was he an apostle. (Certainly, on this latter point, according to the understanding of the fourteen, Arthur was not an apostle because he had not established and nurtured churches.)

Problems were beginning to brew up within R2 at this time, too, and John Noble and Graham Perrins were at loggerheads over the primacy of prophecy and who should submit to whom. At the same time and into 1976, the London Brothers had discovered that David Mansell's private life 'was not totally glorifying to the gospel'. There were problems of mutual trust here, and the Brothers found that Mansell would accept no sanctions from them.

It was in the light of this that John Noble and Maurice Smith went to see the Fort Lauderdale Five in Florida. Ern Baxter promised, according to Maurice Smith, to 'bust the whole David Mansell thing open' when he came to England in the summer of 1976. The major purpose of the meeting, however, was to see if John Noble would agree to submit to Arthur Wallis. Maurice Smith remembers being overawed by their wealth – the swimming pools, the discussion of many thousands of dollars, the glancing at watches like bank managers giving their clients moments of their valuable time.

The notion of 'double honour' has a long history in American Pentecostal circles – the idea that Christian leaders should be apportioned more of the wealth than their followers, by virtue of their leadership. Certainly, Maurice Smith began to realize what many Restoration leaders were to realize, that great things can be achieved through the tithe! But let Maurice tell the story his way:

> They were exasperated with John Noble because he was such a strong man and would not submit to Arthur. John went out to the loo on one occasion. And he had no sooner gone out to the loo when Bob Mumford leant forward and said to me: 'Look, quickly Maurice, while John's in the loo. Obviously, you're not as clear as John

about all this.'

So I said: 'No. I'm open to the fact we might be wrong.'

But he said: 'You see you're not one with him in this. We're all one.'

'Yes,' I said. 'But our oneness does not depend on agreement of doctrine.' (So all this was tearing Bob apart – I like Bob, he's a warm and friendly guy.)

So he said: 'Look Maurice: let's put it like this. Do you think a woman should submit herself to her husband?'

I said: 'Yes. I think there's safety in that.'

'Do you think she should only submit herself to him when he's right?'

I said: 'No. That is not submission; that's doing what you want to do and calling it submission.'

'And what would happen, Maurice,' (because he's a very clever fellow, Bob) 'what would happen, Maurice, if a woman submitted herself to her husband who was often wrong?'

I said: 'I think that she would help to lift him into his place of authority' (because that's how I used to think then) 'in the family. By not undermining his authority she would put him into authority.'

'Exactly!' he said. 'And that is our solution for your country. As God is moving in this House Church way, if John and Bryn will submit it would help to put Arthur Wallis into his authority; even though he has not got that gift, it will help to bring it about and he will bring these two men together.' So he said: 'Maurice, you see it?' (John is still in the loo.)

So I said: 'No. No. No!'

So he said: 'What's the matter, Maurice?'

So I said: 'I can't agree with it because the woman fell in love with the man – it was organic: something happened between them which meant she wanted to willingly let go of some things at some times so the thing would work out. But this isn't happening now. It's a shotgun marriage, Bob. You're forcing this issue.'

'Oh!' (And he clapped his hands in exasperation.)[11]

John Noble and Maurice Smith may have come away from Florida without having resolved the submission issue, but they felt that Baxter was on their side concerning the Mansell trouble. By this time, Bryn Jones was arguing with the Brothers that they were being too judgmental in their attitude to David Mansell and offered to take over the 'covering' role himself. (To this day, the Brothers have never understood Jones's attitude over this matter.)

Baxter's arrival in England certainly had a dramatic effect on the Restoration story, but not the one that John Noble and Maurice Smith were expecting. At the Dales Bible Week, which was a tremendous success, Baxter's presence and contributions were seen as an endorsement for Bryn Jones and his fellow apostles, David Tomlinson and Terry Virgo. Tomlinson recalls that the drama between Bryn and the rest of the fourteen hardly affected him personally. He was never a member of that group, and when the division came he automatically sided with Bryn Jones because he knew him and was involved with him; in no sense can he remember making an objective analysis of the situation at that time.

Although I have not been able to uncover the exact sequence of events, it is clear that Ern Baxter, after meeting and working with Bryn and Arthur, took their part in their handling of the Mansell row, and in their general disagreement with R2. What so alarmed the London Brothers and Graham Perrins was Ern Baxter's attitude when he came down from the Dales to attend a smaller convention at Bath organized by Peter Lyne. Maurice Smith felt 'there was something terribly wrong'. Baxter was uneasy, and on the first night made, the Brothers thought, an appalling contribution that was neither up to his usual standard nor seen by them to be conducted in the spirit of charity. In an earlier chapter, I mentioned Graham Perrins as being a strong personality. The crisis brings this out clearly. Baxter, apparently without any apology or explanation for his contribution, asked the members of R2 what they wanted for the next night. 'Never mind the next night,' Perrins said. 'We want an explanation for tonight, Ern.'

Under pressure to 'come clean' and explain what was going on, Ern Baxter protested that he did not need this kind of aggravation. His wife was seriously ill, and perhaps, he suggested, he would just pack his bag and go right back to America. In the event, he did stay another night, but the Brothers that I have spoken to about this episode claim that he was preaching against them on the platform and not preaching to the congregation.

Arthur Wallis, the architect of Restorationism, and the man who had tried so hard to bring the factions together, was heartbroken at this open show of discord.[12] Maurice Smith remembers him walking and praying all night ('Arthur always prayed until he felt he had an answer'), and in the morning, Arthur had come to see – along with Baxter – that the R2 section of Restorationism was deceived. If I have understood this correctly from John Noble and Gerald Coates, this idea of deception was not a psychological form of deception; they were seen to have been led astray by demonic forces – a 'spirit of deception'.

After this incident, Ern Baxter left England and played virtually no other part in the story after 1977. His contribution, however, was vital. It was he and his colleagues who helped the theological formulation of early Restorationism. His personal ministry was a major boost to the establishment and success of R1. His intervention at Bath was a significant factor in the hastening split between R1 and R2 in October 1976. Ironically, Ern Baxter's influence on Bryn Jones was also coming to an end. Bryn Jones recalls that Arthur Wallis felt that there should be an input from some other source in 1978. The Dales Committee decided to ask Bob Mumford to come. He came and was very much liked. Like Baxter before him, he too was a great success, but he did not have the pioneering influence of his colleague. In 1979, the link between R1 and the American five was severed. It was decided no longer to invite them, and they have not been back since.

David Tomlinson says that the Fort Lauderdale Five, and in particular Ern Baxter, felt that they had a stake in the British scene.[13] They had, after all, made a significant contribution to the initial success of R1. Morally, Tomlinson thinks, Baxter believed that Bryn Jones owed it to him to submit to American authority. Neither Tomlinson nor Noble, however, believe that the Americans were thinking improperly of a takeover. It was simply that they thought God wanted to extend his kingdom through them. If there had been an American operation, it would have probably involved the mainstream denominations; one wonders if they approved of the separatist direction of R1? Tomlinson also wisely points out that if you look at it from Bryn Jones's perspective, you get a different moral picture. The American guests were outstaying their welcome. They had come to the Dales as a result of an invitation by the Bible week committee. In effect, they were 'hired servants'. It was not their place to talk about rights or privileges.

This perspective seems reasonable, and certainly it can be morally defended. I discussed this issue with Bryn Jones, and he confirms that all of his team – and the associated teams – felt that while they were eternally grateful to the Lauderdale group for their input, and while they recognized the prophetic role of the five, in no sense did they accept that they had any 'governmental' authority over them. Bryn was anxious that the work he was involved in should not be written off as merely the satellite of American interest. In short, you can believe that Bryn Jones used the Americans and then dumped them, or you can accept that he acted in both a patriotic and proper way.[14] Whatever the case, the Americans eventually found out, as they already had with John Noble, that Bryn Jones was neither a man to manipulate nor one to submit to their ultimate authority.

The Rending of the Kingdom

Gerald Coates sees October 1976 as the date of the formal split. This was the month when Arthur Wallis wrote a letter to the brothers in R2 disassociating himself from a number of their attitudes and practices. Without exception, the members of R2 saw this as a letter written by Bryn Jones and signed by Arthur. They were both deeply hurt and furious at the accusations made against them. The letter, as they saw it, was tantamount to being 'disfellow-shipped'. In older times, the language of anathemas and excommunication would have been used. The letter was, in effect, the straw that broke the camel's back. From that time onwards, the 'magnificent seven' and 'fabulous fourteen' ceased to exist; the uneasy peace between the North and South was shattered.

However, from R1's perspective, October 1976 does not loom as such a major catastrophe. Their show was now well and truly on the road, and doing very well. The fact that they felt uncomfortable with members of R2 inevitably meant that they would prefer to work on their own, and with their own. Furthermore, a number of leaders in R1 had been brought in from outside the original fourteen leadership. The historical problems did not affect them so personally. Therefore, although the division was regretted – very deeply by a few – the split was not quite the tragedy that it was for R2.

I think it is not difficult for us to understand how John Noble, Gerald Coates, Graham Perrins, George Tarleton, Maurice Smith and others felt. They saw themselves as the pioneers of the kingdom. It was they, so they believed, who had developed the doctrines of apostleship and discipling within the British context. They saw themselves as first, not in terms of honour, but in laying the foundations of a charismatically-ordained Church. Then along came Bryn Jones – a 'Johnny come lately' – who borrowed from them, improved on them, out-manoeuvred them, and then gave them their marching orders.[15]

It was during one of the many meetings at Fairmile Court in 1975 that Bryn Jones announced to the assembled Brothers that R1 was publishing a new journal called *Restoration*. Those involved in *Fulness* were furious. It seemed to those Brothers that a betrayal had taken place – Bryn was going into competition against them. It was as if, some of them thought, Bryn Jones was running up the flag of his own empire. By publishing *Restoration* magazine, he was making a unilateral declaration of independence.[16]

Whether or not this was true, by 1976, thanks partly to Ern Baxter, R1 had suddenly come from nowhere not only to rival R2, but to emerge as the major vehicle for Restorationism in Great Britain. Although I think we can see the announcement of *Restoration* magazine as the beginning of the end, and the Wallis/Jones letter as the end of the generic Restoration movement, these two events are only historic markers in what was really a fundamental difference over the nature of grace. I am not personally so convinced that this was the real underlying problem, but it was perceived to be by many participants. Here, I believe, some personal interpretation is necessary.

Issues of law and grace – Until the mid-1980s, R1 and R2 had virtually no contact with each other following the 1970s split. Consequently, their perceptions of each other in the 1980s have been coloured by historical events and disagreements of the past. Bryn Jones, for example, wonders if they were not always as different as chalk and cheese, but he no longer knows, in any personal or empirical sense, what the leaders of R2 were like then.[17]

Conversely, as Gerald Coates and John Noble have not met Bryn Jones for a long time, they have never really been able to clarify exactly what went wrong between them. Restoration ideology acclaims confrontation as a means of healing, and yet the leaders of both R1 and R2 have chosen not to take that path.

David Tomlinson, however, can claim knowledge of both sides of the divide, because he crossed over from R1 to R2. What he has found is very instructive. On beliefs, there is virtually no difference (although there are a number of doctrines undergoing change in R2). He primarily notices a difference in style and atmosphere. For his money, R1 is too structured and R2 is not structured enough. R2 is more relaxed than R1, and far less intense; there is less pressure to conform to an organizational 'line'. R1 is now basically set on its path. R2 is still fluid and changing.

Such differences of style and *modus operandi* help us, I think, to see a little more clearly what the law and grace debate was about in 1975 and 1976. At Fairmile Court and other places, there was an attempt to thrash out the permissible actions open to Christians. How, in short, do children of the King behave? What does it mean to be no longer 'under law but under grace'? Christians are free in the Spirit, but what is the nature of that freedom? Maurice Smith took the view that living in the Spirit meant that you had been made free from the Old Testament dispensation of law. This was, on the surface, in line with Honor Oak and Brethren teaching. Most evangelicals would declare with St Paul that the shackles of law were broken when sin itself was destroyed. It is not typically the case, however, that the evangelical world has understood this to mean that the law (the Ten Commandments, for example) is no longer operative. Christ came to fulfil the law, they would claim, not to destroy it.

None of the London Brothers ever claimed that Christians could murder, steal or commit adultery. However, John Noble and Gerald Coates did think that masturbation could be a neutral act, and not necessarily a sin. Gerald had written a little booklet, *Law And Grace*, and Arthur Wallis and Bryn Jones saw in this an invitation to licence (so John and Gerald recalled). The booklet is not a call to 'situation ethics', nor an invitation to immorality, but I think it not unfair to say that it could be open to misinterpretation.

Joyce Thurman, probably unintentionally, gives the

impression in her book that this controversy took place at a distance,[18] but the masturbation issue was discussed face to face between the various leaders. Its discussion reveals the underlying difference of style between R1 and R2. Gerald wanted everybody to admit that they masturbated sometimes. One can only imagine what Arthur Wallis and Bryn Jones thought when they were asked about this openly! I recall from my own Pentecostal background what would have been the reaction if such a topic had been raised. (As a matter of fact, you could not raise this particular topic as a teenager, because such practices were not admitted to exist.) Perhaps Gerald's question was an impertinence, prurient, or simply lacking in decency? However Bryn Jones and Arthur Wallis saw it, they did not wish to condone it as a Christian practice.

But too much can be made of this well-publicized dispute. It was only one of a number of issues. Drinking alcohol was also a major bone of contention. Most of the brothers drank alcohol, but Gerald and John counted it as a virtue to declare it openly. Bryn and Arthur were not exactly secret drinkers, but neither did they declare it from the rooftops. Gerald and a number of the London Brothers liked the cinema, theatre and pop music. Others thought this worldly. Gerald believed that most of the leaders enjoyed doing the things that he did. As there was nothing wrong with them, he thought, you should not hide these practices. You should declare them as desirable.

In the older Pentecostal tradition, emphasis had always been put on not doing anything that might cause your brother to stumble. 'Remember the weaker brethren' was often taken to mean not doing things that were lawful in themselves but which were not necessarily expedient. To personalize this and put it into extreme form: Bryn Jones thought that Gerald flaunted his permissiveness, and Gerald thought that Bryn was a hypocrite because he did the same things in secret.

Some of the differences between the leaders of the 'fabulous fourteen' were partly differences of class and culture, and partly differences of moral understanding. Clearly, both Gerald and Bryn's positions can be morally defended, and I do think there is a tendency for the two sides to exaggerate the *substantive* disagreements between them. John Noble does like to drink, and Gerald Coates is 'flashy' and uninhibited in his talk, as extroverts often are. Neither, however, are liberal in their moral beliefs, and their personal lives have attracted no scandal in recent years. Perhaps Gerald's 'flashiness' (does he still have the canary-yellow suit?) and 'froth' were taken by Bryn Jones to be the substance of the man? His friends inside and outside R2 know that Gerald is unashamedly a showman, but they also know that he is generous, kind, totally honest and always open to correction and improvement.

Conversely, I think it likely that the London Brothers did not fully appreciate the older-style Puritanism of Wallis, nor did they fully understand how their liberality would be seen by the people with whom Bryn Jones originally associated and still has a great love for: namely, the classical Pentecostals. Having lived in the Welsh valleys and attended chapel three times on a Sunday, I know from that neck of the woods how alien the London Brothers, Peter Lyne and Graham Perrins looked. Graham, for example, was not only good-looking, but was always dressed in the latest fashions. Gerald's clothes tended to be idiosyncratic bordering on the outrageous. What with the enjoyment of some aspects of modern culture, the risqué jokes and alcoholic chatter,[19] these modern-day charismatics would look like agents of hell to some classical Pentecostals.

This being so, it is understandable that Bryn Jones is cautious in this area. Wishing to be all things to all men – being careful not to offend – can be a positive Christian virtue; hypocrisy may very well be too strong a charge. These issues are still alive today between the older-style Pentecostal denominations and the new independents. Once, when I was chatting with Bryn Jones in his office, I saw a bottle of excellent quality French wine on his filing cabinet. Pointing to it, he remarked, regretfully, that some members of Elim and the Assemblies of God still found it difficult to accept somebody as 'sound' if they indulged in alcohol. The 'demon drink' belief in these denominations is very similar to that of the Salvation Army.

This issue, more than the disagreement over masturbation, in my opinion, highlights what I have called the difference in style between R1 and R2. Bryn Jones drinks moderately, and admits it if he is asked. Gerald Coates drinks moderately, and proclaims it on the radio and in print. The same can be said in investigating the events and issues leading to the split in 1976. R1 have hidden nothing from me but have volunteered no information. R2 have been willing to tell all without the same feeling of reserve.

It remains a curiosity, however, to see why Bryn Jones should want to take David Mansell under his wing. The London Brothers felt that at the moment they were being indicted for turning grace into licence, Bryn Jones was telling them that they were being too judgmental with David Mansell, whom they thought had gone too far. Whatever David Mansell's 'problems' were they are of no concern to us, but in 1976 he agreed to be 'covered' by Bryn Jones. As a result, he left R2 for R1, where he has remained as an important member of Bryn's team, and a significant contributor to *Restoration* magazine.[20]

When Arthur Wallis's letter was sent to the leaders of R2 in October 1976, it was in effect a list of the disagreements between them. There were references to theological issues as well as to the law–grace row. For example, Arthur Wallis felt too much was being claimed, at that time, for apostolic authority. He was not happy, either, with the 'remnant' eschatology that was favoured by Ted Crick (who had already left R2) and Graham Perrins. The serious charge, however, was the suggestion that they were falling into licence, with a hint that they were being led astray by demonic forces. Apparently, this tendency to licence was supposed to include 'associations with hairies' (Ern Baxter seemed to have strong views about long hair at that time).

To an untutored ear, all this may sound like the breaking of covenant, but I suspect that this is not so. From what
I know of Arthur Wallis, I doubt very much whether he
saw the parting of the ways as synonymous with breaking
covenant. John Noble certainly does not: 'I made a
covenant with Bryn which as far as I'm concerned still
stands . . . There was an issue of conscience. (This puts
your working relationship into parenthesis for a time.) I'm
actively working in my own heart to see how this can be
resolved so we can get back together again.'[21]

The failure to hold the Restoration kingdom together
was a personal tragedy for many of the leading apostles
and elders. While for us it is a fascinating and essential
episode in the story of this radical Christianity, it is worth
remembering that for those whose story it is, the split
remains painful if not shameful. Not all the leaders
thought that the split was a disaster. We have already seen
that R1 was not so badly affected as R2, but George
Tarleton now thinks that the split was God-ordained. He
believes that it helped prevent the emergence of a new and
large denomination. This is a minority view, but I think
that most leaders are convinced that much has been
learned by these mistakes.

By 1976 – despite the division – a new radical
Christianity had become established in Great Britain.
Following that time, there was a steady growth of the
Restoration movement. No other Christian grouping, outside the mainline denominations, could boast such a rapid
rise in size and popularity. To accurately chart the course
of R1 and R2 over the years of their growth would take a
full book in itself. Before we look at Restoration teachings,
practices, sociological complexion and historical
antecedents, we can at least catch up with the major developments within the two movements. Such a brief look will
take us up to 1985 and demonstrate in what ways R1 and
R2 continued to diverge.

Recommended Reading

Arthur Wallis, 'Springs of Restoration: Part 2', *Restoration* (Harvestime Publications, Sept/Oct 1980).

Roger William Curl, *Three Communities: a Sociological Study* (unpublished DPhil thesis, Oxford).

Eileen Vincent, *Something's Happening* (Marshalls, 1984).

Joyce V. Thurman, *New Wineskins: a Study of the House Church Movement* (Verlag Peter Lang, 1982), chapter 6.

5

EXTENDING THE KINGDOM 1975–85

After the failures and disappointments of 1976, the
Restoration kingdoms grew amazingly quickly. Despite
further serious divisions (as we shall see), the two movements continue to attract new members and form new
churches. By 1980, evidence that they had really arrived on
the religious scene could be found in the growing opposition to them in some mainstream charismatic and evangelical circles. Much of the criticism at that time was somewhat muted by the lack of information concerning the new
movements, and in particular the failure to distinguish not
only R1 from R2, but both of them from other house
church movements.

The British Council of Churches consultation on the
Renewal in 1979 was typical of much denominational reaction: something was happening that was clamouring for
attention, but few knew what that something was, or what
its significance could be.[1] In the absence of clear information, this situation was not helped by R1 and R2 refusing
to identify themselves in any clear way, and the result was
that rumours about this new movement began to prolifer-
ate. Despite the fact (or perhaps because of the fact) that R1
sets out its doctrinal position very clearly in *Restoration*
magazine and the writings of Arthur Wallis, this has not
prevented controversy concerning the nature of
Restorationist religion.

It is easier to discern a shape and pattern to R1 than to
R2. In many ways, R1 has done a great deal more than R2
to determine the direction in which they are going. This
being so, and because R1 is clearly larger and more insis-

tently Restorationist than R2, we will first look at how they developed after the division.

Restoration One

Exactly one year before the split of October 1976, and following the successful summer Bible week at the Lakes, Bryn Jones became leader of a Pentecostal community that consisted of his own congregation from the independent Holiness Assembly, a former Brethren Assembly, and a charismatic house church. This new and enlarged church has become the home base (R1 does not like the idea of headquarters) of Bryn Jones's apostolic ministry. It was in Bradford that *Restoration* magazine was first started in 1975 as an expression of that new community church. By the end of 1977, *Restoration* expressed not only the work of Bryn Jones, but also his newly 'related' apostles, Terry Virgo and David Tomlinson. Terry was pioneering in the south-east, while David was working in the north-east and the Midlands. The three apostles spent very little time in those days outlining apostolic doctrine or announcing their work with a great fanfare. Instead they were working out in practice Restoration principles and building together their fellowships.

The amount of work and territory they covered was phenomenal. Charismatic groups, small house churches, and sections of Baptist and Pentecostal denominations were eager to come under their 'covering'. Even before they had properly established their British churches, they had become involved in missionary work that has been a hallmark of R1 ever since. Visits to Norway were started as early as 1975. In 1976, David Tomlinson, Terry Virgo, David Mansell and others went to Spain, where they worked in both Protestant and Catholic communities. David Tomlinson recalls the cultural shock of seeing a Catholic charismatic priest with cigar in mouth and glass of wine in one hand, while his free hand was dispensing Pentecostal blessings![2]

Missionary expansion and Church House – The year 1977 was a year of missionary expansion and home consolidation. Bryn Jones and David Mansell went to Kenya, where they pioneered a new church, and the following year on a return visit they came into contact with the new President following the death of Jomo Kenyatta. The missionary work there resulted in many reported miracles of healing. Feeling that they had some entrée into Kenya with their relationships with government officials and the President himself, R1 decided to raise money in various projects designed to help the Kenyan tribes be self-supporting. That same year, Arthur Wallis, Peter Paris, Alan Vincent (now a member of Terry Virgo's team) and Hugh Thompson visited India, where they established contacts and preached Restoration principles. Contacts were also made with South Africa, and later David Mansell and David Tomlinson went to Argentina, where they worked with Orvil Swindoll for a time.[3]

The most significant event in 1977, however, was the purchasing of Church House in Bradford, formerly the Anglican diocesan headquarters. The building was in a terrible condition. Over the next few years, it was first gutted, then reshaped and refurbished to a high professional standard. Many members of the new community gave not only their money, but also their time and talents.

By 1985, this Victorian gothic building was an impressive centre for the Church House Community Fellowship (to give the Bradford church its full title). It housed not only worship and recreational facilities for the 500 or so members, but also boasted administrative offices, a coffee lounge, a bookshop and the gift shop of the Harvestime organization. Harvestime was set up as a commercial enterprise to raise money to support the growing needs of Bryn Jones's team. This organization of religious free enterprise grew in importance for the whole of R1 over the years. It initially concentrated on tapes, gifts and stickers, but by 1984 it was stocking products with greater quality. *School of the Word*, a correspondence Bible course, was the most ambitious project at that time. Run efficiently and professionally – with the latest computers, word-processors and other software packages – this self-supporting business had an annual turnover of around £0.75 million by 1985.

Much of the Harvestime work is carried out at a separate site from Church House. This site, which also houses *Restoration* magazine, radiates calm and efficiency, but also invokes an atmosphere of cottage industry rather than big business. Since the Harvestime shop was opened in late 1977, and the Granary coffee lounge in 1980, Church House itself has become a popular centre in Bradford. In the basement is a full-sized basketball and sports arena surrounded by a gallery. This is sometimes used for plays and musical shows. The shop, coffee lounge and bookstore are on the ground floor. On the first floor (up a wide and commanding staircase) are various offices housing three secretaries, elders and administrative staff. The showpiece, however, is the main hall next to these offices, which seats up to 350 members for the regular weekly meetings. For those who cannot get into the services, there is an overflow room, where an internal televised relay carries the message and blessing to a further 100 members.

The success of the Church House enterprise led to similar projects in other parts of the R1 kingdom. Terry Virgo in Hove bought an old dilapidated church in Clarendon Villas. When I visited it in 1983, it was just nearing completion. The vast and plain hall, rectangular in shape and holding 500 people, dominates the pine-stripped utilitarian offices and anterooms. Bath, Southampton, Leeds and Leicester are also developing large centres.

The growth of such 'plant' are only the major examples of many church buildings and halls owned by R1 house churches. Many churches are still rented, but church purchase is the goal. In addition to churches, there are private houses bought for the leaders. I know of no houses that have been bought outright, but Restoration members have made significant financial contributions. In Hertfordshire in the early 1980s, a school was started, King's School, the building for which was on lease from the county council. In 1980, Riddlesden College was formed and housed in a converted barn. This college, just a few miles from Keighley in Yorkshire, is open to students other than members of R1, but it is very much a Restoration college. Its curriculum is designed for leadership and not for academic success.

This impressive growth rate of church buildings and other supportive organizations has been accompanied by the proliferation of house cell groups. Churches are broken down into such cells, and the house group leaders meet regularly with the elders, who in turn report to the apostles. The house groups are considered an essential component of R1, as members are not encouraged to live outside the fellowship; they are expected to interact with each other on a regular basis outside the church services. Not that these house cells are indispensable – the Bradford groups were suspended in 1984 because people were becoming too attached to them at the expense of the larger church.[4]

Dales Bible Week – From 1978 onwards, *Restoration* magazine began to major on the central doctrines of the new movement. It was not until 1980–81, however, that whole issues of the magazine were given over to discipling and apostleship. By this time, the Dales Bible Week was running not only without visits from the Fort Lauderdale Five, but was topping 8,000 residents a week. This made it a larger Christian convention than any other weekly residential event of any denominational or inter-denominational gathering. Indeed, except for the Christian rock festival Greenbelt, it was larger than any form of residential Christian event in Great Britain, until the success of Spring Harvest a few years later.

The Dales, not surprisingly, became the shop window for Restoration teaching and worship. Its music has had far-reaching effects outside its own circle. All the

Pentecostal denominations, and many Baptist and charismatic mainstream churches, can be found singing 'songs of the kingdom' that originated at the Dales. I visited a large, independent Pentecostal church in the Easter of 1982, which I have visited on previous occasions when in the north-west of England, only to find that the old hymns of Elim and the Assemblies of God had been largely replaced by Restoration songs.

The Dales also became a successful recruitment office for R1. Many fellowships and congregations (mainly from Baptist, Elim and Assemblies of God churches) became Restorationist after visits to the Dales; a good number went on to join R1. The success of the Dales owed much to the preaching power of Bryn Jones, but the continual growth of R1 during the years 1978–83 is proof that it was not a one-man show. During this time, except for his visits to the Dales, Bryn Jones was living in America. He had moved to St Louis, Missouri, where he pioneered Restoration churches. While it has always been true that Bryn Jones is very much the man at the top of his particular segment of R1, he has shown shrewd judgment when it comes to delegating functions. He does not concern himself, as some leaders do, with every little item of administrative and bureaucratic detail. Because he is an apostle, he does not assume that he is therefore an entrepreneur, a manager, or an administrator.

In June 1983, Bryn Jones, somewhat unexpectedly, returned to Bradford 'for good'. Rumours surrounded his return, but rumours attach themselves to Bryn Jones with the same persistence as records of miraculous happenings. In the face of stories I had heard concerning disagreements of practice, personality clashes, and the accumulation of personal wealth while he was in America, Bryn Jones was able to dispel one rumour that stated that he owned a house in St Louis worth £250,000. He pointed out that he did not own a house in America.[5]

Reorganization and evangelistic campaigning – During 1981 and 1982, criticisms were growing within the mainstream churches and Pentecostal denominations that R1 was 'stealing sheep' from existing churches, instead of obtaining converts from among non-Christians.[6] Similar claims existed against R2; both groups tended to see the issue not as one of 'poaching', but of simply 'growing greener pasture'. This was a rather unfortunate choice of image, given the connotations of what happens to people who think that the 'grass is always greener on the other side'. Whether this criticism is valid or not, from 1983 onwards, R1 showed a definite change in direction. They dismantled the massive Dales Week organization by halving its size and moving into the regions with smaller residential weeks and weekends; and they commenced, following this reorganization, the beginnings of evangelistic campaigns in the large provincial cities.

In preparation for these new changes, which had always been envisaged by Bryn Jones, the apostles formed around them teams to help a more effective Restoration ministry. These men were prophets, evangelists, teachers and pastors who assisted the apostle. However, at this stage, these teams do not seem to have been a formalized diaconate surrounding the apostle, which would be an episcopal model, neither do they seem clearly to have fitted the ministries which R1 saw stemming from Ephesians chapter 4 (which would be a charismatic apostolic model). Suffice it to say that the teams consisted of leaders of the movement whose functions were sometimes, and sometimes not, clearly defined.

The year 1983 saw the first new-style Dales Bible Week, and also the first Welsh Bible Week. These were repeated in 1984, and with the Downs Week still running at Plumpton, Sussex, some 12,000 people were resident at Restorationist camps; several thousand day visitors attended. In addition to these massive camps (the whole combined might of the British Council of Churches could not produce more than 1,000 people at its youth camp in

Lincoln), there were residential weekends held in Cheshire, Shaftesbury, Bury St Edmunds and Chelmsford.

In 1984, evangelistic outreaches were held in Birmingham, Leicester and Leeds. This first organized assault by the 'restored kingdom' upon the secular world (what Bryn Jones calls 'the other 95 per cent') was begun only when leaders felt that the kingdom base was now secured. In the heart of enemy territory (that is, the devil's world, or Babylon) the foundations for the restored kingdom had been laid. The initial results from these short campaigns have been encouraging rather than spectacular. For example, 2,000 people turned up to hear Bryn Jones in March 1984 at Leicester's De Montfort Hall. After the subsequent 'follow-up', it is believed that there were 150 converts. A further 350 converts were claimed during a four-month period in Yorkshire.[7]

While these results were modest by the standards of Billy Graham and George Jeffreys of fifty years ago, we should remember that Bryn Jones was starting off as a virtual unknown as far as the British population was concerned. Even if these Restoration evangelistic campaigns were primarily designed to bring new converts into R1, the very fact that they existed also attracted many from the evangelical constituency, whose major criticism against R1 until that time had been that it had not engaged in evangelism.

By 1985, R1 seems to have had around 12,000–15,000 members, and several thousand other people interested in Restoration principles, but still in their churches.[8] This was a phenomenal achievement, making them, after only ten years, almost half the size of the Elim Pentecostal churches. R1 had become well organized, financially secure, and led by thoughtful and powerful leaders. They seemed to be poised to make a major breakthrough in British life.

However, we need to keep a sense of proportion. R1 was still only a tiny fraction of the religious population of Great Britain, which itself made up only some ten per cent of the general population of over sixty million people.

Restorationism also needs to be seen against a meteoric rise in the number of Mormons over the same period. Although the Mormons have been in this country since the nineteenth century, it is only since the mid-1970s that they have seen a rapid rise in membership. In 1985, the Church of the Latter Day Saints had well over 100,000 members in Great Britain (and their leaders would put it much higher).[9] Unlike the house church movement, the Mormons have received very little attention either from the media or from Christian Church figures.

Divisions in R1 – Not only is R1 still small by the denominational standards of the mainline churches, it has yet to demonstrate that it can remain stable without wholesale defections. Splits of various kinds have occurred ever since the division took place in 1976 between the leaders of R1 and R2.

Peter Paris, who left Wally North to join Bryn Jones in Bradford, fell out with the Welshman in 1978. He moved to Little Rock, Arkansas, where he came under Ern Baxter's 'covering' for a while. Part of the problem was that Peter Paris maintained relationships with Maurice Smith and John Noble. After Paris fell out with Jones, his name was removed from the editorial board of *Restoration* magazine. Following this, a considerable number of individuals and families also left R1 complaining of too much rigidity, legalism and heavy-handedness.[10] A number of these people ended up in R2.

The most serious division, however, that significantly depleted the numbers of R1 and weakened the leadership, was the defection of David Tomlinson and his churches to R2. At the Dales Bible Week in 1982, I noticed that David was absent from the leaders' platform for most of the time – he was being sanctioned for his dissent with Bryn Jones. Soon afterwards, he decided to withdraw from R1, and his name was also removed from the editorial associates of *Restoration* magazine.

Tomlinson had been a genuine pioneer in the north-east

and Midlands. Those under his pastoral care were very loyal to him, and most of them chose to stay with their shepherd. In many ways, his disagreement with Bryn Jones echoes the division of 1976. Differences with Bryn Jones were more a question of style, method of leadership and emphasis of doctrine, rather than major doctrinal disagreements. Tomlinson is almost the opposite in personality to Bryn Jones. Bryn (to use psychological terminology) is the classical convergent thinker. He presses on regardless of opposition and setbacks, running a tight ship all the way. David is a divergent thinker. He is always rethinking his position, always seeing new angles and aspects to doctrines and practices, always learning and changing. He was the perfect foil and check to Bryn Jones, and Jones's incisiveness was the counter-balance to Tomlinson's caution. The attraction of opposites, however, so easily leads to opposition, and the same power that attracts becomes the power that repels.

The absence of David Tomlinson has caused, many would argue, a serious imbalance in the life of R1. Many people there miss him, and he is still greatly respected by such people as David Matthew (the respect is mutual), the editor of *Restoration*. However, he is glad to be free of R1. He had felt, for a number of years, that R1 was already a denomination. In its desire to be the kingdom – to be truly the place of God's people – he felt R1 had adopted a 'fortress mentality' and was turning its back not only on the rest of Christendom, but also on the whole of modern culture.

Restoration Two

If, on following the story of R1, we can discern purposefulness and firm direction (despite the defections and clouds of rumour), a first glance at R2 seems to reveal partial disintegration and a perpetual running around in circles. First impressions are always useful, even if they are at best superficial. The collapse of the 'fabulous fourteen' seems to have caused no more than a hiccup in the life of R1, but its effect on R2 was traumatic. For a long time there seemed to be no unity of purpose. The firmest decision that seems to have been taken was consciously not to try to ape R1 by setting up a bigger and better Dales. The split had brought some relief. David Mansell was gone, and with the absence of Bryn Jones and Arthur Wallis, some of the London Brothers thought the atmosphere lighter. Perhaps the 'good times' of the Royal Albert Hall would return?

In the event, although the anarchic animus was still at work in R2, it was experienced more as a twitch and a stretching than a full flowing of power: R2 was alive but creaking. Morally and spiritually the leaders gave each other support, but co-ordinated efforts seemed to be difficult to sustain. This was partially due to the way apostleship worked in R2. Once churches were established, covenanted relationships assured and 'covering' arrangements understood, both house churches and house groups were expected to get on with it.

John Noble, for example, organized his own team, set up churches, and left elders to run their own affairs. His was the ultimate authority, but he did not see it as his place to delve into the minutiae of everyday kingdom life. 'Father in God' he might have been, but he did expect his children to grow up and have enough independence to run their own lives. Not that nothing went on in Collier Row, in Romford, Essex, where he had his stronghold. Up on the hill – the fellowship held to the image of kingdom light shining forth from the mountain top – members moved into the same streets and became neighbours. Similar formations – which Nick Butterworth was later to characterize as ghettos – took place in Petersfield, Cardiff, Cobham and Yeovil.

Gerald Coates started up 'Kingdom Life' in Cobham, where praise and worship reflected the glory days of the Royal Albert Hall. Gerald's sense of drama and style developed in those meetings, and many hundreds of people attended. Some evangelicals found the meetings shallow, emotionally manipulative and lacking in traditional evangelical content. 'It was just religious showbiz,' someone reported to me. Another saw it as a platform to promote Gerald Coates. The majority of people, however, found the meetings liberating and stimulating; fun but spiritual. There is no doubt that by 1981 Gerald Coates had more friends than enemies. The success of Cobham was parochial in the sense that it reflected what Gerald was doing, with support from John, rather than influencing R2 as a whole.

The weakening of relationships – It is very difficult, looking back at the late 1970s, to see R2 as an entity at all. In discipling terms, Gerald looked to John Noble as the senior apostle, but other leaders were less submissive. Gradually, and without much of the drama that took place in R1, relationships began to weaken. John MacLauchlan had a disagreement with John Noble as to who had the primary responsibility for the flock in Yeovil. He also, along with Graham Perrins, began to develop ideas of the primacy of the prophet in the end-time kingdom. By the end of the 1970s, R2 no longer formed a unity based on an alliance between the London Brothers and the western leaders. Peter Lyne departed for New Zealand, Ian McCullogh went off on his own and ended up with one community, relating to no one except some obscure American shepherd. John MacLauchlan and Graham Perrins decided to work together and no longer 'relate' to John Noble and Gerald Coates.

Up until 1979, *Fulness* magazine had been the major focus for the, by now, damaged kingdom of R2. With the departure of Graham Perrins into his Cardiff stronghold, *Fulness* ceased. Nick Butterworth valiantly tried to edit a new journal in the early 1980s. *Dovetail*, as it was called, did not really live up to its name. There seemed to be little editorial co-ordination, and it was a bits and pieces magazine compared to the earlier *Fulness*. George Tarleton was still around, but remained, as he always had been, a law unto himself. By 1981–82, R2 had two faces: what was left of the original Restoration movement was really no more than a weakened London Brothers (Terry Virgo and David Mansell now being in R1).

For the rest, there were isolated pockets of Restorationist-style groups, which included Graham Perrins and John MacLauchlan, who related together and with Wayne Drain in America. There was also Ian McCullogh's church, and a few floating communities that flitted from apostle to prophet. None of these disparate groups formed any kind of co-ordinated movement, although some of these R2 churches were more authoritarian and demanding than the churches under John Noble and Gerald Coates (see chapter 13).

Unlike R1, R2 showed less interest in buildings (at least until 1985). They primarily rented their churches and halls. In 1980, John Noble did start an independent school which was always difficult to finance. A number of Christian business ventures were tried, but they seemed to have the habit of going off half-cock. The Rainbow company was started by John Noble in 1983. After a very poor start, it seemed to be finding its feet by late 1984. I think it not unfair to say that R2 was not the efficient business machine that characterized R1 in the same period of time. George Tarleton finds this one of the most endearing qualities of R2.

By 1983, Graham Perrins and John MacLauchlan had fallen out. Reports that Graham Perrins had 'gone off the rails' began to filter through to the London Brothers. It appears that Graham Perrins was man enough to admit mistakes had been made, and the communities under his direction had reportedly stabilized. This cannot be said of John MacLauchlan's churches, where there were defections, complaints of false prophecy and undue heavy-handedness.

Remarkably, while R2 could boast neither co-ordinated efforts nor a clear-cut programme during these years, it continued to grow. Landmarks are difficult to find, but there were significant events and interesting experiments. For example, in the two years that Graham Perrins and John MacLauchlan worked fruitfully together (from the end of 1979 until 1982), they produced a remarkable journal that I think will become a collectors' item. Perrins always had a reputation for wide reading, and John MacLauchlan's Greek and historical scholarship had been a byword in Restoration circles for years. The magazine they produced, *Proclaim*, not only published shocking and radical views concerning the nature of prophecy, it also contained a level of genuine scholarship that cannot be found in any other Restoration publication that I have read.

Gerald Coates joined the Evangelical Alliance, and with his interest in media and pop culture became instrumental in the Spring Harvest and Banquet organizations. This move of Gerald, coupled with John Noble forming links with Catholic charismatics from 1982, demonstrates a desire to relate their style of Restorationism with the rest of neo-Pentecostalism.

By 1983, with the arrival of David Tomlinson and his churches, R2 recovered its nerve and its sense of direction. Indeed, Tomlinson's appearance heralded the emergence of R2 in its new and mature form. The old London Brothers–Peter Lyne–Graham Perrins axis having shattered, what remained was a remnant of the London Brothers and refugees from R1. There was a celebration and dedication of commitment in 1983 with R2's first attempt at a Dales-style camp. Festival 83 was held for a week at the Staffordshire Showground, and although it was not a financial success, it succeeded as a demonstration of identity and spiritual seriousness. 1983 was a good year for Gerald with the publication of his book, *What on Earth is this Kingdom?* and his subsequent interviews on Radio 4 and local radio stations. To the many churches under the newly-constituted leadership,[11] there was a feeling of moving on to a new phase.

Developments in 1984 and 85 – In the event, 1984 turned out to be as significant and as traumatic a year for R2 as it was for R1. By now David Tomlinson, John Noble, and Gerald Coates (and Peter Fenwick, who formerly worked with Peter Paris) were working closely together while remaining autonomous and publishing their own house magazines. There was a new searching for how kingdom principles could be applied to a more evangelistic and pioneering effort. David Tomlinson took a bold step – to move into the inner London areas and establish new churches. There was an eagerness to learn from past mistakes, holding onto the essentials of Restoration revelation, but disregarding what they saw as exclusivist and legalistic tendencies.

Festival 84 was held at Stafford, and was a huge success. It was attended by over 4,000 exuberant people. The format was similar to the Dales, but its workshops and seminars were far broader in content and more controversial and provocative than Dales teaching. Dales Bible Week can be likened to a military camp, but Festival was more like a spiritual Butlins. Certainly, the R1 refugees felt they had escaped into a holiday camp: women could and did say that they did not always want to stay at home. Some of them showed an interest in leadership, and issues of racism, unemployment and peace were discussed by many groups with a seriousness and interest that would not have shamed the British Council of Churches. And yet, at the moment when, for the first time for years, the newly rejuvenated (and admittedly partly reconstituted) R2 was emerging as a more united force, it suffered its own defections.

1984 had not started well for Collier Row, with a bad school report by Her Majesty's Inspectors. It was not a damning report: the community spirit and primary provision were praised. It did suggest, however, that the school had bitten off more than it could chew; the secondary schooling curriculum and teaching was not up to scratch.[12] More seriously for John Noble, Maurice Smith decided to break with him, and at the same time, Nick Butterworth pulled his churches out from the covering umbrella of John Noble's leadership. A number of other members from the Essex fellowships also decided to leave.

One of the issues revolved around a greater financial commitment that John Noble wanted, to help both Rainbow and more concerted team work. Complaints were made by some that John had become too authoritarian. This is a charge that John denies. Perhaps it was the case that he was the victim of leaving his followers too much to their own devices; they had become used to the status quo, and did not seem prepared to offer any greater commitment. Nick Butterworth believes that Collier Row and its fellowships had become a ghetto. He claims that he woke up one day and realized that he did not know anyone in his street except kingdom people.[13] It was time, he thought, to quit what had become a holy huddle.

Both he and Maurice Smith felt that the discipling doctrines were wrong, and that the whole psychology of Restoration (both R1 and R2) was based on insisting that there was always something within people which needed improving. They decided to abandon such principles and preach that Jesus is happy with people just the way they are. Influenced by Norman Grubb ('an old friend') and the American Union Life movement, Maurice insisted that he had not joined that movement and had no intention of doing so in the future. He launched out on his own in a new full-time ministry at the end of 1985, which he jokingly told me might become known as 'the nebulous church'.[14]

George Tarleton, on the other hand, decided to throw in his hand completely, and retire not only from R2, but from full-time Christian work. He loved many of the brethren, and in particular John Noble, but felt that there had been too much delusion in what they were doing. He felt that R2 was itself taking the road to denominationalism.

R2 had not had the spectacular success of R1 by the close of 1985, and yet it was not surrounded by the same clouds of rumour and scandal as the larger Restoration kingdom. The Tomlinson–Noble–Coates axis, at the core of R2, numbered some 8,000–10,000. If we include all the other fellow travellers of the time – Peter Fenwick's churches, for example – we might be able to double that figure.[15] Leadership was strong and member commitment high. The real question for them, in 1985, was not how big or small they would become, but which direction they would take: further away from the mainstream into a sectarian enclave, or back into the central flow of British religious life and culture?

There is a limit to how far an interpretive narrative can take one into understanding a new phenomenon. It will have been obvious that while I have not denied the importance of seeing Restorationists as living members of the kingdom of God, I have used the notion of 'kingdom' as a metaphor to describe the new movements. Having used this metaphor in an extended way to see in what manner the kingdom of Restoration was established, I wish now to extend it further to see how we can understand and evaluate its significance. My central contention is that Restoration is a radical kingdom. An examination of its doctrines, an investigation into its historical antecedents, and a look at its sociological complexion will help us establish the nature of this radicality.

Recommended Reading

'The Dales Dilemma: Church Splitters or Kingdom Builders?' *Buzz* magazine (August 1984).

Pioneer Bulletin, Vol. 1, Issue 3 (Pioneer Enterprises Ltd.).

Ross Peart, 'The House Church', *Methodist Recorder* (9th February 1984).

Gerald Coates, *What on Earth is this Kingdom?* (Kingsway, 1983).

Eileen Vincent, *Something's Happening* (Marshalls, 1984).

Word to the World, Voice of the Harvestime Team, Issue 1, 1984 (Harvestime Publications).

Part Two

The Radical Kingdom
An Evaluation of Restorationism until 1985

6

THE RADICAL PRINCIPLES OF RESTORATION (PART ONE)

On Radicality

It was the philosopher Ludwig Wittgenstein who claimed in his later works that the meanings of words are related to their usage. To discover the meaning of a word, he said, it is not enough to use a dictionary or lexicon – terminology can only be understood by examining the ways people use it. While this theory has its difficulties, it is certainly a useful insight when we come to investigate idiomatic language used by religious movements (or the jargon of social scientists, for that matter!). This approach is also useful when we examine words and phrases in our culture that have extended usages and multiple meanings.

The word 'radical', for example, is particularly problematic. Ever since it became associated with the Whigs, and later with Liberalism and Socialism, 'radical' has become very difficult to disassociate from politics of a reformist or revolutionary kind. In calling Restorationism 'radical Christianity', I want to make it clear that I am invoking no political meaning. Indeed, politically speaking, Restorationism is neither radically left wing nor right wing; like so many enthusiastic religious movements, Restorationism tends to be apolitical.[1]

Another extended usage of 'radical' is to make it synonymous with 'liberal' and apply the term to either morality or theology. If we take this to mean 'against tradition', and think of such examples as situational ethics and demythologising theology, then Restoration is clearly not

radical at all in this sense. On the whole, its moral and theological positions are conservative, and as we shall see, the
majority of its doctrines clearly belong to the conservative
evangelicalism of classical Pentecostalism.

So far, my use of the term 'radical' is in harmony with
the Restorationists themselves. Arthur Wallis, however, in
his book *The Radical Christian*,[2] discusses radicality in a far
more ideological and comprehensive way than I shall be
able to do. I feel it more useful to define and 'operationalize' the notion of radical in a way which I can then apply
with some certainty and explanatory power. (Another way
of understanding this is to realize that Arthur is writing
from the inside; my perspective is that of the outsider.) Let
me, at least, start with Arthur's usage.

Arthur points out that the word 'radical' has its origins
in the Latin *radix*, or root. He sees the radical Christian as
one who returns to the origins, roots or sources of pure
Christianity. The radical Christian, then, is not one who
turns away from the tradition, but is one who returns to
the pure tradition. This tradition he sees as totally committed Christianity both in personal and corporate terms. For
Arthur, the true Christian is by definition one who stands
absolutely for truth and refuses compromise. 'Or to put it
differently, when it comes to important issues he refuses to
sit on the fence or adopt a "wait-and-see" policy. It's right
or it's wrong. It's true or it's false. It's light or it's darkness.
He cannot go along with those who, for personal consider-
ations, are content to live in the twilight.'[3] In the kingdom
of God, Wallis claims, 'radicalism means unswerving righteousness'.

This return to pure, biblical Christianity, in Wallis's
understanding, is radical in a twin sense. Firstly, it is radical because it is a turning round (*metanoia*) and going back
to a Christianity of the New Testament. This, as we shall
see, entails going back to a Christianity that precedes
denominationalism in order to go beyond denominationalism. Secondly, it is radical because the true disciples of
the Jesus of the New Testament are seen to treat the root

problem of all social and political ills: the wickedness of the human heart. Put together this twin notion of radicality leads us to see a Christian who is committed to eradicating sin, error, apostasy and compromise. He is also one who stands for righteousness, truth and unswerving commitment to God's reign and rule(s) in his kingdom.

The Restorationists' claim, that they have restored the pattern of New Testament Christianity, is certainly radical enough. Personally, I find the claim less than convincing,[4] but the problem with Arthur's definition is not that I cannot personally give wholehearted assent to the claims inherent in it, but that his understanding of 'radical' is too comprehensive for me to operationalize in a strictly defined way. I propose, therefore, to limit and narrow my understanding of 'radical', so that I can use it in a non-theological way.

I believe that an examination of the doctrines and practices of both R1 and R2 demonstrates that we can usefully apply the term 'radical' if we keep in mind that this kingdom Christianity entails a comprehensive degree of social control by leaders, and a strong personal commitment by members not normally found in Christianity. Restoration religion circumscribes the lives of its followers to a far greater extent than is typical not only in the mainline denominations but also in the majority of Pentecostal churches.

In typical evangelical churches, believers are expected to 'give their hearts to Jesus', and there is an expectation that some demands will be made on free time. Restorationists, however, are prepared to give their all to the kingdom, whether it be time, money, personal possessions or skills. Being an Anglican or a Baptist can be a part-time pursuit (almost a leisure activity). To become a Restorationist is to adopt a total way of life.

For this reason, it is not enough simply to lump R1 and R2 with fundamentalism and dismiss them as yet another addition to Protestant sectarianism. In the United States there has been a considerable rise in fundamentalism throughout the 1980s and 1990s. But being a fundamental-ist or a 'Bible-belter' does not necessarily lead to a radical alternative to the American way of life. All too often it is seen as synonymous with it. A particularly interesting aspect of Billy Graham's 'Mission England' in 1984 was the way in which he confided to Christian leaders that many of the new conservatives in American religion were blind to the evils of American society. R2 is still working out its relationship to British secular culture, but R1 is quite clear that it belongs to an alternative society.

The fact that Restorationism circumscribes the lives of its adherents every bit as much as the Salvation Army is not only sociological evidence of its radicality, it is also a demonstration that its theological claims are radical too. Salvation Army control is related to its hierarchical organi-zation, which is self-consciously modelled on the secular army: orders are given at the top and passed down the line. In the Restoration churches, claims are made not only to belong to the Lord's army, but also to be subjects of the King in a theocratic state. Theocracy is not unique in Protestant history, but it is rare in the modern world.

To recapitulate: while it is not my intention to disprove the thesis that Restorationists have restored New Testament Christianity, neither do I intend to substantiate that claim as evidence of its radicality. I shall discuss Restorationist Christianity as radical in two interrelated ways. Firstly, against the conventional wisdom of denom-inational Christianity, it insists that the charismatic gifts of the early Church have been restored and that God has re-established his control over the kingdom through a theoc-racy of apostles. Secondly, a belief in the restored theocra-cy has led to an ordering and control of believers' lives not typically found in conventional Christianity.

Restorationists claim that the Christianity which they practise is to be seen as the New Testament norm both in terms of Church government and individual commitment. By contemporary denominational standards, their beliefs and practices clearly deviate from the normative behaviour of most mainline Christians. In this narrow sense they are indisputably radical. I do not mean this to be seen as a polite way of saying that Restorationism is sectarian. It is that too – from a sociological standpoint at least – as I shall later argue. But even from a sectarian perspective, Restoration makes claims and demands upon its members that are not typical of many such movements. It is clear, then, that Restoration is neither 'run of the mill', nor just another Pentecostal movement. Its beliefs are radical in its claims, and its organization is radical in the effect it has on believers' lives.

The Christian Context of Restoration

To locate the principles of Restorationists is to recognize that they belong firmly to evangelical Protestantism. Furthermore, most of their beliefs and practices are identical to classical Pentecostalism. Both R1 and R2 resemble the traditional Pentecostal denominations more than the Renewalism of neo-Pentecostalism. This is true because their theology of the 'baptism of the Holy Spirit', and their total commitment to adult baptism, is no different from their classical counterparts. Their eschatology too has its origins in Pentecostalism, and to a certain extent in Brethrenism.

Classical Pentecostals pioneered lively and spontaneous liturgies. The coupling of informality with serious ideological content has been taken over by the Restorationists and revamped into their own style. So similar in many ways is Restorationism (as indeed have been aspects of the Renewal) to classical Pentecostalism, that a first glance fails to notice the difference. Many of the members of Elim and the Assemblies of God who have attended the Dales Bible Week felt immediately at home. If anything they felt more at home than in their own churches, because the Dales generated greater expectations of God's blessings, more excitement, and a real feeling of revival.

I think it important that before we concentrate on the

few distinctive and radical doctrines of Restoration, we realize how close they are to their older Pentecostal cousins. Restorationists accept the Bible as the infallible Word of God in all matters of doctrine and religious practice. They are literalists in matters of interpretation, whether it be the miraculous stories of the New Testament, tales of Old Testament heroes, or understanding the Creation story of Genesis as an historical account.

They not only reject the scholarship of modernist theologians, but they are not, on the whole, versed in issues of hermeneutics, historical criticism or demythologising tenets. I think it not unfair to describe them as fundamentalists (though they do not like the term), rather than conservative evangelicals. This distinction is a vital one because while fundamentalists – within Protestantism – will be evangelical by definition, a conservative evangelical might well be able to accommodate some forms of higher criticism and evolutionary theory while remaining committed to the essential truths of the incarnation, life, death and resurrection of Christ.[5] Many evangelicals, also, would not wish to identify themselves with a firm commitment to a particular eschatological theory.

Restorationists, like all fundamentalists, counterbalance their literalness with a wide use of typology, analogy and ingenious speculations concerning the end of the world. Adventism dominates all forms of Pentecostalism, and a commitment to and expectation of the imminent return of the Lord Jesus is the backdrop against which the drama of Pentecostal life is played. Restorationists are by no means in agreement on all interpretations of the second coming, and in that they are no different from other Pentecostal groups.

Like all Pentecostals, Restorationists believe that one becomes a Christian by the regeneration of the 'new birth'. Christian life cannot begin until Christ has been accepted as Saviour. This acceptance, based on the belief in the vicarious death and resurrection of Christ, is the passport to the Church which consists of born-again believers. The same issues of faith and grace are debated in Restoration as in the rest of Pentecostalism. The majority of Restorationists are tacitly Arminian – overtly so in Bradford – in the sense that like many of the early Methodists, self-will and personal faith are stressed more than doctrines of grace and election. (This is not true of Hove, where the leading pastor there – under Terry Virgo – has a strong Calvinistic emphasis which stems from his earlier days in the Baptist Union.)

Restorationists are aggressively Baptist. I say 'aggressively', because Restoration leaders are anxious to stress that believers' baptism is not an option for Christians, but an essential part of the restored Church. While I have met two vigorously argued cases against infant baptism,[6] and heard many vehement sermons against it from R1 leaders, I have never seen any evidence that they know what the biblical and historical defence of the traditional practice could be.[7] The proselytising attitude to believers' baptism has clearly divided Restorationists from many Catholic, Anglican, Presbyterian and Methodist Renewalists. I have seen Anglicans rebaptized at the Dales. The fact that this takes place is evidence of the strength of feeling that Restorationists possess over this issue. It is another example of how they are closer to classical Pentecostalism than the Charismatic Renewal *per se*.

It could be argued that their Baptist views owe as much to Brethrenism as Pentecostalism. The same could be said of their general attitude to sacraments. The doctrine of the Lord's Table seems to be identical to Brethren usage. Like all Brethren and Pentecostals, they abhor ritualism and sacramentalism of any kind.

Their view that the 'baptism of the Holy Spirit' is a second experience quite separate from conversion is taken from classical Pentecostalism.[8] They believe that the 'baptism' is the initiation into the power of the Holy Ghost. Most Restorationists believe that the initial sign, or evidence, of the baptism is speaking in tongues. There is no dogmatic ruling on this, however. Following other

Pentecostalists, Restorationists have emphasized the gifts of the Spirit as outlined by St Paul in 1 Corinthians chapter 12. Great emphasis is placed on divine healing and the deliverance of people from the possessive and oppressive power of demons. In this respect, Restorationists can be said to major on demons and 'deliverance ministry' far more than Elim and the Assemblies of God. There has been considerable input from America in this area, both in terms of the older-style revivalist Pentecostalism and the newer Independents.

Most classical Pentecostals are nominally trinitarian in belief, but few groups have a developed doctrine of the Trinity. This applies also to Restorationists. It is not even clear that the old dispute that we noticed earlier in regard to Chard, concerning the correct formula for baptism, is yet resolved. I have heard the Holy Trinity invoked at water baptism, but reliable informants have told me that some baptisms use the name of Jesus only. An interesting feature of classical Pentecostalism and Restorationism is that despite the emphasis on the Spirit, most theology tends to be Christocentric. Prayers are rarely addressed to the Holy Spirit, and never at all to the Holy Trinity. It might seem that given the close similarities between themselves and classical Pentecostalism, Restorationists see themselves as belonging in that camp. This is not so. Restorationists admit to a filial relationship, but that is all. They think that the classical Pentecostals fell into the error of denominationalism on the one hand, while on the other hand they failed to see the full implications of the restoration of the charismatic gifts. Restorationists believe that God is saying something new to Christians and something more radical even than the Pentecostal belief in revival.

They see the great revivals of classical Pentecostalism as the first phase of restoring the supernatural gifts of the Holy Spirit to the Church. The second, short phase, was the Charismatic Renewal, when God demonstrated that Holy Ghost power could not be contained within the sect or denomination. The third and final phase, was the restoration of the kingdom of God, which has been absent in its full power since New Testament times. This restoration of the kingdom is to be the final chapter in the history of the Church in preparation for Christ's bodily return to earth, and the establishment of a new heaven and a new world: 'the time of universal restoration'.

The Restored Church as an Eschatological Imperative

The key to understanding the emergence and significance of the Restoration movement, as Restorationists understand it themselves, is eschatology. Following Edward Irving and the early Brethren movement, a section of the evangelical world has inherited a fascination with certain interpretations of the last things. In America, under the influence of the Millerites and the early Mormons and Jehovah's Witnesses, eschatology became a burning topic among many non-Christian sects, too. Today, Christadelphians, Seventh Day Adventists and most Pentecostal movements share with these sects a concern to understand history in the light of an eschatological doctrine.[9]

John Nelson Darby, perhaps the most dynamic of early Brethren leaders, believed that the second coming of Christ would be preceded by 'wars and rumours of wars'. Following Darby, a considerable consensus developed in non-conformist evangelicalism that the end-time would be characterized by such wars, but also moral depravity, natural disasters and religious decline. In recent years, with the arrival of 'the bomb', and a growing concern with ecological problems, this thesis has continued to thrive.

One of the central controversies has centred around the issue as to whether Christians will be whisked away from all the troubles and tribulations of the last days, perhaps in a secret rapture – as Darby and Irving thought – in the air with Christ and the saints of history. The role of the antichrist (seen either as an actual person or an evil system) has been just one of the many enigmas in a prophetic jig-saw that few have claimed fully to understand.

Against the 'doom and gloom brigade', who have tend-ed to hold onto a remnant eschatology, in which only a few true Christians would be saved, have arisen the counter-vailing groups who emphasize 'the latter rain'. This was a movement that gained prominence in classical Pentecostal circles, and the central idea was the belief that a worldwide revival would herald the return of Christ. The 'first rain' was interpreted as Pentecost and the beginning of the Christian dispensation. The 'second rain' – the latter rain – was understood as a restoration of Pentecostal power to the Church before the end of time. There was a latter rain movement in Canadian and American Pentecostalism in the 1950s, which no doubt influenced Arthur Wallis. In Great Britain today, the charismatic leader Colin Urquhart belongs in this tradition.

The early Restorationists, like many Renewalists, saw the charismatic movement as a sign of the latter rain. As the movement developed, however, they saw the Renewal as just a few 'showers of blessing' before the real deluge. The nature of this deluge began to take on an interesting and concrete expression. God, it was claimed, would not let his Church be swamped by sin, or by the forces of the evil one. On the contrary, he would restore the Church to her original splendour. But this would entail not only revisiting her with charismatic gifts, but also equipping her with the government and ordinances of God's kingdom.

This kingdom would not be of this world (Babylon, the whore city, is the image often used for the world), but would exist in this world as an alternative society, run according to God's rules, and staffed by his devoted fol-lowers. Graham Perrins has tended to emphasize the peo-ple of the kingdom as a prophetic people, both pointing to and in part realizing the eschaton. The majority of Restorationists, however, especially in R1, see God's peo-ple as those who fulfil God's original plan for Adam. This plan was to populate the earth with men and women made in his image. Since the fall, and since the failure of the Old Covenant with Israel, Christ – the new Adam – has initiated the covenant of the New Israel. Henceforth, the people of God – both Jew and Gentile joined to Christ as the head of the Church – have continued God's plan to populate the earth. In the last days, God will make it possible for his people to multiply, fill the whole earth, and become rulers in his kingdom.

Despite the apostasy of the Church, then, the kingdom of God is destined to be restored. Denominations will be abolished and the new Church will establish a substantial and glorious witness to the power and holiness of God. His people, in the last days, will prosper and become victorious over their enemies. The rest of the world, which will begin to disintegrate during these last days, will look on in wonder.

God's kingdom is to be understood as 'the stone cut without hands' of Nebuchadnezzar's famous vision of the kingdoms of the earth. In this vision of the image composed of gold, silver, iron, and iron and clay (representing historical epochs) the stone was dashed against the image, which was smashed to pieces. The stone became a great mountain and filled the earth. Daniel interpreted the stone in this way:

> And in the days of these kings shall the God of heaven set up a kingdom, which shall never be destroyed: and the kingdom shall not be left to other people, but it shall break in pieces and consume all these kingdoms, and it shall stand for ever.[10]

As the great restored kingdom begins rapidly to grow, so it will meet great opposition. The so-called 'great tribulation' is to be endured by the saints in the Restoration schema before the second coming. Most Restorationists believe that the secret rapture of the Church, which allows the saints to miss the tribulation, is an unfounded biblical inference. They believe, however, that the kingdom of

God, which will be attacked by the antichrist and his forces, will withstand all opposition. Indeed, the very establishment of God's alternative society, they believe, will inevitably polarize the world into the forces of good and evil.

All this is not quite as black and white as it seems. Those not in the kingdom will recognize it for what it is: the dwelling place of the people of God. David Matthew, the editor of *Restoration* magazine, foresees the day when the politicians and workers of the world will come to kingdom people cap in hand.[11] Conversely, all those living within the shadow of the kingdom are not necessarily in the Church.

On first meeting kingdom people, I thought that 'kingdom' and 'Church' were interchangeable terms in Restorationist circles. Apparently, this is not so. The kingdom of God is to be understood not as a place, but as the rule of God. God's laws and precepts are to be written in the hearts of men and women, and adhered to in practice in a corporate and not merely in an individual way. God's alternative society exists wherever God's rule is obeyed. The kingdom enters the world through the Church, which acts like a portal or a door. Once established, this kingdom derives its spiritual authority supremely through King Jesus, but also through his body, the Church.

In one image used by Restorationists, the Church is seen as the cutting edge of the kingdom. Another image is the hardened tip of the arrow. In short, the Church leads and the kingdom follows. I assume the logic of this position is that members of the Church are *ipso facto* members of the kingdom, but that members of the kingdom need not necessarily be members of the Church. (Children would fit this category, for example, in Restorationist churches. This is one of the consequences, as Edward Irving saw, of conversion experience and not infant baptism being the initiation into the Church.)

The Church, then, is to usher in the kingdom of God prior to the historical return of Christ to earth. The return of the King completes the full restoration of the kingdom on earth. Some evangelicals will no doubt see this as pre-empting God's sovereignty: 'How can Jesus come like a thief in the night,' they might ask, 'if the kingdom has to wait to be properly established?' Others might see this as tantamount to saying, 'Even so, come quickly Lord Jesus, but not yet because we haven't finished the job.'

Restorationists do not claim that God is bound by their eschatology; they are merely demonstrating their commitment to the promises of God's Word, as they understand them. Furthermore, they insist that God is merciful and wishes, if possible, for all to be saved. At the very least, therefore, the Church should be seen not as a little band of the faithful huddling together like some sect awaiting their final release from a hostile world: it will be powerful and strong, awaiting the return of the King. The Church militant and defiant is the message of Restoration; not the Church defeated:

We are the army of God
As a church we stand in God's armour.
The pow'rs of darkness are trembling
As Jesus our captain goes before us.[12]

The Restorationist adventism is essentially post-millennial, but millennialism is not an essential theme in their vision of the last things. Christ will return when the Church is perfect ('the Bride without blemish') and the kingdom restored. He will come as King and take his rightful place: 'And every knee shall bow, and every tongue shall confess to God.' Whether he will then reign with his saints for a thousand years, or whether Christ's historical return heralds the end of time seems less clear. I think most Restorationists think there will be a gap between the return of the King, and the full 'restoration of all things' in eternity. The essential thrust of their adventism, however, is the establishment of a mighty kingdom of God prior to the return of Christ.

Not all Restorationists hold to such a strong eschatological position as outlined above; but despite disagreement over details, most members of R1 and R2 hold to some version of it. I would describe the version that I have outlined as the classic Restorationist vision. It is not only the dominant eschatology of R1, but it is the vision with which Arthur Wallis inspired the 'magnificent seven' and the 'fabulous fourteen' in the 1970s.

Graham Perrins and John MacLauchlan have increasingly, since those days, veered away from the idea of doing prophecy to becoming prophetic. One consequence of this would seem to be a concentration on the prophetic role and the bringing forth of prophecy. The extreme version of this is that the prophet declares it, and it is! This prophetic emphasis has replaced the more traditional Pentecostal concern to piece together a correct interpretation of the end things. Members in R2 seem less caught up with eschatology than R1. I suspect that David Tomlinson, for example, is wary of insisting on too strong a Restorationist eschatology. (Both R1 and R2 tend to see eschatology in terms of adventism rather than a theological doctrine of the final judgment *per se*.)

The significance of Restoration eschatology is not that either R1 or R2 has a 'correct' line which everybody holds dogmatically. Its significance lies in the vision of Church life and kingdom order that the eschatology inspires. The eschatological vision has not been added to Restorationism after it became established: it preceded the movement and provided the motivating force for the establishment of the Restoration kingdom(s).

The vision of a powerful and resplendent Church standing high on the mountain like a beacon paradoxically offering both hope and warning to a lost world, is also seen as a judgment on the Church. Or, to be more accurate, it pronounces a judgment on what men and women have tried to do to God's Church. The eschatological view of the fulfilment of God's plan, therefore, has also provided Restorationists with a means for both interpreting and judging Church history. Reading the eschaton back into history led the Restorationists to the conviction that the original glory of God's Church had been dimmed; consequently the power of the kingdom had been virtually switched off. The restoration of that power was a gradual process culminating today in the reappearance of a re-energized and charismatically-ordained Church.

Denominational Apostasy and the Reunification of the Church

Whether one reads the history of the remnant Church in the early *Fulness* magazines, the prophetic history of the *Proclaim* journal, or the nine-part 'Church Adrift' series in *Restoration*, one will not find an account of Church history that accords with conventional scholarship. Neither is there anything to cheer the heart of anyone from an Orthodox or Catholic tradition. Many Protestants too will be unable to identify with the way in which the Church has been presented.

It might seem as if the writers are unaware of the Greek fathers, and have certainly not read their Kelly.[13] Perhaps they do not know that Calvin and Charles Wesley were saturated in the theology and spirituality of the Chalcedonian thinkers? Perhaps, too, the writers do not really know their Catholic history? Whether they do or not, it is a mistake to understand the interpretation of Church history by Restorationists as an intellectualist exercise.[14] They are concerned with discerning the survival and gradual restoration of the true Church – amidst the apostasy of denominational history.

Looking at Figure 1, it can be seen that Restorationists believe that the Church took a nose dive at the end of the New Testament canon. After a brief attempt at rousing itself under the Montanists, it hit rock bottom by AD 600, and stayed there until the Reformation. The failure of the early Church is seen primarily as an abandonment of the sacred and inviolable rules of Scripture for the maintenance of normal (that is, charismatic) Church life. In a short time after the death of the apostles, extra-biblical doctrines concerning the nature and power of the Church began to circulate. Beliefs in ritualistic and sacramentalist theologies (seen by Restorationists as magic or superstition) and ecclesiastical systems of episcopacy began to distort the gospel. In short, the Church fell into error, and the power of the Holy Spirit was withdrawn.

Restorationists see the Reformation as recovering the supremacy of Scripture over Church traditions. They also see with the emergence of the Anabaptist movement, the recovery of believers' baptism (which they see as a New Testament practice). The recovery continues and accelerates with the outbreak of Puritanism, religious enthusiasm and the growth of evangelicalism. A milestone in this recovery is seen to be the Methodist movement. It is particularly interesting that the Salvation Army and Brethrenism are highlighted as stepping stones to Restorationism.

The twentieth century is primarily seen as the century of the recovery of the gifts of the Holy Spirit, and latterly the restoration of apostolic ministries. Watchman Nee is cited by all Restorationists as a genuine apostle and precursor of both the house church movement, and Restoration *per se*. (Watchman Nee was no Pentecostalist: he has also been claimed as a mentor by the Exclusive Brethren!) Billy Graham is praised too for his mass evangelistic efforts.

Throughout this Restorationist view of Church history, a consistent theme is the apostasy of the historic denominations and the failure to adhere to New Testament principles. Although the Reformation is hailed as the beginning of the recovery, Protestantism is indicted for failing to return to a unified Church. Protestant denominations are viewed as churches perpetuating their own distinctive doctrines and failing to repent of the sin of divisiveness.

It is significant that the religious movements most admired in the past are the movements of enthusiasm.

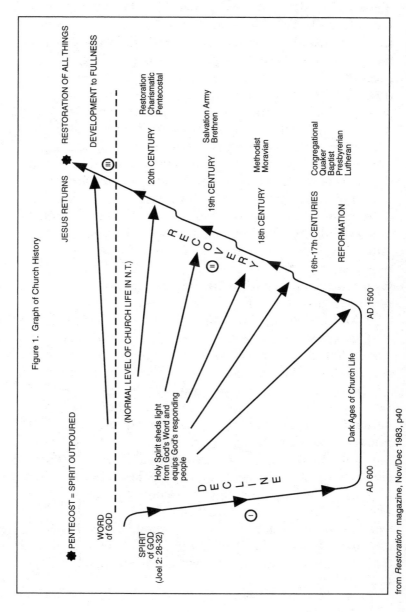

Figure 1. Graph of Church History

from *Restoration* magazine, Nov/Dec 1983, p40

Figure 1

145

David Matthew firmly places himself in that tradition: 'Personally, I like to think that, had I lived in a bygone era, I would have been an enthusiastic Montanist, Clunyite, Reformer, Anabaptist, Wesleyan or Pentecostal.'[15] Many members from R1 and R2 have told me of their 'radical roots', and they all see these roots in the sort of movements described by David Matthew.

John Noble pointed out to me[16] that the emergence of new denominations that encapsulated new truths (or rather recovered old ones) was a sin on the one hand because these movements gradually established new and divisive church structures; on the other hand these churches – in bits and pieces – brought back the forgotten truths of the gospel. God the Holy Spirit, in other words, revealed himself to humankind in small portions, according to the faith of believers. Now that the truth is out for all to see, however (now that the full power of the Holy Spirit has been returned to the Church), denominations are not only no longer necessary, they are a hindrance to the work of God. The new wine of the Spirit cannot be contained in the old denominational structures. New flexible and biblically principled structures need to emerge to contain and mature the new wine.

The attack upon denominations really has a twofold movement. Firstly, it is insisted, denominations have perverted the teachings of the New Testament. Secondly, it is pointed out, many churches are made up of people who are not Christian at all. Infant baptism is seen as pernicious, not only because it is said to be unbiblical, but because it allows people to be in denominations and participate in Communion without having to be regenerate. The Church, as Restorationists understand it, is not a social structure surrounding declared articles of faith. It is the 'body of Christ', and only those who are born again belong to that body.

Not only the historic denominations are seen to be in error, all denominations fall short of being what was in 'God's heart from the beginning': a people of God linked organically to the new Adam, Jesus Christ. God wants only the Church. He does not want denominational expressions of it.

Brethren readers will find much of this familiar territory. In many ways, the Restorationist thesis is an updated and Pentecostal version of E. H. Broadbent's *The Pilgrim Church*.[17] In this work, Broadbent attempts to trace the faithful witnesses down the centuries; witnesses who have carried aloft the torch of the gospel. The general image of the Church is the spluttering candle kept alight amidst the blackness and perfidiousness of denominational Christianity. For Broadbent, the Brethren movement – in the words of another Brethren classic – is the 'great recovery'.[18] Restoration sees the torch taken from the Brethren by the Pentecostal movement. By now the spluttering light has become as bright as the Olympic flame. With the coming of Restoration, the flame ignites to become the white heat of pure Pentecostal power.

That Restorationist churches (not only R1 and R2, but international counterparts in the 'shepherding movement') are seen as the foci of God's final chapter in the history of His people – and thus the whole world – can be seen in the list of recovered truths of the twentieth century as declared in *Restoration* magazine:

(1) The baptism in the Holy Spirit.
(2) The return of the gifts of the Spirit for both corporate and individual life.
(3) A belief in a worldwide end-time revival.
(4) The restoration of apostolic and prophetic ministries as a major means of bringing about the unity of the Church.
(5) The establishment of apostolic teams to supplement and complement the work of apostles.
(6) The growth of discipling practices, under godly leaders, in the local churches.
(7) A recognition that denominations are not in God's plan, and are ultimately unrenewable.

(8) New freedom in worship and praise.[19]

'A plague on all your houses' declare the true radicals of Restoration, who wish to shake off the dust of conventional Christianity from their feet. Their desire is to replace denominations by the Church. Their radicality springs from their zealous concern with truth and purity. If, for example, David Matthew's 'Church Adrift' series sounds strident, it is because it is written with the deliberate aim of shaking people out of their complacency. The series is not so much an historical overview of the Church as a prophetic denunciation of heresy, betrayal and 'lukewarmness' in the Church. Burning conviction is a phrase that aptly characterizes both David Matthew and Arthur Wallis.

Restorationists declare themselves to be not a new denomination, but the alternative to denominationalism. They wish to be simply the Church. The Church is understood as operating on two levels, or possessing two modes. The universal Church is simply all those who are born again who together make up the body of Christ. The second mode is the operative one: it is the local church. The local church is the place where people who are related to each other organically by their shared membership in the body, share a common life according to the precepts of the New Testament. Locality ranges from the 'house cell', local community church, to a celebration event such as the Dales Bible Week.

Restorationists believe that it is possible to be a member of the body of Christ (as are all people who have experienced the new birth), but not be moving in the vanguard of God's people. Kingdom people do not constitute all those who are 'saved', but are God's shock troops. For them, the only Church worth belonging to is the Church militant. They often like to see themselves as a battleship ready for war; denominations are viewed as luxury cruisers. Restorationists are convinced that Christians who are willing to listen to 'what God is saying to the Church today', will recognize that he desires all men and women to be not passengers in the Church, but enlisted warriors.

To revert to kingdom language: members of the Church are not destined to be slaves in the kingdom of God, but rulers. To rule, however, is also to learn to obey. Personal and denominational sin are the result of rebellion. Rebellion has no place in the ordered life of the kingdom, or the King's army. To be kingdom people is to learn to follow only God and his anointed leaders. A truly united Church can only exist on the voluntary principle of covenanted relationships under God. To become a Christian of the kingdom, therefore, means voluntarily abandoning individualism and self-interest, and freely choosing to become subjects of King Jesus and accountable to his chosen apostles and leaders.

The way forward to Church unity, Restorationists are convinced, is through the re-establishment of charismatically-ordained apostles. Only such an anointed leadership can ensure that Restoration will unite the Church. As far as R1 and R2 are concerned, denominationalism has had its day.

Recommended Reading

Arthur Wallis, *The Radical Christian* (Eastbourne: Kingsway, 1981).

E. H. Broadbent, *The Pilgrim Church* (London: Pickering & Inglis, 1931).

David Matthew, 'The Lessons of Church History', Part 8, *Restoration* (March/April 1984).

David Matthew, *Church Adrift: Where in the World are we Going?* (London: Marshall Pickering, 1985).

Martin Scott, *The Theology of the So-Called 'New Church Movement'*: An Analysis of the Eschatology (unpublished MTh thesis, Brunel University, 1997).

7

THE RADICAL PRINCIPLES OF RESTORATION (PART TWO)

Restorationist Ecclesiology: the Kingdom as a Theocracy

Ecclesiology is often seen as a minor adjunct of theology. The doctrine of Church order, however, not only has major implications for the status of ecclesiastical structures, it has also been a major cause of schism in Christendom. The understanding of papal authority, for example, and its relationship to the inspirational and governing power of the Holy Spirit, is, perhaps, the primary conflict between the Catholic West and the Orthodox East. Within Protestantism, episcopal, congregational and presbyterian structures have developed as a result of fundamental differences in ecclesiology.

Restorationists, having declared that denominations are not in the plan of God, and having insisted that the Church is entering its last phase, when it will be 'as it was in the beginning', attempted to reintroduce what they believed to be the apostolic structure of the New Testament. Their system could be described as a charismatic episcopacy. Leadership does bear some similarity to bishops and priests in the way in which Restoration elders relate to apostles. There is, however, no hint of apostolic succession: apostles are ordained, or anointed, solely by God. For this reason, I think Restorationist leadership can better be described as a charismatic apostolate.

The reintroduction of apostles – The decision to reintroduce apostles was not an intellectualist one. As we have already seen, apostleship emerged in the early 1970s when leaders recognized that God had anointed and sanctified what was already a *de facto* apostleship. However, the establishment of apostles and prophets by Restorationists has not been purely inspirational and mystical. Because Restorationists are Bible people and because scholarship is not despised when seen to be God-inspired, they have presented their case as an apologia.

Restorationists recognize, along with most Church scholars, that the issue of religious orders is extremely complicated. It is difficult to know, for example, from the New Testament texts alone how exactly the orders of the diaconate and the presbytery (or elders) worked in conjunction with apostles. Many scholars think that the early Church, during or soon after the scriptural canon, developed an episcopal system where bishops became the overseers of districts or dioceses. Bishops came to be linked with apostleship (in the sense of delegated authority from the original apostles – St Paul appointing Timothy, for example). Elders became identified with priesthood. Religious orders also included deacons, deaconesses and readers.

The relationship between these orders, and the exact status of the presbyterate as a second order of clergy – as distinct from a third order of laity (deacons/readers) – still taxes and fascinates Church historians. It would seem from the scriptural canon and the early Church records that there was a fluidity of leadership and a certain interchangeability of roles. (Women, however, while being in the diaconate, seem never to have been members of the presbyterate.)

Restorationists show no interest in the first few centuries of Church history. They insist that the pattern for Church order can be, and must be, discerned from Scripture alone. For them, the foundational scriptures for Church order are to be found in Ephesians 4:8–12. The key verses, as we have noticed twice already, are 11 and 12:

> It was he who gave some to be apostles, some to be
> prophets, some to be evangelists, and some to be pas-
> tors and teachers, to prepare God's people for works of
> service, so that the body of Christ may be built up . . .
> (NIV)

Sometimes referred to as the 'fivefold ministries',
Restorationists are convinced that this is the only correct
New Testament pattern for Church leadership. Strictly
speaking, they do not like the idea of a priestly order,
because they are not happy to make too much of the distinction between clergy and laity. They prefer the idea of
function in the body of Christ – stressing the priesthood of
all believers. But while they do not use priestly terminology, they do believe firmly in authority in a constituted
hierarchy. The ministries in Ephesians chapter 4, for example, are understood as being under the apostle. The apostle is God's delegate, or anointed one.

Restorationists are well aware that not only is it controversial to claim that this pattern for the Church has been
restored, but also that apostleship in the New Testament
itself had different meanings. Firstly, and supremely, they
claim, Christ is the first apostle: he is unique; the sent one
of God. The writer to the Hebrews declares that Christ is
'the apostle and high priest whom we confess' (Heb 3:1).
Secondly, they identify the twelve disciples of Jesus as the
unique band of apostles who witness to the life, death and
resurrection of the Lord. These apostles (who, of course, do
not include Judas Iscariot, but do include his replacement,
Matthias) are identified as the 'twelve apostles of the
Lamb' (Rev 21:14). Because of their unique relationship
with the Lord Jesus, these men will be the foundation
stones of the New Jerusalem, interlocked with the cornerstone who is Christ.

Restorationists claim that Ephesians chapter 4 refers to
neither of these usages: there is a third group of apostles
who are God's appointed gifts to his Church. First among
these was Paul. In addition, James, the brother of Jesus,

Barnabas and Timothy are also cited as examples of this group. These men are seen as apostles appointed after Pentecost as charismatic delegates from the ascended Christ. The twelve were commissioned in Christ's earthly lifetime, but the second group of apostles are Pentecostal appointments. The gifts of the Spirit as outlined in 1 Corinthians 12 are therefore not the only charismata. The offices of apostles, prophets, evangelists, pastors and teachers are themselves 'gifts of the ascended Christ'.[1]

A variety of charismatic ministries – Having identified the apostles of Ephesians chapter 4 as a group distinct from the twelve, and Christ himself, Restorationists then ask, what is an apostle's function in the Church? The answer they give, in the words of St Paul, is that he is a 'skilled master builder' (1 Cor 3:10, NEB). By this they mean that the apostle is one who lays the foundations of a church – a local community – and is ultimately responsible for ensuring that the stones of the 'building' are put together in the correct manner according to the will of the divine architect. This foundational and overseeing ministry, and the extended metaphor of the building, clearly lend themselves well to the image of the kingdom. Apostles are master builders of the kingdom.

God uses multiple charismatic ministries, however. Evangelists are needed to challenge people with the gospel. Apostles ensure that the kingdom is being properly constructed. Teachers are needed to teach and impart the correct understanding of kingdom principles. Pastors, or elders, are men who will care for, or shepherd, the flock in each locality. Prophets bring the inspired word to the whole Church. Citing 1 Corinthians 12:28, Restorationists point out that within the kingdom, prophets are to be second only to apostles (close as they are to the 'heart and will of God'). It is difficult to find an adequate analogy to express this relationship. Shall we say that the apostle is the chief executive, and the prophet the advertising 'whizz-kid'?

I feel a more appropriate image would be to see the apostle as king, and the prophet as court jester or 'holy fool'. From my brief conversation with David Mansell, who is a prophet in R1, I think he would prefer the more intellectual notion of adviser or wise-man to the king.

Restorationists point out that the New Testament clearly reveals apostles as men who missioned, travelled and founded new churches. Their responsibility in the Church, therefore, was trans-local. Elders were men who worked at the local level and were accountable to the wider responsibility of the apostles. In practice, New Testament apostles sometimes acted as prophets and teachers in addition to their primary function as overseers. Restorationists also feel that apostles were surrounded by a team of helpers.

This is a later interpretation by Restorationists, who in the mid-1970s tended to stress simply the function of an apostle, prophet, teacher, etc., without much emphasis on a team of charismatic leadership. The restoration of apostolic teams, they believe, gives the lie to the criticism that apostolic leadership is a one-man ministry. This emphasis on the team is a major development in Restorationist thought. They understand the team as a flexible instrument: people will join and leave the team according to the needs that arise. The team, as it were, takes on the mantle of the apostle and becomes endowed with his anointing. To be in Bryn Jones's or Tony Morton's team is to exercise apostolic authority in some sense.

Restorationists do not see teams as something they have invented. They claim that the epistles of Paul are full of examples of team membership:

'I have sent Tychicus to you . . .' (Eph 6:21–22).
'I hope to send Timothy to you . . .' (Phil 2:19).
'I thought it necessary to send Epaphroditus . . .' (Phil 2:25).
'I have sent Onesimus . . .' (Col 4:9).
'Make every effort to come to me . . .' (2 Tim 4:9).

'Pick up Mark and bring him . . .' (2 Tim 4:11).
'When I send Artemas . . .' (Titus 3:12).[2]

God's master plan for his kingdom – A charismatically-ordained Church is, then, for Restorationists a Church not only established and run according to the teachings of the apostles of the New Testament, but also governed by present-day apostles and their related ministries. The leaders of the New Testament were men who were anointed and sent by God. Qualification for leadership, today as then, is neither intellect nor training, but Christian character and charisma (in the Pentecostal sense). God does not despise learning, as evidenced by his choosing Paul, but it was not a condition of his calling. To be leaders, men should be able to run their own households and be full of the fruits of the Spirit. The man who exercises proper authority over his family is obviously fit, with God's anointing, to oversee churches (see 1 Thessalonians 2:8–11).

Apostles were not optional for the Early Church: they were the master builders of God's master plan for his kingdom. Nowhere, Restorationists proclaim, does Scripture ever suggest that apostles were meant to cease with the death of the twelve. On the contrary, all the internal biblical evidence points to apostolic structure as being the norm for Christian life. Part of the apostasy of the first-century Church was to abandon God's plan for successfully building his kingdom. Unbiblical ecclesiastical structures go hand-in-hand with extra-biblical doctrines of sacramentalism, infant baptism and ritualism.

It is possible, Restorationists agree, to be a Christian in a church without apostles and prophets, but it is not possible for that church to become what God would have it to be. The master plan is that the kingdom shall grow and fill the whole earth. Only a kingdom built on kingdom principles and run by God's appointed men can achieve such a goal. In the words of Robert Brow: 'If the true church of Jesus Christ is to grow faster than the population explosion, we will need to produce, recognize and use Pauline apostles.'[3]

Restorationists recognize that apostles do not fit into the spirit of the age. Modern man has become accustomed to consensus agreements and democratic methods as a means of reaching corporate decisions. While they accept that such methods have their place, in politics for example, Restorationists do not see them having any place in God's kingdom. A kingdom run on divine principles and ruled by God's delegates is by definition a theocracy.

God alone is sovereign. It is he who chooses apostles. Authority in the kingdom has its source in King Jesus, who until his return to reign victoriously over his restored kingdom, has delegated authority to apostles. It is precisely because denominations have abandoned apostles – the guardians of the gifts of the Spirit – that Christendom has been almost overcome by the evil one. In the absence of Holy Ghost power, churches have been swayed by 'every wind of doctrine'. The rot can only be stopped by a 'structure of authority directly from the throne of God'.[4]

Jesus, declared Ern Baxter,[5] never set up a system of government or Church order. Instead, 'he poured his life into twelve men'. In their turn, the apostles did not initiate a set of rules for the early Church: they established relationships within the Christian community based on mutual submission and a voluntary denial of selfhood for the sake of the brethren. In short, they made disciples too.

Spiritual Authority and the Nature of Discipling

The idea that the spiritual authority of the apostles and elders can reach right down into the minutiae of everyday life, affecting Christians' personal and social lives, may not seem to be necessarily entailed by an apostolic structure. In Restorationist thinking, however, what have become known as 'discipling doctrines', 'relatedness', or 'shepherding principles', are so directly bound up with apostleship doctrines that they do not distinguish between the two.

As an outsider, it took me quite a long time to realize

this. To me, the doctrines look quite separate. You can have a strong shepherding movement without having to have apostles. You can certainly have doctrines of apostles without any commitment to Restorationist submission teachings. In the other apostolic structures of recent times, such as the Catholic Apostolic Church and the Apostolic Church, apostolic rule has never carried the comprehensive authority which can be found in Restorationism.

Terry Virgo thinks that the restoration of apostles is the most important and distinctive feature of Restoration.[6] With respect, I think that what makes Restoration more distinctive – and certainly more radical – is the way that the charismatic apostolate has gone beyond simply restoring apostolic structures to establishing a far more complex and interwoven system of relationships. The reason, I think, that most Restorationists do not divide apostleship from shepherding, is because historically they melded together these separate doctrines into a new synthesis that became the unique hallmark of Restorationism. (Arthur Wallis is adamant that Restorationists did not learn apostleship from the Americans.)

As these theories are analytically distinct, I have decided to deal with discipling doctrines separately. This is solely for the sake of clarity and exemplification. Clearly, Restorationists see these doctrines as one set of principles, not two. Though they are not logically connected, they can, as we shall see, be understood as one coherent system.

The obedience of discipleship – The aim of discipleship is not to bring everybody in line, or impose ideology from the top onto those below. The aim is to make sure that each person in the Restoration movement (including apostles) is open to correction and admonition within the context of loving relationships. 'Those whom the Lord loves he chastises' is extended or projected into the context of Christian personal relations.

However, the notion of admonition or chastisement is not to be understood as bondage, or authoritarian domination. Such methods, declares Restoration teaching, are the devilish counterfeits of the cults. The very idea of correction is possible precisely because it is in the nature of a Christian to be a disciple. A disciple is a learner, the follower of a master, or one who is spiritually more mature. Restorationists in R1 and R2 often describe such a person as 'one who is a little further along the path'. The true disciple desires to become like the teacher; ideally, like Christ himself.

Restorationists believe that a Christian who is not prepared to be a disciple is no Christian at all. The word disciple is mentioned 269 times in the New Testament, Ern Baxter told the Lakes Bible Week in 1975. He went on to say that the meaning of discipleship is made clear by the Lord Jesus himself: 'If anyone comes to me and does not hate his father and mother, his wife and children, his brothers and sisters – yes, even his own life – he cannot be my disciple' (Luke 14:26). And again: 'If anyone would come after me, he must deny himself and take up his cross and follow me' (Matt 16:24).

To be a disciple, then, from the ultimate authority of Christ's own lips, is to love God above all else. This is the radical heart of the gospel for every believer. Jesus demands nothing less than that a follower becomes like him not only in his glory, but in his suffering and sacrifice: 'take up the cross'. This radical sense of following, this discipleship, is designed 'not to manipulate people but to mature them spiritually'.[7] To be under anointed and God-constituted authority is to be a learner. Only learners, those in obedience, can reach the sort of spiritual maturity where they can cease drinking the milk fit only for babes, and partake of the strong meat of adulthood. Only then can they become leaders of the kingdom.

In the United States, discipling doctrines have found their way into some lay Catholic communities. These covenanted and charismatic communities have recognized, more readily than many Protestants, how close discipling is to their own tradition. This is so, because in many ways such a radical discipleship is not usually associated with the lives and homes of ordinary people – it is usually seen as belonging to monasticism. Whether one thinks of the harsh asceticism of St Antony of Egypt, or the spiritual exercises of the hermits and desert fathers, or the kenoticism of the early Franciscans, one thinks of all these people as under a rule of obedience. Reading the *Philokalia*,[8] for example, one can see that it is permeated with practices and spiritual exercises designed to break the 'spirit of rebellion', foster total obedience (often through a spiritual master) and break the iron hold of egoism.

Restoration writers do not invoke such practices. (One leader in R2 felt that the leaders in R1 were overweight, and could do with a dose of asceticism!) They do not like the distinction between the committed dedication of certain clergy and monks, and the lives of ordinary Christians. All believers, they feel, should be saints. In this respect, Restorationists fit far more closely the Puritanism of early Calvinism than the asceticism of Catholicism. To a certain extent, it could be argued, enthusiasm and evangelicalism – from the eighteenth century onwards – did not always show the unswerving attachment to righteousness that we find in so many of the seventeenth-century Puritans. The corporate sense of covenant with God certainly disappeared. I do not think it stretches it too far to see Restorationists as modern-day Pentecostal Puritans.

Covenanted relationships and delegated authority – The belief in a corporate covenant between God and his people is a dominant theme in discipleship doctrine. Gerald Coates rarely uses the terms 'discipling' or 'shepherding', but often refers to the work in R2 as one of 'covenanted relationships'. A disciple is one who shares a common life with others of like mind and heart. This community of committed Christians, who are all disciples 'under authority', is expressed by the sharing of the bread and wine of the Lord's Table. Covenant implies a solemn oath, and discipleship is not to be entered into lightly. When a new member of Restoration submits himself to one who has authority over him, this submission is to Christ himself.[9]

We have already seen, in looking at the charismatic apostolate, that apostolic authority and its concomitant ministries are modes of authority established by God's anointing. This being so, discipleship doctrine sees such authority as sacrosanct; only the God who has raised up this authority can bring it down. Disciples should submit to those set over them. This has echoes of similar arguments in favour of the divine right of kings. Many Restorationists have tried to demonstrate the anointing of apostolic and eldership appointments as a parallel to the anointing of King David in the Old Testament. We have already encountered this comparison between apostles and David in our earlier narrative section. Suffice it to say here, that David is a key figure in Restoration hermeneutics and typology. His life is followed in minute detail and used as a model for apostolic leadership.[10]

Some Restorationists insist that delegated authority should be obeyed because it is God's authority, not because the delegate is always right. The Basingstoke communities, in particular, stress this, but so too do most leaders in R1. We have already seen, in Maurice Smith's discussion with Bob Mumford,[11] that it was thought that a woman should submit herself to her husband because a husband is God's delegate for the wife and family, regardless of whether he acts rightly and fairly or not.

In discipling doctrine generally, God's delegated authority goes further than the supernatural authority of apostles. Husbands are seen as the head of the family, including the wife. Parents are God's delegates over children. Political authorities too are seen as God's delegates. The state, in short, should be obeyed. In conversation with Restorationists, it is clear that the distinction between Caesar and God applies to the state. There is no question, therefore, of having to submit to a Hitler without a murmur. It is clear, however, that political and social action do not figure highly on a Restorationist list of moral imperatives.[12]

The influence of Watchman Nee – A great deal of Restorationist understanding of authority, especially spiritual authority, comes from Watchman Nee. While Nee could not be described as a Restorationist or even a Pentecostalist, his influence upon both the American and British discipling movement is considerable. Nee was a controversial figure in Chinese religious life between the two World Wars. Greatly influenced by Western missionaries, Nee nevertheless pioneered a house church movement throughout China. Violently opposed to Communism, even today the movement that he founded, the 'Little Flock', is still *persona non grata* with the authorities.

Nee's style in translation is turgid, and not altogether clear. Most Restorationists seem well-versed in his book *Spiritual Authority*,[13] but seem unaware of many of his other works. Neither do many of them seem to know that his spirituality is far closer to Darbyism (Exclusive Brethrenism) than their own. It is ironic that one of the seminal thinkers of early Restorationism, David Lillie, has been the one to point out that the 'Little Flock' developed into an authoritarian denomination after the death of Nee.[14]

There is no denying, however, that Watchman Nee is one of the most interesting and remarkable – although mysterious – religious figures of the twentieth century. We are all indebted to Angus Kinnear's thorough and scholarly book on Nee;[15] without it we would know very little about him.

Spiritual Authority is replete with 'hard sayings'. On the question of whether people should trust and follow wrong authority, Nee says:

> If God dares to entrust His authority to men, then we can dare to obey. Whether the one in authority is right or wrong does not concern us since he has to be responsible directly to God. The obedient needs only to obey; the Lord will not hold us responsible for any mistaken

obedience, rather will He hold the delegated authority responsible for his erroneous act. Insubordination, however, is rebellion, and for this the one under authority must answer to God.[16]

In a more telling aphorism he remarks: 'All who are insubordinate to God's indirect authorities are not in subjection to God's direct authority.'[17]

Two themes develop out of Nee's conception of authority which are fundamental to Restorationist discipleship doctrine. Firstly, as in the above quotations, we see that rebellion against God's delegates is rebellion against God himself. Rebellion is understood by Nee, and Restorationists, to be the essence of sin. Secondly, Nee, as a counterbalance to the power of God's delegates, insists that (at least in the case of Christian leaders) spiritual authority carries with it not only enormous responsibilities but dire consequences if mistakes are made. I think it important that we examine each doctrine in turn.

'The essence of salvation is subjection', said Ern Baxter at the Lakes Bible Week in 1975. By this he meant that without submitting to Jesus Christ, and without admonition and correction being accepted from God's delegates, true discipleship cannot be achieved. Pride and rebellion are masked behind the secular virtues of an independent and individualistic spirit. Rebellion is the hallmark of the world, but an anathema in the kingdom. The marks of that kingdom are harmony, love and doing the will of God.

'Brokenness' is a term used frequently in evangelical circles. It means allowing God to take over your life after he has broken down your wilfulness and egoism. There is a Russian Orthodox saying: 'God will bring you to himself by either breaking your heart, or every bone in your body.' While this is, hopefully, not to be taken too literally, it captures the essence of being broken in a spiritual sense; for it means that God will eventually bring his disciples to a place where there is no more rebellion or resistance to the divine love. Brokenness is that moment in spiritual experience that allows the next step of surrender to God.

Restorationists see that brokenness is hard for the average Christian to accept because we have been weaned on doctrines of self-sufficiency and such notions as 'standing on your own two feet' and 'being yourself'. Furthermore, and fundamentally more problematic, the childish petulance that refuses to accept parental and school authority becomes the adult wilfulness of self-reliance. Discipleship, therefore, stresses the need to break rebellion in the child so that character can be built. Breaking down bad habits, anti-social traits, sinful ways and a rebellious heart is a necessary prerequisite for building up characters to be fitted into the kingdom of God.

To discipline children into the precepts and rules of God's kingdom is not seen as enough by Restorationists. Many of the Christians who join a Restorationist church are seen as having practised rebellion all their lives. Restoration principles have to be imparted through teaching. Just as a Protestant receives instruction before embracing Catholicism, so converts to God's restored kingdom must undertake a commitment course. As Eileen Vincent puts it:

> It is not assumed that those coming into the churches automatically know how to bring up their children or how to have successful marriages. These practical topics are carefully taught and, through close discipling, the new understanding is woven into the fabric of a new style of living.[18]

It is at this juncture that the other side of the discipling coin needs to be looked at in order to avoid a distorted picture. As Nee made clear, spiritual authority carries with it a fearful responsibility. He is very careful to insist that the husband acts towards his wife with love and respect; that parents treat their children with justice; and spiritual leaders truly discern the will of God. Apostles and elders are considered in Restoration circles – at least in principle – to be servants of the people, not dictators over them. Much has been given them by God, and much will be asked of them in return.

Nee, even more so than Restorationists, pays great attention to the qualities necessary to enter leadership. Many of these qualities are the spiritual fruits outlined in Galatians 5:22–23 – 'love, joy, peace, patience, kindness, goodness, faithfulness, gentleness and self-control'. Nee lays particular emphasis on self-control. Nee and the Restorationists both agree that no one can simply set themselves up and say: 'I am your leader: submit to me'. Spiritual authority has to be recognized.

Both R1 and R2 are very clear on this point. Authority has to be accepted voluntarily by church members, otherwise it has no validity or power. Both groups also agree, following Nee and the Fort Lauderdale Five, that all leaders must themselves be under authority. Even apostles must be judged by their peers. This is, of course, the same in principle as the collegiality of bishops. It was the claim by the Latin West that the Bishop of Rome held a unique position among the ancient sees – greater even than *primus inter pares* – that broke up the order and unity of the ancient Church.

Restoration apostles are under an authority greater than collegial correction. The Scriptures are to remain the ultimate authority in matters of doctrine. All prophecies, statements of doctrines by apostles, and discipling instructions by elders, are to be submitted to Scripture for authentication.

David Tomlinson adds another safeguard, which I have not found in Nee, Trudinger or Prince's seminal document on discipleship. He states:

No one has such authority that he cannot be questioned or challenged. Even children should be allowed the privilege of dialoguing about an issue provided they do it in a right attitude. It is important that those being discipled feel that they will be seriously heard in their misgivings, and not merely swept aside. True men of God are aware that God does speak 'through the mouths of babes and sucklings'.[19]

'And little old ladies', I know Gerald Coates would want me to add.

Tithing and the 'double honour' – Restorationists strongly believe that the overall context within which discipling operates is loving relationships. To be shepherded, or 'covered',[20] cannot be done through a cold, unfeeling covenant. Covenanted relationships are not legal contracts – they are personal commitments.

Restorationists do not find the image of hierarchical relationships helpful. They feel that a shepherd is paternal. A 'father in God' is a quite different creature from an executive, general, or even a scout master. Military men give orders, but apostles, prophets and elders bring conviction. Disciples cannot be corrected from above, they can only be corrected from within.

One of the ways in which disciples can express their love and support for the leadership is to support them financially. Tithing has a long and controversial history in Pentecostalism, and as a doctrine it does not belong to discipling *per se*. But just as Restorationists do not divide apostleship from shepherding (as I have done for the sake of explication) neither do they see tithing as a separate issue from good discipleship. Again, this may well be because, historically, tithing was introduced into some areas of Restorationism as part of the discipling package received from the Fort Lauderdale Five. I would not want to insist on this, however: tithing was around in the house church movement long before Ern Baxter arrived at Capel Bible Week. Indeed Arthur Wallis insisted that tithing was taught before any American input.

Under the Judaic law, Derek Prince points out, tithing was the means for supporting the priestly orders.[21] Restorationists assume that tithing was a practice in the New Testament. Certainly it was the case that St Paul taught that shepherds were entitled to material support from their flocks (1 Cor 9:7). Prince takes this to mean financial support. (He does not mention that Paul claimed the right, but refused to take it!)

Tithing, then, is the means for supporting full-time ministries and part-time leaders. Tithing should be given to leaders to administer as they see fit. But tithes in themselves will not be enough to meet the full needs of the flock. Money for new buildings, new methods of communication, computers for God's businesses, and musical instruments for his praise will need to come from special offerings. Tithing is a demonstration of commitment to kingdom leadership. Special offerings, and the profits from business ventures, are proof of commitment to the kingdom as a whole.

Prince puts up a case for ruling elders to receive 'double honour'. 'Let the elders that rule well be counted worthy of double honour, especially they who labour in the word and doctrine. For the scripture saith, Thou shalt not muzzle the ox that treadeth out the corn. And, the labourer is worthy of his reward' (1 Tim 5:17–18, KJV). These texts have a long and notorious history in the American Bible belt. They have been taken to mean that leaders have the right to considerably more money than their followers.

On the whole, however, this interpretation is not favoured in England (where it has no history). If it exists in print from within either R1 or R2, I have not seen it. I believe that a more typical understanding of financial support for leadership is that they should be properly supported financially; kept comfortable, but not made wealthy. Restorationism does not preach a gospel of poverty,[22] but it has not yet started preaching a gospel of personal prosperity.[23]

Kingdom People on the Move

The problem with looking at doctrines analytically is that

they take on a static and unchanging quality. In reality, Restorationist principles – whilst remaining basically the same as I have outlined them above – are constantly undergoing minor changes and modifications. Restorationists also differ a great deal over details, despite holding a common core of distinctive doctrines. John Noble has been particularly anxious to keep moving on, making adjustments, checking Scripture, and if necessary being prepared to bring in sweeping changes in the future. Restorationism is, after all, supremely a movement of the Spirit. As such it cannot be nailed down too firmly to a fixed position.

In my view, the eschatological vision and distinctive principles of kingdom theocracy have transformed what might have been a fairly typical (though middle-class) form of Pentecostalism into a movement that claims a more radical cutting edge.

If, however, I have given the impression that Restoration, in being so serious and Puritanical, is glum and boring, then I had better correct that impression by highlighting another principle of the kingdom. 'Folk' (to use a favourite Restorationist term) are expected to have a good time. It is not only kingdom doctrines that show some signs of movement. Kingdom people spend a good deal of their time jumping, dancing and leaping. What is known as 'body worship', or free expression in worship, is seen as a sign of the kingdom. David, that great Restorationist archetype, 'danced before the Lord'. It is expected that the Holy Spirit will affect the body and emotions, too, not only the mind and will.

I think that in R1, the style of worship is seen not as cultural or optional, but as a fruit of the Spirit. As God is working to restore his ministries of apostles, so too he is restoring true praise and worship. Many people in R2 feel the same way, but a number of leaders would not want to make a Restorationist worshipping-style into a cardinal Restorationist principle. It is a cherished principle, however, both in R1 and R2, that God's people are a worshipping people. There is a great deal of emphasis on celebration and adoration. The Church itself is seen to operate on three local levels: the house cell, the local church, and the coming together of churches for celebration (Dales and Festival, for example).

The moving, feet-tapping people are caught up in the eschatological vision with which we started. Restoration is seen essentially as a movement of the people of God. It has no headquarters and no earthly head. King Jesus is the Lord of the kingdom, and he has delegated his authority to the apostles, prophets, evangelists, teachers, and elders. When such anointed authority is established, and covenanted relationships adopted, the New Testament order of the kingdom can begin. But this new wine cannot be contained in the old wine skins (denominations): it demands new and flexible structures founded on old and inviolable New Testament principles.

Each local church that becomes established on kingdom lines is a microcosm of the whole Church. If it is established aright, and the foundations are truly laid, the building will be both the place of, and witness to, God's alternative society. Apostles with their trans-local responsibilities will recognize other apostles when they arise under God's anointing. In the future, what started off as isolated and unconnected churches will become a mass movement. Just as the house cells and front-room churches sprang up overnight, so shall that mycelial structure be repeated on a larger scale.

Within the great cities of the world, large communities will be set up as an offence to Babylon and the apostate Church. Because of sound Christian principles in business and stewardship, Restorationist enterprises will flourish. Modern communications, such as video, cable and satellite television, will beam God's end-time message around the world. This, it should be said, is a much greater theme in R1 than R2.

As a dying and decaying world sees the health, vigour and security of the kingdom, people will flock to the

Restoration standard in increasing numbers. The kingdom will not be a sanctuary; it will be a mighty fortress. The image of Nehemiah restoring the broken walls of Jerusalem towers over Restoration thinking. Jerusalem the city is itself a biblical image of kingdom. Everywhere the little microcosms of the kingdom, and the larger communities, businesses and enterprises, will grow up together, become more closely knit ('jointed together' is another favourite phrase), until the kingdom reaches its full and perfect structure. The microcosms become the macrocosm – the mountain fills the earth – and the King returns to lead his powerful and holy army in the final battle against the evil one.

That is what kingdom people are moving towards, insists the Restorationist vision. God's disciples are essentially pioneers not settlers. Denominations breed rigidity into Christians – they can no longer move on. Anointed leaders, committed and 'covered' relationships, and flexible church structures all denote a mission people – not wandering aimlessly like the children of the Old Covenant through the desert, but towards the last battle of the end-time.

> The church of God is moving,
> The church of God is moving.

People on the move are not restless, because they are people with a mission; they are in harmony with each other and under the clear direction of the King. Restorationists want to move on with the whole of God's people. They believe that they are in the vanguard of God's purpose for this (the final) generation. In that sense, paradoxically, they are a people set apart who call Christians to themselves. They fervently believe that as their numbers swell, and the growing ranks show that they have the discipline and formation to qualify for God's army, denominational Christians will desert their demoralized barracks and join the crusade.

Restorationists want to teach Christians and new

believers their principles. But most of all they want them to catch their vision. 'Christians unite!' sounds the battle cry. 'We have nothing to lose but our institutions!'

Recommended Reading

Derek Prince, *Discipleship, Shepherding, Commitment* (D. Prince Publishing, 1976).

Ron Trudinger, *Built to Last* (Eastbourne: Kingsway, 1982).

Arthur Wallis, 'Apostles Today? Why Not!', *Restoration* (November/December 1981).

David Tomlinson, 'Is Discipling Biblical?', *Restoration* (July/August 1980).

Terry Virgo, *Restoration in the Church* (Eastbourne: Kingsway, 1985).

Angus. I. Kinnear, *Against the Tide: the Story of Watchman Nee* (1973).

Max Turner, 'Ecclesiology in the Major "Apostolic" Restorationist Churches in the United Kingdom', *Vox Evangelica* (Vol. XIX, 1989).

8

THE STRUCTURE AND SHAPE OF KINGDOM LIFE

As early as 1974, Bryn Jones circulated a cyclostyled letter, warning many of the house churches not to get carried away with thoughts of the second coming of Christ. The Church's job, he pointed out, is to build the kingdom until the King chooses to come. Since that time, while it remains true that Restorationists expect the coming of Christ to be imminent, their response to the return of Jesus is to estab- lish – as quickly as possible – the kingdom as an alterna- tive society to the secular world.

Putting kingdom principles into practice, however, has inevitably led to a certain amount of adaption of those principles: the obduracy of reality has a habit of cooling visionary fire. One of the major differences that now exists between R1 and R2, is that R2 is self-consciously coming to terms with its adaption, whilst R1 feels itself still to be on course and is not consciously aware that maybe things are not going according to the master plan.

Both R1 and R2 admit that they still have a long way to go. The Church, as they envisage it, has not grown in size and power to become a 'mountain' to fill Great Britain, let alone the whole earth. What has happened is that Restorationism has become a significant religious move- ment in Britain in just over ten years, with its own organi- zational shape, practices, successes, and failures.

To say that Restorationism has a clearly defined shape needs some clarification. Both R1 and R2 are still in the early stages of formation. There is a fluidity of organiza- tional structure that has not yet hardened into a fixed mould. We should keep in mind the image of a kaleidoscope: peering through it presents us with a clear pattern and order. But with a twist of the scope, the pattern dissolves and a new picture emerges. In short, I believe that Restoration's organizational structure can be understood, but the structure is volatile. What I can describe as the structure and order of 1985 will probably have changed in ten years' time.[1] To predict what the new structures will be is as difficult as guessing what new shape will emerge from the movements of coloured glass in the kaleidoscope.

Ephesians 4 as an Organizational Model

Restorationism, by adopting the ecclesiology of Ephesians chapter 4, adopts with it an organizational pattern. To put it this way is not to present it as Restorationists would do themselves. They would say that to accept God's theocracy is to enter into a series of covenanted relationships with those leaders that God has ordained should rule in his Church. To talk of organizations or structures leads one, very soon they feel, to talk of denominations. R1 still rigorously denies that identification. If we are a denomination, they say, where is our headquarters? R2 also insists that they have no centrally ruling body. The Apostolic Church, like the Restorationists, also bases its organization on the ecclesiology of Ephesians chapter 4, but clearly has a headquarters situated in Penygroes, South Wales. Restorationists see this as evidence of denominationalism.

To resist being labelled 'a denomination' is understandable because, as we have seen, Restoration is motivated by the desire to go beyond denominations. Denominations are not in God's plan. He wants Christians of this last generation to restore the kingdom. An essential, if not *the* essential, ingredient of this restoration is the re-establishment of apostolic ministries.

There are two different questions here. Firstly, is Restorationism a new denomination? And secondly, can the two groups that I have identified as R1 and R2 be said to have an organizational structure? Put this way, I do not believe that Restorationists would wish to (or be able to) deny that their work has a structure, but they would still resist the notion that they have become denominationalized. I do not think that we can fairly assess Restorationism as a denominational formation until we have explored the way in which – in practice – Restoration works. For the rest of this chapter, therefore, while I will be attempting to identify the structure and practices of Restorationism, I shall for the time being put the question of denominationalism on one side.

To recapitulate: the full list of ministries outlined in Ephesians chapter 4 comprises apostles, prophets, evangelists, pastors and teachers. In practice, the foundation of the Restoration kingdom has primarily been laid by apostles working on a regional basis, and elders working on a local level. Since 1980, both R1 and R2 have built up apostolic teams.[2] These are groups of men, as we noted earlier, who work with the apostle on a regional or trans-local basis. It is by no means clear how the membership of teams coincides with the ministries of Ephesians chapter 4.

Apostles – Of all the various ministries that have been established, the apostolic ministry seems to me to be the most clearly defined. R1, for example, consists of groups of churches who are all accountable to a number of apostles, who either founded them from scratch, or took over the senior 'covering' role when asked. Each apostle is responsible for a chain of churches. While each chain is separate, they are linked together at the top by a mutual recognition of ministry amongst the apostles. The apostles, then, have separate areas of responsibility, agreed territorial boundaries, and considerable – though not total – autonomy. Churches from the different chains sometimes meet together at such celebration events as Dales, Downs and the Welsh Bible Week.

Apostles are easily identified because of their role and because they are so few. In R1, the leading apostles are Bryn and Keri Jones, who are based in Bradford, with some fifty to sixty churches under their direction;[3] Terry Virgo, who is based in Hove, and responsible for some forty churches or more; and Tony Morton, who is a more recent apostle, based at Southampton, with some seventeen to twenty churches under his direction. The number of apostles is by no means fixed. It varies according to need, as well as to defections – remembering that David Tomlinson was once an apostle in R1.

There is talk that Tony Ling may be a future apostle. But apostles are not names conjured out of a hat; they have to prove themselves as *de facto* apostles before they become recognized formally as apostolic leaders. A number of people have asked me whether Keri Jones fits this model. One person thought that Keri was a sort of suffragan bishop to Bryn Jones. Others have seen Keri's position as nepotism – climbing to power on the back of Bryn. This is, I think, unfair. Keri Jones may not, so far, have had the same impact as his brother, but he did come to his position by right. He pioneered a number of churches in his native South Wales. I think it true to say, however, that his authority and work seem to be clearly linked to Bryn's authority.

In this respect, Bryn and Keri Jones are merely carrying on a long tradition in Welsh Pentecostalism where brothers have often worked together. Before the First World War, the Williams brothers were instrumental in founding the Apostolic Church. A little later, one thinks of the Jeffreys brothers and the beginnings of the Elim and Assemblies of God movements. Stephen, the elder brother, had all the fireworks, but George eventually emerged as both the most stable and the most able leader. I am not suggesting that history will repeat itself in the case of Restoration. Nevertheless, Keri Jones is a very thoughtful and warm personality. Whereas Bryn seems to attract either total loyalty to him, or distrust, everybody seems to like Keri Jones. At the very least, in my opinion, he is a leader to watch for the future.

The apostles in R1 are very much the men at the top.

They deal not only with policy and finance, but also matters of discipline and excommunication. Apostleship operates through mutual recognition in a framework of covenanted relationships. All the apostles' names appear as editorial associates of *Restoration* magazine, and they support each other in joint ventures, and sometimes travel abroad together. In practice, Bryn Jones appears the senior apostle and would appear to 'cover' the others.

The fact that David Tomlinson could be sanctioned by Bryn suggests that Bryn is *primus inter pares*. David does not know who, if anybody, disciplines Bryn.[4] Too much can be made of Bryn's authority, however. Neither Terry Virgo nor Tony Morton are facsimiles of Bryn; nor do their churches run on exactly the same lines as the Bradford churches. Indeed, the covenanted relationships between the apostles are tentative, as the defection of David Tomlinson demonstrates.

Apostleship works in a similar way in R2. John Noble and David Tomlinson are clearly apostles in the R1 sense. Gerald Coates is too, but while he works on a trans-local basis and has an input (as he puts it) into many house groups and fellowships, he also works in many non-restored churches.[5] I mention this because while Gerald is happy to be associated with the house church movement and its leadership, he is actively involved outside it. This looks to be the way that John Noble and David Tomlinson will also work in the future. R2 has, at the moment, no focus ideologically in the sense of a magazine. The apostles meet regularly, but mainly on an *ad hoc* basis.

Elders – In practice, eldership has become the combined role of pastor and teacher. Usually, but not always, elders are responsible for shepherding the flock in the local church. Occasionally, leaders of house groups are seen as elders, and some elders join apostolic teams without their new role being clearly defined. But on the whole, elders are pastors of churches. The Early Church of the first three centuries tended to identify eldership with priesthood.

The contemporary 'Restored Church' identifies elders with pastors. This, so it seems to me, is increasingly the picture that has emerged in the first half of the 1980s; it was not so clear in the second half of the 1970s.

Elders in both R1 and R2 regularly meet together with their respective apostles. They can wield considerable power in their local churches, but they are overseen by apostles, and sometimes by members of apostolic teams. They implement the policy and ideas of the apostles in the locality, and also constantly report back on developments and problems in the local church. Elders meet with the apostles in retreats, and there are usually special seminars for these leaders at the Dales, Downs, Festival and other Restorationist residential gatherings.

The eldership is the backbone of the Restoration movement. They are the ones who shepherd (discipline and exhort) the flock, and feed (teach and promote kingdom principles) the sheep. I have come across a number of examples where elders have engaged in activities not really approved of by the apostles. Apostles in both R1 and R2 are busy men, and are often ministering in other countries. Consequently, some elders are not always monitored as closely as apostles would like. On the whole, I think that the system of control over the eldership is considerably tighter in R1 than R2. A small number of sexual scandals have come to light in R1, but without a doubt the majority of the elders are conscientious, committed Christians who take their responsibilities very seriously.

Ironically, R2, whose system of control is weaker than R1, have had a number of heavy-handed elders who have not always been picked up by apostles. Abuse of elders' considerable power (remembering Watchman Nee's warnings on this matter) is of considerable concern to all the apostles with whom I talked. Bryn Jones, for example, invited me to investigate and report back any stories of misconduct I could find.[6] Both the formal authority and *de facto* power of elders cannot be understood by the Ephesians ecclesiology alone; the authority of elders derives not only from apostles but also through the acceptance by Restoration members of discipling doctrines. This is crucial, as we will see later. The Ephesians ecclesiology without the discipling doctrines is unusual, but would not promote the radicality that we find in Restorationist churches.

The Other Ministries of Ephesians Chapter 4

Apostles and elders, rather like bishops and priests in the historic churches, have emerged as the primary ministries of the restored churches. Leaders of house groups, and those who take on some leadership function within the local church, could be said to perform the function of a diaconate. These people, however, are seen as those learning in leadership. They have no formal position and there is no developed teaching in Restoration circles concerning a tier of authority below eldership. All members belong to the 'priesthood of all believers', but some are more priestly than others (particularly in R1).

Prophets – The teaching concerning prophets, evangelists and teachers is clear, but in practice, these ministries of Ephesians chapter 4 have not emerged in any great number. There are a great many prophecies and interpretations of tongues in Restoration churches, for example, but few formally constituted prophets (or informally recognized prophets, for that matter). In Bryn Jones's churches, many people prophesy, but prophecies have to be submitted to the elders, who then decide whether to release the message to the congregation or not. The early anarchic Pentecostalism is now absent from most Restorationist churches. It is not uncommon in R2, however, for prophetic words and interpretations of tongues to burst forth before permission is asked from the elders and apostles. The same is still true in many areas of R1.

To my knowledge, most local churches would not claim to have one or more resident prophets. In practice, some people are recognized as having the prophetic word more than others, but they do not emerge with the authority of the prophet, which, according to Restorationist teaching, is second only to the apostle. In R2, as we saw earlier, Maurice Smith was widely accepted as a prophet to John Noble's apostleship. The leading prophet in R1 has been David Mansell, who, until he gave it up, combined the role of elder at Turner's Hall with an itinerant position as prophet and conference speaker on Bryn Jones's team. Mansell's ministry has been particularly linked with Bryn Jones.

Interchange of role is the key to understanding prophets, teachers and evangelists in Restoration. Bryn Jones, for example, is widely accepted as having a prophetic gift. He prophesied over the separating (Restorationists do not like the idea of ordination) of George Tarleton as apostle and David Mansell as prophet at Chingford Fellowship on 7th April 1974.

Terry Virgo is seen as possessing the charism of a teacher and so too are Hugh Thompson and David Matthew. Thompson and Matthew are also elders and members of Bryn's team. The latter fact definitely raises their status in the movement, but quite what that status means in terms of Ephesians is not clear. What is clear is Arthur Wallis's role as the undisputed senior statesman and teacher of the Restoration movement. He is so highly regarded that I believe that most members of R2 also accept him in that role.

Evangelists – Evangelists have not really emerged as a separate category in either R1 or R2. Both Bryn and Keri Jones are excellent platform speakers, and so too is David Tomlinson. R2 has an elder called Rodney Kingston who lives in Worthing. He has undoubted evangelistic gifts, but whether he is seen as an evangelist *per se*, I think is unlikely.[7]

The 'big guns' of evangelism, teaching ministry and prophecy do seem mainly to exist in R1. In R2, David

Tomlinson is an all-rounder: he is a pioneering apostle, an evangelist and teacher. John Noble is a builder and nurturer of churches, and an innovator of ideas. He is not seen as an evangelist. Gerald Coates qualifies as an apostle, but though he teaches and evangelizes, his great ministry does not seem to appear in the Ephesians chapter 4 list. Gerald is a sort of spiritual supremo: he conducts and compères conventions and large meetings with consummate skill. He is the best communicator – particularly with the media – that the Restoration movement has got.

Apostolic teams – Unwittingly, I think the establishment of apostolic teams in both R1 and R2 has added another tier to Restorationist organization. Members of the teams, in becoming associated with the apostles, are endowed with apostolic authority. They are released from their local strongholds to become involved in both regional and international ministries. This also alters the apostle's function: he is now not only the spiritual leader of the churches under his control, he is the leader of a team. The team helps him to evangelize and make local and national decisions; they act as messengers between the eldership and the apostle and promote both the ideological and commercial aspects of the kingdom. The team is composed of men whose leadership is neither exactly that of the apostleship nor exactly that of the eldership. Or to put it another way: the men take on their new status because they are members of the apostolic team, and not because they are elders or because they fit into the ministries of Ephesians chapter 4.

I do not intend these remarks to be critical, because I hold no special brief for the Ephesians model, but I do think that team development has altered the structure of leadership within the Restoration movement. I think that both Bryn Jones and Arthur Wallis would want to say that the ministries of Ephesians are essential ministries for the Church, but these should not be interpreted too rigidly. Elders who join apostolic teams remain elders, but assist the apostle in whatever capacity their natural talents and their supernatural gifts allow.

R2's teams are not as high-powered as R1's. Or, to be more accurate, they are more low-key. Teams in R1, and in particular Bryn Jones's team, were developed as a result of a conviction that an evangelistic thrust was needed to bring the people into the kingdom. Teams are seen as a vital part of Restoration vision: they are a sign that the kingdom is going onto the offensive.

R2, however, has not really taken evangelism terribly seriously. Their teams, therefore, have arisen to provide a support network for the apostles in their shepherding of churches and bridge-building with mainline denominations. Gerald Coates, for example, has a team that cannot really be seen in terms of a development of Ephesians chapter 4. His team are an eclectic bunch who help Gerald organize various functions, events and everyday administrative affairs. I remember meeting Gerald one day with a team member who was introduced to me as an administrative assistant.

The Structure and Practice of Shepherding

In practice, it seems to me, Restorationists have not majored on all the ministries of Ephesians chapter 4. They have created an organization whose leadership is invested in apostles, apostolic teams and elders. If the apostles and elders are the foundation stones and bricks of the kingdom, it is shepherding that provides the mortar. In the Catholic Apostolic Church (as we will see), the adoption of the ministries of Ephesians chapter 4 eventually led to a formal ecclesiastical denomination with the orders of apostles, angels (bishops), priests, prophets and deacons. If Restorationism had been created around apostles and elders as formal or official ranks within the movement, then what would have emerged would have been a hierarchical Church in formal terms only – that is, an apostolate whose jurisdiction was confined to ecclesiastical matters alone.

The adoption of discipling doctrines, however, alters the formal ordering of the Ephesians ministries, and turns them into a paternalistic network of structured relationships. These relationships extend beyond the church and enter into the homes and communities of believers. To say that this involves a structure again needs some clarification. Restorationists say that discipling is not a structure but a set of personal relationships voluntarily entered into. This is not untrue, but it is misleading. Firstly, not all relationships are voluntary, because children are covered by their parents whether they like it or not. But more importantly, the personal relationships take place within a clearly defined matrix.

Children do not shepherd parents, wives do not discipline husbands, elders do not cover prophets, and prophets, while they might admonish, do not rule apostles. God's kingdom is a theocracy, and the spiritual principles which guide it are hierarchical. There is an assumption that shepherds are more mature than sheep, but this is really a very tentative principle in Restoration. There is no guarantee that apostles are spiritually more mature than elderly ladies in the back pew, any more than one can safely assume that husbands are more mature than their wives. The ranks and orders of the kingdom are primarily understood, as we saw in the last chapter, as God's order. Apostles, prophets, elders, husbands, parents, are all the indirect but delegated authority of God himself. It is for this reason that I think we have to understand shepherding as a structure and an organizational shape, as well as a set of practices.

An outsider who casually dropped into a Restorationist meeting or celebration event would not pick up this structure. He would notice the freedom of worship, individualistic expression, and the exercise of the spiritual gifts of 1 Corinthians 12. There would be no use of formal titles, because apostles and elders are called by their first names. (George Tarleton, when he was an apostle in R2, did self-mockingly refer to himself as 'St George'!) But the absence of formal titles only masks the reality of the power and authority of the apostles and elders within the movement.

I think the evidence shows that, in both R1 and R2, shepherding has been more pervasive than the ministries of Ephesians chapter 4. Shepherding adds two dimensions to kingdom life that are missing in the ecclesiology of Ephesians. Firstly, it transforms the formal ecclesiastical authority of the apostles and elders into an informal system of paternal relationships. This informalism does not undermine the formal authority; on the contrary, its very humanness reinforces it. Secondly, shepherding extends the influence and control of leaders into every corner of the alternative society. In doing so, it blurs the traditional distinction between church and home. When converts join Restoration, they do not become members of a new church; they leave the secular world for a sacred society.

I do not intend to enter into controversies in this chapter concerning possible abuses of discipling. Horror stories certainly abound, but to deal with them now would distort the general picture. I will deal with such stories and other controversial issues within Restorationism in chapter 13 and Appendix 2.

The extent and level of eldership control – This area is difficult to determine. Shepherding is all-pervasive in the movement, but it is patchy in its application. When new members complete their commitment courses and become members of their local Restoration church, they enter into a counselling arrangement with the elder. He in turn may assign a mature Christian, such as a cell group leader, to take on a shepherding role. Within the local church, however, the elder is always the senior counsellor. To be counselled means to be taught the principles of kingdom life, and to put yourself in the position of learner. Members are expected to put into practice kingdom principles in their everyday lives, and to be open to correction, admonition and improvement.

In principle, there are no areas of members' lives which

are exempt from investigation. The usual distinction in churches between spiritual matters and personal responsibilities does not exist in Restoration. Personal issues become a matter of concern to elders and counsellors, especially if they are perceived to hinder personal and spiritual growth. Smoking, for example, is not seen as a personal matter: it is kingdom business.

Teenagers will be counselled not only against premarital sex, but against engaging in any activity which is seen to contradict kingdom principles. Right attitudes of wives to husbands, and husbands' attitudes to work and the world are constantly checked. The elder may often be used to arbitrate between personal rivalries and disputes in the church. A common misunderstanding of shepherding is the idea that elders spend all their time giving orders to their congregations. A much more typical method is open and frank discussion of problems between elders and members. Such discussion is typically in private. Conversation may be heated, and confrontation is often seen to be necessary. Usually, problems are resolved to everybody's satisfaction.

The confessional and counselling aspects of shepherding are not usually ritualistic or formal occasions (although I have heard of a number of cases in R1 which could be described as a formal 'carpeting'). Most discipling takes place within close personal relationships. There are some similarities with the confessional practices of Catholicism and the secular methods of psychiatry, but there are a number of essential differences. For example, one does not typically ask the priest or psychiatrist whether you should marry so and so, or whether you should take job Y instead of X.

In R1, while elders do not tell women which men to marry, it is expected that engaged couples will discuss their forthcoming marriage with elders. Elders certainly would not approve of marrying non-Christians (or self-confessed Christians from traditions that deny the 'born-again' experience). People, on the whole, are also dissuaded from moving homes or jobs if they take them away from the Restoration ambit. I have heard many (unsubstantiated) rumours that elders have told couples when to have sex and how many children they can have. It is certainly true that it is not considered inappropriate for elders (and apostles) to seek to influence and direct the financial, social and moral lives of Restoration members.

Another essential difference between discipling and other counselling methods is that discipleship has a bottom line. The line is that in the local church, ultimate authority lies with the elder. (A priest can also invoke a bottom line, of course – he can refuse absolution.) It is only when the elder invokes the bottom line that the whole discipleship system is liable to break down. Either the authority of the elder (or apostle) is accepted, with the possibility of mounting resentment and the likelihood of future rebellion, or members leave. It is usually only when Restorationists leave the kingdom after failing to agree with their leaders that we hear of how terrible discipling is in practice.

Typically, the bottom line is not invoked in Restoration churches. The majority of counselling involves the elder in giving advice and offering methods and means for overcoming problems. How to improve your prayer life, for example; or how to improve your temper. Members will be exhorted to tithe more graciously, become more active in the Church, learn to cope with the unsaved at work, or an uncaring husband at home. The overall intention of counselling is to make people more responsible, and more spiritually mature. All the leaders insist on this and claim that the scare stories are the sort of rumours everyone hears, but no one can substantiate. Whether it is true, in practice, that shepherding leads to maturity is a matter of conjecture. It seems likely that paternalism breeds dependency, and shepherding, instead of producing Christian leaders, merely produces sheep. (Arthur Wallis, on the other hand, wonders if any other Christian group has produced so many leaders.) Perhaps this is merely a long-term worry of mine, or simply a prejudice; the evidence for the effects of shepherding is notoriously difficult to find.

When I visited the Dales Bible Week in 1982, and Festival in 1984, I asked a number of people to describe their experience of discipling to me. None of them gave me any examples of what they considered to be heavy-handedness or inappropriate counselling. One woman told me that the elder had helped save her marriage. A teenage boy claimed that his house group leader, and the group as a whole, had helped him to overcome racist feelings. One boy told how the leader of his community church had helped him stay off heroin and pot. The general image of the elder seems to be the elder brother, or one who is more spiritually mature. Perhaps it is natural that committed believers are unlikely to discuss serious tensions and difficulties with an outsider. But the fact remains that believers often see discipling as a positive benefit.

David Tomlinson gave a good example of discipling problems, and how to deal with them, on Radio 4's documentary, *Front Room Gospel*.[8] A couple joined one of his churches with debt hanging permanently round their necks:

House group leaders tried to find why their lives were so up and down, and of course found out that they had all these worries all the time, and were constantly going into commitments that they could not keep. Now, as far as we can see, love and faithfulness, and brotherhood, demands that we help each other in those sort of areas. And so, in the context of a loving, caring, trusting relationship, one person can say to another: 'You've really got to stop this; and before you go and get into any more commitments – before you take on any more hire purchase agreements – you must come and share it with me . . . That's not to say that we are going to lock you up in the church dungeon if you don't, or excommunicate you if you don't. But it is a case for saying that if you want to get out of your problems, you are going to have to open up your life for someone to help you.

To introduce David Tomlinson here is to introduce a major factor in shepherding which I do not think can be ignored. David Tomlinson can talk with some confidence in the way that he does because he has the sort of personality that seeks to avoid confrontation, invoking bottom lines, and falling out with people. He is a mature, secure person, who does not feel the need to use his apostolic authority to get his own way, ride roughshod over others, or make impossible demands on members. The personality factor inevitably influences both the content and manner of discipleship. In the fat file that I have collected on discipling abuses, authoritarian and insecure personalities is a dominant theme.

One former member of R2 told me that he had adopted a rule of thumb that helped him judge the maturity and sensibility of leaders. He would score them out of ten. If they said to him: 'Bill' (a pseudonym), 'how are things going? Can I help?' he would give them ten. But if they said to him: 'Bill, God wants you to sort yourself out', he would give them five. Frequently, according to Bill, they would say to him: 'Listen to what God is saying.' This would merit a score of three. Occasionally, they would insist: 'This is God's word for you, Bill: you must receive it' (the implication being, Bill felt, that if he did not receive this word, something nasty would happen to him). This approach scored zero in Bill's book. According to Bill, the more insecure leaders were, the more they would invoke heavenly backing for their advice.

While I am obviously in no position to endorse Bill's original personality theory, I do think that there is no doubt that shepherding is a system that is open to abuse. Many people want to condemn the system outright as unbiblical or totalitarian. But even supporters of shepherding recognize the dangers. The very fact that it reaches into every corner of a believer's life demonstrates that it can be a source of tension and evil as well as a power for good. George Tarleton, former apostle in R2, pointed out to me that discipling is not simply a problem at the eldership level. Who oversees unscrupulous apostles? George believes that the majority of apostles, prophets and elders are good, conscientious people. However, some of them, he believes, are deluded and potentially dangerous. And there are one or two leaders throughout Restorationism as a whole, he believes, who are what he described to me as 'wrong 'uns'.

The role of women – Looking at the role of women, and particularly wives, in Restoration circles, it is noticeable that R1 and the Basingstoke communities are more committed to the traditional role view than R2. Women are not encouraged to go out to work, and wives are expected to submit to their husbands regardless of whether their husbands are right or not. From a feminist perspective, this information will be all one need know to condemn kingdom life as yet another bastion of male privilege. Joyce Thurman, who was involved with the house church movement when she wrote her book, *New Wineskins*, told me that she found attitudes to women the hardest thing to take. Joyce and her husband are now Roman Catholics (of a charismatic variety) and she finds women far more free and less restricted than those in R1.

In practice, however, the situation is by no means uniform in R1. There is a lot of lip service paid to the submission of wives in the home. According to the doctrine, in the home the man is God's delegated leader. Wives can and do, however, go over the heads of their husbands to the elders. Elders, while respecting God's order in the home, and while teaching the submission of wives to husbands, also remind the men that they are supposed to be the head of the wife as Christ is head of the Church. In R2, in particular, this is often understood not only to mean that the husband should be caring and respectful, but also that he should encourage mutuality of ministry in the home.

A young wife in Terry Virgo's church in Hove gives her assent to the idea of submitting to her husband, but it is worth noting how she interprets this:

I don't think it's an authoritarian thing at all. I know that Steve really loves me, and he does not order me to do things. But because I know he loves me just as much as Christ loves the Church, I can relax and be myself fully in that. And yet at the same time, I know that I don't bear the brunt of the total responsibility for the family. He is the head, and I'm happy to be in partnership with him in that.[9]

The submissiveness of wives has as much to do with their social class as their Restorationist ideology. In R1, and more so in R2, there are many middle-class wives who were already in professional employment when they joined the kingdom. Becoming Restorationists did not lead to the wholesale abandoning of professional careers. Many of the women in Restoration are better educated than their leaders. Ron Trudinger may write about the submissiveness of women in *Built to Last*, and he may be quoted with relish by the men in R1, but some women, while accepting the titular shepherding of their husbands, maintain considerable autonomy. Having said that, it remains true that there are many women who claim that they are content with their lot. I have met wives who see themselves fulfilling a spiritual function or ministry in the home, and feel that a woman's place is in the home.

Within R2, there is a definite mood of emancipation among women. At Festival 84, I heard women publicly say that they wished to be more involved in healing, water baptism, teaching, preaching and forms of leadership other than 'women's work'. Often in R2, like R1, women's leadership tends to be among women. Most women that I have talked to agree that the man is the head of the home, and that elders should be men. Nevertheless, many of them thought that women could and should play a more active part in Christian leadership.

It might be thought that this issue has nothing to do with how shepherding works. But it has: Restoration has been built up on what leaders see as the spiritual order of the kingdom. Christ is the high priest, and all leaders are men. The only shepherding role allocated to women is among other women (under the ultimate authority of men) and children. For women to become more active in leadership, a change in perception of God's order will need to take place.

John Noble's wife, Christine, has always been involved with John's work. John sees Christine as a partner, and not an underling. One of the reasons that I take with a pinch of salt the claim that John is too authoritarian is his relationship with his wife. I am sure that Christine would not mind me saying that she is not the 'model' submissive wife. I remember one incident at Festival 84, when I shared the platform with Christine Noble on 'the role of women today'. Christine had been waxing lyrical about what women were going to do when they finally got away from male domination. Then calling out to John, who was sitting in the middle of the large audience, she said: 'Is that all right, dear?' The whole crowd, including John, erupted with laughter.

I cannot imagine this happening in R1. Such incidents are not trivial, for they tell us a great deal about the difference between R1 and R2, and the way in which the structure of shepherding is more open to change in R2. Christine's comments and attitude are enough to cause a shiver throughout the whole of R1: women expressing themselves in this way smacks of rebellion in the kingdom. And, of course, in a way they are right.

Children and shepherding – The position of children within the structure of shepherding is interesting. On the one hand they are encouraged to become 'born again' at a very early age, but on the other hand their status in the kingdom up until the conversion experience is not absolutely clear. Once born again, children are encouraged to be baptized with the Holy Spirit. It is not uncommon for seven- and eight-year-olds to speak in tongues and prophesy. The children are also encouraged to dance and sing with considerable freedom of expression. But because for Restorationists, like many evangelicals, initiation into the Church is conversion, children up until that time are not in the Church but living in the shadow of the kingdom. Shepherding and training for children in kingdom principles must begin, Restorationists feel, before conversion and throughout their formative years.

Ern Baxter's influence is clearly noticeable in this area. When he was at the Lakes and Dales Bible Weeks, he stressed the importance of physical punishment: 'to break the rebellion of the child'. He taught that the hand should not be used, because the hand should always be the touch of love; and because hitting with the hand can often damage the child. It was recommended to use the strap or a cane, but never while the parent was in anger: 'in order that you won't build up resentment'.

Maurice Smith recalls that this advice permeated R2 as well as R1. He remembers a leader living near him buying up a large bundle of canes, which he gave out to members. Ted Rotherham, who until recently was a local leader in the extended branch of R2, regrets the use he made of physical punishment. So too does Maurice Smith. One father in R2 admitted to me that he had thrashed his son in temper; in practice, as he had discovered, it is very difficult systematically to beat someone in cold blood. I recall a letter in an edition of *Restoration* where a woman wrote in, thankful that she had a special wooden spoon which she used for punishment. She hung it on the wall (presumably its visibility had a deterrent effect).

Today, attitudes are changing in this area. Shepherding of children is still a major theme, but methods of correction are not so uniform. Some people, such as David Tomlinson, never did take much notice of this stress on physical punishment. However, leaders in the newly-constituted R2 felt it necessary to put on a seminar at Festival 84 to discuss alternatives to physical punishment. John Noble's school reserves the right to corporal punishment, but the government report notes that the sanction has never been used. I think it not unfair to say that it is normative to use physical punishment within the homes of R1 (and to a lesser extent R2), but it is not compulsory.

On the whole, the structure of shepherding is clear in Restorationism. From the apostle down to the small child, covering arrangements exist for all members. Virtually everybody seems to be under some delegated authority. This being so, there is a remarkable fit between the principles and practice of shepherding. More so, I believe, than the fit between the theory and practice of the Ephesians chapter 4 ministries.

Formally, Restorationism may be a charismatic apostolate, but in practice Restorationism operates as a network of interpersonal yet paternalistic relationships. The idea of a pyramid structure, or a totalitarian organization run from the top, is misleading. Restorationism is not yet a formal institution with a clearly delineated bureaucracy. Power and authority exist at all levels of the network; they are not invested totally in one man. Discipling gives Restorationism its dynamic and specialness. It is the shepherding structure, above all else, that makes kingdom people radical people. To use a sociological phrase, the level of social control is far greater than in the average Christian church. Restorationists say, correctly, that the control exists within the context of a freely entered and voluntary covenant.

Some evangelicals do not find this reassuring. They point out that the same thing could be said of the cults such as the Moonies and Scientology.[10] Certainly, a number of questions are being asked by worried observers. Do apostles accept admonition and criticism from below? (David Matthew says that Bryn Jones does).[11] Who monitors the apostles? Are abuses merely aberrations from good practice, or are they in the nature of the system itself?

Meeting Together

If apostolic ministries in conjunction with comprehensive

192

discipling methods provide the basic matrix within which Restoration exists, it must not be forgotten that kingdom life is focused in a number of settings. Ideally, many Restorationists in R1 would like to be able to turn their backs totally upon the world, but this is not possible because most people work primarily in secular society. R2 does not seem so convinced that all modern culture is evil, and even R1 members enjoy some leisure activities outside the 'alternative society'. In both R1 and R2, however, the focus of the kingdom in everyday life is the home, the cell or house group, and the local church. In some cases, as we have seen, this is extended to Restorationist schools.

House groups and extended families – The Christian home is the nursery of the kingdom. It is in godly family relationships between the husband, wife and their children that the reality of kingdom life is practised. Both R1 and R2 are proud of the fact that much of the shepherding input goes into the family. The house groups are in many ways what sociologists call extended families, except that instead of mother and father and children being augmented by grandparents and other kinfolk, they are extended by kingdom people who live in close proximity. The house group is an expression of the family extended into community. Many kingdom people move into the same street. Together they worship, debate and have fun (and rows) together. Strong friendships are formed and the emphasis is on sharing a common life.

In a way, then, kingdom people form communities by association – they self-consciously create pockets of the kingdom wherever they go. This is another demonstration of Restorationist radicality. People in the Charismatic Renewal, Baptist or Pentecostal Churches, do not typically move in with each other (or next door to each other).

The local church – Increasingly, however, especially in large sections of R1, the house group is being superseded by the local church. It is difficult to generalize, but in Bryn

Jones's churches, for example, the house group is of diminishing concern. More and more time is being spent in church. The building of larger and larger churches in the cities is seen as part of the vision of a light that is both an invitation and a warning to the world. Certainly, R1 is anxious not to hide its light under a bushel: it wants to make a public show of strength. House cells persist and remain as an important daily contact with fellow believers, but it is the church that is the major focus of the local Restoration community.

Celebration events – Local leaders, both elders of churches and house group leaders, regularly meet with apostles or members of apostolic teams. Retreats and regional sessions are regular events. For everybody, however, their liturgical year is punctuated by the celebration occasions. These events perform a similar function to the conventions of earlier Pentecostal movements: they are a special time when God is believed to move and bless in a particularly powerful way. Unlike the day outing of Elim members to the Royal Albert Hall every Easter, or the weekend Easter convention at Bethshan tabernacle in Manchester, Restoration events tend to be residential; the whole family goes along. In the great Dales Bible Week, or Festival week, when you are mixing with literally thousands of kingdom people, there is a feeling of excitement, expectancy and revival in the air.

The celebrations are regional events which go beyond locality. Hence they are expressions of the larger Church and pointers to the eschatological vision of filling the whole earth with the kingdom of God and the final 'restoration of all things'. Celebrations give Restorationists the feeling that they belong to a massive movement. The tiny house cell rooted in the burgeoning local church flowers into the full glory of the restored kingdom. The big events are not simply things that Restorationists happen to attend: they are essential expressions of personal faith and commitment. They are also essential to the overall shape and structure of the kingdom. As one elder put it: 'Can you imagine heaven without the banquet?'

In R2, which for the moment is marginally smaller than R1, the new Festival venue is a means of bringing churches together which normally never meet. It is also an opportunity to express solidarity between the different streams of churches who are linked to the apostolic leadership. R1 tends, increasingly, to stick to regions. Downs Week is really Terry Virgo's patch. The Dales and the Wales Bible Weeks are primarily Bryn and Keri Jones's concern. However, there is an intermingling of churches and leadership at these celebrations. They demonstrate that Terry Virgo, Tony Morton and Bryn Jones are working together and supporting each other's work.[12]

R1 goes in for far more jamborees than R2. Furthermore, Church House in Bradford acts as a focus once a month for the many fellowships in the outlying districts. R1 does not invite leaders in R2 to their celebrations. R1 leaders do not come to R2 celebrations. Moves are being made to make mutual acceptance of ministries between R1 and R2 a reality and not just a formal agreement. (I think it is going too far to say that even a formal agreement exists.) There are to-ings and fro-ings between some of Terry Virgo's churches and Gerald Coates's, but whether this will come to anything is too early to say. In many ways, R1 and R2 are so clearly moving apart that it will take a miracle for Bryn Jones and Gerald Coates to share a platform together.[13] The separateness of the celebration events highlights clearly that the Restoration kingdom is a kingdom divided: it has two shapes, not one.

Celebration events are special occasions that promote the solidarity of kingdom people, but they are not ghetto events. On the contrary, celebrations are a demonstration of kingdom power to all who wish to come. The Dales Bible Week, for example, has always been an interdenominational occasion. Probably half the people there are not from Restoration churches (this is one of the reasons that I earlier overestimated the size of R1).[14] All of the big residential conventions of Restoration are the showpieces and recruitment offices of the kingdom.

But how does one get into the kingdom? What sort of people will you find there? What sort of life does one lead? How much will it cost you? If you do not like it, can you leave (without hassle)? For those who would like an answer to such questions, perhaps because you would like to join, or simply because you are curious to know what kingdom people do, may I suggest a quick tour in, around, and out of the kingdom.

Recommended Reading

There is virtually nothing, though one can glean a little from Eileen Vincent's *Something's Happening* (London: Marshalls, 1984).

9

A KINGDOM TOUR[1]

I am in a position to take you on an exclusive tour to the Restoration alternative society (courtesy of Kingdom Tours). But be warned: this is not the sort of package holiday for the lazy; it is a trip for intrepid travellers.

In principle, anyone can apply for a visa to enter the kingdom, but I am afraid that some of you will be disappointed and refused entry. Years ago, when the kingdom was just starting, it was not so difficult to get in, but now you will have to undergo a commitment course. Commitment courses are not everybody's cup of tea, but at least they offer you the opportunity to decide whether you really want to go. There is no excuse, when you enter the kingdom, for saying, 'I did not really know what it was all about.'

How to Get into the Kingdom

Before applying for your visa, you have to know where the official recruitment offices are. There is no problem, for they are all over the place. Firstly, look around your locality and you will probably find a church with the words 'Community' and/or 'Fellowship' in the title. Be careful, though: you could easily stumble upon something that looks like Restoration but is not. Ask the right questions: 'Do you believe in delegated authority?'; 'Who is your apostle?'; 'What does Dales Bible Week, or Festival mean to you?' Once you have satisfied yourself that you have got the right place (remembering to check whether you have R1 or R2), stick around, attend the services, and if you decide that you want to go on the tour, they will approach you with the method of applying for your visa (in other words, entering a commitment course).

Although this is a perfectly legitimate way to get on the tour, I must confess that it is not the way most people get to go. Usually people prefer more organized approaches to the recruitment offices. Most of the people who enter the kingdom are already Christians from denominations or independent house groups, who want to live a more radical life. Many of them were involved in the charismatic movement. Sometimes whole churches, and sections of churches, apply to be 'covered' by one of the apostles of the kingdom. This often happens after a visit to the Dales Bible Week, or a similar event. It is more likely, therefore, that you will wish to join the tour in the company of your friends and fellow-Christians.

Another popular approach to the visa problem is to invite a team of consultants from Restorationist churches to come and teach you about the kingdom. This can happen, and does happen, in churches within the Baptist Union, and traditional Pentecostal churches. A small minority – though an increasing minority – are asking to join the tour as a result of a conversion experience either from evangelistic meetings, or from hearing of the kingdom from a permanent resident. This approach is particularly welcomed by Restorationist leaders, as a number of them have told me that those without any previous denominational experience settle down into the kingdom with less trouble. However you choose to come into contact with the kingdom – or however it thrusts itself upon you – ultimately you cannot avoid having to undergo your commitment course in order to obtain your entry visa.

Commitment courses do vary considerably around the country, and all of them, regardless of whether they are in R1 or R2 and are formal or informal, take several weeks to complete. If you think that you would prefer to visit R2 (because you think it is easier to get in) then you may be in for a shock. You will probably have to complete a foundation course on conversion, water baptism, gifts of the Spirit, tithing and shepherding. Here is an example from the Romford Fellowship:

> In this brief look at spiritual authority we will be touching on submission and shepherding. The spirit of this age is anarchy, independence, rebellion, and anti-authority, and we must always guard that the church is not affected by this. An essential element in the care and concern necessary in church building is spiritual authority by God's delegated authority. Submitting to spiritual authority, in another person whom I can accept as appointed by God, is at the heart of restoration life and growth in church.

Is that too heavy for you? Well if it is, then I am afraid that you cannot come on the tour. John Noble may want you to fill in a questionnaire to make sure you really want to go (for Restorationists do not want fly-by-nights). But whether you want to enter the kingdom through the recruitment offices of R1 or R2, you will have to be taught the principles of kingdom living in advance. You will be expected to do a fair bit of reading, join in group discussions, and ask questions. After having had some weeks to pray and seriously consider taking the tour, you then have to make a decision. Maybe you will feel pressurized by your local church or fellowship to go, or not to go, but in the end it is you who have to make up your mind. Once you make your commitment to go, and once the leaders of your commitment course accept your commitment, they will give you your visa. Kingdom Tours is now happy to take you into the kingdom. (Rumour has it that there are still pockets of the kingdom where commitment courses do not yet exist.)

What Sort of People Will You be Travelling With?

One of the good things about Kingdom Tours is that you travel with a nice class of people. Mind you, you could feel a bit out of it if you travel to the wrong part of the kingdom. If you go down to Cobham, for example, and you are a 'chip butty' person, you will find that they are all middle class down there. But don't worry, the kingdom accepts all types of persons regardless of class, race or previous experience. As long as you have got your visa, you will be all right. In Bradford and Middlesbrough you will find that communities are much more mixed in their social class.

If you are self-consciously middle class, then you might like to know that the kingdom boasts a very high proportion of professional classes both north and south. These include many small-businessmen, estate agents and civil servants. There are a great many teachers in schools and further education. Nurses are everywhere, and there is no shortage of doctors, solicitors and accountants. Bryn Jones can boast four PhDs in his church (in various disciplines), and a great many elders have degrees or higher education of some kind (however, most of the apostles do not).[2] What the psychologists like to call the divergent thinkers – the abstract and conceptual intelligentsia – do seem to be in short supply. There are technicians and engineers, but few philosophers, social scientists or postgraduate theologians. If you are a skilled worker, with a trade, then be warned. Your tour is likely to be a busman's holiday: the kingdom needs people like you.

Maybe all this 'class' stuff leaves you cold. What difference can social class possibly make in the kingdom? (the same as anywhere else, David Tomlinson would say). But perhaps age profile worries you? You will be welcome in the kingdom if you are old, but one of the most interesting and surprising features on entering the kingdom is to find how many young people there are. Most churches in Great Britain have an imbalance of old to young (and women to men). The kingdom is replete with children, teenagers, almost as many men as women, and seems to specialize in young couples with families. Around the Cobham and West Sussex areas, for example, the community dimension of the kingdom is especially attractive to young couples with no extended families to help support them socially and financially.

This sense of community will also appeal to you if you are unemployed, old, ill or lonely. If you want to remain socially isolated, or keep numerous and close relationships in the secular world, then frankly I do not think there is much point in taking the trip. Kingdom life, in practice, tends to be a reality shared among kingdom people.

If you are black, you will be welcome (though George Tarleton warns that there is covert racism around). Intermarriage is quite common, and is certainly not frowned upon. There are not many West Indians or Asians in Restoration, but numbers are on the increase. If you live in London's inner city, look out for David Tomlinson. He will be especially interested if you are working class as well. Basically, David is fed up with the kingdom being only white middle-class house church people. He feels it is in danger of becoming a cosy club for the better off.

Divorcees get a special welcome in the kingdom (which is not common in many evangelical circles). You won't get the usual pious patter, either, about 'God loving you and accepting you – but you can never marry again'. Remarriage in the kingdom is not an automatic certainty, but it is becoming increasingly common.[3] If you are homosexual or lesbian, however, you will not be welcome unless you are prepared to become heterosexual (or, at least, not practise homosexuality). Kingdom people believe that you can be supernaturally 'delivered' from sexual perversions. A major leader has declared to his friends that his sexual orientation was changed by God.

What Sort of Life Will You Lead?

The adage 'When in Rome' is particularly apposite in the kingdom. As I pointed out earlier, you cannot enter on a package tour. Package tour operators cater for 'little Englanders' who go to Spain to eat fish and chips and

drink English beer; they do all they can to preserve a sem-
blance of the homeland in the foreign country. This will
not do in the kingdom: once you are in, you must leave the
old world behind. You will be expected to behave according to the laws and customs of your hosts.

You will spend a great deal of time in worship while
you are in the kingdom. The chances are that many of you
were first attracted to Restoration by the music.[4] Proof that
the kingdom generates its own styles and is not merely
derivative, is the number of original songs that have been
written. If you are a follower of Billy Graham,and attended Mission England in 1984, you will already be well
acquainted with kingdom songs: the *Mission England Praise*
book is full of them.[5] You will soon learn all the words and
tunes. I remember in 1982, shortly after I had commenced
my own kingdom tour, that I used to wake up in the night
with the choruses jangling in my head.

Those of you from the more traditional Pentecostal
backgrounds will find the songs in the kingdom not so
sentimental and personal as the ones you are used to
singing. This is even more noticeable in R1 than R2. 'Jesus,
Jesus, Jesus, sweetest name I know (I know, I know)' is far
more likely to be replaced by songs centred on God the
Father and King:

> Father we love you,
> We worship and adore you.
> Glorify your name in all the earth.
> Glorify your name,
> Glorify your name,
> Glorify your name in all the earth.[6]

Many of the songs invoke the glory and majesty of God
(and the all-powerful judge, the *Pantokrator*, is a dominant
motif). Psalms and scriptural verses are often set to modern music, though the style is more modern anthem and
march than rock or jazz. You will also hear groups and
soloists, and like many of the people who perform at the

Christian Greenbelt festival, these songs tend to be middle-of-the-road rock, or American modern country music.

If you go to the Welsh Bible Week you may find dancing is more restrained than it used to be, because egoistical dancers – since the Dales – were spoiling it for the others. In most corners of the kingdom, however, you will be able to dance and use your body in worship. In every part of the Restored kingdom you will find clapping, hands raised (and shaking), and extempore crying and praying. Worship is primarily understood as a corporate activity – the subjects of the King worship him together as the people of God. The Restorationist style of worship will not appeal to anybody who prefers traditional liturgies. But as these issues are dealt with in the commitment courses, I can assume that traditionalists will not apply for visas. (One elder in R2 told me that he longed for a formalized liturgy as a contrast to the freer style!)

Worship in church and the house group will be Pentecostal worship. 'Signs and wonders' are normal in the kingdom, and you will find expectations are high that God will heal the sick and deliver people from demons. You may wonder why there seems to be so much demon activity in the kingdom. Unlike you, the devil does not need a visa to get in. The kingdom is not yet in its spiritual fullness, and sin, while it is not expected to abound, certainly exists. You will discover when you first start the tour that people will naturally expect that you may be smuggling in more than a few secret sins. Elders will determine whether your sin or problem is of demonic origin or some other source.

Demons do not seem to be so prevalent in the kingdom as a few years ago. This is not because the kingdom is now full of holier people, but because many leaders are more careful in seeing demons behind every sickness and trouble. David Mansell, so a number of people have said, has a grasp of psychological principles as well as a fundamentalist doctrine of demons. David Tomlinson makes a distinction between a belief in demons in principle, and actual demonic attacks. He feels that some Restorationists tend to treat demons like the proverbial 'reds under the bed'.

If there is some disagreement on the influence of demons among kingdom people, you will find a general acceptance of the importance of the gifts of the Spirit. You will be expected to pray for such gifts; elders will help you to exercise the gift of tongues and prophecy. If you are slightly worried, even though you have completed your commitment course, that the signs and wonders may be a bit over the top (perhaps you have heard non-kingdom people use the word 'extreme'), then you will find them very similar to the practices of the charismatics in the mainstream churches.[7]

You will certainly find that a lot of your time in the kingdom will be spent socially mixing with fellow Christians. To get the most out of the kingdom – indeed, to demonstrate that you are a kingdom person – you become a member of a community church and a house group. That is why a short stay is not really possible. You cannot be a part-time kingdom person, and if you wish to go on tour you have to be prepared for a long stay and take all your money and goods with you. (I did not say the tour was cheap.)

The kingdom encourages parents and children to be involved in church meetings. Crèches are organized both by the local church and the house groups. If you get into financial difficulties, you will find that your close friends in the house group, and others from the church, will help you out. David Tomlinson and a few families, for example, wanted to move into London, but could not afford the house prices. Festival 84 took an offering of £25,000 for them. A fellowship from the Midlands came down and did all the internal work of plastering and plumbing as a gift to the apostle.

In case you are thinking that such generosity is only for the leaders (and I would be a liar if I did not tell you that they seem to get the biggest financial rewards), it works on the local level too. You could be helped with mortgage payments, debts, and even school fees. Terry Virgo gives an example of what mutual support means in practice:

> A young man had a chip pan fire in his kitchen, and before nightfall – though the fire had really destroyed most of the kitchen and spoilt a lot of the house – before nightfall, there was a new gas cooker installed and operating by the other members of the cell group who came in and worked hard all evening.[8]

Admittedly, some people find the close atmosphere of mutual support groups stultifying. Others find the close scrutiny of the shepherd inhibiting. Even if you have completed your commitment course, and have a general idea of what kingdom life is like, the only way you will ever know how it works out in practice is to practise it.

It is not the case that once you enter kingdom territory you will never be involved with anybody or anything outside. In R1 and R2 you will find that members go to the cinema, and go out for meals; usually they go with other Restoration members, but not always. In R2, the local church and house groups remain the primary focus of social life, but increasingly other social venues are looked to, such as concerts, pubs, holiday outings. R2 is obviously keen to be more involved in mainstream happenings than R1. John Noble and Gerald Coates, and many of their fellow Restorationists, were to be seen at the Westminster Central Hall in October 1984. There, a 'Third Wave' conference had been organized to introduce John Wimber and a team of over 200 from California to the Christians of London.

Tony Morton, and a number of Terry Virgo's team were also there. This is probably the greatest intermingling of mainstream charismatics and house church people to date.[9] However, do not expect much extra-kingdom activity if you visit Bryn Jones's branch of R1. David Matthew will tell you that this is a deliberate policy by Bryn's team. Their churches seem to be the most socially exclusivist, and spend virtually no time with Christians from outside their own fellowships. The reason, says David, is that they want their churches to be a cutting edge, an offence and a challenge if you will, to the denominational churches. However, both Bradford churches – along with R1 and the whole of R2 – supported Mission England and Mission London.[10]

How Much Will the Restoration Kingdom Cost You?

The answer to this question obviously depends on whether we are talking about money, personal freedom or psychological stability. You will have learned from your commitment courses that there will be a spiritual cost. Becoming members of the kingdom – soldiers of the King – is to turn your back on self-interest and on being a comfortable member of secular society or mainstream Christianity. People such as Nick Butterworth and Maurice Smith will tell you that this 'spiritual cost' is just a jargon phrase, meaning that your personal freedom will be invaded, and legalism not freedom will be your lot. Many people, who are still happy in the kingdom, see this as the sour grapes of the disillusioned. To talk of spiritual and psychological costs would take another investigation and merit a further book, but for the purpose of our brief tour I will restrict myself to the practical issue of money.

Here, the commitment courses are quite honest. No one who has opted to go on Kingdom Tours can possibly claim that they did not know how much it would cost them. Tithing is a universal custom in the kingdom.

The practice of tithing, however, varies from church to church. Some people tithe on their gross incomes, and others on their net incomes. To pay the tithe is to demonstrate that you are a serious believer. Not to pay the tithe is evidence of rebellion, dissatisfaction and a flouting of kingdom authority. The simple fact is that most people pay up without a murmur. People do sometimes get into financial difficulties, but usually they are helped out. As many of the permanent residents are middle class on incomes above the national average, most of them manage quite well. Tithing takes a great act of faith (and it is of course a heartache for the tight-fisted).

Your tithe will be used primarily to support your local elder and apostolic teams. One rule of thumb that seems to have been adopted in Terry Virgo's churches, is for each local community to pay an average of their earnings to the elder. However, many of the elders get less than that. If you want to know what your local elder and apostle earns, you had better ask them. Bryn Jones, for example, was earning £13,500 a year plus car in 1985.[11] Such a sum is not unusual in Restoration circles. While this would seem a fortune to the pastors in the traditional Pentecostal denominations (and not bad for Anglican vicars either), it may very well be that real wages are higher than that.

Fees and expenses for trips abroad, tax relief, 'love offerings', cars, money for housing, and personal gifts, may be extra payments or the fringe benefits of the job. George Tarleton admits that leaders are comfortable and well looked after. Church members may voluntarily do jobs around the house, or be assigned tasks of gardening, painting and decorating. These issues are obviously questions of individual conscience by leaders (and perhaps of interest to exposé journalists).[12]

The kingdom is an expanding empire. As it grows, it acquires new plant, machinery and new leaders. All have to be paid for. R1 is fortunate to rely partially on efficient business organization, but the bulk of the money still comes from members. The primary method of raising money in addition to the tithe is the special offering.

The amount that you will be expected to put into these offerings will depend on your faith, generosity and financial means.[13] Special offerings are usually asked for specific purposes or needs. They will not always be for kingdom uses. R1 raised some £58,000 for the Italian earthquake victims, for example. Usually, however, money will be for supporting Restoration missionary work, helping apostolic teams in evangelistic and international work, developing video and audio systems of communication, and helping with housing for leaders.

You will discover that a great deal of effort has gone into the methodology of fund-raising. This is necessary in our culture, as there is a great deal of pain associated with giving away money! The majority of members give without stint in the belief that they are furthering the kingdom and will be supported by God (and each other) if they should personally run short. When special offerings are called for, either locally or regionally, it is not uncommon for a prophet, or an elder with a word of prophecy, to announce the sum of money that he believes God would have the congregation meet. If, say, the target is £20,000 and only £18,000 is raised, it is not unusual for a slip of paper to be handed up to the platform. The leader will announce that a generous giver has raised the extra revenue to meet the target. The announcement is greeted with salutations of 'Amen!' and 'Thank you Lord!'

If this strikes you as stage-managed or rather American, then I wonder how you will react to the 'heap offering'? This is linked to the idea of the 'hilarious giver': 'the Lord loves a cheerful giver'. They had a heap offering at the Welsh Bible Week in 1984. People were encouraged to think of giving away money as fun. And so to joyful and playful music, members (and guests) danced and jumped their way to the front and deposited money in a heap. The idea of giving as 'so much fun' obviously worked in this case, because the final amount raised, an informant told me, was £90,000.[14]

Perhaps we can see this simply as the razzle-dazzle of American methods. But not all fund-raising is of this type. At the Dales in 1982, the platform speaker asked for financial support for leaders. Quietly and without fuss, £5,000 was raised. Bryn Jones's churches seem to raise more money than the rest of R1 and R2. Nevertheless, all Restorationist churches can gather huge sums of money compared to many mainstream churches. Perhaps we ought to remember, however, that the Church of England is the second largest landowner in England, and many established churches have investments and stock. Restorationist churches have nothing but their members' generosity.

You will find that the majority of Restorationist members support their leaders because they want to extend the kingdom, and not because they want to keep a lot of 'fat cats' in luxury. I think it probable that we shall see some of the money being invested in cable and satellite television before very long. If Bryn Jones is not one of the first to establish the 'electronic church' in Great Britain, I will be surprised.[15]

Leaving the Kingdom

Some of you who may want to start off visiting R1, may eventually decide to settle in R2. It seems to be a mainly one-way traffic. I certainly know of no major defections from R2 to R1. Many of you who decide to take advantage of Kingdom Tours will no doubt soon apply for permanent residence. But what about those of you who might want to leave? Here, I have to make a confession. The kingdom does not automatically issue exit visas. Perhaps you think this is crazy, and that this extended metaphor of the tour has gone far enough. After all, if you do not like the kingdom, you will leave. Who will stop you? But here a word of warning is in order: it is not quite so easy in practice.

In the first place, people with whom you have been closely associated, who have become your friends with whom you have spent many hours in prayer, worship and fellowship, are not happy simply to let you go. This is true of all deeply committed religious groups. Try asking the Catholic priest, for example, who decided to give up holy orders, what pressures he was subjected to before he could get out? (Incidentally, there is nothing intrinsically evil in this. It is just that turning your back on a vocational priesthood is no small matter.) Many Restorationists do not look upon other denominations as alternatives to their own movements. They see them as, at best, marginally involved in the kingdom. To leave the fellowship and return to the world or another church, they often say, is to risk being sniped at by the devil. Demons may sometimes creep into the kingdom, but outside it they are everywhere.

Such a picture may seem strange to someone like Gerald Coates, who is worldly-wise by Restorationist standards and is continuously seeking rapprochement with other religious groups. It is certainly not the case that leaders deliberately keep believers in constant fear of the outside world (although George Tarleton would qualify this a little). But it is the case that many people I have met in R1 and R2 spend so much time together that they are afraid of the outside world.[16]

And so the first problem to face if you want to leave, is that fellowships are unlikely to let you go without a real effort to keep you inside. I know that this is true of many religious groups, including the classical Pentecostals, but in most places the social and moral controls are miniscule compared to the discipleship and close community living of Restoration. Most dissidents in religious institutions simply get up and leave when they lose commitment. But for some Restorationists, this involves far more than leaving the local church.

Many people who really give Restoration a try will probably have moved into the same street as the local cell group. Some may have become involved in joint mortgage schemes, or borrowed money. To pull away from such involvement means a radical change to your whole way of life. It may involve legal proceedings and financial wrangles, if you insist on leaving. If you stay put, but discontinue fellowship, it may lead to ostracism and bitterness.

Of course, you could be lucky. The fellowship may have recognized that you were really only a tourist; a spiritual dilettante, who was at best a fellow traveller, but never really a member of the kingdom. You can be assured that if you persist in flouting kingdom authority, you will be expelled. John Noble is a big man and would not only let you go, but would try to stay friends with you even if there was a major ideological rift between you. But it is important to understand how the apostles and the ordinary members of Restoration feel when a genuine member (as opposed to an interloper or someone passing through) leaves the kingdom. It is as if the father in the story of the prodigal son sees the boy choose to return to the swine.

Leaving the kingdom, then, is as hard as entering it. This is not because Restorationists are narrow, unpleasant and spiteful people. On the contrary, the difficulty of getting in, and getting out again, is evidence of the seriousness of commitment which the kingdom entails. As I have been trying to demonstrate throughout this book, the kingdom is for radicals. I can take you imaginatively on a brief tour, but in reality, Restorationism is the opposite to Canon Ivor Smith-Cameron's house church. There you are welcome to pop in for a quick snack. In the Restorationist kingdom, it is the full banquet or nothing.

10

IS THE RESTORATION MOVEMENT A DENOMINATION?

I do not intend in this chapter to make any prescriptive statements about denominationalism. That is to say, I am not concerned with saying whether denominations are good or bad. When Michael Harper, for example, points out[1] that the house churches (he means R1 and R2) are a new denomination, he is not so much stating a fact as making an accusation. A new denomination for Michael Harper, and for most leaders in the Charismatic Renewal, is a disaster and a tragedy. The question I do want to discuss at some length in this chapter, is a descriptive one: is Restorationism a denomination or not?

Denomination and Sect as Sociological Categories

To talk about denominations, sects (or even cults) is really to talk about sorts of religious organizations or movements; it is not to enter into theological controversies. Theology is the knowledge and study of God. Insofar as that knowledge leads to a concern with God's working in the world – his 'economy', to use a theological category – then, of course, his Church is a theological issue. To talk of the Church as the body of Christ, or the relationship of the Holy Spirit to the Church, soon brings us back to issues of ecclesiology and prescriptivism: how should God's Church be ordered?

I think it is expedient to duck such issues here, simply because we can decide whether Restorationism is a denomination or not without having to enter such controversies. Most people, when they think about denominations – how they are formed and what relationship they have to other religious structures – do not immediately start thinking theologically. If they think systematically, they may think in terms of organizational typology. This has been a major interest in the sociology of religion. As a considerable body of knowledge and reasonably clear-cut criteria for identifying religious movements now exists, I intend to approach the denominational question within this framework.

We can start, as sociologists so often do, with some observations from common sense. If you were to ask most people in Britain to name religious denominations, they would probably think of the Church of England, Roman Catholicism, the Methodists and Baptists. Perhaps they might mention the United Reformed Church. The last is the odd one out of this company for two reasons. Firstly, it has only been in existence for a few years (compared to the others). Secondly, the United Reformed Church is probably unique in British religious history as it is a denomination that was not formed as a result of a revival, or a schism; neither has it emerged from a long identification with our past religious heritage. Instead of being sanctioned either by tradition, schism or enthusiasm, it was formed out of three existing denominations which desired to come together as a witness to Church unity. Thus, the English Presbyterian movement, the Congregationalists, and the Churches of Christ became a denomination by fiat: by general consensus the URC was born.[2]

That this is so should alert us to the fact that denominations are not always born out of enthusiastic and sectarian movements which then cool down into denominational respectability. Denominations can emerge in that way, of course, the Quaker movement being a good example. Methodism was certainly born out of schism and religious revival, but the modern Baptist movement (whose roots are only partly in the Anabaptists) was formed more out of doctrinal differences than revivalism. We can note that, with the exception of very rare churches like the United

Reformed Church, denominations can only be said to be denominations when they have been around for a while. By the mid-nineteenth century, for example, Methodism had certainly come out of the cold, and was accepted by other denominations as a respectable and responsible Church.

On this criterion alone, it is far too premature to call the Restoration movement a new denomination. Denominations do not appear overnight; they slowly emerge until they are seen by existing denominations to be serious contenders (or perhaps even partners) in Christendom. In my opinion, this is about as far as common sense will take us. Sociologists want to go further. 'What is a denomination?' they ask, 'And how do we compare it with other religious structures?'

Weber and Troeltsch: Church and sect – The modern origins of this question go back to the German sociologist, Max Weber. He suggested a dichotomy between Church and sect. He saw the Church as 'a sort of trust foundation for supernatural ends, an institution, necessarily including both the just and the unjust . . .' The sect, on the other hand, he saw as the 'believer's church . . . solely as a community of personal believers of the reborn, and only these . . .'[3]

Particularly through the influence of Weber's student, Troeltsch, this dichotomy became the basis of much of the subsequent work in religious typologies. The sect was seen as a body of voluntary believers that stood for distinct theological doctrines. It refused to compromise its religious teachings (particularly the belief that it held the unique or most enlightened path to salvation). It refused, also, to compromise with 'the world'. Conversely, many of the earlier sociologists felt, the Church as an organization was universalist in its teaching, but the voluntary principle was unimportant (you are born in the Church); and the world was not something to shun but something to be accommodated. The Church, then, was broad in its teachings, and sought to dispense supernatural blessings. Its compromise with the secular world (and hence the established political order), resulted in a built-in conservatism. National Churches, in particular the historic churches of the Catholic, Orthodox and Anglican persuasions, are the embodiment of 'churchness'.

Now while much of this early work was crude and in some ways inconsistent, as we will see, it is glaringly obvious from this information that Restorationism does not only fit the description of 'sect' far more closely than 'Church', but Restorationists themselves, on these criteria, would see themselves as sectarian. Their very attack on denominationalism is that churches contain believers and non-believers, and that these churches are compromising churches.

When I first broached the subject of sectarianism with David Matthew, he was understandably none too pleased with the idea. But in fact, the real problem with the word 'sect' is not that it cannot be defended as a useful typology, but that it carries with it negative connotations. In short, to repeat an earlier point, it is used prescriptively and not descriptively. To use it prescriptively is to talk of sectarian spirits (the spirit of divisiveness, the spirit of separatism). In this sense of the word, there are many sectarian people in traditional denominations. Some evangelicals – and many broad churchmen – see the charismatic movement within the denominations as sectarian, even though the charismatics have not hived off to form a new denominational structure. On the same criterion, no one could accuse John Noble, for example, of being sectarian: he would walk over broken glass to maintain fellowship with people. Many Restorationists are not the sort of people who want to cut themselves off from the rest of Christendom as 'holier than thou' people.

The growth and development of sects – To be able to use 'sect' as a descriptive category, however, we have to clear up some of the obvious weaknesses of the earlier sociological approaches. Troeltsch, for example, tended to identify sects with the poor and disinherited of society, and churches with the relatively affluent. At least this distinction did give the opportunity for seeing the possibility of a movement from a sectarian organization to a church (what we would call, these days, 'denomination'). Methodism seems to exhibit such a movement, for example. Unfortunately, Troeltsch tended to oversimplify.

This becomes clear if we look at America. There we see a pattern of denominationalism, but no established Church. Many of the denominations, however, while (perhaps) not so universalist in their theology as Weber's understanding of Church, are closer to the Church-type than the sect-type organization. H. Richard Niebuhr sees the denomination as endemic in American society, because of his belief that

> by its very nature the sectarian type of organization is valid only for one generation. The children born to the voluntary members of the first generation begin to make the sect a Church long before they have arrived at the years of discretion. For with their coming, the sect must take on the character of an educational and disciplinary institution, with the purpose of bringing the new generation into conformity with ideals and customs which have become tradition.[4]

Niebuhr, and a number of American sociologists after him, see all denominations as advanced forms of sects. The sect, with its radical, uncompromising stance, and with a membership from the lower strata of society, inevitably in time becomes the more affluent middle-class denomination that makes an accommodation with the world. The real problem with this approach is that while it fits some sects and denominations, it does not fit all of them. (It also fits America better than Europe.) What we can detect in many sectarian churches is that although they tend to lose the fervour of the first generation, the second and subsequent generations still adhere to specific (and sometimes unique) doctrines. They also attempt, quite successfully, to resist the compromising tendencies of denominations.

The first big problem that a sect has to face is the possibility that it may not survive the first generation. Sometimes, we can detect the beginnings of a sectarian formation (such as the group that surrounded Edward Irving when he was excommunicated from the Church of Scotland) without having any certainty that it will come to anything. Looking at Restorationism at the present time, for example, I believe that there is strong evidence for the emergence of at least one, and probably two, sectarian formations. I can be bolder than that and say that R1 has, even now, all the hallmarks of a new sect. For a sect to become anything, however, it has successfully to make the transition from the first to the second generation. To do this it has to demonstrate stability, continuity with the first generation, a recognized authority structure, and yet maintain its specialness and distinctive doctrines and practices (or adopt new revelations). If it is able to do this, it does not become a denomination; it becomes an established sect.

The established sect becomes a stable – and possibly quite large – sect that never quite becomes mainline. Which is to say that it never becomes absorbed into the more integrated Church–world compromise of so many denominations. Certainly, it is possible for an established sect to go on to become a denomination; the many American Baptist churches are good examples of this development. Professor David Martin argues, I think correctly, that Methodism was a schismatic offshoot of Anglicanism, but its orientation to the world and its strong universalist appeal has always been closer to Weber's sense of Church rather than sect. Methodism is not, then, necessarily a good British example of the transition from sect to denomination (Church). What is interesting about British sects is how many of them have become established, but have remained faithful to the doctrines of their founding fathers.

Even Quakerism, for example, while moving away from an enthusiastic and evangelical beginning to a quietist and eventually reforming sect, has held onto much of the simplicity of its Church structure and liturgical practices. The Salvation Army, too, despite its almost universal recognition, has maintained its original and unusual military structure. With its uniforms and brass bands (whatever happened to the 'Joystrings'?) and its temperance ideology, it clearly still bears all the trappings of its nineteenth-century origins.

The fact that earlier I could cite the Quakers as still a sect, highlights the possibility, against Troeltsch, that sects need not be organizations of the poor. But if suggesting 'The Friends' as a sect rather than a Church-type denomination is pushing it a bit, they are not the only example of middle-class sects. Both the Exclusive and Plymouth Brethren (though more so the Open Brethren these days) have been middle-class movements. The same is true of the Catholic Apostolics. It remains true, however, that the majority of sects begin in relative poverty. The established sects also typically show an upswing in social mobility and affluence.

The Pentecostal sects in Britain are good examples of this. Indeed, they are excellent examples of sect development from tentative beginnings to established formation. Elim and the Assemblies of God, which were established and secure by the late 1920s, may have lost the fervour of those early days – nobody today would claim that they are living in revival – but they have remained faithful to their early vision. The same is also true of the smaller Apostolic Church and the Apostolic Faith Church sects. They all still stress the specialness and uniqueness of their doctrines.

Sectarian structures – Having tried to introduce some elementary sociological ideas in the area of religious typology, however, I think it is now essential to concentrate on sectarian structures themselves. To say, for example, that sects are groups of Christians committed to the voluntary principle in religion and stand against compromising with the world, is not to tell us much. Clearly there are many different forms of religious sects, a number of which are not Christian. Some sects, such as Elim, are essentially 'conversionist' sects in the sense that they wish to bring people to Christ and into the baptism of the Holy Spirit. They do not claim, like the Mormons do, to be the only true Church; rather they stress their special emphasis as a Pentecostal church. Quakers, on the other hand, stress the 'reformation' of society rather than personal salvation. Some sects have, if not exclusively, primarily stressed the 'revolutionary' transformation of this world into a glorious millennium. Adventism of various kinds runs through the Millerites of the nineteenth century, the Jehovah's Witnesses, and in Christian organizations such as the Christadelphians.

Other sects have stressed perfect knowledge (*gnosis*) or techniques of divination and healing; the Spiritualists and Scientologists come to mind. A few sects have been 'utopian', such as the Oneida Community, which attempted to build heaven on earth. Most significantly, many sects have often showed conflicting tendencies towards reformation, revolutionism, conversionism and utopianism. Just as the enthusiastic Quakers developed into quietists (Bryan Wilson would say 'introversionists'), so did the Catholic Apostolic Church quickly move from a Pentecostal enthusiasm into a sacramental High Church, but still with a muted Pentecostalism. Many Pentecostal sects in America have exhibited different aspects of sectarian ideologies in the earlier stages of development, but usually a dominant and consistent set of ideas develops. I mention these changes, because it is one thing to identify a sect, but it is quite another thing to identify the way in which a sect will develop.

Who could have predicted, for example, that the Children of God sect, which started out as a fairly typical – though communitarian – version of fundamentalist evangelicalism, would have moved into left-wing politics, adopted a resident prophet, put 'hookers for Jesus' out on the streets, and ended up promoting paedophilia?

To quote the Children of God here gives us a clue as to why so many Christians in sectarian formations reject the notion that they are a sect. It is not that they will not (in time) 'come clean' and admit that they are a denomination of some kind, but because they object to being lumped together by sociologists with the cults and non-Christian groups. I think that this is a perfectly understandable reaction. However, there is a misunderstanding here. Sociologists do not call Christian groups 'sects' because such groups are necessarily weird or heretical. On the contrary, most sociologists are aware that many sects are in fact more orthodox and traditional than many so-called mainline denominations. Sects have resisted rationalism and modernism far better than many of the denominations, and in particular the Church of England and Methodism.

Sociologists link non-Christian and Christian religious movements together because of their organizational similarities and their general antipathy towards secular society. Sectarian classifications are not theological classifications in any way. The Jehovah's Witnesses, for example, are sociologically similar to the Christadelphians, but theological distinct. To call the Jehovah's Witnesses 'heretics' is perfectly in order within the prescriptive bounds of orthodox Christianity – but it is out of order for a descriptive sociology.

Characteristics and Restorationism

Bryan Wilson's approach to sectarian typology is to search for a cluster of typical characteristics (he is well aware that there are always exceptions to generalizations). Wilson suggests that the sect is typified by the following:

a) it is a voluntary association;
b) membership is by proof to the sect authorities of some special merit, such as knowledge of doctrine or conversion experience;
c) exclusiveness is emphasized and expulsion of deviants exercised;
d) the self-conception is of an elect, or gathered remnant with special enlightenment;
e) personal perfection – however defined – is the expected level of aspiration;
f) there is ideally a priesthood of all believers;
g) there is a high level of lay participation;
h) the member is allowed to express his commitment spontaneously;
i) the sect is hostile or indifferent to the secular society and state;
j) the commitment of the sectarian is always more total and more clearly defined than that of the member of other religious organizations;
k) sects have a totalitarian rather than a segmental hold over their members, and their ideology tends to keep the sectarian apart from 'the world'. The ideological orientation to secular society is dictated by the sect, or member behaviour is strictly specified.[5]

Wilson recognizes that these are ideal characteristics: in practice there will be both variations on these themes and also some will be stressed far more than others. We would expect, for example, a well-established sect like Elim, which is close to being a denomination without becoming one,[6] to be less totalitarian in its control than the sect in the full flush of its youthful struggle for identity.

Before trying to establish what kind of sect Restoration might be, let us go through Bryan Wilson's sectarian characteristics and see how they apply to Restorationism:

a) Voluntary association – both R1 and R2 are committed freely to accept God and be shepherded by his delegated authorities.

b) Membership as special merit – leaders have to be convinced that members are regenerate – born again – and that doctrine is fully understood as a result of a commitment course (whether formally or informally conducted).

c) Exclusiveness – this is emphasized far more in R1 than R2, but both stress distinctness.

d) Conception of elect or remnant – children of the kingdom, special shock troops of the King, with superior teaching to other churches is a strong theme.

e) Personal perfection – the rooting out of selfishness and rebellion is what discipling is all about.

f) Priesthood of all believers – this is a cardinal doctrine, but with an apostolic structure, there is a hierarchy of priesthood.

g) High level of lay participation – there are no part-timers in the kingdom.

h) Express commitment freely – this is encouraged and expected, especially in worship.

i) Hostility to secular society – more true of R1 than R2, but sections of R2 also see the world as 'Babylon'.

j) Commitment more total than other religious groups – this is a primary characteristic of the radical Christians in Restoration.

k) Totalitarian hold – far more true of Restoration than not only denominations, but other Pentecostal sects.

There are other recognizable signs of sectarian formation in Restoration, but they are more clearly marked in R1 than R2. These are: the move from house fellowships to church and community fellowships; the establishment of a clear hierarchy; the development of teams; setting up business organizations; buying up local churches and buildings; buying large churches as foci for apostolic leadership; gathering together the local churches in regions, and at large venues, such as the Dales and Festival; adopting common liturgical styles and a Restorationist argot; a growing hostility to Restorationism from other sects and denominations.

All these are signs not that a new denomination of a sectarian nature is now established, but that it is in the process of becoming established. To say more than that is to go beyond the evidence. R1 does not perceive itself as a sect. R2 perceives R1 as a denomination, but not itself. Other Pentecostal movements see these branches of the house church movement as a denomination (or fast on the way to becoming one). All these perceptions are rarely descriptive. It seems to me that there are a variety of reasons why these groups see Restorationism the way they do. For R1 to admit that they have become a sect is to admit that they have failed. R2, if they admit that they are denominationalized, are accepting that they are no better than R1. Pentecostal sects, already established, want no more rivals in an oversubscribed and highly competitive small market. Those in the Charismatic Renewal see the new 'denominations' draining the spiritual energy from the mainline churches. For them, a new denominational structure is both a folly and a betrayal.

I think it absolutely essential, however, that we do not dismiss the Restorationist claim not to be a new denomination or sect out of hand. In other words, there are still some factual matters left to be resolved. For example, Restorationists often say that they cannot be a new denomination because they have no constitution or declared articles of faith. This is true in a formal sense only. The Restoration articles of faith are clear enough, and the commitment courses may not ask new members to sign on the dotted line, but the rules are public knowledge.

But Restorationists also claim that they have no headquarters. This is also true (for now), but sects do not always have a headquarters. The Open Brethren have never had a constitution or a headquarters, but that does not alter the fact that they are an established sect. The reason that they can be considered so is not because they are not a significant force in Christianity, but because they failed to achieve their original goal.[7] That goal, like Restorationism's, was to turn their back upon denominationalism and become no less than 'the Church'.

Restorationists would agree that the Brethren movement failed. They see this related to the absence of the gifts of the Spirit, and a refusal to accept that apostles and prophets are ordained by God for the Church of today. This time, Restorationists feel, the earlier Brethren vision of going beyond denominations in order to found the universal Church, will succeed. The very fact that Restorationists believe this poses a very interesting problem in our understanding of sects. Does not this idea of theirs – the search for universality and comprehensiveness – sound far more like Weber's Church than sect? Most sects arise clinging to one idea, or special doctrine. Often salvation is seen as belonging exclusively to themselves, or they see their own movement as possessing the most perfect expression of it. Sects that turn their back upon the world usually do so with a rising sense of their own self-importance and uniqueness. The Restorationist vision does not seem to be sectarian in this sense at all. They want to fill the whole world with the kingdom; and they hope that the whole of divided Christendom will be swallowed up in the restored Church.

Bryan Wilson points out that a few special sects do indeed look, on the surface, as if they are churches. Such religious movements, he maintains, are radical reformers or 'restored churches' (his phrase not mine)[8] who seek to bring back a pure unsullied religion which has been lost. In practice, however, they compete with other churches, sometimes aggressively, and become separatist. Their rejection of other religious denominations and structures warrants their inclusion as sects. He cites two historical examples of restorationist sects: the Catholic Apostolic Church, and Brethrenism.

I believe that modern-day Restoration is the third

restorationist sect to emerge in Britain in the last 150 years, and the first of the twentieth century. In many ways, Restorationism is a synthesis of the Pentecostalism and apostolic structure of Irving's followers, and the anti-denominationalism, simplicity and evangelicalism of the Brethren. All three movements reject the old wineskins of the traditional denominations. All three movements, inter-estingly, are primarily middle class. Modern Restorationism, however, does not have the upper-class flavour of the earlier movements. Neither can we under-stand it without seeing it in relation to denominational Pentecostalism. It is this Pentecostalism that provides the glue that makes the synthesis stick.

In the next two chapters I want to look at modern Restoration in the light of these three movements: early Brethrenism, Irving and the beginnings of the Catholic Apostolic Church, and the first few years of classical Pentecostalism. The historical perspective lends substance to Bryan Wilson's abstract typologies, and also enables us to understand more fully the nature of restorationist sects.

Adjusting to the Possibility of Failure

To end this chapter, however, in order to correct what might seem to be a slur on the intelligence of Restoration leaders, I should point out that many leaders have given these matters a great deal of thought. They all know that movements fail, and they have read Church history as much as anyone. John Noble, for example, realized the dangers of denominationalism back in 1974. He holds a view on sectarian development which is quite common in Restoration circles. Like David Matthew, he sees the emer-gence of new religious movements as a means used by the Holy Spirit to promote aspects of truth that have been lost or neglected.

Furthermore, what sociologists might use as a criterion of sectarianism, he might want to see as evidence of bring-ing truth out of an apostate Church. Indeed, I think Arthur

Wallis would reject much of my argument on the sociology of sectarianism not only because sociology is still thought of as demonic[9] or subversive of faith in some evangelical circles, but also because he would see the coming out – the radical separation – as a work of God's Spirit. Denominations have basically had it for Arthur. God is calling his people out, and no amount of sociologizing is going to alter that!

My sociologizing, however, is not designed to 'rubbish' the work or belittle it.[10] I have deliberately avoided prescriptivism. On the basis of a sociology and history (as we shall see) of religious movements, it simply has to be said – using these criteria alone – that the Restoration movement is the crucible for at least one and possibly two emerging sects.

Bryn Jones accepts that the earlier revivalist movements foundered, and that the Pentecostal churches failed to continue their momentum. (I think that Pentecostalism was a renewalism that went wrong rather than a full-blown restorationism.) He believes that the Renewal movement can never radically repair the damage done to the Church by denominationalism. Bryn's perspective on revivals shows that he has a sense of history. God, he claims, is calling the Church to himself. All the great revivals of the past are foretastes of the true deluge of the latter rain. The people involved in these movements (like himself) were certain that they were in the final generation. They were all convinced that their revival would be the final chapter in the gospel story.

Despite these facts, as Bryn sees them, he is convinced that his churches are involved in part of that final chapter. He told me that he would not, he could not, admit that they were going to go the same way as the rest of Church history. I have no doubt that Bryn, David Matthew and all the leaders of R1 are convinced that God is on course and that they are with him.[11] But Bryn is no fool. It is not in his nature to court failure. He is a man with a vision, and the idealist in him sees nothing less than God's Church filling the earth in preparation for the King's return. Nevertheless, he knows that revival is not dependent on him. As a last word on the matter, he said to me that whether he was right about his own work, or whether he personally would fail (and even if Restoration became another denomination), God would not give up on his Church. His plans would continue: the kingdom would be restored, and revival would sweep the world.

R2, I feel, might be prepared to settle for less than moving on to build the final kingdom. The pioneers could become settlers. David Tomlinson, for example, who is already convinced that R1 is a denomination, is aware that R2 could also become one. He does not want it to do so, and he is by no means convinced that it will become so. Nevertheless, he would be able to adjust to a lesser victory as long as he felt that he was personally doing God's will.

The biggest problem for Restorationists, it seems to me, is not whether their movement will become denominationalized, but whether they will be able to cope with the fact of it should it arrive. Denominationalism is a sly process, it sneaks up on you and catches you unawares. When you are an active and committed member of a new religious movement, you are often the last to know that you have been caught.

Recommended Reading

Bryan Wilson, *Religious Sects* (London: Weidenfeld & Nicolson, 1970).

Andrew Walker, 'From Revival to Restoration', *Social Compass* (1985).

Peter L. Berger, *The Sacred Canopy: Elements of a Sociological Theory of Religion* (New York: Doubleday, 1967).

David Martin and Peter Mullen, *Strange Gifts: A Guide to Charismatic Renewal* (Oxford: Blackwell 1984).

11

CATHOLIC APOSTOLICS AND CHRISTIAN BRETHREN AS THE FORERUNNERS OF RESTORATIONISM

Edward Irving, the Catholic Apostolic Church and Brethrenism are not typically treated together by historians. In my opinion, this is a mistake. Both movements were a response to the upheavals of society caused by the French Revolution and what Thomas Carlyle termed 'industrialism'. Irving and the early Brethren leaders were appalled at the disintegration of the Church into competitive denominations that seemed, to them, devoid of the glory of Christ. Furthermore, there are interesting and important historical and theological overlaps between the two groups. For these reasons, I intend to look at them together.

Irving(ism) and Early Brethrenism[1]

What eventually became the Catholic Apostolic Church, and a group of Christians who preferred to be called 'Christians' or 'Christian Brethren', were two movements which were born out of an eschatological conviction. This conviction, stated baldly, was the belief that the second coming of Christ was imminent.

Prior to the early nineteenth century, the general view of adventism among many Protestants was the belief that Christ would return at some date in the future after the world had been rid of Pope and Turk, and subsequent to the Jews being restored to Palestine.[2] The hope of the Christian, therefore, was death, and certainly not a hope in an imminent return of Christ to rule in a glorious kingdom. The millennium, in their schema, was usually seen as belonging to history prior to the *parousia*.

For those who like their history tinged with irony, the developments in adventist theory, following the French Revolution, and having such major consequences in Protestant nonconformity, were dominated by the thinking of three Jesuits. Indeed, the beginning of the nineteenth century witnessed the origin of a modern brand of prophetic interpretation which has fascinated evangelical groups ever since. (There were, of course, waves of adventism in the late Middle Ages and in the early seventeenth century.)

W. Cuninghame, in 1813, had published a prophetic work claiming that Christ would return to the earth, personally, before a millennium became established upon earth. This 'futurism' was denied by a growing number of supporters of the writings of Alcazar, a Jesuit priest who had died in 1613. He had argued that the prophecies of the book of Revelation had already been fulfilled at the time of ancient Rome. This 'historicism' saw Nero as antichrist (later versions opted for Caligula), Rome as Babylon, and the millennium as commencing with the defeat of imperial paganism by an imperial Christianity in the person of Constantine.[3]

Cuninghame's futurism, however, was supported by two other Jesuit writers. Riberia, who died in 1591, taught that antichrist would be an actual person who would build a new temple in Jerusalem, forbid Christianity, be acknowledged as leader of the Jews, and eventually become conqueror of the world. This would all be done in a space of a literal three-and-a-half years. Perhaps the single greatest influence on Protestant adventism came from a book that first appeared in English in 1826, to be followed in 1827 by a two-volume edition translated and with a long foreword by Edward Irving. Ostensibly written by a converted Jew, Ben-Ezra, and entitled *The Coming of Messiah in Glory and Majesty*, the book was in fact written by a Chilean Jesuit, Manuel de Lucunza, who died in 1801.

In Lucunza's futuristic schema, we get the idea of the antichrist as a confederacy of persons, a great deal of emphasis on the destiny of the Jews seen in terms of a separate covenant with God, and Jerusalem as the centre of God's reunion with mankind. When Jesus bodily returns to earth, he will not come initially in power and glory, but secretly for the saints. This 'secret rapture'[4] was to be a 'meeting in the air', where the dead saints and the living faithful servants of Christ would be caught up to meet him. This interpretation of Lucunza leaves the judgments and the wrath of God to fall upon the unjust, while the so-called 'great tribulation' would be missed by the saints. The tribulation would be survived by some people who would refuse to blame God for their troubles and repent of their sins. These people would constitute the rank and file of the millennial kingdom on earth, which would be ruled by the returned saints and Christ himself.

Variations on these Jesuit speculations have dominated fundamentalist and some evangelical groups ever since. In Elim and the Assemblies of God, for example, a rather lurid novel, *The Mark of the Beast*, was all the rage before the Second World War. I read it as a young boy, but had no idea (and probably nor did the author) that the prophetic theories in the book stemmed primarily from the Jesuits! The futurism to which Irving and Darby (the leading Brethren founder) subscribed, was not really a 'latter rain' eschatology. On the contrary, despite a conviction that God would restore his Church in the face of apostasy, this was seen against the background of appalling world disasters and destruction. Irving saw the Church revived again, 'terrible as an army of banners', but he did not expect it to become a mountain that would fill the whole earth. The vision of destruction which Irving and Darby both envisaged is precisely what modern Restoration opposes.

The Albury and Powerscourt Conferences – What crystallized this vision of the 'last things' into firm convictions which became a major impetus (I believe, *the* major impetus) behind the Brethren movement and the so-called Irvingites, were two conferences held over a number of years. Out of the Albury conferences in Surrey in 1826–30, and Irving's congregation in London, emerged the group called the Catholic Apostolic Church. The other conferences at Powerscourt in Ireland in 1831–34, gave shape to the movement of Brethrenism.[5] By this time, Brethrenism was already in existence in embryo, as the Plymouth church, for example, was already functioning.

The people gathered at Powerscourt were mainly – but not exclusively – disaffected Anglican evangelicals. The Albury circle were more broadly based, and included not only Anglicans but Presbyterians and Independents. Henry Drummond, who originated the Albury conferences, was an evangelical, and so too was the Revd Armstrong (both of whom would become apostles in the new church). However, Edward Irving was neither an evangelical nor a low churchman. His Scottish Presbyterianism was of a high church variety both in terms of a doctrine of sacraments and holy orders. Interestingly, too, John Nelson Darby, the most dynamic and controversial of the early Brethren, held to a high church theology as far as ecclesiology was concerned.[6]

The members of both conferences were from the middle classes and aristocracy. Many participants were excellent scholars. Albury could boast a world scholar in Hebrew, but many people from both conferences were proficient in Greek and Hebrew and well-versed in theology and philosophy. The Powerscourt group, despite being more uniform than the Albury set, were marginally better educated. Benjamin Newton was, in my opinion, the finest scholar the Brethren movement produced, until Darby hounded him out in 1845. The most adventurous and wide-ranging thinker of either group was Edward Irving, whose incarnational and trinitarian doctrines so excited Samuel Coleridge that he described him as having 'the heart and unction' of Martin Luther.[7]

The two conferences are, in fact, connected personally. Lady Powerscourt attended the Albury conferences. The journal of this young widow reveals her to be closer to the mystical and Pentecostal doctrines of Irving in some respects than the more conventional evangelicalism of Brethrenism. Irving himself visited Lady Powerscourt in Ireland. Shortly afterwards, a smaller, private version of Powerscourt began before the full conferences commenced in 1831.

A number of Irving's followers attended Powerscourt, although we do not know their names. Brethren historians, on the whole, have not been anxious to show the connections between Irving and Brethrenism. One writer, Timothy Stunt, has made an attempt to show some interesting personal connections.[8] Bulteel at Oxford, for example, was a clergyman who resigned in protest against the apostasy of the Church of England. He was supported by Newton and Darby. Later he joined Irving's circle, and after the great man's death in 1834, he became a member of the Catholic Apostolic Church. When he became disillusioned with this movement in later years, he again made contact with the Brethren. The Revd Armstrong, before he became an apostle in the Catholic Apostolic Church, worked for a time with one of the leading Plymouth Brethren, Dowglass. This gentleman later left the Plymouth church and the Brethren movement, and supported the Catholic Apostolic Church for the rest of his life.

John Nelson Darby, who was to become the leader of the exclusive branch of Brethrenism, taught the doctrine of the 'secret rapture'. He denied that he took this from Irving, but on this issue and many other aspects of futurism,[9] it must be said that many of the Powerscourt ideas were very similar to those promulgated through the *Morning Watch* – Drummond's own quarterly journal, but also a vehicle for many of Irving's later views.

More broadly, Stunt points out, both the 'Irvingites' and the Brethren were movements in search of purity. For both of them, the Church had gone wrong. They taught separation from the world, and expected the imminent return of Christ. Neither group, in the first instance, held to a narrow individualistic pietism based on biblical authority alone. They believed in a high doctrine of the Church under the direction of the Holy Spirit. To this, one could add that both groups had a strong commitment to a universal, catholic Church.[10] They both believed that they were movements for the unity of the Church.

The question of charismatic gifts – The early Brethren were not aggressively Baptist, and a number of the Anglican members, including Darby, did not see believers' baptism as a cardinal teaching. It is not the case that Albury was Pentecostalist and Powerscourt was not. On the contrary, interest in the restored gifts divided Albury as well as Powerscourt. We can see from the Powerscourt reports that there was considerable interest in the possibility that divine healing and the charismatic gifts of the Spirit might be a sign of the imminent return of Christ. One of the Brethren's great leaders, Captain Percy Hall, was particularly keen on the possibility of a new Pentecost. Darby himself (though never Newton) was by no means closed to this possibility.

When news reached Albury in 1830 that there had been an outbreak of tongues at Rosneath and healing at Row in Scotland, there was intense excitement. Irving had already presented a very powerful theological argument in favour of the gifts, based on his trinitarian and incarnational works.[11] He was desperately anxious to discover whether the Scottish phenomena were really the work of the Holy Spirit or some demonic counterfeit. The Albury group sent an investigative team, which included Cardale, who was to become the leading apostle in the Catholic Apostolic Church. Darby also decided to go to Scotland to see the 'miracles' for himself.

The Albury team came back convinced that the Holy Spirit had been restored to the Church. From that moment, until tongues broke out in Regent Square Church in

October 1831, Irving and some 600 people daily prayed for an outpouring of the Spirit in London. Darby, on the other hand, was not convinced of the genuineness of the gifts. He did not like some of the biblical prophecies and doctrines given in 'the power', and as they agreed with Irving's speculative theology rather than his own, he withheld support. A little later, Newton attended an Irving Pentecostal service (he does not tell us whether it was at Regent Square or Newman Street). The atmosphere there, he felt, was not from God, and he found that he was not able to concentrate on Christ's atonement.

However, what clinched it for the Brethren – and ended any latent Pentecostalism that there might have been – was the discovery that Irving's Christology was heretical. In fact, Irving had already been tried for heresy by the London Presbytery of the Church of Scotland in 1830. He was found guilty of believing in the sinfulness of Christ's nature. In 1833, after the outbreak of Holy Ghost manifestations at Regent Square, Irving was again tried at Annan in Scotland, where he had been ordained. The charges were the same and so was the verdict; this time, however, Irving was excommunicated.

Nothing hurt Irving and his circle more than the confessions of a man called Baxter, who in his *Narrative of Facts* revealed that, after supporting Irving, and having been one of the leading prophets in the new group, he discovered to his horror that Edward Irving taught heresy concerning our Lord's human nature. This discovery immediately led to the end of his 'delusion', and he never again found that he could speak in 'the power' (as the Irvingites called being under the influence of the Spirit). For the rest of his life, Baxter remained a respectable evangelical layman, but a consistent and persistent opponent of Irvingism.

Irving's so called heresy was the peccability (or liability to sin) of Christ in his human nature. Darby, in revolting against this notion, was not only joining the majority of the evangelical world at that time, but he was also, like Baxter, seeing a direct link between Irving's heresy in Christology and the issue of Pentecostalism *per se*. Newton also condemned Irving on both counts, but in fact his doctrine of the incarnation was far closer to Irving's than Darby's theology. This proved to be his undoing, because Darby was able to use this as an excuse for railroading him out of Plymouth. There are some very important theological issues which we cannot go into here, but I would like to comment on them briefly.

Irving and the early Brethren – It does not surprise me that when the Exclusive Brethren in the 1930s made their last attempt as a Christian group to become influenced by an outsider, they chose Watchman Nee. Nee was involved with the Exclusives for a time, until they ostracized him for consorting with Open Brethren. His spirituality owed much to a Darbyite theology. Both Nee and Darby tended to treat Christ's human nature as unreal. This docetism, as it is called, with its strong (almost gnostic) sense of the evil of matter, is precisely what Irving had been fighting against. Newton thought that he overstated his case, but he too thought that the ancient teachings of the Church should be preserved: that Christ in becoming human became a real man, not a facsimile of a man, nor clothed in the unfallen flesh of Adam.

At the very least, the long-standing belief in Brethren circles that Irving was a heretic, and that this *ipso facto* made Pentecostalism suspect, needs challenging. Professor Tom Torrance and Professor Colin Gunton are just two notable conservative theologians who would defend Irving's orthodoxy. They realize, in a way in which many Protestants do not, that Irving's doctrine is in line with the early Greek fathers and primitive Calvinism, as opposed to the teachings of Augustine and much later evangelical thought.[12] (Perhaps it is more curious that classical Pentecostals, neo-Pentecostals, and house church radicals have, on the whole, tended to ignore Irving. This is mainly due to lack of knowledge of his teachings and theology, but it is also partly due to the fact that Irving was a high churchman in the strict Calvinist tradition. Modern Pentecostalism has its roots in the low churchmanship of the Holiness movements.)

Irving and the early Brethren leaders both wanted to return to a New Testament Church. They both believed that God was restoring his kingdom through them. From a modern Restorationist point of view, it must look like a lost opportunity that the Brethren and Irving's followers never joined together. If they had, there is no doubt that what would have emerged would have looked very much like Restorationism. The differences between Irving, his followers, and the Brethren, however, were considerable.

The Brethren movement was initially a Christian reformation of great simplicity. 'Irvingism' is really the nickname of the church that grew up around Irving, but which Irving did not found (as Bryan Wilson incorrectly states).[13] The correct name for Irvingism is not 'Irvingites' but the Catholic Apostolic Church. This movement is complex and only marginally connected to Edward Irving himself, who died in 1834. Nevertheless, Irving's own doctrines shaped much of that Church, and so it is worth comparing his understanding of the restored Church with the early Brethren.

The Brethren were solid evangelicals; they were low church in practice (though some of them were high church in theology). Irving disliked what he saw of evangelicalism. He thought it was tainted with the rationalistic doctrines of the Enlightenment, and too taken up with good works and missionary societies. He thought also that evangelicalism treated the Bible as an idol as surely as the Catholics treated the Church as an idol. Methodism he saw as subjective, sentimental and awash in an Arminianism that put faith and self-will before the sovereignty of God. Brethrenism was itself mildly Calvinistic, but in later years it became increasingly attached to the sort of holiness, evangelism and spirituality that was to be found in the Keswick conventions.

Darby, in particular, but most Brethren, too, were iconoclastic on the issue of holy orders. They took the priesthood of all believers literally. There was a genuine commitment to the end of clericalism, and a dislike of any constituted priesthood. Irving, on the other hand, was strongly attached to ordained ministry, and his belief in the purity of holy orders stemmed from primitive Presbyterianism in Scotland and earlier Catholic teachings.

Irving, the Catholic Apostolic Church, and the early Brethren were totally convinced that the Holy Spirit should direct the Church. But the Brethren did not see, unlike their rival restorationists, that this would involve either a commitment to the ecclesiology of Ephesians chapter 4, or a return to the supernaturalism of the Acts of the Apostles. Once Irvingism had been rejected by the Brethren, their doctrine of the Holy Spirit developed more along the lines of Quaker pietism than enthusiastic Pentecostalism.

The unity of the Church, Irving thought initially, would take place within the historic denominations. Catholic Apostolics saw themselves as part of the historic Church – as a witness and signpost to the Christianity of the New Testament. The Brethren saw unity being restored not by the establishment of a new sect, but by the re-establishment of the true Church. When I heard Terry Virgo say on Radio 4 that the Bible only talks of two shapes of the Church – the universal Church of the born again, and the local church where believers meet – he was reiterating Brethren teaching.[14]

Irving believed that Roman Catholicism (not Catholics) was beyond redemption, because it was founded on a false ecclesiology: that the high priest of the Church was not Christ, but his earthly representative, the vicar or Pope of Rome. However, Irving warmed towards the episcopacy of the Church of England, which he recognized as a sister Church to his own Church of Scotland. He believed, on the whole, that Protestantism would preserve a remnant of the faithful. The Brethren were taken with the remnant theology, too, but they believed that denominations were simply not in the plan of God.

In an interesting way, both Irving and the early Brethren – like the later Restorationists – saw the Lord's Table as a central issue of discipleship. For the Brethren, the breaking of bread was the essence of the Church. It was the bond, or covenant, of members of the body of Christ. (Some 150 years later, John Noble told me that the essence of the nascent Restoration movement was breaking bread together, and not doctrines.) Sharing the common table, and following the apostles' teaching – as the Acts of the Apostles records of the early Christians – was the clear and simple ideal of Brethrenism. Evangelical as they were, however, the catholicity of their churchmanship was not matched by a catholic doctrine of sacraments. Irving would have none of this. For him, such doctrines denied both the reality of the mystical body, and the physical means of grace whereby Christians could be united to their head, who is Christ. Irving, in short, believed in the real presence of Christ in the Eucharist – although like the Orthodox, and some Presbyterians before him, he refused to see this in the technical terms of 'essence', 'accident' and 'transubstantiation'.

Developments in Irvingism

Irving's sacramentalism did not include confession (which the Catholic Apostolics also excluded), but it did include a belief in the sacramental efficacy of infant baptism. All these aspects of Irving's teachings, which are so often neglected, explain why, after his death, the Catholic Apostolic Church seemed to turn its back on enthusiasm and opt for what looked more like Tractarianism. In fact, Pentecostalism did continue, but in an orderly fashion, with set times in the formal liturgy for the utterances of the Holy Spirit.

Towards the end of his life, Irving did seem to believe in a charismatic apostolate. Having said that, we do not know how far he had worked out the full implications of this. Like modern-day Restorationists, the apostles of 'Irvingism' were called by prophecy, although in a seemingly arbitrary way. Henry Drummond, the banker and member of parliament, acting in 'the power', called out a Mr Cardale to be the first apostle. 'Art thou not an apostle!' were the rhetorical words. By 1832, Cardale and Drummond were both apostles. Irving's circle believed that the correct order of the Church was apostles, prophets, angels,[15] priests, evangelists, deacons and readers. This full range of holy orders was developed after Irving's death. Before he died, Irving was to discover that the circle was the tail that wagged the dog. He genuinely tried, but found it difficult to submit to the new apostolic authority. After he was excommunicated from the Church of Scotland, Irving was forbidden to officiate as a priest in the CAC until he was re-ordained by the apostles. Irving was called to be an angel, and he presided over the church at Newman Street, but under the authority of the emerging apostleship.

Irving's health rapidly failed in 1833, and in the following year, with the blessing of Cardale, he set off for his native Scotland to start a new work there. That October, Irving entered Glasgow clearly dying. On the 7th or 8th of December he died. He was buried in the crypt of Glasgow Cathedral, under the stained-glass window of John the Baptist.

Like Arthur Wallis, so many years later, Irving was passed over as an apostle. He was the catalyst of the Catholic Apostolic Church, which reverenced him as a John the Baptist, but not a founder of the Church. What eventually became the mature Church is surely one of the most unique movements in sectarian history.

It was decided that there were to be only twelve apostles, who would have full authority in all matters doctrinal, liturgical and financial. (Unlike the Brethren, the Catholic Apostolics tithe.) Many of the excesses and confusions of the first few years – this is their own perception – were curbed, and gradually the new Church became established. At first, as they had been so influenced by Irving, the liturgical style resembled the staid order of Regent Square. Soon, however, all vestiges of Presbyterianism disappeared from the church services. They were replaced by a developed liturgy, complete with incense, lights and vestments, and based on Orthodox, Catholic and Protestant forms.

The Church held onto Irving's 'heretical' Christology, his Reformed Catholicism and his biblical prophecies. They developed prophetic interpretations of their own, and eventually melded together scriptural literalism and sacramental Catholicism with a muted Pentecostalism – and a number of unique views of their own.

Most significantly, it was decided to choose only twelve apostles as evidence of the restored 'twelve apostles of the Lamb'. They did not accept later interpretations of Ephesians chapter 4, which saw the possibility of more apostles. (Today's Restorationists, for example, see no limit in principle to the number of apostles.) The Catholic Apostolic Church sought to legitimate their choice of only twelve apostles by this text: 'And round about the throne were four and twenty seats: and upon the seats I saw four and twenty elders sitting, clothed in white raiment; and they had on their heads crowns of gold' (Rev 4:4 AV). The Tractarian leader, Edward Pusey, wrote: 'Yet it is, on the very surface, a large claim, that the Twelve Apostles should be revived in the nineteenth century, in the persons of twelve English Gentlemen.'[16]

The apostles were 'separated by the Holy Spirit' from their secular jobs or priestly charges, and all moved to Albury, which became the headquarters of the new Church. The Catholic Apostolic Church did not see itself as a new sect – and it never has done. Like their contemporaries, the early Brethren, and like their modern Restorationist counterparts, they were reluctant to be called anything. They eventually accepted the title 'Catholic and Apostolic Church' as a result of an accident.

A government official, engaged in some form of census, asked a leading member of the Church what his denomination was called. His reply was that he belonged to the 'Catholic and Apostolic Church'.

I cannot go into all the many liturgical and theological innovations of the apostles, their successes and failures. It would be easy to poke fun at what seems to be a classical case of Victorian eccentricity. But the curious thing about the Catholic Apostolic Church is that the more you research it, visit the churches, and talk to the last few remaining members, the more you discover a dignity and a genuine spirituality that will not be denied.

The twelve apostles ordained angels and priests, but left no provision for a second generation of believers. They thought that Christ would return before they all died out. Throughout the nineteenth century, the new Church continued to grow in Great Britain, Europe, and to a small extent in America. At its height, the approximate size of the movement was some 30,000 people.

In 1901, the last apostle died. Henceforth, without apostolic authority, there could be no more ordinations. Other Churches had paid little attention to the Catholic Apostolic Church, and with the death of the last apostle, the movement gradually declined (though a sectarian offshoot continues to thrive in Europe). The year 1902 saw the beginning of the 'silence' – 'And when he had opened the seventh seal, there was silence in heaven about the space of half an hour' (Rev 8:1 AV). During this silence, which is said to be the last moment of human history, the members of the Catholic Apostolic Church have quietly waited for the return of their Lord. They no longer proselytize, and throughout the twentieth century, as the last angels and priests have died, one by one the parishes have closed. In an act of generosity and solidarity with the universal Church, many Catholic Apostolic Church members were sent back to the historic churches. In 1971, the last officiating priest died, and the liturgy of what had become a worshipping Church in the historic tradition ceased. Today, a handful of members still meet at Paddington and Gordon Square. The litany of intercession is still followed on behalf of the universal Church. Like Milton, members of the Catholic Apostolic Church insist, 'they also serve who only stand and wait'.

I have met some Catholic Apostolics who see the outbreak of the Welsh Revival in 1904, and the later Pentecostal movements, as a sign of hope that God would fill all his Church (and not just their part) with his Spirit. One lady told me that she thought that Colin Urquhart seemed to be a man of God. Other Catholic Apostolics prefer the spirituality of the Orthodox Church to Pentecostal enthusiasm, and a number have joined the Greek Orthodox Church. I certainly believe that the Catholic Apostolic Church has had an internal spiritual history that is quite genuine, but its external role in Christendom has not been to restore the kingdom, but to establish a sect. An old lady of ninety kindly allowed me to interview her. She was married to one of the last priests in the church. When I asked her whether she thought the Catholic Apostolic Church had become a denomination, she said: 'Well I suppose we did, but we never meant to be.'

Developments in Brethrenism

And what happened to the fine ideals of the Brethren? At its best, those ideals remain today. Donald Tinder's article, 'The Brethren Movement in the World Today', for example, exhibits those ideals. In practice, however, Brethrenism ran into a serious problem soon after its formation. Its seeming simplicity turned out to be a delusion. The breaking of bread with fellow Christians is one thing, but how do we know who are our fellow Christians? Or, put another way: if the common table is not to be defiled, heretical and unworthy Christians must not be allowed to pollute the holy meal. The last supper is marred by the presence of Judas; partakers of the one loaf must be true Christians only. (If this sounds more like a Catholic doctrine than an evangelical one, it certainly has its counterpart in sacramental liturgies. The Eastern Orthodox, for example, still jealously guard the 'heavenly mysteries' from the heterodox.)

Within the Brethren ranks, the drive for purity became more dominant than the drive for unity. To some extent, Darby's great idealism and vision of one Church resisting the devil and apostasy, carried with it a quest for purity. Just as today, Restorationists cannot envisage a true Church as one that includes the unjust or unregenerate, neither could Darby stand heresy or sin of any kind. This man of extraordinary talents could not resist playing Witchfinder General.

The split between Exclusive and Open Brethren – In the Early Church, a distinction was always made between dogmatic statements, theological opinion and pious opinion. On the fundamentals of the faith, concerning the incarnation, life, death and resurrection of Jesus Christ, and the doctrine of the Holy Trinity, there had to be one undivided faith. There was room, however, for disagreement on matters of an important but not essentially dogmatic kind. Darby, to the cost of the Brethren movement, failed to recognize such distinctions.

Darby and Newton had coped with a number of disagreements between them. Darby was irate because Newton was not too taken with his theories of dispensationalism. Whilst the Powerscourt conferences were continuing in Ireland, Newton was holding meetings in Plymouth. Newton would have no truck with a secret rapture, and was convinced that the return of Christ would be a single event. Darby saw the second coming in two stages. First, Christ would come to meet the saints in the air, and secondly, he would return in glory with the saints to judge an apostate Church and the godless world. At first, tensions between the two men provoked no more than an agreement to disagree.

In 1845, a follower of Darby discovered some notes taken down by a lady during one of Newton's sermons. These notes seemed to reiterate the doctrines of Irving on our Lord's human nature. Newton was rigorously pursued by Darby over this matter, and was eventually forced publicly to recant. He published a full confession of his errors, but, as Harold Rowdon points out, Darby regarded Newton's confession as 'little more than an effort to throw dust in the eyes of the reader'.[17] Newton lost the support of many of his fellow elders at Plymouth. In 1847, he withdrew from the assembly, and played no further part in Brethren history.

The following year brought the split that led to the division of the movement into the Exclusive and the Open or Plymouth Brethren. In Bethesda Chapel, Bristol, Müller and Craik, two of the main leaders of the new movement, received a request from two brothers to receive them into fellowship. These men had been in Plymouth. Some Bethesda elders objected. The Woodfalls brothers were examined to test their orthodoxy. They passed the test and were admitted to fellowship and to share in the Lord's table. Darby, who was passing through Bristol on his way to Exeter in April 1848, made it quite clear that he found this judgment unacceptable. He saw it as a means of sneaking Newton's theology through the back door. He insisted that Newton should be publicly condemned.

On 29th June 1848, a statement known as 'The Letter of the Ten' was read out at Bethesda. In it, the elders there refused to say any more concerning Newton's doctrines. Soon Müller and Craik were at loggerheads with Darby over this matter. On 26th August, Darby published a circular to Brethren assemblies, urging them to isolate Bethesda. The majority of assemblies sided with Darby, but a sizeable proportion of churches refused to support him.

In a very short time, the churches that gathered around Darby became more and more obsessed with the question of Christian purity. 'Care meetings' or tribunals were set up to vet members' orthodoxy. The Open Brethren were accused of antinomianism, and Plymouth Brethren accused the Darbyites of legalism. (All this almost makes the accusations of R1 and R2 against each other seem like an action replay.)

Characteristics of Brethrenism – Darbyism, or Exclusivism as it is usually called, has tended towards central control with power residing in one man or an oligarchy – Darby, Kelly, the Taylors and others – but it has never really discovered a totally workable and successful system. Splits and schisms have been endemic in the movement. In Bryan Wilson's terminology, the Exclusivists have become an 'introversionist' sect, stressing separation from not only the world but other Christians.

Today, there are only a few thousand Exclusives left in Great Britain.[18] Since the movement came under the influence of the American Taylor dynasty, there has been considerable scandal and confusion amongst the saints. I was impressed, however, by a paper that Bryan Wilson gave at the London School of Economics in 1984. He said that despite media portrayal as heartless bigots, and a strong antipathy towards them from the Open Brethren, the Exclusives were in fact a jolly and happy lot in many ways. The families, he pointed out, were characterized by a great sense of fun and togetherness (although this does not apply in a family where a member has rejected the faith).

We need reminding in our brief review of Brethrenism that no one was more committed than Darby to the restoration of a New Testament Church that would replace denominationalism. In the early days of the movement, he was a man of vision as well as bigotry. Despite his inability to accept criticism and tolerate deviations from his own theological system, he was a tireless worker of great intellectual talents. Although he wrote some of the worst English prose that I have ever read, he could write snappy religious pamphlets and coin memorable hymns. From the

Greek, he translated a new version of the English Bible, and one in German.

Darby was capable of cruelty and unpleasantness towards his enemies. But the man who destroyed Newton was also the man who was invariably kind to children and people in distress. The story is told of him that on board ship, in order to give a mother rest from a child that would not stop crying, he took the child under his greatcoat and walked with him all night.

It is a pity that Pickering's *Chief Men Among the Brethren*[19] should exclude Newton. Aristocratic and authoritarian he may have been, but he was also an outstanding leader. So many of the first generation of Brethren were men of leadership, culture, intelligence and principle. Anthony Norris Groves, perhaps the wisest and most catholic of all Brethren, was saintly. One thinks also of Lord Congleton, who despised luxury and social class; he would not even have carpets in his house. Captain Percy Hall also stands out. He resigned from the Royal Navy because he could not square his commission with his belief that war was against God's will.

The Christian Brethren were primarily a small but significant exodus from the Church of England. Within a few years, they had turned their back upon her ecclesiastical and sacramental traditions. Believers' baptism quickly became the norm, and some of the earlier catholicity narrowed to form a sort of strict and principled evangelicalism. True to their origins, the Open Brethren have kept the Lord's table open to all who confess Jesus Christ as Lord. Over the years, the Brethren have remained a well-heeled religious movement, but have contributed generously to many missionary and Bible societies.

In the twentieth century, the Brethren have been involved in many interdenominational activities of an evangelical kind. Eric Hutchings, for example, was a Brethren evangelist who had considerable success in the early 1960s. Brethren have often been the unsung heroes in interdenominational evangelical work throughout the world. Unlike many other evangelical groups, Brethrenism has maintained a high level of conservative scholarship. (The work of Professor F. F. Bruce is a good example.) The *Christian Brethren Review* is a fine journal of impeccable scholarship.

If I have been seen to digress to say much about the positive worth of the Brethren (and the Catholic Apostolics), it is because I am anxious to show that I do not think their work is in vain, or of no consequence. I do think, however, that the Brethren movement has not succeeded in its original aims. The 68,000 or so Open Brethren in Great Britain have maintained their commitment to local autonomy, and have consciously resisted denominationalism. However, a certain uniformity of practice and doctrine has become established which merits the term 'sect'. Many Brethren have remained conversionist, but some assemblies are more closed and conservative than others. Pentecostalism has remained a thorn in their sides since the early days of the Catholic Apostolic Church. Bitterly opposed to classical Pentecostalism, some assemblies have been more open to Charismatic Renewal. Modern Restorationism, more than any other form of Pentecostalism, poses a major threat to the Brethren. As we have seen throughout this book, Restoration is replete with ex-Brethren personnel.

Despite the superficial similarities with the Catholic Apostolic ecclesiology, Restoration is really closer to Brethrenism in terms of doctrine and organization on the local level. Indeed, from them they inherit their evangelicalism, anti-denominationalism, anti-clericalism, and principled views on baptism. Having male-dominated ministries and local elders also owes much to the Brethren, as does the emphasis on the purity of church and separation from the world. Restoration is the direct successor of neither Brethrenism nor 'Irvingism', but it is an amalgam of both.[20] The missing ingredient that binds together the first two restorationist movements into the third and new Restorationism is the classical Pentecostalism and Holiness movements of the twentieth century.

Recommended Reading

Harold H. Rowdon, *The Origins of the Brethren* (London:
  Pickering & Inglis, 1967).

Timothy Stunt, 'Irvingite Pentecostalism and the Early
  Brethren', *Christian Brethren Review*, No. 10, December 1965.

Andrew L. Drummond, Edward Irving and His Circle
  (Cambridge: James Clarke & Co. Ltd., 1936).

Andrew Walker, 'Will No One Stand Up for Edward Irving?' *The
  Listener* (6th December 1984).

Columba Flegg, *'Gathered Under Apostles:' A Study of the
  Catholic Apostolic Church* (Oxford University Press, 1992).

12

CLASSICAL PENTECOSTALISM AND RESTORATIONISM

The Beginnings

The outbreak of tongues at Row in Scotland, and Regent Square in London, predates the modern Pentecostal movement by some seventy years. It is generally accepted by Pentecostals that the birth of Pentecostalism began in 1906 at the Azusa Street Mission, Los Angeles.[1] The crucible for American Pentecostalism was the Holiness sects of the nineteenth century. With their Methodist origins, the two-way path of conversion and sanctification became eventually the 'born again' experience and the 'second blessing'. This second religious experience, or initiation, became the full-blown 'baptism in the Holy Spirit' of Pentecostalism. That Pentecostalism as a mass movement should have its roots firmly in the soil of a Holiness spirituality would not have pleased Irving. He considered such enthusiasm to be sentimental and theologically arid.[2]

In Europe, the picture is a little more complicated. Anglican evangelicalism and Lutheranism played their part, but so too did numerous Holiness movements. The Salvation Army, for example, with its Pentecostal hymnology – 'Let the fire fall, let the fire fall' – combined with the Keswick Conventions (commencing in 1875) to provide a major Holiness momentum. Two Holiness groups, the Pillar of Fire and the Pentecostal League, contained many churches which were only a breath away from a new tongues movement.

Catherine Price of Brixton is credited as the first speaker in tongues of British Pentecostalism. The 1907 date for this event, however, needs to be seen against a much more significant cause of Pentecostalism: the Welsh Revival. This phenomenon, so similar to the American Holiness revivals of C. G. Finney, was nevertheless more than a Holiness revival. Starting in 1904, and continuing in bursts until the Great War, this wave of enthusiasm broke down the traditional barriers between Wesleyans and Calvinists. The revivals had considerable social and political consequences, and had a social communitarian dimension so often lacking in the pietistic Holiness Camp Meetings of North America.

The Welsh Revival, coinciding with the great reformist Liberal government of 1905–09, provided part of the fuel for what was to be the last great secular power surge of British nonconformity. ('No Rome on the rates!' shouted the Welsh radicals against the 1902 Balfour Education Act.) It also provided power for the nascent Pentecostal movement. Many of its leaders were converted through the preaching of Evan Roberts, the most successful of the many Welsh evangelists, or his associates. George and Stephen Jeffreys of Elim, D. P. Williams of the Apostolic Church, and Donald Gee of the Assemblies of God, are the most prominent examples.

The Anglican vicar, Alexander A. Boddy, from All Saints, Monkwearmouth, was also associated with the Welsh Revival. It was at his church in Sunderland, and under the influence of an English-born Norwegian, T. B. Barrat (who was directly influenced by the Los Angeles revival), that British Pentecostalism got under way in 1907. The early years of the Pentecostal movement are marked by a mushrooming of independent groups, rivalries and opposition from mainline denominations. It is impossible to go into these developments here, but it will be worthwhile to examine the origins of the Apostolic Church, and to look at events in the denominationalism of Elim and the Assemblies of God.

The Apostolic Church

A dispute arose in South Wales concerning the institution-alization and content of prophecy. Most of the new Pentecostals saw prophecy as an ecstatic utterance to be used for the exhortation and edification of the local church. At Penygroes, however, it was believed that prophecy was to give direction to the Church and should be instituted as an ordinance of Church government along with the offices of apostle, evangelist and elder. W. J. Williams became a prophet, and his brother (those Welsh brothers again!) an apostle. Soon other Welsh churches joined the growing movement founded firmly and self-consciously on Ephesians chapter 4. In 1918, the Burning Bush Assembly in Scotland joined, and later, English churches were established.

The Williams brothers had no idea that the new Apostolic Church had interpreted Ephesians chapter 4 in a similar way to Edward Irving and the Catholic Apostolic Church. Their discovery of this fact increased their sense of awe and conviction that this time God would call out a New Testament Church in all her glory.

But while the Apostolic Church developed the most authoritarian and hierarchical organization within British Pentecostalism (until modern Restorationism), there is little similarity with the earlier Irving experiment. No angels or priesthood emerged. Instead, there was, in descending order: apostle, prophet, shepherd (pastor), teacher, evangelist, elder, deacon and deaconness. The high church-manship of the early Brethren and Irving is missing. So too is the catholicity and universality of those movements. The Apostolic Church was born in sectarianism, and, despite a strong commitment to world mission, there was a built-in separation from the start. This separation was somewhat foisted upon them, because the rest of British Pentecostalism has never really accepted them.[3] Because sectarianism and separatism were built in to the Apostolic Church, I do not think, sociologically speaking, that the

Apostolic Church qualifies as a full-blown Restorationist sect.

Nevertheless, they certainly set the scene for modern Restorationism, and are a vital link with the nineteenth-century movements. Restoration today has partly recaptured the universalist spirit of their restorationist precursors, but their organization and theology is far closer to the Apostolic Church. Apostle Williams did not identify apostleship with either the twelve apostles of the Lamb (Rev 21:14) or the twenty-four elders before the throne (Rev 4:4). He saw a revived apostolate in exactly the same way as modern Restoration.

Because Bryn and Keri Jones hail from Aberdare, and as Arthur Wallis and David Lillie were directly influenced by former leaders within the Apostolic Church, I think it is not unreasonable to postulate that the linkage between the two movements is a substantial one as far as ecclesiological theory is concerned. If this is true, then it reinforces Bryn Jones's insistence, and John Noble's, that their thinking was already partially formed before the Americans arrived.[4] (But did the Apostolic Church influence Ortiz and the Fort Lauderdale Five?)

Discipling or shepherding doctrines have never existed in the Apostolic Church, but the apostolate contains an authority and casuistic power not typical in the majority of classical Pentecostal Churches (although things are changing now). Unlike modern Restorationism, it has remained primarily a working-class movement. Its earlier history and development was marred by prophetic rivalries. Increasingly, over the years, the prophets have been subjected to apostolic and elder control. Apostles were first called by prophecy (this seems to be a universal feature of charismatic apostolates) and emerged as leaders for life.

Clearly, the Apostolic Church is closer to modern Restorationism than any other Pentecostal group from the classical era. The Apostolics today, however, are far more denominationally conscious, and far more centralized than the Restorationists. Penygroes in South Wales is now the headquarters of the world Apostolic movement. If I may be allowed a subjective note: the Apostolic Church and Restoration look very similar, but in feel and tone they are quite different. Restoration (R2 in particular) is theologically similar to classical Pentecostalism, but its spirituality tends to reflect the cosy middle-classness of the Charismatic Renewal.

On Radio 4, in the programme *Front Room Gospel*, I gave the unintentionally misleading impression that the Apostolic Church was an insignificant sect. This is not so if you look at it in a world context (rather than a European context, as I was doing). We have a genuine curiosity here. In Great Britain, the Apostolic Church has never really established itself as a major established sect. Today, they have no more than 5,000 adherents. England has some sixty-seven congregations, some of them numbering only a few dozen worshippers. Scotland has twenty-nine congregations (Hollenweger thought more than forty, fifteen years ago), Northern Ireland thirteen, and Wales sixty-one congregations.[5]

At first glance, this is surprising. It is certainly not the case that Apostolic meetings are boring. On the contrary, to be impressionistic again, the Apostolic churches that I have attended in Wales were the most emotionally intense that I have ever experienced in Pentecostalism outside Black churches. I recall wonderful *hwyl* preaching and elegant prophecies. Perhaps there is a clue here. The Apostolics in Wales seem to have encapsulated the old Welsh revivalism in an institutional form. There is something essentially Welsh chapel about the Apostolic Church that you cannot find in Elim and the Assemblies of God. The main cause for their relative lack of success in Britain, however, is their authoritarian structure, and what many people see as an extreme form of Pentecostalism. Donald Gee's view of the Apostolic Church is one I hear from many classical Pentecostals in regard to modern Restorationism: 'To bestow New Testament titles of offices upon men and women and then consider that by doing so we are creating apostolic assemblies parallel to those of the Primitive Church is very much like children playing at churches.'[6]

The Apostolic Church has made some modest gains in Europe, but in Africa they have been a phenomenal success. In Nigeria (the home of so many messianic and cross-cultural cults) they have some 3,000 congregations, and hundreds more in other countries of the Third World. As a missionary operation, therefore, the Apostolic Church is a great success, but operating from a weak home base. There is obviously a cultural factor here. The special emphasis on the prophetic word, and the institutionalism of the charismatic gifts is alien to the individualism and democratic traditions of Western culture. Conversely, the success of ecstatic authoritarianism is to be expected amongst the weakened and dispossessed members of Nigeria's competing tribal structure.

The Apostolic Church may very well offer an organizational lesson for Restoration. Can the Restoration structure, which is even more paternalistic and controlled – despite its middle-classness – ever grow beyond a certain level? How can Restorationists persuade the British people, in any substantial numbers, to forsake self-reliance and individualism for a system of paternalism? The Apostolic Church faced with a conflict between the prophets and apostles (which the Catholic Apostolic Church faced before them) settled in favour of a dominating apostolate. This led to a certain amount of inbred rigidity and inward-lookingness: the conversionist sect abroad is virtually an introversionist sect at home.

The charismatic ecclesiology has not failed as an organizational structure, but it does seem to have built-in deficiencies as far as church growth is concerned. In our culture, at least, charismatic apostolates have so far never succeeded in heading a religious movement of any great size. In this respect, the growth of the more evangelistic apostolic teams of R1 may offer greater flexibility. This partly depends, as it did for the Brethren, on whether the evangelistic thrust is greater than the drive for certainty and purity. In the Apostolic Church, apostles are chosen for life. This itself is a recipe for rigidity – for it soon turns the new wineskins back into the old. Apostles for life face similar problems to trade union presidents who are elected for life. What happens when personal popularity is no longer recognized and charisma disappears? The answer is that you are left with the legalistic authority of the office. The charismatic apostolate too easily becomes the priestly magisterium.

Issues of authority, charismatic leadership and bureaucratic organization are at the heart of the institutionalization of Elim. To look at Elim and the Assemblies of God is to look at the most successful of Pentecostal denominations in Britain, and also the last two significant Christian sects to have become established since the First World War. Looking at these classical Pentecostalists, Restorationism may very well be looking at its future.

Elim and the Assemblies of God

If the Welsh Revival provided the immediate resources for Pentecostalism, it would not be true to say that the new movement started in a sectarian fashion. On the contrary, the Pentecostal Missionary Union, which was founded in 1909 to support the growing band of missionaries and provide them with some training, was an organization within the churches. Or to be more precise, it was an organization like the Fountain Trust, which operated within the context of the existing denominations, with input from the Independents.

Alexander Boddy saw Pentecostalism very much in the same terms as does Michael Harper today; and he remained an Anglican vicar all his life. Many other Pentecostalists within the mainline churches saw the movement in ecumenical terms. However, there were so many different groups and organizations that it was perhaps inevitable that some should crystallize into sectarian formations.

A group of independent churches that eventually became known as the Assemblies of God had many successful evangelists such as Smith Wigglesworth and Nelson J. Parr. But the two men who really dominated early Pentecostalism, after Boddy, are Stephen and George Jeffreys. I have to agree with Walter Hollenweger's assessment that it is unlikely that British Pentecostalism has ever produced a more naturally talented pair.[7]

Stephen and George Jeffreys – The brothers were brought up in Maesteg. Stephen was a miner and George a salesman in the Co-op. Stephen, by all accounts, was a spectacular preacher. He was often carried away by passion and patches of rhetorical eloquence, amidst a not altogether carefully structured sermon. His reputation as a healer was also considerable. In 1912, he became a full-time evangelist, often supported by his brother George, who was also beginning to strike out on his own.

In 1913, George, and a small group from Wales, attended a conference of Pentecostals at Boddy's church in Sunderland. As a result of this conference, George was invited to Ireland. And it was there, in 1915, that the Elim Evangelistic Band was formed to preach the foursquare gospel of 'Christ the Saviour, Healer, Baptizer, and Coming King'. Elim began in Ireland, and by 1922 there were some twenty-two churches. George, however, made frequent visits to Wales and England, and gradually, but not spectacularly, the movement began to grow.

On the mainland, many small independent Pentecostal churches also began to be formed (sometimes in houses), and it became increasingly clear that Pentecost was not going to survive in the mainline churches. Strictly speaking, it never became established in the major denominations. Despite the upper-middle-class leadership of Boddy and one of the famous 'Cambridge seven', Cecil Polhill, the majority of established and 'respectable' Christians rejected the new charisma. Both these Independents and the newly formed Elim churches were almost exclusively working-class. An anti-intellectualism was often seen as a hallmark of the Spirit.

Meanwhile the Elim Evangelistic Band was consolidating. Dominated by the authoritative George Jeffreys (who was later to become authoritarian), and aided by the talented E. J. Phillips (who was putting a little organization into the outfit), the Foursquare Gospellers were making a name for themselves. Stephen Jeffreys was soon to fall out with George and ended up preaching in the Assemblies of God. But he did not seem to have the temperament for discipline or denominational exactitude. He remained a law unto himself, but made a considerable personal impact wherever he went.

Crucial dates: 1924 and 1926 – Two dates were crucial in those early days. In 1924, George Jeffreys and his team were out of the country. The Pentecostal Union was abolished and the Assemblies of God came into being as a loose-knit federation of some seventy-seven Assemblies. Jeffreys and the Elimites were invited to join, but they decided to go their own way, as it seemed to them that 'God's blessing was resting upon the movement'.[8] To be fair to George, he had made moves to create an umbrella organization in 1922, but the failure to unite the burgeoning Pentecostal movement into one organization was certainly a failure to create the potential for a mass movement.

Henceforth the Assemblies of God grew, but as a federation of congregational churches. Elim became increasingly centralized in a presbyterian-style church. At first it was dominated by Principal George Jeffreys, as he became known, and later by the bureaucratic style of E. J. Phillips and the 'headquarters'. (Headquarters almost had a Salvation Army military sense at first.) Ecclesiological and personality differences were the main causes of division between the Assemblies and Elim. The only doctrinal difference, which remains to this day, was that the

Assemblies of God insisted that the 'baptism of the Holy Spirit' was always accompanied by the sign or seal of *glossolalia*; Elim refused to accept phenomena as the external evidence of the inner divine experience.

The births of Elim and the Assemblies of God are different in kind from the origins of Irvingism, Brethrenism and the later Restoration. Essentially, these other groups were middle-class and 'come-outers'; doctrine and conviction rather than evangelistic revival drove them out. Admittedly, Irving's congregation experienced supernatural manifestations, and Restorationism arose in a revivalistic milieu (first created by the Renewal). But none of these groups was born out of a revival; most members were existing Christians, not new converts. Elim and the Assemblies had their fair share of converts from existing denominations, but many of the ordinary rank and file members became Christians as a result of evangelistic crusades. Classical Pentecostalism, in short, was far more evangelistic than its neo-Pentecostal counterparts of the 1980s (and it still is). But it was 1926 that marked the take-off point for George Jeffreys, and confirmed the rightness of his decision, as he thought, to go it alone.

In that year, unexpectedly, the famous and controversial woman evangelist, Aimée Semple McPherson, visited Britain from America. George, ever the pragmatist and opportunist, took the bold step of hiring the Royal Albert Hall. It was packed, and although Mrs McPherson's Hollywood style did not endear her to the British public, she received enormous media attention. The publicity rubbed off on George. In almost no time, he was able to fill the Albert Hall, the Birmingham City Hall and the great Crystal Palace (before it was burnt down) without any help from Americans.

The American connection was a crucial boost to the Elim movement, just as it proved to be at the Lakes Bible Week fifty years later, when Ern Baxter arrived. Not that George (any more than Bryn) needed American backing to make him shine. He was a phenomenal evangelist. His sermons were short, biblical, orthodox and beautifully constructed. His voice, as records testify, was rich and musical. His style, on the whole, was reverent, and he had none of the wildness of his brother, nor the gimmickry of Aimée Semple McPherson.[9]

For a while, the daily press loved this 'mystic of Maesteg'. He was Britain's most successful evangelist of the 1920s and 1930s. The healings associated with his ministry were seemingly authenticated in a way not typically seen in Pentecostal circles today. The *Daily Express* once recorded that over seventy healings took place at one Easter Monday rally at the Royal Albert Hall. Sometimes, on these occasions, the Principal and other pastors would baptize by immersion 100 or more converts in a specially constructed tank. During a three-week campaign in Birmingham, over 10,000 people were converted to Christ. Many joined Elim, but many more went back to their own denominations or joined a mainstream church for the first time.

Smith Wigglesworth and Stephen Jeffreys also held many successful campaigns, but none of them were quite of the order of the Principal. George Jeffreys was a shy man outside the pulpit. He never married. Despite his rather effeminate looks in his early days (at least against his miner brother), and despite occasional whiffs of scandal surrounding his sexuality, there is not the slightest historical evidence that Jeffreys was homosexual. (As Restorationist leaders know today, no charismatic leader escapes the rumour machine.) During the height of his power in the late 1920s and 1930s, George Jeffreys gained a stature of spiritual authority, so that many Elimites, and others, admit that Jeffreys had great personal presence as well as an engaging public persona.

And then, in a way, it all went wrong. Bryan Wilson's excellent account of the Elim movement[10] sees this as the inevitable clash between charismatic leadership and emerging bureaucratic organization. Elimites have accused Wilson of taking Jeffreys' side against them, by talking mainly to the followers who went with Jeffreys to form a new church, the Bible Pattern Fellowship. Today, however, Wilson's account is given greater credence than it was. Not that everyone goes along with Wilson's account. Some Elim members, who are old enough to remember, prefer to see Jeffreys' fall in terms of spiritual pride, doctrinal deviation, and even personality disorder. It would be true to say, however, that all Elimites, while admitting that something went wrong with Jeffreys, recognize him as a great man. The story of Jeffreys' 'fall' has only recently been told from an Elim perspective,[11] though not everyone agrees with this account (nor mine in the first edition of this book!).[12]

The 'fall' of George Jeffreys – Elim as a denomination was formed as the Elim Pentecostal Alliance in 1926. It was later simply called the Elim Church. More and more churches were bought as a result of evangelistic campaigns. (I remember Pastor Brewster, who was a successful evangelist with Elim after the Second World War, used to buy a church first, and then hold a 'Great Revival and Healing Campaign' to fill it.) A committee of pastors controlled the daily issues of finance, discipline, and (to a certain extent) doctrine.

While Jeffreys went up and down the country with his team, Elim was consolidating as a denomination behind its figurehead. I think it likely that Jeffreys did wake up to the fact that the tail was wagging the dog (shades of Irving). He became distressed, by the end of the 1930s, at the centralized control, and urged a move towards congregationalism. But there are some contradictions here. At the very moment that Jeffreys was insisting on greater lay participation and local autonomy, his own increasingly authoritarian personality came into play. He was also eager to make the beliefs of British Israelism an acceptable doctrine of Elim. Whether he was aware of the neo-fascist overtones possible in such a position – especially as war with Germany loomed – I cannot say.

The first Secretary of the Assemblies of God, Nelson J. Parr, told me in 1970, not long before he died, that British Israelism destroyed George Jeffreys. 'His theories about the long-lost tribes of Israel,' Parr said, 'became more important to him than the gospel.' I think it may well be true that British Israelism unhinged Jeffreys a little, in the same way that Dr Chalmers claimed that biblical prophecy 'unshipped' Irving. But I think this issue has been exaggerated. Jeffreys was a diabetic, which was a well-kept secret of the healer for many years. His ill health and unsettled personality,[13] combined with a genuine dislike of the bureaucratic centralization, were multi-causal factors in his downfall. From an organizational point of view, I think that Bryan Wilson, following the German sociologist Max Weber, was right: sooner or later, charismatic personal authority gives way to more institutional forms.

It was in 1939 that Jeffreys resigned from the Elim movement, and after some delay founded the Bible Pattern Church Fellowship (to give it its full title). On the surface this new movement looks to have Restoration overtones, because Jeffreys wanted a church founded on biblical principles alone. In reality, the new sect was a kind of Pentecostal congregationalism with British Israelism attached. Despite his great popular appeal within Elim – the rank and file members knew little of the conflicts at the top – the new movement never really got off the ground. He made a personal appeal to the pastors in Elim, but many who left to join him soon returned to the parent body. The few churches that made up the new federation returned to Elim in the early 1960s after George's death. (At least the buildings reverted to Elim; not necessarily the small membership of the short-lived Bible Pattern Church Fellowship.)

Whatever the true cause of Jeffreys' departure from Elim, the split between the Principal and Elim led to the disappearance of the evangelist's great popularity – although he remained active in the 1940s and 1950s, and was still greatly respected in European Pentecostal circles.

Elim survived this crisis in its relatively short history, and has matured into an established sect. Its centralized structure seems to have protected it from Restorationist incursions rather better than the local autonomy of the churches in the Assemblies of God.

The Assemblies themselves grew larger than Elim in the number of churches they established. They estimate that they have some 60,000 members today; I cannot find evidence for such a number and believe that this is a considerable miscalculation.[14] Nevertheless, with its popular Bible College at Mattersey Hall, salaried pastors, and lively evangelistic style, the Assemblies of God has developed into a stable sect. Its stability has been considerably rocked by Restorationism in the last five years, but there is no sign that it will imminently capitulate to the new Pentecostalism.

No mention of the Assemblies of God would be complete without reference to Donald Gee. This man, who so wished that he had had a university education, was in fact endowed with great musical and intellectual gifts. He never pretended that the Pentecostal movement had succeeded, and he wanted the Assemblies of God to join the World Council of Churches. Gee was an excellent example of a person who belonged to a sect, but who was totally devoid of the sectarian spirit.

History is cruel. I think it a shame that George Jeffreys, who was probably Britain's most successful evangelist and healer of the twentieth century,[15] should have been completely forgotten. Like Irving before him, the final events of his life obscured his success. Unlike Irving, however, who at least died infamously, George Jeffreys died a nonentity.

The Historical Lessons for Restoration

Elim and the Assemblies of God were able to grow to their present stability and size (I think 25,000–30,000, and 35,000–40,000 respectively)[16] as a result of emerging beyond the revivalism of the first generation into the relative security of established sects. The initial impetus of classical Pentecostalism, which was a revival with a strong evangelistic emphasis, failed to consolidate the new charismatic organizations into one movement. We have briefly looked at the three main sects that grew out of the early revivals (there were other smaller and short-lived groups), and have noted that Elim itself split. The Assemblies of God have consistently shed churches in various directions (most recently to R1). Such evidence poses the question: is Pentecostalism schismatic by its very nature? While I feel that Restorationists would want to answer with an emphatic 'No!', many of them recognize that the historical omens, at the very least, are not favourable.

Restorationism did not begin like classical Pentecostalism. The fuel for the movement, both in terms of rank and file members and the spiritual energy, originated in the Renewal,[17] whereas the ideology, organization, and leadership lay outside the Renewal. This, at least, has some similarities with the nascent renewalism of Boddy and the early Pentecostalists.

The failure, however, to move over to a large-scale and successful evangelistic movement may lead Restoration to become no more than a small introversionist sect of the size and significance of the Apostolic Church in Britain. The emergence of teams, especially in R1, at least points to an evangelistic development. There seems to be a tension here. On the one hand, Bradford, the most centralized, organized and separatist group, is also the most evangelistic. R1 as a whole, as it is presently constituted, is more evangelistic than the more liberal and ecumenical R2.[18] It is too early to tell whether conversionist or introversionist tendencies will win out. Despite its Pentecostalism, Restorationism not only resembles the ideological restorationism of Brethrenism more than it resembles Elim and the Assemblies of God, but also its development is closer to nineteenth-century restorationism.

Modern Restorationism, however, starts from a far

narrower religious base than the nineteenth-century movements. In short, the new groups have been predicated
upon a classical Pentecostalism, Independents, and a neo-
Pentecostalism from within the mainline churches. But
neither the Anglican, Methodist, nor Catholic Churches
have provided major input. Most personnel have come
from the Baptist Union, the Open Brethren, classical
Pentecostalism, and earlier house churches such as Wally
North's fellowships and Chard.

The neo-Pentecostalism (which is itself a mutation from
the classical style) is essentially overshadowed, therefore,
by sectarian inputs. Figure 2 (p 270) shows how we can
relate Restoration to present sectarian groups and nineteenth-century movements. The historical perspective
demonstrates that the third bite of the Restoration cherry is
from a more sectarian point than earlier movements.
Indeed, the third bite has to be seen in the light of classical
Pentecostalism. Restoration is not a direct descendant of
Brethrenism or Irvingism: it would not have come to life
without the theology and experience of twentieth-century
Pentecostalism. It is this Pentecostalism that mediates, or
binds together the two earlier restoration movements into
its modern form.

The history of Elim and the Assemblies of God is crucial
to an understanding of Restoration, not because their origins are similar, but because, it seems to me, the evidence
points to the possibility that at least some Restorationist
formations will end up in the classical Pentecostal camp. If
R2 makes too many overtures to the mainstream churches,
it will simply be sucked back into the Renewal. R1 will
either grow through evangelistic endeavour, or shrink to
become an introversionist sect. Even if Terry Virgo and
Tony Morton cease to relate to Bryn Jones, their organizations are too large to disband. Their future is either to disappear within the first generation or survive in some other
sectarian form; perhaps with people from R2. The
Bradford group already have a built-in headquarters at
Church House, a strong organization, firm and charis-

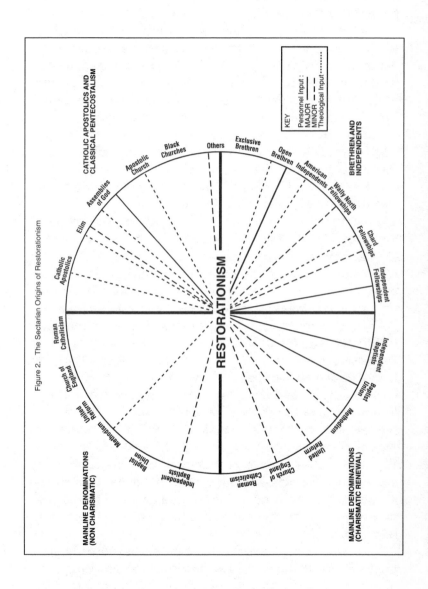

Figure 2. The Sectarian Origins of Restorationism

Figure 2

matic leadership, and money. They look dangerously like a sect within a sect. If R1 disintegrates in its present form, the Bradford core will survive on its own.

The point I am trying to make, sociologically speaking, is that there is no middle ground between the sects and the denominations. Whichever way Restoration goes, whether it be to adopt a more modest conversionism such as Elim, or the introversionism of the Exclusives, while it stays outside the mainstream, it will remain a sect.

Colin Urquhart, one of Britain's best-known charismatic leaders, has recognized, correctly in my opinion, that there are two parallel structures of Pentecostalism: the classical sects and house churches outside the mainstream, and the Renewal inside. I think, however, that he is mistaken in thinking that he holds the middle ground between the two. His Bethany Community, and the new Bible College in Sussex, are far more likely, whether he likes it or not, to take him into sectarian territory. Indeed, Colin's books and sermons are not so much reflective of Anglican renewalism as reminiscent of 1950s American revivalism.

If Restorationism still wishes to become 'the mountain' to fill the whole earth, then it will have to go onto an aggressive evangelistic offensive. So far, neither R1 nor R2 have conducted campaigns anywhere near the scale of George Jeffreys and the Elim evangelistic team. Ironically, to date, restorationist sects have not grown at the rate of the less universalistic conversionist sects of Elim and the Assemblies of God. The desire to re-establish the New Testament Church order, for committed Christians only, has led to an inward-looking approach that tends to inhibit Church growth. Modern Restorationism, like its restorationist precursors, resembles a movement fallen between two stools.

In many ways, however, Restoration has already succeeded wonderfully well. The historical evidence suggests that it is unlikely that it will do better than the other groups. History, however, offers lessons to be learned. It is not a predictor of events; neither does it exist by inviolable rules. I do not wish Restorationism to end up as a certain kind of sectarian formation just so that I can say I was right. On the contrary, nothing would give me greater joy than for the laws of history and the fallible sociological categories of men to be blown apart by the gale force of the Spirit.[19]

Recommended Reading

Desmond Cartwright, *The Beloved Evangelists: the Lives of Stephen and George Jeffreys* (London: Marshalls, 1986).
Donald Gee, *Wind and Flame* (AOG Publishing House, 1967).
Walter J. Hollenweger, *The Pentecostals* (London: SCM, 1972).
Bryan Wilson, *Sects and Society* (London: Greenwood Press, 1978).

13

THE KINGDOM UNDER ATTACK

One of the most significant ways that Restoration can demonstrate that it has really arrived on the religious scene with a vengeance is the fact that it is increasingly being opposed and resisted. This is not simply because it is new – it is because it is radical. Opposition has not come, on the whole, from secular opponents. Non-Christian parents have expressed concern for their children,[1] and as I mentioned at the beginning of the book, the national press has been sniffing around hoping for a sensational exposé. Restorationism cannot really expect to avoid the full glare of publicity, because it is a high-risk religion. By that, I mean that it avoids cosy, safe evangelicalism, and opts for a radical alternative to mainstream religion. Its high charismatic profile, Americanized business methods, and above all, its commitment to paternalistic yet intense relationships, inevitably means that it is always walking in the shadow of sensationalism and scandal. Some Restorationists, I know, see the press (including the religious trade press) as vultures just waiting for something to go wrong, so that they can swoop in and make a killing.

To date, however, the major opposition to Restorationism has come from fellow Pentecostalists and evangelical groups. Much of this criticism has been muted. A number of evangelical leaders, for example, expressed 'grave concern' to me, but were not prepared to be quoted or see their names in print. Classical Pentecostals have been particularly reticent in this respect.

A far bigger problem for me, as a researcher, is that many of the criticisms levelled at Restorationism have been based either on hearsay evidence, or, if based on direct experience, have lacked corroborating evidence (such as documentation, further witnesses, etc.). For example, David Tomlinson related the story of the elder who supposedly possessed the front door keys to everybody's home in his fellowship.[2] I have heard this story in four different places, but nobody has been able to find me the bunch of keys or the keeper of the keys. And again, I was told the story of a young woman who was apparently told by the elder that she was not to use contraception; the informant was unable to provide me with the name of the woman, or the fellowship to which she belonged!

Furthermore, when people have been prepared to talk to me, I have had to take into consideration, if they have recently left R1 or R2, that their disillusionment can lead to a bitterness that distorts what really happened to them in the kingdom. Taking all these factors into account, there are four criticisms, it seems to me, that present a serious challenge to Restorationism. None of these challenges are invented by me. I have selected them as the four most coherent and persistent attacks I have heard against the Restoration kingdom.

1. Restorationism is Destroying the Charismatic Renewal

The problem here is that charismatic leaders are rarely specific when they accuse house churches of being sectarian. Do they mean R1 or R2, or do they mean churches outside this rubric? Consider Tom Walker, one of the leading Anglican Renewalists in Birmingham:

> I'm concerned with the house church movement because it seems to me that a movement that pulls believing Christians out of established churches is going against what the Spirit is saying to churches all over the world. And that is, that there should be new life and a real unity within the established churches.[3]

When I talked with the Revd Tom Walker, while he could not necessarily give me a definition of the house church movement, he could give me examples. In particular, he was concerned with the Dales Bible Week phenomenon. Having talked with Douglas McBain and Michael Harper,[4] they are obviously worried about those house churches that stress distinctiveness of doctrine, and in particular shepherding principles. However, even this is misleading, because both these leaders of the Renewal are seeking a *rapprochement* with the John Noble, Gerald Coates and David Tomlinson fellowships. It is really the Bradford churches of R1 that they are bothered about, and groups like the Basingstoke communities.

Since I commenced this book, new evidence has come to light that the Renewal is consolidating and growing at the grass roots level (at least in the Church of England).[5] Therefore, the accusation against Restorationism is not that it has completely sunk the Renewal, but that it is always launching torpedoes against it. From the renewalist standpoint, the *raison d'être* of their movement is that it promotes an organic (as opposed to bureaucratic) ecumenism: the renewal of the local churches is a call to the unity of the Church. God the Holy Spirit, they feel, wishes to revive existing structures and prevent the creation of new sectarian enclaves.

This 'reformism' is precisely what radical Restorationism rejects. Renewalists see new structures as competing with the existing churches. This competition they see as dividing the body of Christ and weakening the power of the Holy Spirit. Renewalists reluctantly accept the classical Pentecostalists (despite a middle-class bias), because they were there first. But the establishment of house churches they see as a betrayal of all that the Renewal has stood for.

It is a matter of fact that a great many of the rank and file members of the Restoration movement were involved in the Renewal. However, few were members of the historic churches (though I have met former Anglicans and

Catholics). Or to be more accurate, few congregations or large groups moved over from the historic churches, or indeed Methodism and the United Reformed Church. Those former renewalists who came over to Restorationism wholesale, often did so as a result of a visit to the Dales Bible Week, or Downs Week. Leaders of the Renewal perceive R1 as more enticing to the neo-Pentecostals of the mainstream churches than R2. Bryn Jones denies that his churches have advocated that Christians should leave denominations. Consider his reply to such an accusation:

> Such a thing has never been preached to my knowledge. I have made it very clear on a number of occasions that where a denominational church is against the authority of Scripture or things of the Holy Spirit, there is no obligation on any Christian to stay in that church.[6]

But there is a certain ingenuousness here. There can be no doubt on reading Arthur Wallis's book, *The Radical Christian*, or the 'Church Adrift' series in *Restoration* magazine, that R1 believes that all denominations fail to live up to this criterion. Denominations are not in God's plans; the Church cannot be renewed from within the existing organizational structures; apostolic and discipling structures are the essential not the secondary features of Church structure.

If Restorationists do begin to say that the Church can be renewed from within, after all, what reasons do they have to continue their separate existence? In America, the Fort Lauderdale Five succeeded, for a time, in integrating their shepherding system inside some mainline Churches. This is precisely why the discipling issue was so much more divisive in the United States than it has been in Britain: it split the Renewal from within. British Restorationism has peeled off layers of the Renewal from without. As I was at some pains to point out earlier in this book, Restorationism is not a mutation from the Renewal. Despite overlapping with renewalism, its existence was separate from the start.

In fact, Bryn Jones makes a point of not having apostolic control over congregations or groups within the mainline Churches. It would appear, however, that Terry Virgo has a more flexible arrangement with groups still inside Independent and Baptist Union churches (see chapter 15).

Since I started researching this book in the 1980s, I have seen some convergence between R2 and mainstream renewalism. A mutual recognition of ministry, an acceptance of the *de facto* reality and an acceptance of each other's territory, may yet lead to some reintegration of house churches with the renewal of the mainline denominations. I cannot see this happening in R1. But although reintegration may not be on the cards for R1, greater cooperation is certainly hoped for among some of Terry Virgo's elders.

I think it true to say that most Restorationists do not see themselves as deliberately setting out to destroy the Renewal. It is more the case, they feel, that God is showing them something about the nature of his Church that renewalists are not yet seeing. Arthur Wallis is unequivocal on this issue of divisiveness. For him, it is a question of truth: Christ came not to bring peace but a sword:

> I think that one always has to bear in mind that truth is always divisive. When the truth of the gospel comes it divides between those who receive that truth and become Christians, and those who reject that truth. When the charismatic movement came, the truth concerning the Holy Spirit became a divisive point. And we feel that we are simply proclaiming – with no intention to divide – what God has shown to us about the Church. Some receive it, and some do not.[7]

Radical Restorationists do not deny that Renewalists are 'born again' and Spirit-filled Christians. But they do feel that they are out of step with God's purpose 'for this generation'.

I agree with Michael Harper that Restorationism took some of the heat away from the Renewal movement, especially after the closure of the Fountain Trust in 1980. Between 1980 and 1982, the Dales Bible Week became a major focus for many nomadic Pentecostalists, and some disaffected Renewalists. By the end of 1984, however, after the visit of John Wimber from California to Great Britain, and after evidence began to show that the Renewal was still consolidating, Restorationism seemed to be slightly less of a threat.

But in fairness to Restorationists, it must be said that it is oversimplistic to suggest that they are dividers while Renewalists are unifiers. Caustic critics of the Renewal, such as the Revd Peter Mullen, claim that the Renewal does not form new churches, but divides congregations.[8] The parish church can consist of the 'in group', and be divided into those with the 'baptism' and those without it. I attended a Catholic church a few years ago where there was a church within the church. Natural reconcilers like Tom Walker and Michael Harper within the Church of England know that the tensions within any form of Pentecostalism are liable to switch from being creative to become destructive. It has yet to be proven, in my opinion, whether Pentecostalism in its 'posher' charismatic form can be successfully grafted – on a long-term basis – into traditional churches without causing schism. In this respect, history is more on the side of the Restorationists than those in the Renewal.

2. Restorationists Deliberately 'Poach' Church Members and Divide Congregations Against Themselves

This is a very serious claim, and is really an extension of the first challenge. There are two things that can be said with certainty. First, it is the case that a majority of Restorationists are 'come-outers' from the denominations, independent assemblies and established sects. Secondly, it is not the case that there is a conspiracy, an elaborate plan, or a concerted effort to break up other churches.

It is true to say, however, that churches and fellowships are sometimes broken up – often before the new break-away group calls in an apostle to oversee them. I know of a number of cases where apostolic direction has been sub-sequent to a split or local schism. More straightforwardly, what happens is this: the new teaching arrives in the local church and gradually it takes root. Either the whole con-gregation is wooed over, or a sizeable minority leave. That power battles arise, and unpleasantness and unhappiness occur, is without doubt. The churches which feel most vul-nerable to incursions or takeovers (as they see it) are con-gregational-style assemblies which are relatively autonomous, and democratic in leadership.

Even centralized churches have been vulnerable. Six Elim churches, for example, have seceded from the parent body, and a sizeable number of individuals. But it is the Assemblies of God, Evangelical Free Baptists, Brethren Assemblies, and churches of the Baptist Union that have been the most affected. The heartland of the Renewal (Anglicanism and Catholicism) has barely been touched. A number of leaders in the locally-structured churches have been bitter because their democratic processes have been abused, they feel, by a religious group that practises no democracy within its own ranks. When Dr David Russell was General Secretary of the Baptist Union, he received a number of complaints from long-standing Baptist mem-bers who said that they had been, in effect, ousted from their own churches. As his successor, the Revd Bernard Green put it:

We have even got a situation where half a church has left and set up in rivalry in the building next door. Now, even allowing for our respect of their integrity, that seems to us to create a picture of the Church which does not always reflect love as the first gift of the Holy Spirit. I think of one particular church (which I must not name) where all membership was cancelled and people were told that they could only be members in the future if they signed a covenant which was newly written; one clause of which was 'I promise to give total obedience to the leaders of the church'. These people refused to sign, and they were excommunicated immediately.[9]

Pastor George Canty of Elim (now retired, but still an itinerant evangelist) highlighted the problem of walking out of a church and leaving the rest of the congregation saddled with the mortgage debts on the church building.[10] The issue of trust deeds and debts is a major factor in these disputes. But these cases are rather vague. I would like to offer two case studies which are more specific.

Goos Vedder and Hoole Baptist Church – The first case study involves Goos Vedder, who is now a member of Bryn Jones's team.[11] In 1974, this Dutch evangelist and fellow worker with 'God's Smuggler', Brother Andrew, was invited to pastor Hoole Baptist Church. He was already known and liked there. Within a year, however, many of the Baptists complained at the charismatic emphasis, and the influx of new people who supported this new style of ministry. Unlike Bernard Green's story, the new people had not become church members and had no right to vote. A church meeting was eventually held, and there was a vote of no confidence in the pastor. Half the meeting supported the motion, but as a two-thirds majority is needed to remove a pastor, a situation of stalemate prevailed. Goos Vedder sought advice from the local Baptist superintendent, but he could offer no solution to the problem.

Goos Vedder then went to see Bryn Jones, whom he had known for some years. Eventually he decided to leave the church, explaining to the congregation that there was no point in him staying if there was not total confidence in his leadership. He did not, however, give the statutory three months' notice, but left almost at once. He announced from the pulpit that if there were any of the congregation who felt towards him as a sheep towards a shepherd, they were welcome to join him.

A week later, a fellowship commenced in the local arts centre. At first, a large group of 100 or more turned up to support him. From the start, Goos Vedder made it clear that the church would be run on shepherding lines (remembering that Ern Baxter had not yet been to the Lakes). Many left at this news. In January 1975, Bryn Jones, Keri Jones and Peter Paris came to commission Goos as pastor of the new church.

The fellowship sank to about thirty in number, but then began to consolidate and grow. This story of Goos Vedder is interesting because it allows us to see the problems from both perspectives. One charismatic pastor still in the Baptist Union complained to me bitterly: 'If they must go, they must, but why do they always have to take a group of followers to support them?' This is a fairly typical reaction to such stories, and it is certainly true that once a faction has been established, it is usually resolvable only by schism. In Goos Vedder's case, however, he was in a particularly difficult position. He was the formally constituted pastor, and the democratic meeting had not secured enough votes to remove him. And it is at this juncture that we see the radical cutting edge of Restorationism. If the Church will not obey the voice of the Holy Spirit, then it will be left to its own devices.

We can recall Edward Irving when he was excommunicated from the Church of Scotland at the Annan presbytery: 'As many as will obey the voice of the Holy Ghost, let them depart.'[12] Or again, when the trustees of Regent Square locked him out of the church in London: 'Surely disappointment and defeat will rest upon it for ever. God will not bless it.'[13] Vedder's appeal, therefore, is to obey the voice of the Holy Spirit. We are back to Arthur Wallis: 'truth is always divisive'. To stand for truth, purity of gospel and ministry, often cuts across personal relationships and friendships. The Puritan radicals of the seventeenth century believed in love, but they dared not risk being polluted by an apostate Church that refused to heed God's message. Darby believed in one world Church, but he could not accept a lukewarm or heretical believer at the common table.

One could argue that Vedder was forced out, or that he did the decent thing and left. Whether you think it was a decent thing to set up a rival church depends on whether you think people were obeying the voice of the Spirit, or 'the rebellious murmurings of the heart'.

John and Liz Race and the Emmanuel Community Fellowship – My second case study involves a fellowship that had already broken away from the local Baptist church. John and Liz Race, who gave me this story, have done so because they feel that it is essential that people know the way in which recruitment and commitment programmes operate in practice. Giving me their names, as they have done, is to risk further ostracism, they feel, from people who are still their friends, but who no longer share religious worship with them. Unlike most other stories of this nature that I have received, this one was well documented, thought out and reflective. It obviously took great courage for them to give their version of events. They felt that names should not be fictionalized, but they accept that other people in the story may very well interpret events differently. Essentially, John and Liz Race are charismatic evangelicals; they see Restorationism as something potentially dangerous and sinister.[14]

After a group of people left Romford Baptist Church to join John Noble's fellowships (John Race does not say when), a small group who stayed formed a charismatic core within the existing church. In time, the charismatic group gained supporters, including an elder, a few deacons and the church secretary. This secretary, Brian Smith, opened up his house to the group and became one of the leaders. Some thirty or so people would meet for praise and exercise of the spiritual gifts. Some members of Romford Baptist Church knew nothing of this activity.

Tension arose between the pastor, Norman Wright, and the group. (Revd Wright was President of the Baptist Union, 1985–86.) Apparently, he was deeply upset about remarks accusing him of 'grieving the Holy Spirit'.

It was suggested by him that the group should be disbanded or curtail its activities. After much prayer, soul-searching and fasting, John tells us, the group began to re-form outside the Baptist church. John and Liz removed their son from the Sunday school, but they did not formally resign from the church. In the summer of 1983, after a visit to the Shepton Mallet Bible Week (R1), Brian Smith formed a caretaker leadership of himself and five other men. This was supposed to help them through the transition from a disbanded group to a new fellowship. Peter Birchinall, a much-respected elder at Romford Baptist Church, resigned and joined the leadership of the new group.

In September of that year, the new group started meeting for worship in the YMCA. They called themselves Emmanuel Community Church. John and Liz Race insist that neither they nor many of the group had any idea at the time that choosing the title 'Community Church' was in any way associated with the Restoration movement. A month later, it was agreed to establish links with John Singleton and the North London Community Church (which was then one of London's fastest-growing churches). There seems to have been some confusion as to whether links should be made with R1 or R2. Originally, they had talked of bringing in Tony Morton and Arthur Wallis. That they decided to choose John Singleton is interesting. He was at one time associated with Bryn Jones and David Mansell, but had by then branched out on his own. I think it safe to say that he is now firmly in R2, as I saw him and his wife at Festival 84.

It was suggested that John and his team should be brought in as consultants – at least, that is how John Race saw them. The Emmanuel Community Church was told that these men 'were humble men of God who were farther along the road that they were now travelling'. The group were told that they would be taught 'restoration principles' and how to 'build relationally'.

At first, says John Race, it was by no means clear what this new radical teaching was all about. By the end of October 1983, Peter Birchinall left the fellowship and returned to Romford Baptist Church, because he was not happy with these new teachings. John Race believes that Brian Smith already knew what Restorationism stood for because he read *Restoration* magazine, and had attended the Dales Bible Week. At this time, says John Race, the full implications of Restorationism were not spelled out to the group. Indeed, for the next month, John recalls, Singleton and his colleagues talked much about love, sharing and being radical, but nothing specifically Restorationist was discussed. During this time, however, John and Liz read Ron Trudinger's book, *Built to Last*, and began to understand, with deep concern, what Restorationism was about. Here are some of John's notes:

1. The concept of delegated authority and submission to leadership. Trudinger writes (p 126): 'Every man needs another man with delegated authority as a shepherd over his personal life. Every leader then, himself needs a leader – a voice from God, we may say.' This passage concerned me very much. The phrase 'over his personal life' is unscriptural and open to abuse in practice. It places men as mediators between God and men. Extremely dangerous.

2. The concentration of power in the leadership. The removal of decision-making from the church members. Trudinger writes (p 117): 'In a restoration church, the elders or the leaders in plurality, are the door of the fold.'

John and Liz were particularly worried about the insistence on tithing. John wrote in his notes: 'A new legalism was being imposed. Christians should obey the dictates of their conscience and should be free to distribute their money as they felt led. There is no New Testament support for tithing.' John also disliked a section in Trudinger's book where he says: 'So in a community of God's pattern each one is committed. There are no peripherals.' John felt that it was unhealthy to build a fellowship without a fringe membership. He thought that the ideology of 'no peripherals' would alienate the faint-hearted.

These points, and many more, were raised at a special meeting held in Brian Smith's house. John Singleton and David Hall were there from the North London Community Church. According to John Race, the book was more or less dismissed by the North London team. The Emmanuel Fellowship was told that its teachings were not going to be implemented. (A number of leaders in R2 do, in fact, consider Trudinger's book to be extreme.) After the meeting, Liz told John: 'We may have won a battle, but we have not won the war.'

'How right she was,' said John. Soon afterwards, the group returned to those very same principles of commitment and shepherding that had earlier been dismissed. No cell groups or home groups were established during this time, but the group were told that they would be established after commitment had been made to the new principles. John thought that there was a lot of double talk around.

Commitment had two sides to it. On the one hand, it was said to be a commitment to one another, a commitment to God and the Bible. The bottom line or the undertow was that commitment really meant being committed to the leadership and being willing to do what you were told. There was much talk about being free in worship and community. On the other side this meant you would be free provided you had the blessing of the leadership. On the one hand we were told that we were not going to have any authoritarianism or heavy disciplining. On the other side we were taught submission, delegated authority and the pitfalls of ecclesiastical democracy. Democracy became something of a dirty word. Theocracy was the way ahead.

John and Liz Race sent me their comprehensive commitment course. After completing it, they felt unable to make a further commitment, and withdrew from the emerging new Restorationist church. John took a rather personal line. He thought that Peter Birchinall was a stable and sensible person. After his voluntary withdrawal, he felt the remaining leadership was too autocratic. John felt that the dividing line between theocracy and autocracy was too thin. Despite the grand theological structure, the whole thing was a golden opportunity for the power-seeking, and for authoritarian personalities.

John and Liz Race would like to remain friends with members of the Emmanuel Community Church, but they are convinced that Restoration principles are wrong and dangerous. They object to the way the teaching was introduced; they felt that they were hoodwinked to a certain extent. Finally, they felt it was wrong and divisive to make the congregation, which had worked so closely together, either agree to the new thing or to get out.

There are, of course, many ways to interpret John and Liz's story. I can see no evidence, for example, that John Singleton and his team did anything improper. They responded to an invitation by the Emmanuel Community Church to come and run a commitment course on Restorationism. However covert this might have been at first – or, if you prefer, after the 'softly softly' approach – it was clear by the end of the course what Restorationism entailed. I put it to John Race that the real damage was done not by John Singleton, but by the group themselves when they decided to set themselves up as the charismatic group within the Romford Baptist Church. That is where the division started, not at Emmanuel Community Church.

You could argue that Restorationists typically exploit

such divisions. But in this particular case, although John's story exemplifies how Restorationism can move in and take over a fellowship, it also demonstrates that the work of division and separation had begun before Brian Smith took over. I am not sure whether John really favours this interpretation, but he does feel that things got a lot worse when Brian Smith became leader. Restorationism was not a ground-swell movement within the community, says John, it was pushed from the top.[15]

If Restorationism is built on a spiritual rebellion, and not on truth and holiness, as Gene Edwards claims,[16] then we can note that the problems that Bernard Green and John Race discuss are rampant within the Restoration kingdoms themselves. David Tomlinson told me that he abhorred the sectarian spirit that sought to divide and break up churches. He pointed out that he had written to Bryn Jones and begged him not to set up an R1 church in Birmingham, where there was a thriving fellowship under his care. Cardiff seems to have churches from the extended R2 and R1. Gerald Coates admitted that he had a small group that was probably seen as a thorn in Tony Morton's side in Shirley, Southampton. There have certainly been tensions between Terry Virgo and some of Gerald's and John Noble's churches. Some leaders from R2, I know, see Maurice Smith as a pied piper, as he calls people out from under their noses.

Every time R1 or R2 fragments, the issues of division and 'poaching' come home to roost. R2 leaders do not see themselves as poaching members from R1. Neither do R1 leaders see themselves as competing with R2. Nevertheless, there is covert rivalry. All this is strangely reminiscent of the development of the Exclusives and Open Brethren 120 years ago.

Two things need to be said in concluding this section. First, the blame for divisiveness that has taken place in the formation of Restorationism cannot be placed entirely on the shoulders of the new groups. Hardened attitudes have existed on both sides. Very often, Restorationism only moved in when divisions had already occurred. It is far more typical of Restorationist leaders that they are invited into new fellowships than that they move in.

Secondly, as Rosemary Hartill reminded Bernard Green, 'People in glass houses should not throw stones'.[17] Only a short while back, in the history of the Church, the Pentecostals seceded from the mainline churches. They claim that they were driven out, or that the Spirit 'bade them go'. Only a few years before them, the Brethren separated from the Church of England, primarily because of principles. Restorationists claim that they are doing the same. The Baptist movement itself has its modern origins in the seventeenth century, when, like the Methodists 100 years later, they could no longer relate to the historic tradition.

Restorationists believe that they are building the Church. They believe that this cannot be done from within the existing religious frameworks, so they have moved outside them to try something new. If Restorationists, in peering back at these groups, may dimly perceive their own future, these historic denominations in looking at Restorationism are seeing their own past. An argument many Baptists and Methodists have put to me is that today things are different: we do not need to divide any more; ecumenism is the thing. This is not only sociologically naive, but logically untenable. The same argument could have been put, and probably was, at every subsequent divide of the Protestant Reformation. If Restorationists are to be blamed for stealing sheep, dividing congregations and splitting churches, then it is difficult to see how this differs from the schismatic behaviour of established and respectable churches in the early days of their development.

3. Restorationists are Doctrinally Deviant and Self-Deluded

Curiously, these two criticisms are often presented in juxtaposition. This is so, I think, because there is the suspicion by some that the shepherding system breeds dependency by followers and delusions of grandeur in leaders. I do not feel sufficiently trained in psychology to comment on this in any elaborate way. I can say, however, that I have seen no evidence to suggest that Restorationism breeds a certain kind of personality. I share with Eileen Barker both the conviction and experience that people labelled as 'brainwashed' or 'weird' turn out on investigation to be just like anybody else.[18] If it is the case that Restorationism attracts a particular type of person, then it will require a large-scale psychological study to determine this.

I have heard recently that people have been leaving the American Shepherding movement in droves. It is alleged that there are many psychologically damaged people.[19] Peter Mullen is collecting a file of case studies both inside the Renewal and the house churches. I do not wish to appear too sanguine concerning this issue, but I prefer to reserve my judgment until the evidence is a lot clearer than it is now.

This idea of 'damage' is usually aimed at the discipleship doctrines. And some critics of Restoration see a connection between psychological effects and doctrinal deviation. Classical Pentecostals, in particular, insist that the movement that prides itself on abandoning extrabiblical teaching, is itself built upon non-biblical teaching. This view is shared by many Renewalists. They claim that Scripture simply does not support the discipleship as taught and practised by Restorationists. Unfortunately, this argument tends to be a non-sequitur both for Restorationists and their opponents. One group insists it is biblical, and the other group insists that it is not. It is sufficient to note, however, that Restorationists are out on a limb on this one. Evangelicals, classical and neo-Pentecostals are not persuaded that shepherding structures can be deduced from biblical principles. Without being way out on a limb, of course, Restorationism would have little reason for claiming distinctness and special revelation. Without a commitment to covenanted relationships, Restorationists would not be radicals.

This is particularly true when linked to the charismatic apostolate. The general view of apostolic structures within Elim and the Assemblies of God, as we have seen in chapter 12, is that they are fictional creations with no relationship to the power or legitimacy of the New Testament offices. Anglicans such as Tom Smail and Michael Harper believe that there is a uniqueness about the original twelve and a special place for Paul.[20] The so-called apostles of the 'risen Christ', such as Timothy and Barnabas, they understand in an episcopal sense of bishops, and not in a charismatic sense of anointed ones. (Though, of course, these particular examples may very well have been men with charismata.) Such a view, which is similar to that held by most Catholic and Orthodox groups, could never be acceptable to Restorationists, because it tacitly accepts some kind of apostolic succession. If it gained ground in Restoration circles, the whole legitimacy of their position would be denied. The Brethren coped with these issues by a radical anti-clericalism that denied the priesthood altogether.

A number of Brethren have told me that the Restorationists are clericalists, albeit in a charismatic form. Apostles, prophets and elders are in effect, they claim, holy orders. While I think there is a great deal to commend this argument, I do not think that it is the case that Restorationists really think in these terms. The reason, I believe, lies in the absence of the high church theology which underlay the earlier restoration movements. Modern Restoration, in theory, holds to universality and catholicity, but their immediate roots are in classical Pentecostalism and modern Brethrenism (as far as their churchmanship is concerned). The full ecclesiastical implications of a restored apostolate have not really fired their imagination in the way they did the Catholic Apostolic Church.

A criticism that I have heard from such disparate

groups as the Ichthus house churches, classical Pentecostals and Baptists, is one I first heard from Maurice Smith: Restorationism is an extreme form of legalism. This legalism, he believes, characterizes both R1 and R2 and any other shepherding system. Maurice Smith thinks that legalism is repressive and builds up resentments and rebellions. Specifically, he believes Restorationism breeds guilt by always stressing the shortcomings of believers. Striving for perfection, under delegated authority, he believes leads to a sense of inadequacy and perhaps despair.

It is certainly true that the anarchic freedom of the early days gave way to a strong authority imposed from the top downwards. I think it also true to say that Restorationism's strong sense of community and solidarity does not leave much room for personal deviancy in the kingdom. But I believe that it is untrue to say that life in the kingdom is bound by rules and regulations at every turn. I am not sure, for example, whether Maurice Smith is aware of the changes taking place in R2 since he left. Nor do I think that it is possible to generalize about the kingdom. The application of Restoration principles is patchy and reflects personality factors of leaders and social class to a certain extent.

Perhaps one of the most serious criticisms of doctrinal deviation and its relationship to self-delusion comes from former apostle, George Tarleton.[21] George believes that doctrinal and psychological factors have combined to ruin what he believes was a genuine movement of the Holy Spirit. I spent some hours talking on the phone to George, and it was obviously a painful experience for him first to recognize, and then accept, that he had been deluded. He kindly sent me a written statement or testament on 'The One That Got Away':

One of the main reasons I quit was the growing awareness that the freedom – which had given this movement its dynamic – was being eroded away. The 'freedom' it now boasts of is only when it is compared with something formal. Britain's poverty trap can look like heaven if you're starving in Africa.

Tithing was the warning bell that law was back with us again. Under the euphemism of a 'kingdom principle', this unbiblical practice was imposed by Bible lovers. The letter was replacing the Spirit. Institutionalism was setting in. A new denomination was being born.

That was really sad – realizing that we had given birth to another sect. Especially when one of the main aspects of our vision was that there was one church. The reality was that there were thousands of sects and we were adding to that number. Nothing is more painful than the death of an illusion.

The greatest damage was done by the submission trip which the leaders went on. Due to a lack of spiritual authority, submission to men was imposed on the church. These men merely passed on their insecurities, their modified middle-class values, and a christianized form of right-wing politics. (How anyone with an ounce of discernment can see Mrs Thatcher as a prophet is beyond me!)

Then there were my 'liberal' views about the authority of the Bible, the place of women and the humanity of Christ. They were beginning to be a source of embarrassment. Slowly it dawned on me that the doctrines people cling to are those which suit their personality.

When creative praise degenerated into a series of action replays, when individuality was being strangled to death by submission, when impressing became more important than expressing, I knew it was time to leave. Discarding my siege mentality, I had to get out of the ghetto. Away from the doctrinal dualism which saw everything as either of God or the devil.

The last message I was allowed to deliver at a large gathering was a plea to stop evangelizing the world and start loving it. Well I have now taken refuge in that world, setting up my stall in the market place. From here my view of the world has changed. I see God deeply involved with it. Far from writing it off, he's changing it because of the love affair he has with this world of ours.

When George Tarleton left R2, he took no followers with him. He has moved down to the New Forest and taken a secular job. His telephone is ex-directory and his address unavailable. He is convinced that the splits and factions of the Restoration kingdom are ultimately God's will: they will prevent a really large denomination being formed.

4. Restoration is Not Brotherly Love: it is Big Brotherly[22]

When we were preparing for the programme *Front Room Gospel* at the BBC, inevitably – as it was 1984 – the question of 'Big Brother' cropped up. By far the most serious criticism against Restorationism is that it operates a system of sinister control over members' minds and lives. I can state unequivocally that most of the stories circulating about Restoration are either lies, expressed but not yet realized fears, or exaggerated accounts. Shepherding, in the majority of cases, takes place within admittedly paternalistic yet caring relationships.

In preparing for the Radio 4 programme, however, I did come across a definite syndrome: there were people who were frightened to talk, or who felt that talking would only damage the good they felt still existed in the movement. I received a number of complaints and letters concerning the Basingstoke churches, for example, but absolutely nobody would talk on radio. And then Rosemary Hartill received a letter from a man in Basingstoke that contained some hard-hitting observations and some shocking stories. Before we went on the air in March 1984, he too had withdrawn, saying he had changed his mind.

A number of friends and people I trust, have handed

me stories that led me to believe that in the kingdom not all was sweetness and light. These stories, however, were virtually impossible to check out. Following Bryn Jones's invitation, for example, to report on discipling abuses in R1, I have not been able to find one story that stands up. Because of the number of complaints I received, and the people who delivered them to me, it is my personal opinion that the discipling controversy is going to stay around for a long while yet. Pockets of abuse do exist, I am convinced.

The Basingstoke *Gazette* carried out its own investigations in 1982.[23] Like me, they found that the majority of people refused either to talk, or to give names. Only Mrs Dominique Lawson would allow her name to be used. She joined the Community Church in the mid-1970s. At first she was grateful for the way her husband was helped financially, because he was unemployed at the time. Gradually, she claimed, the church took over their lives. 'We had to look happy and smiling, even if we were not feeling like it. We had to seem united and happy, when underneath it was just awful.' She claimed (although this is not what I would call hard evidence) that members had to consult leaders if they wanted to change their jobs, their cars or their homes. Eventually the Lawsons wanted to move, and they were told that the time was not right. They moved anyway, and left the church. A deputation arrived and tried to persuade them to rejoin. 'They said that outside the church we would not survive,' said Mrs Lawson.

I have met people whose experience seems similar to Mrs Lawson's. But such stories are not typical. Clearly, some of the people I have discussed this with in R1 and R2 were as outraged as I was at such stories. A number of leaders knew of such stories in other groups, but preferred to turn a blind eye because the persons concerned were not under their authority. This has a slightly humorous side to it for anybody from a Catholic or Orthodox tradition. It seems that the problem of jurisdictions has been inherited by Protestant sectarianism after all; apostles can no more tell other apostles what to do than diocesan bishops!

After the first broadcast of *Front Room Gospel* in March 1984, some letters reached me containing stories, allegations, and in some cases stronger evidence of discipling abuse. A few people agreed to be named. One man came to see me whose story was quite different from the others. It involved not only him, but most of his church. The story was different for another reason. He not only came to see me for a day, but he brought with him a written statement, carefully thought out, together with copious correspondence between himself, his apostle/prophet, and other letters between himself and Gerald Coates. In addition, he brought some tapes of the man to whom he had submitted his life. These tapes included informal conversations (as well as formal addresses) on how to successfully discipline wayward members.

The apostle concerned is from my extended use of R2, and we have met him before as one of the 'fabulous fourteen'. His name is John MacLauchlan. In view of the serious nature of the allegations made against him, I contacted John MacLauchlan, who kindly replied to the substance of the complainant's allegations – made in some detail in his written statement. The complainant is called Ted Rotherham. He is well known in R2 circles, as he was around from the early days of the Leprosy Mission. Although never a national leader, he was a respected elder of a small church in Surrey.

It is not my intention in this case study to say that every word of Ted Rotherham's story is true. He is prepared to defend every word of it, even though he realizes that it makes him out to be a dupe. I believe that he is a man of integrity, and is concerned that others do not make the same mistakes as he did. It is not my intention either to suggest that John MacLauchlan is a wicked gentleman. He denies absolutely Ted's version of events. I do not believe that John MacLauchlan is a liar; both he and Ted perceive each other and the world in a totally different way. As they no longer share the same *Weltanschauung*, it is perhaps not surprising that they cannot agree on the nature and facts of the dispute between them. What Ted's story illustrates – and it is essentially Ted's story that we shall be looking at, not my version of it – is the potential dangers and problems of a discipling system.

After the split of Restorationism into R1 and R2 in 1976, John MacLauchlan and Graham Perrins continued to see themselves in an apostolic role, but tended to conflate, in practice, the offices of apostle and prophet. From about this time, Ted Rotherham's church came under John MacLauchlan's influence, and they were proud to be associated with a man whose reputation as a scholar and level-headed person was high in Restoration circles. Ted's Camberley church in Surrey continued to have fellowship with Gerald Coates, who was very popular with the people there. Ted takes up the story:

> It was in the autumn of 1979 that I was summoned to see John Mac at his home near Yeovil. He asked me a question: 'Who is your father, Gerald Coates or me?' I did not feel the need to make such a choice but was told: 'It's either Gerald or me.' At that time I was not aware of the division between them and with some reservations had to choose John for his long-standing input into my life.

Ted began to realize that some leaders were competing for leadership. His church was told to withdraw their small financial support for Gerald, and stop 'relating' to him. In February 1981, a conference was held at John Mac's home. There, Ted says, he was asked to relinquish all authority to John. Ted again:

> He then laid out his objectives to have concentrated input with monthly visits to bring us in line with the same ministry as his own fellowships at Yeovil. This consisted of personal foundations, corporate foundations, tithing, giving oneself, and attitudes in daily liv-

ing. We were told that if these aspects of teaching were not changing our lives that we would have to move to Yeovil within twelve months. I was very uncomfortable with this statement and said so and began challenging John on many areas of his direction, and was subsequently told that the word of God to us was that we would have to move and that we would never have another word.

My wife and I were in complete turmoil and desperate to know what we should do. We had decided not to go; a few others said that they would submit to John and could not agree with us to stay. The majority stood with us but were very confused as the fellowship had now been dissolved and I had stood down after twelve years' leadership in what was a very loving and friendly fellowship.

Ted went to see Gerald Coates, who, although he sympathized with Ted, felt that Ted had to sort it out for himself. I discussed this with Gerald, and I do not think he was saying to Ted: 'You've made your bed, now lie in it', but I do think he was saying to Ted: 'You've submitted to another man's authority; sort it out with him.' In the event, Ted and his wife decided to capitulate and confess their wrongdoing to John Mac. Ted continues:

I was told to apologize to everyone in the church for my actions and put my house on the market right away. The move was on and by now we were all moving with the exception of two young men. There were the problems of jobs, children at 'A' and 'O' levels. We encouraged my wife's elderly parents to sell their home and move away with us to the West country.

Ted felt that now everything would be all right. John had assured him that the move would not affect his shepherding relationship with the fellowship. A move was effected to Martock in Somerset. In a few weeks, a local house church leader, Keith Impey, called on Ted and informed him that he was no longer to have responsibility for the Camberley church. Those who had not yet made the move would now, like Ted, submit to Keith as John's delegate. John could only be contacted, Ted was told, through Keith's mediation. Ted insists that John MacLauchlan had promised him close personal contact after the move, which would include regular lunches and consultations. In the event, says Ted, it was nine months before he saw John. Ted felt humiliated.

> Some were now moving into Martock whilst others were told to move to Yeovil and we began to meet at Keith's house. I was a sheep amongst my own sheep, having to get permission for what I should and should not do, being directed to help with the decor and garden of other leaders.

Ted and some others were encouraged to give money from the sale of their houses to help others move down from Camberley. Keith, according to Ted, told them that they were not getting jobs because they were not giving money when directed. False prophecies were often given, says Ted, and when they failed they were told that God had changed his mind. He remembers an incident of a girl who was told that she would not get a job because she had not mastered a smoking habit. The prophecy was given as a 'word' (*rhema*) direct from God. The girl did get a job.

After some twelve months, when Ted felt cut off, isolated and humiliated, he and his wife decided that enough was enough. Through one man, they realized, they had come to believe that they were the unique expression of the Prophetic Church on Earth. Yeovil was to be the centre of the true Church radiating out to the whole world. Ted recalls: 'I had lost my leadership, function, sheep, job, friends, financial help, and was very disillusioned.' On 25th March 1983, Ted decided to finish with submission to men and cast himself on Christ alone. Several days later,

John MacLauchlan rang to say that he could no longer cover Ted and his wife, but they were welcome to choose somebody else from Yeovil. Ted made it clear that he would submit to nobody. John then replied: 'In that case I will not allow anyone access to you because of your actions.'

The ill-feeling continued, claims Ted, and he was asked to move out of the area so that he would not attract others to himself. He asked John MacLauchlan what was the scriptural basis for not allowing others to see him. 'Ted,' he replied, 'you should know that we don't work from scriptural principles.'

Ted and his wife are still in Martock. They claim that others are now coming out and that the prophet's kingdom is breaking up. Ted insists that the basic problem in his life has been looking to external authority to lead him into truth. All his attention, he says, was given to making the effort to live up to other people's expectations. Ted is now part of Maurice Smith's support group for, as they see it, the casualties of shepherding. Whether Maurice's 'new thing' will turn out to be yet another twist in the sectarian spiral remains to be seen.

Ted hopes that his story (and this is a very shortened version) will help prevent others from being deluded and duped. He sees submission and discipling practices as a trap:

Having the desire to know and please God, and enjoy fellowship with others, you commit yourself to 'the Fellowship' and subsequently 'the Authority' of those 'over' you. No longer do you act independently, but through the leader by direct intervention, or seeking advice and guidance from him. Should this conflict with your own feelings, the choice you face is to do what you feel is right and face the consequences, or deny 'your spirit' and give way to the one over you. The latter denies direct communication with God and embraces a structure held together by Law, leading to fear and condemnation.

John MacLauchlan wrote to me on 1st December 1984, and Keith Impey on 3rd December. Both categorically deny Ted Rotherham's account. John MacLauchlan (first paragraph):

> Dear Andrew, Thanks for your letter and copy of Ted's material. There are really so many inaccuracies and outright lies in Ted's account that I can see no profit in commenting on them in detail. The Lord has not taught us to defend ourselves in such circumstances. Ted will account for his statements to a higher authority than ourselves!

Keith Impey (paragraphs five and six):

> For a man who was so confused and attacking anything and anybody in sight at that time, it is ironical that he can remember with so much clarity exactly what was said and done.
>
> In truth and reality, he cannot and he only has his impressions upon which he is basing his comments. Those impressions are born out of bitterness and resentment. They do not represent the real issues and the facts.

John MacLauchlan did make some personal accusations off the record, but then Ted Rotherham also made some personal accusations off the record about John.

Ted Rotherham felt it right that John MacLauchlan should have the right to reply, but warned me that John was extremely plausible, intelligent and believable. John MacLauchlan wrote in paragraph four:

> I must say that I think it unwise to publish an account such as Ted has written for you. He is a plausible man who has done much harm to the work here. My main

mistake with him was to leave him in leadership as long as I did in the hope that he would mature and stabilize.

Neither John MacLauchlan nor Keith Impey actually rebut any of the specific facts (except one – see below) of Ted's account. John explains why in the final part of his letter: 'I trust that your readers will accept that I consider it inappropriate to enter into controversy in the forum of your book, over the specific allegations made by Ted.' What John does do is offer us, in contrast to Ted, his view of the Yeovil fellowships:

> We remain 'unaligned' with any group. I have always (publicly, including during the days of the so-called 'fourteen') opposed any moves towards national leadership or organization. We would not call ourselves a 'House Church' (we meet in all sorts of buildings!) but simply Christians meeting together in the Yeovil area. We acknowledge without reserve God's moving with groups of all kinds, and have no exalted opinion of ourselves. There are many approaches that would not be appropriate or God's will for us, but we respect the right of each group to build as God directs, and would not dream of criticizing them. The body of Christ in a universal sense has many varied members.
>
> We resist all attempts at producing or imposing uniformity among the churches. Our unity must be based on mutual respect and recognition, not on anyone's attempt to modify all others to harmonize with his views. There is no 'New Testament church pattern', as the church is an evolving entity, called onward by the word of God towards a consummation in Christ that we can only at present glimpse. (It is this refusal to accept that a New Testament pattern is currently binding on us that is misrepresented by Ted.)[24]

What readers will realize, I am sure, is that they are being presented with two different versions of reality. Even such a strong case as Ted Rotherham's story is by no means clear cut. Without a great deal more material witnesses, corroborating evidence, etc., it is very difficult for us, in any objective sense, to decide which version we choose to believe. Personally, I am convinced that both Ted and John presented me with the truth as they see it. This book is not a court of law, and it is not for us to decide who is right and who is wrong.

It is the purpose of this book, however, to attempt to investigate every aspect of kingdom life. While I do not feel that it is my place to arbitrate, I do feel that it is proper that I should air the sort of complaints that exist against Restorationism. John MacLauchlan put himself in my hands as far as editing his letter is concerned (last paragraph), and Ted Rotherham gave me full permission to edit as I saw fit. Ted's complaint was the best documented of any I received, but it is not unique; there are six other stories on my files which differ in detail and the personnel involved, but are similar in complaint.

The Restoration kingdom, both R1 and R2, is a radical kingdom, and radicals attract opposition in a way in which conventional Christians do not. Some Restorationists see criticisms as attacks of the devil. But it is my experience that many Christians outside the kingdom are not so much censorious as curious. This curiosity is sometimes married to anxiety. Most people simply want to know what the Restorationist kingdom is really all about. The kingdom is not really under attack from without (though it has many rebellions from within), but it is being seriously probed.[25]

Recommended Reading

George Tarleton, *Birth of a Christian Anarchist* (private publication, Pendragon Press, 1993).

'Shepherds or Sheep Stealers?', *Buzz* magazine (August 1984).

Gene Edwards, *A Tale of Three Kings* (California: Christian Books, 1980).

Michael Harper, *That We May Be One* (Hodder & Stoughton, 1981).

Alan Munden, 'Encountering the House Church Movement: A Different Kind of Christianity', *Anvil*, Vol. 1, No. 3, 1984.

Joyce Thurman, *New Wineskins: a Study of the House Church Movement* (Verlag Peter Lang, 1982).

Part Three

The Breakdown of the Kingdom
1985–90

14

THE BEGINNING OF RESTORATIONIST DECLINE

Recruitment and Demography[1]

After 1985, Restorationism ceased to be a runaway success as far as growth is concerned. There were admittedly some significant growth areas,[2] but on the whole it slowed down either to a steady trickle of converts, or stopped growing altogether. The primary reason for this was the ending of wholesale defection from other churches. Despite the stemming of this flow of committed Christians, the number of first-time converts increased in virtually all areas of R1 and R2. In the March/April 1986 edition of *Restoration* magazine, the editor, David Matthew, reported that 'sheep stealing' from other churches was a myth. He cited as evidence for this assertion that, on the basis of a survey conducted by him, 55.3 per cent of all new membership for 1985 was made up of new converts and recommitted nominal believers.

No doubt some people would put this down as sheer propaganda, but I think his figures are accurate enough. Not only is David Matthew an intelligent graduate, but he is a scrupulously honest person, and I have always found him open and unafraid of criticism. But I think these figures are reliable not only because I trust David Matthew, but also because they bear out my own independent enquiries within R1 and R2. There is no doubt that new converts were on the increase after 1985, comprising a proportion of at least 25 per cent, and in some cases 50 per cent, of all new members.

But we have to look at the issue of first-time converts

and new patterns of recruitment with a measure of sobriety. In the first place, while people are happy to talk about percentages, nobody I have talked to has any hard evidence of actual numbers. Even if it is true that 55 per cent joined the fellowships of Bryn Jones in 1985, we have no idea from the *Restoration* article itself how many people this percentage refers to. It is indeed significant that over half the people who joined were new Christians, but it would be even more significant if the actual numbers who joined were hundreds and thousands, as opposed to tens and fifties.

Furthermore, and this is a more important point, we not only need to know how many new Christians were joining, but also how many established Christians were leaving. It is clear from my own research that many people passed through the Restorationist churches and moved on to new and independent house churches, or returned to the mainstream.[3]

I do not have any strong evidence that any particular segment of Restoration shrank at an alarming rate during this period,[4] but the overall picture is clear: growth was either static or sluggish. Part of the problem for getting reliable figures resides in the psychological problem that churches find it easier to remember how many new members have joined them than how many old ones have left!

Judging the overall numbers after 1985 is virtually impossible, as many churches chose not to reveal the full extent of their membership. Furthermore, Restorationism became flanked by many new independent churches, which made an input into R1 and R2, but also drew people out. Restorationism certainly retained a hard core of committed and stable members, but became soft around the edges; consequently people continually crumbled away. Personally, I doubt if there have ever been more than 40,000 hard core Restorationists, and I believe that in numerical terms they had peaked by 1984–85.[5]

If the overall pattern of recruitment and the size of Restoration is fairly clear by the second half of the decade, so too are the demographic factors. Restoration was primarily lower-middle to middle-class, but much more so in the south than in the north. While Cobham in Surrey remained almost exclusively middle-class, R1's churches in the north were broader-based. Indeed, I have been to churches in the East Midlands that are more working-class than middle-class.

Historically, Restorationism has not been a woman's religion, and while there are more women than men in the rank and file, there is not the sort of imbalance that one often finds in the historic churches. On the other hand, although Bryn Jones and David Tomlinson (to name but two apostles) made significant efforts to recruit ethnic minorities, Restorationism remained predominantly White. This is, of course, also true of most Protestant mainstream Churches in Great Britain.

Of greater demographic interest is age. Restorationism has been a young religion with a young population. There have not been a significant number of old people, nor single people of marrying age (although one-parent families are welcomed).[6] Restorationism has majored on young families and it is truly the case that both R1 and R2 can be said to be family churches (this is clearly observable at Cobham in Surrey and Hove in Sussex). Numerically, teenagers became a more significant group than they were before 1985, because they had become the young adults that were once the small children growing up in the first flush of Restoration's success. However, they were a discontented lot in some ways. David Tomlinson felt that many of them were bored with charismatic religion, or at least with Restoration. Teenagers became the most vulnerable group in the movement and the one from which most people will probably defect in the future.

External Factors in Restoration's Decline

We will see in the next two chapters how internal divisions

within Restorationism help explain their relative decline, but I believe the primary causes of the loss of momentum were external. These causes are crucially important for our understanding of the history of kingdom Christianity, for they demonstrate that Restorationism was already a spent force by the time the revivals of the 1990s exploded upon the evangelical world.

Clive Calver and the Evangelical Alliance – Ironically, one of the key factors in the slowing down of the Restorationist movement was its incorporation into the Evangelical Alliance. By 1989, virtually all Restorationist leaders had joined the Alliance, Bryn Jones being the notable exception. Persuading the new radicals to join the EA was a great coup for its General Secretary, Clive Calver, but it did somewhat draw their sting. The distinctiveness of Restorationists lay in their separation from others, and while joining in is morally laudable, it does not always make good sociological sense if you wish to survive as a radical Church.

The Evangelical Alliance was formed in 1846 and not only predates the British Council of Churches by many years but was probably the prototype for many worldwide national councils of Churches. In 1966, however, it survived a major crisis. This crisis was precipitated by Dr Martyn Lloyd-Jones of Westminster Chapel. He wished for evangelicals everywhere to leave their historic denominations and join together. This was vigorously opposed by many evangelicals within the mainstream Churches, notably Revd Dr John Stott, then of All Souls, Langham Place. The separatist tendencies of Westminster Chapel held appeal for those from a Brethren background, Independents and some Congregationalists. In some ways, I believe that the separatist movement of the 1960s was to have its counterpart in Restorationism in the 1980s.

However, in 1983, Gordon Landreth, the General Secretary of the EA, left and was replaced by Clive Calver, a professional evangelist with Youth for Christ. Clive's approach was dramatic. He asked the old guard to step down and, sweeping the Aegean stables clean, began with a completely new team and a new agenda. Clive was himself from a new church and had been brought to Christ through the ministry of Roger Forster of Ichthus. Roger had always been in favour of evangelistic co-operation, and while he was new church through and through, he favoured alliances rather than separatist movements. Indeed, Roger was critical of early Restoration for not being evangelistic and being too separatist.[7]

Clive Calver followed him in this and encouraged all who were truly evangelical – regardless of their denominational status – to join the Alliance. When Clive left British Youth For Christ, he left behind him a well-organized and successful movement. He had already demonstrated, therefore, both his activism and his organizational ability when he became General Secretary. In a short time, under his leadership, the EA not only picked up, but it has since become the major umbrella organization for activist and new evangelical churches, as well as the older evangelical groups in the mainstream Churches.

Clive's view when he moved into the EA was that it was not representative enough of British evangelicalism. In 1989, he claimed that the Alliance was made up of roughly 50 per cent charismatic and 50 per cent non-charismatic evangelicals.[8] Clive understood the EA not to be a power bloc, but he did hope that it would provide the infrastructure for the many activities of (what he claims) is an evangelical constituency of one million members.[9] As he put it himself: 'The EA has been described not as a "piece of the jigsaw", but rather the table on which the jigsaw pieces come together.'[10]

Restorationists were invited to join the other jigsaw pieces on the table, for the sake of a unified and coherent evangelical Church. Not only did Clive, on behalf of the EA, offer Restorationists a refuge and reference point to other evangelicals, he actually encouraged them to join, participate and lead. Nearly all R2 churches did join, as well as many hundreds of independent new churches (excluding Bugbroke and Derek Brown's churches, stemming from his Aldershot base). Many of Terry Virgo's churches also joined.

The EA is a democratic organization and Clive Calver has to abide by the rules of his general council. These rules state that no churches may join the Alliance unless a) they agree to a common doctrinal statement, and b) they are in good relationship with other evangelical churches. The fact that Clive was able to bring in many of the Restorationist churches between 1985 and 1989 is evidence of the lessening tension with other fellowships. It is also evidence that one of the earlier charges against the Restorationists, that they 'poached' from other churches – a charge Clive himself made at one point – was dropped, or at least was muted.

It needs to be remembered that for many years the Elim and the Assemblies of God movements did not belong to the Evangelical Alliance, and for decades they felt it was wrong for them to join. The fact that most Restorationists after 1985 wanted to be associated with a larger organization than themselves, one that also included non-charismatics, shows how far they, like the classical Pentecostals, had moved as a movement, and how much they had become willing to be accepted as part of the evangelical family.

Belonging to the EA not only gave Restorationists legitimacy, it also gave them a voice. Indeed, more than a voice. For since the late 1980s to the present day, the new churches' star (including Restorationists) has been in the ascendancy within the EA. It may even be that the sheer size and weight of new churches within the Alliance may have had the opposite effect to that desired. That is to say, rather than the EA bringing the new churches into the mainstream, the new churches may have taken the EA into a more sectarian (and some would say triumphalist) direction. If this is an accurate portrayal of what has happened to the EA, then in a way that he had not quite anticipated,

Martyn Lloyd-Jones may have succeeded in his separatist plan – though not with the sort of evangelicals that he had in mind.[11]

Spring Harvest – Clive Calver may have become a dynamic and successful leader of the EA, but in my opinion, since 1982/83 he has been responsible, along with his old friend Pete Meadows,[12] for the greatest success of evangelical and charismatic Christianity in Great Britain since the initial Pentecostal revivals in the first half of this century. This success was the establishment of the Spring Harvest residential holiday camps,[13] which by 1990 numbered some 80,000 people.[14] Spring Harvest, more than any other factor, has been, I believe, the single most important cause in the decline of Restorationism.

Interestingly, some Restorationist leaders saw themselves as precursors to Spring Harvest (see chapter 16), but in no sense can they claim any credit for it. Indeed, Clive Calver is quite adamant that Restorationism had no direct impact on Spring Harvest. Nor, more specifically, did the Dales Bible Week, which Clive had never visited when I spoke to him in 1989.[15] Both Clive Calver and Pete Meadows insist that Spring Harvest was conceived as something quite different to the Dales, and indeed in some senses as opposite to it.[16]

As Spring Harvest is so important to our story, we had better let Clive tell of its beginnings and growth. Clive's interview with me on this matter was refreshingly candid.

> I believe that Spring Harvest is totally different to the Dales, and it was always intended to be different. If you want the facts, Pete Meadows and I (and I hope Pete will admit it) started off trying to start an alternative to Keswick. And we said we did. Not because we had anything against Keswick, but because we felt that our generation needed an expression of corporate spiritual life and it certainly was not a charismatic one. I remember being the only person on the Spring Harvest platform

with my arms in the air (probably because Graham Kendrick was playing the guitar at the time). Spring Harvest did not start off as a charismatic event: it started off as being a teaching/training event. And its major thrust was young people.[17]

When Spring Harvest began in the late 1970s, some 2,700 people attended. In 1990, this number had grown to around 80,000 in England and Scotland, making it probably the largest residential event of its kind in the world. Within the charismatic constituency, there is certainly nothing comparable to it in the United States. The scale of Spring Harvest's success can also be measured against the Dales Bible Week and Greenbelt. When I reported for BBC radio on the Dales in 1982, it could boast some 8,000 people. Only Greenbelt at that time could be said to have been a bigger Christian residential event, with some 20,000 people or more.

It is difficult to be certain about what made Spring Harvest so successful, for there is no doubt that there has been nothing like it in British evangelical history. What is significant, it seems to me, is that its very size is evidence of the growth of charismatic Christianity over recent years. Spring Harvest became an event that was perceived by vast numbers of people to meet their needs. Clive believes that its initial success was due to the fact that while he and Pete Meadows all along intended it to be an evangelical event, they designed it to be one in which evangelicals and charismatics alike could come along and be themselves.

My own view is that the event quickly came to be seen as one in which the family could come together in a holiday atmosphere. Establishing the sites at Minehead in Somerset and Skegness on the north-east coast made it possible to have fun and faith at the same time. The event also provided a venue in which the seminars were not only diverse and at different intellectual levels, but also attempted to question the agenda of the Church. The ability to pay for major 'star' speakers such as Tony Campolo and Luis Palau did not do the organization any harm either.

One of the greatest successes of Spring Harvest was its laid-back style and its worship.[18] There were alternative worshipping venues for those who did not like the 'big top' atmosphere, but the large nightly celebrations were fuelled by the sort of music that came out of the Dales and Downs Weeks. More importantly, it was dominated by the worship songs of Graham Kendrick, who in my opinion has had a greater influence on British Christianity than all the new church leaders put together.

To go to Spring Harvest was to experience Restorationist style excitement, without having to buy its theology. You could get baptized in the Spirit or be healed without having to sign up for a Restorationist instruction course. You could follow charismatic leaders without having to be shepherded, and attend lectures on Ephesians chapter 4 without having to come under apostolic authority. In short, Spring Harvest offered virtually everything that Restoration was offering in terms of style, worship and enthusiasm. But its far greater choice and diversity appealed to the British public in a way in which the more authoritarian and specific doctrines of Restoration did not.[19] Sociologically, if you will, Spring Harvest was more in tune with the pluralism of late modernity than Restorationism, whose radical discipleship was always going to have minority appeal in the Thatcher era.

Clive Calver does admit that Restorationists have had a personal input into Spring Harvest. In this respect, it owes a debt to certain people, but as individuals and not as purveyors of Restorationism. Spring Harvest not only outshone Restorationist jamborees but also offered its leaders the chance to participate in the larger evangelical movement and make their mark. Along with Roger and Faith Forster, people such as John and Christine Noble, David Tomlinson, Peter Fenwick, Terry Virgo, Philip Mohabir and Gerald Coates made an important contribution to the ongoing success of Spring Harvest.[20] This has also led to the acceptance of new church people by mainstream evangelicals as 'one of us'.

In other words, although it may be true that Spring Harvest contributed to the slowing down of the Restorationist movement, it also facilitated its assimilation into the larger Christian community. I have not found any evidence of sour grapes among Restorationists concerning Spring Harvest and its growing influence at their own expense. Most of them want to be involved with it, and many now go with their families. Furthermore, it has softened them and made them more open to co-operation with other Christians. It is through Spring Harvest and the Evangelical Alliance, as well as his own ventures, that Gerald Coates has been able to move from Restorationist controversialist to a national charismatic leader.

Further External Factors that Accelerated Restorationist Decline

John Wimber – Beginning in the early 1980s and stemming from the missiological work of Peter Wagner at Fuller seminary in California, there was talk among charismatics of a 'third wave' of revival. The first wave was seen as classical Pentecostalism, and the second wave as the Charismatic Renewal. The third wave would be an even bigger religious awakening that would embrace charismatics of all hues and would be characterized by 'signs and wonders' that would bring the unconverted into the kingdom of God.

Of course, Restorationism in its early years saw itself as the third and final wave in Church and human history.[21] But as we will see in chapters 15 and 16, in the late 1980s neither Bryn Jones, Terry Virgo, nor R2 leaders considered that the revival they had hoped for had yet arrived. In fact, talk of third waves has been almost exclusively associated in Great Britain with the ministry of John Wimber rather than Restorationism. I attended Wimber's 'Third Wave' conference in 1984 at Westminster Central Hall, where I interviewed him for the BBC, and in 1985 (on behalf of publishers Hodder & Stoughton) I interviewed him and David Pytches in front of a large audience which had come to hear him speak and present his first major book in this country, *Power Evangelism*.[22] From such close proximity, it was clear that Wimber had become the most popular charismatic personality in town, and after 1985, under his influence, the Renewal movement began to recover from the battering it had received from the radical attacks of Restorationist Christianity.

From that time, despite, or because of, the inevitable controversy that surrounds miraculous ministries, Wimber became a major force in British Christianity, especially among Anglicans. I do not think that it is exaggerating too much to say that Wimber, and the style and methodology of the Vineyard Fellowships, has been the greatest influence in mainstream Renewal since the ministry of the late Canon David Watson and the hey-day of the Fountain Trust in the 1970s.

Wimber's success had two effects on Restorationism:

- Along with Spring Harvest and the growing authori ty of the Evangelical Alliance, Wimber's ministry took the heat and energy away from the Restorationist movement. In so doing, it fuelled the mainstream Renewal, and slowed down the defections to the new churches that had been taking place in the years 1978–85.[23]
- Wimberism also penetrated deep into the Restorationist movement itself, influencing many of the R2 fellowships and, as we will see in chapter 15, having a major impact on Terry Virgo's churches.

The knock-on effect of the Wimber input was to draw Terry and others into the mainstream Renewal, but it had little beneficial effect on Restorationism in terms of either its own growth or the influence of its distinctive ideology.

Some Restorationists resisted Wimber's approach. There is little evidence to show that Bryn followed Wimber in any direct way, and I have heard well-argued critiques of his 'signs and wonders' methodology from elders in Gerald's churches, as well as leaders from David Tomlinson's and Peter Fenwick's churches.[24]

John Wimber has always been controversial, not because of his personality, which was genial, but because his approach was both different from the older-style Pentecostal movements and the mainline Anglican and Catholic Renewalists.[25] In the 1980s, many classical Pentecostals and some of the new Independents did not know how to take to him (although never more so than during his brief partnership with the so-called Kansas City Prophets, and especially the two most well-known ones, Bob Jones and Paul Cain).[26]

Wimber had two great assets, in my opinion, which give him the edge over most contemporary charismatic leaders in the 1980s. The first one was, as already mentioned, his genial personality. He was extremely likeable and quite unlike the more aggressive Bible-Belters of the Mid West.[27] His laid-back Californian style and his willingness to work inside and alongside historic Christianity, endeared him both to the mainline and the independent sectors alike. Secondly, Wimber was aware of the deficiencies of his approach and tried very hard to obtain a balance between practice and theory. He did show in his books a genuine attempt to do some theology, and there was a reflective side to his work which is not typical of the charismatic stars.[28] In terms of influence, I would say that Wimber had greater impact on British charismatic religion than any of the Restorationist leaders in the late 1980s. The only person who came close to him from the new churches, in my opinion, is Roger Forster.

Prayer for revival and Pentecostal realignments – There was another phenomenon at work in Britain over the last third of the decade, and spilling into the 1990s, which probably came to its full fruition during the Toronto Blessing sensation of 1994–95. This phenomenon was a new-found evangelical co-operation, fuelled by the growing desire for revival (in the old-fashioned sense of thousands of converts being brought to Christ). Virtually everybody in charismatic and evangelical activism seemed to be involved in praying for revival. There was a great expectation in Britain, far more than there was in the early 1980s, that there was going to be a national revival on a scale even greater than the great Welsh outpouring of 1904 and the subsequent Pentecostal movements.

This revivalistic fervour was not only talked about in the house journals of Elim, the Assemblies of God, Restorationism, etc., but also spilled over into interdenominational activity. I recall seeing an advert for a major conference on revival at Birmingham in the late 1980s which was supported by the classical Pentecostalists, Renewalists and Independents. The conference was attended by R1 and R2 (Bryn had been present at an earlier one). Commending the conference were a list of charismatics who represented virtually the whole Pentecostal spectrum. They were John Noble, John Wimber, Don Double, Nick Cuthbert, Colin Urquhart and Derek Prince.[29]

What began to happen in Great Britain was something new.[30] We were seeing all the diverse charismatic movements co-operating together for the common cause of revival. To be sure, there are some historical parallels for such a radical co-operation of different Churches. We can think of the Congregational Union prior to 1846, or the Pentecostal Holiness League at the turn of the century, or indeed the congregational formation of the Assemblies of God in the 1920s. But none of them included such diversity as could be seen in the co-operation between Renewalists (whether Wimberite or not), classical Pentecostalists and the many Independents (including Restorationists). We must also include in this new-found camaraderie, those many evangelical Churches, in particular the

Baptists and Brethren, who are not formally charismatic at all.[31]

It is not that the older style 'crusades' became a thing of the past. The great success of Billy Graham's 'Mission 89' is proof of that. But what was beginning to happen, and was to continue well into the 1990s, was a networking that was far more inclusive of charismatics and evangelicals than was typical in the immediate past. For a short while – ten years at the most – the Restorationist movement had taken away much of the energy and ecumenical drive from the Renewal. By 1989, the flow was going back into the mainstream, carrying much of Restorationism with it, but leaving some segments outside.

Elsewhere I have called the new co-operation of charismatics, which began at the end of the 1980s, as the 'fourth wave'.[32] I did so because the 'third wave', in effect, was a change of charismatic emphasis rather than the birth of a new movement. What the third wave did presage, however, was a radical blurring of the lines between the classical, Renewalist and Independent charismatic sectors. This amounted to a newly-discovered togetherness, which augmented revivalistic excitation in the early 1990s until it burst with the Toronto Blessing in 1994. If we may characterize the realignment of British charismatic interests as a fourth wave, we must do so in the knowledge that it was primarily a Protestant affair and that it peaked with Toronto.[33]

What I think is of particular interest in the British context is that by 1990 the charismatic scene had become not only a more co-operative movement, but also an increasingly integrated Christian market. A small group of powerful producers were supplying the spiritual (and shopping) needs of large numbers of religious consumers. So much so, that we can usefully talk of the development of a Protestant charismatic monopoly (Catholic renewalists had little stake in this enterprise economy, except as occasional consumers).

I have tried to indicate something of the supply side of

this monopoly in Figure 3 (p 316) by showing some of the interconnected rings of charismatic influence. This influence was organizational and somewhat incestuous (wheels within wheels) and reached religious consumers at significant arenas of consumption throughout the country. These arenas ranged from festivals and celebrations (in this respect Spring Harvest has been both an arena of production and consumption), networks, and strategic churches. Examples of networks would be Ichthus and New Frontiers. Strategic churches were those churches that were seen both to be a focus of blessing and an influence on the larger charismatic scene. A few examples would be Bethshan Tabernacle in Newcastle, Sunderland Christian Fellowship,[34] St Thomas Crooks Sheffield, St Andrew's Chorleywood, Kensington Temple and Holy Trinity Brompton in London.[35]

I am not suggesting, for a moment, that this Christian market was either a total or a planned monopoly.[36] However, its existence partly explains how, when it broke in 1995, the Toronto Blessing was able to spread so quickly, and why Restorationists, like everybody else, got carried along by the tide.

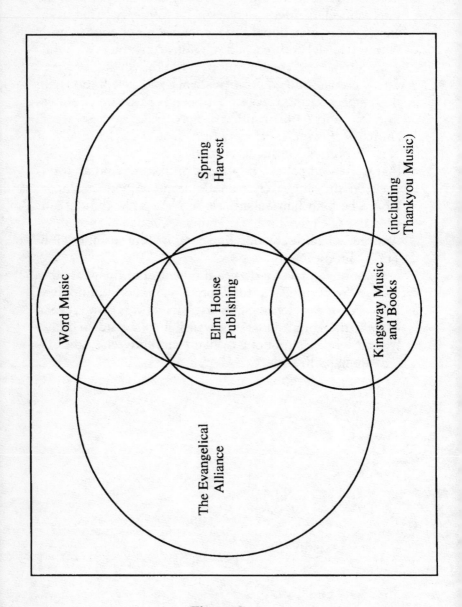

Figure 3.
Interconnected rings of Charismatic influence by 1990

Recommended Reading

A Million People (EA mimeographic publication 1993).

Donald Bridge, *Power Evangelism and the Word of God* (Leicester: IVP, 1987).

Andrew Walker, 'Charismatic and Pentecostal Religion', ed. A. McGrath, *Blackwell Encyclopaedia of Contemporary Christian Thought* (Oxford: Blackwell, 1993) pp 110–14.

Pete Ward, *Growing Up Evangelical* (London: SPCK, 1995) chapter 5.

John Wimber, *Power Evangelism* (London: Hodder & Stoughton, 1985).

15

THE CHANGING CHARACTER OF R1

Going Separate Ways

The external events which slowed down Restorationism after 1985 were matched by internal changes. Within R1, for example, Bryn Jones, Terry Virgo and Tony Morton ceased to 'relate' together and went their separate ways. Terry and Tony's names disappeared from the editorial associates of *Restoration* magazine, and the three apostles no longer enjoyed a close working relationship.

This is not as dramatic as it sounds. There was no break in friendship as there had been in 1983, when David Tomlinson felt he could no longer work with Bryn. No anathemas were hurled, nor accusations made of betrayal. Bryn Jones understood the break as a 'releasing' of his fellow apostles to a wider and more independent ministry. This might seem to support the view that Bryn, acting as *primus inter pares*, let his fellow co-workers go with his blessing. Such a view is misleading, for it suggests a formal split was precipitated by a theocratic decision from the senior apostle. Terry and Tony saw it simply in terms of agreeing to work less together so that they could continue to extend their ministries within their own spheres of influence.

Terry is quite clear that while he owes a great debt to Bryn, he was never 'under his authority'.[1] He cannot be said to have broken 'covenanted relationship' – 'we talk of committed relationships down here'[2] – because no such thing existed. Furthermore, Terry has argued, his churches in the south-east never reflected the Bradford style, and

'David Mansell had more impact upon my life than Bryn did.'[3]

The break-up of Bryn, Terry and Tony did, however, alter the nature of R1. In the first place, the sense of a corporate enterprise was somewhat lost. There may not have been a schism, but there was a loss of momentum with the breakdown of this Restorationist coalition. Secondly, as we will shortly see, the ending of the coalition may have slowed down the initial impact of Restoration on British religious culture, but Terry's 'release' seemed to galvanize him into new efforts and send him in significant new directions. I believe that the 1985 separation of Bryn and Terry did not, however, radically alter their ideological convictions and they both (to this day) remain committed Restorationists in the R1 mould.[4]

Tony Morton, on the other hand, always an independent thinker, since the break moved more in the direction of R2 than staying within R1. This was not so much in the sense that he established working relationships with John Noble, Gerald Coates and David Tomlinson, but more that he adopted a more open-ended theology and a freer *modus operandi*.[5] His Cornerstone Ministries has continued to grow and the parent church in Southampton is one of the largest new churches in the country.

There were some Restorationists who bewailed the break-up of the triumvirate. Elders from one of the churches that were soon to reject Bryn's apostolic authority believed that Terry and Tony had a positive influence on the Bradford leader. Once they went their own way, the elders felt, Bryn was no longer subject to outside counsel and became more isolated and dictatorial in style.[6] On the whole, however, the ending of the special working relationship led to very little debate among Restorationists. No crisis was perceived to have occurred and local church life continued much as before.

Crisis, then, may not be the best word to describe the R1 divide after 1985, but the break certainly brought many changes. We can look at some of the more significant of these by concentrating on the ministries of Bryn and Terry between 1985 and 1990.

Bryn Jones: from Bradford to Nettle Hill

If you were to ask anyone in the evangelical world in the early 1980s what they knew about Restoration churches, the chances are that it would be Bryn Jones that would spring to mind, *Restoration* magazine, Bradford and the Dales Bible Week. By the late 1980s, however, Terry Virgo and New Frontiers probably best represented the Restoration movement.[7] Bryn Jones seemed to become, outside his own circles at least, almost invisible.

Some might argue that Bryn made a mistake in dismantling the Dales Bible Week after 1982. It was in effect to empty the most enticing shop window of Restorationist wares in Great Britain. Or again, others might say that Bryn's age and weight were against him. Reaching middle age and carrying more weight than he should, he became tired and the energy began to fade away. All these arguments – and I have heard them all – seem plausible enough, but they are wrong. The fading into the background by Bryn Jones was not due to loss of charisma, or putting on too much weight.[8] It was a conscious decision based on Bryn Jones's conviction that he had radically to restructure his organization if it were to have a long-term impact.

This was not at all clear looking in from the outside at that time: there seemed to be a higgledy-piggledy approach to things. In 1984 and 1985 there was a brief flurry of traditional evangelical activity in campaign style. There was what appeared to be a flirting with televangelism after 1985 with Dales Television. Then there was the much-heralded £4 million move to Leicester in 1987, which never materialized.[9] All of these might be thought of as false starts before eventually in 1990 the Bradford headquarters was dismantled and operations were moved to Nettle Hill in the Midlands. However, while former members of Bryn's churches are all too happy to see things in this light, I think the phrase 'fits and starts' is a fairer and more accurate description of what took place and more usefully explains the experimental nature of some of the new directions.

From the mid-1980s onwards, Bryn Jones and his colleagues began to think through their future direction. This had a certain introverted feel about it, or an in-house affair in the sense of putting the house in order. The Wales Bible Week for a time became a kind of 'holy convocation', at which, during 1986 and 1987 at least, the meetings were organized primarily for committed members of Restorationist churches. There was much praying and heart-searching by the leaders, who were looking for the way forward. This heart-searching eventually led to relocating the Bradford operations in the Midlands. As the Nettle Hill brochure put it, 'In 1986 the Covenant Ministries team curtailed their itinerant ministry for six months' prayer and waiting upon the Lord. During that time God clearly directed that the base for their ministry should be relocated in the Midlands.'

Dales Television – Before we consider that move, mention should be made of the beginning of Dales TV. According to former members of Bryn's churches, whom I interviewed in the north of England, they were fired up by the vision of televangelism (the Swaggert and Bakker debacles in the United States were yet to happen). They told me that since the days of Ern Baxter in the late 1970s, they had been led to believe that they were the shock troops of the kingdom, a spiritual SAS, who were going to take the nation for God. The Dales Television Company, set up in 1985, was, they thought, the means to accomplish that task.

In the event, the launch of Dales TV was not a great success and some saw this failure as a disaster. They thought they were poised for a great leap forward with satellite broadcasting, only to fall flat on their faces because of its relative failure. A significant number of people left Bryn's 'covering' during this time, because they thought he was inept. Too much was promised, some of them felt, and too little was delivered.[10]

This particular charge strikes me as unfair. Perhaps the rhetoric was strong and the expectation high, but even apostles and prophets do not have infallible knowledge of satellite TV, let alone forthcoming decisions on the deregulation of independent broadcasting. Officially, the satellite broadcasts were seen as a pilot project 'to test our ability to produce regular programmes of broadcasting quality'.[11] As late as 1989, Bryn was quite sanguine about how things would turn out. 'I think that anyone involved in TV knows that it is in a state of flux right now. It is hard to predict. It is almost a month-by-month, feel-the-pulse way of telling about the future of broadcasting.'[12]

Dales TV did sign up for a twenty-six programme contract with a European satellite company to be beamed across Europe from Oslo in Norway. As David Matthew admitted, 'this was not altogether successful'.[13] There were a number of reasons for this. First, reception for satellite television in Europe was variable and the whole system was still undergoing teething problems. Secondly, the Dales programme was transmitted after midnight. Thirdly, not many people in Europe had satellite television at that time. Fourthly, of those who did, many did not speak English. Last, but not least, Dales TV was starting from scratch and did not have the experience or honed skills necessary to make an impact through this medium.

Nevertheless, the twenty-six programmes were completed and David Matthew told me of many enquiries. 'In Norway, in particular, we know of people converted and committed to local churches as a result.'[14] Even before the move to the Midlands, Dales TV became more geared to producing videos for evangelistic efforts (*Living on the Edge* was one series, for example). Equipment and studios were also hired out to reputable television companies.[15]

This explains how Dales TV was kept in business, but it does not explain where the initial investment money came from. Andrew Tyler in *Time Out* magazine thought there was an initial £300,000 investment, but was not sure how the money was raised.[16] Bryn Jones, on the other hand, told me that the initial investment was well under £200,000. 'The reason for that is that we already had a sound studio downstairs. We just moved into it. There was not the big capital investment that other studios had in setting up. The only thing we had to set up was the equipment costs and the outside broadcasting unit.'[17] As for the source of the money, some of it came from tithes and private offerings. Large amounts came from 'heap offerings'.

Restructuring and moving – By 1987, Bradford could not only boast the impressive Church House complex and Restorationist offices – it had also acquired a huge new church. This church, designed in what the Americans call the 'warehouse style', was called 'Abundant Life'. The 'health and wealth' sounding title seems to reflect what appeared to be a growing interest in the so-called American Faith Movement of Kenneth Hagin and Kenneth Copeland.[18] This interest seems to be confirmed by events at the Welsh Bible Week in 1987, when according to witnesses with whom I talked, Mrs Buddy Harrison, who was the daughter of Kenneth Hagin, prophesied (with her head covered) over Bryn and Keri. Under her anointing and power they were 'slain in the spirit' and fell to the floor.[19]

Perhaps of greater significance at the convocation was the fact that many people for the first time were to share Bryn's vision of the restructured and relocated organization. Others, not at the Bible Week, heard of this move by receiving the fund-raising brochure for the site at Leicester. Entitled 'Building for the Future', the leaflet was glossy and professional. The artist's impression of the complex included an auditorium for 1,500 people, a television studio, warehousing, business and administrative offices. The organization was to comprise Help Africa, Dales Television, Go! Teams, Restoration Music and Covenant College (the replacement for Riddleston College in Yorkshire).

Not everybody liked the new plan. The leaders of one of the northern churches which left Restoration looked on it as a bid for denominationalism. Others in a university town felt that it was yet another example of Bryn's team taking precedence over the local churches.[20] Such people, however, were in the minority. Most people in the Bradford network seemed content that it was God's plan for the future. My own view in 1987 was that the plan was too grandiose and expensive, but at least it was clear that what was beginning to emerge from Bryn's network was something akin to the American south-west evangelistic organizations that were part mission and teaching complexes, with supporting church networks. By the mid-1980s, Bryn Jones had considerable experience of American methods (having, for example, been in St Louis for a while).[21]

At the time, I also thought that the Covenant Ministries team surrounding Bryn were becoming a bureaucratic tier between the apostle and the local churches. I saw the whole new structure as top-heavy (it seemed as if there were going to be twenty-seven members in the team), financially insecure and volatile. To me it looked as if the team would become a barrier or buffer between Bryn and the churches. This is certainly how the disgruntled Restorationists saw it. One irate elder believed that the team was increasingly impersonal and kept Bryn away from the local churches. Restoration, the elder said, was supposed to be based on a paternal, filial model of personal relationships. 'What kind of family is it,' he asked, 'when you don't see dad?'[22]

On the financial level, I could not see how a network in Great Britain with less than 8,000 members could financially sustain such an ambitious programme, especially if the churches shrunk in numbers.[23] In the event, many of my concerns and criticisms were to prove academic, because the move to Leicester never took place. Leicester Council did not approve the plans and a new site was found near Coventry. It was another three years before the final move to Nettle Hill, but the organization which emerged at that time was a far more streamlined operation with more of a campus than a business feel to it. The team (in 1989 at least) under the auspices of Covenant Ministries became eight men – Bryn and Keri Jones (apostles), David Mansell and Tony Ling (with prophetic ministries), and the others included Ivor Hopkins, Gwyn Daniel, Alan Scotland and Ron Tempest. There were two administrators, Gareth Duffy and Richard Bartrop. There were also significant jobs for David Matthew and Roger Day.

In an interview with Bryn Jones, I discovered that the British churches were augmented by a significant American network, with churches also in Norway and other parts of the world. Furthermore, the new enterprise was founded on investment and business success, as well as church donations. Sociologically, after the move to Nettle Hill in 1990, the churches and Covenant Ministries – and their sister organizations – might be said to have been so tightly knit together that they formed a sect in the making. But Bryn's vision was (and still remains) to establish an enabling mission for the whole Church, rather than found a denomination.[24]

This can be seen in the various groups and activities that became established at Nettle Hill. At the heart of things was Covenant Ministries, whose purpose was both to establish and encourage a network of churches around the world, but with the core churches established in Britain. Covenant College was created not to be a Bible School for Restorationist leaders (which would have been a significant indication of denominational establishment), but as a college open to all for full-time and part-time training in biblical studies. Perhaps of greater influence was the establishment of modular training courses, using a distance learning training programme of video and audio tapes, work manuals and books.

Rather like American summer schools, Covenant College also housed ACTS (Accelerated Christian

Leadership Training Seminars). These intense courses were aimed at church leaders who were too busy to follow longer periods of study. Nettle Hill also offered training and conference facilities, the Dales Television studios and Help International – a relief and development charity, providing practical help for those living in poverty, regardless of their religious status.

Changing emphases in Bryn's churches – A perennial temptation for all movements which talk of God's rule and dominion is to adopt an over-realized eschatology and begin to lay out a religious and social programme as if the kingdom had already come among us. One such theology which made a splash in the 1980s was Reconstructionism – a movement based on a detailed programme, reconstructing the Old Testament covenant with all its theocratic implications (not least the ancient Jewish injunction to execute practising homosexuals!).[25] A number of Restorationists flirted with this theology, but never Bryn and his churches.[26]

On the surface this might seem strange, as there is strong evidence to show that Bradford became more overtly post-millennial in the 1980s.[27] Reconstructionism, however, is deeply right-wing, and although Bryn appeared from the mid-1980s to adopt a version of prosperity teaching (of which more later), his own moral and political predilection has been to side with the poor and the oppressed. Perhaps he was influenced in this by his father's Marxist idealism[28] and his antipathy to American conduct when he was a missionary in Guyana in the 1960s. But the roots of Bryn's own idealism may go back to his experience of poverty during his childhood in South Wales. I have seen Bryn cry at recalling going to school with cardboard covering the holes in his boots.[29]

Whatever the case, Bryn's churches were increasingly showing a concern for social justice issues in the late 1980s, with a regular section in *Restoration* magazine on world views, which read more like reports from Christian Aid sources than typical evangelical dispatches. And this was no mere posturing, as the 'Cry Freedom' boxes in the magazine, supporting South African liberation, demonstrated. Ever since a major article by David Mansell in 1983, *Restoration* had not only refused to adopt a pro-Zionist approach to Israeli politics, but it also, from the late 1980s, increasingly displayed active support for Palestinian liberation.[30]

The sophistication and passion of some of these articles perhaps echoed Bryn's own studies at Bradford University, where he obtained an MA in Peace Studies in 1990 (and is still registered for a doctorate there). He would also, during his studies, have come into contact with Catholic liberationists and anti-imperialists, but his stance against militarism goes back many years before that.[31]

Help for the poor, involvement in international relations, and critiques of Western imperialism cannot be seen as epiphenomenal to Covenant Ministries from the late 1980s onwards. It was part of the world vision of a team that wished to go beyond the parochial concerns of local church and religious life. This became clearer in the 1990s with the establishment of the Institute for World Concerns.[32] Bryn was quite clear in 1989 that in many evangelical circles there existed an 'ugly kind of righteousness' (we agreed to call it moralism) that was indifferent to social justice. As he put it:

> If I have something to say on anything concerning human rights, humanity as a whole, the dignity of man, etc., I'll say it. If you said to me, 'Bryn, who do you admire as espousing passionately your convictions on these issues?', I would have to say Dr Martin Luther King Jnr. Everything I have heard of his speeches, everything I have heard of his philosophical stance – I could say amen to it all.[33]

At the same time that Covenant Ministries was increasingly concerned with social and political issues, it also appeared to be promoting some of the principles of the Faith Movement. This was the view of one of the most notorious Faith preachers at that time, Michael Bassett.[34] We could be forgiven for finding this plausible, because we have already seen the connection between Bryn, Keri and Kenneth Hagin. Kenneth Copeland also enjoyed some fellowship with leaders in R1. Certainly, prosperity-sounding articles peppered *Restoration* magazine in the late 1980s.[35] There was even a minor division in one of the Restoration churches in Bath over the prosperity issue.

If it is going too far to say that Covenant Ministries espoused a full-blown prosperity doctrine, there was a disjunction, it seems to me, between a leftist-looking social programme and a rightist-looking self-help programme that seemed to owe more to American Republicanism than Karl Marx.[36] (One of the northern elders whom I interviewed thought Bryn was a Thatcherite!) Bryn Jones certainly believes in self-help programmes and is convinced that the poor do not want to be ministered to by anyone in poverty. Being poor, he feels, is no solution to institutional poverty. Like the American evangelists, Oral Roberts and Jimmy Bakker, Bryn comes from a poor background and also, like them, he does not want to return to poverty.

Bryn is quite up-front about the fact that he has made 'lots of money' on property and business ventures, even though he is in no sense a businessman.[37] When he lived in Yorkshire, he owned several expensive classical cars, enjoyed fine food and lived in an impressive grand home called Riddleston Hall (restored by workmen that Bryn took from the dole queue).

On the other hand, Bryn's generosity is legendary. He has helped out many families and individuals in the sense of underwriting their salaries or financial commitments. I was visiting Oral Roberts University in Tulsa, Oklahoma, in 1988, when one of the staff there told me how Bryn had once stuffed $500 into his hand because he had heard that he had fallen on hard times. One day, Steve Goddard, the former editor of *Buzz* magazine, was stopped by Bryn, who thrust £200 into his hand because he heard he was finding it hard to get a job. (Steve was too astonished, he told me, to hand the money back.)

This personal generosity, as we have already seen, is backed by a genuine concern for the poor and for social justice. And to be fair to Bryn and his team, although they do seem to favour a version of prosperity theology, it is mercifully free of the idiosyncratic atonement theories of Copeland and Hagin, with their almost gnostic view of faith as a force to be manipulated by the spiritual elite, but unknown to and unusable by the poor in their despair and degradation.

Not that prosperity doctrines, even amended and reformed ones, do not have obvious institutional benefits in a movement like Restoration. There is a tendency to invite followers financially to back their leaders in the form of tithes and gifts, in return for God's favours.[38] Clearly, a theology of generosity that is tied in to a conviction that God supplies all our needs, also has moral dangers: not least, in its American form, the imposition of moral guilt on those who fail to prosper.

But, as is usually the case with Bryn Jones, he is eclectic, taking what he wants, as with Ern Baxter's doctrines, and discarding the rest. Perhaps the short answer to the seeming mutual incompatibility of centre-left social programmes with right self-help proposals and prosperity promises, is that they reflect the life of a very complex character on the one hand, and the 'fly by the seat of your pants' theology on the other hand. 'Stuff' gets put together on the hoof when a religious movement is flourishing and only later does it get sorted out. In 1990, Bryn Jones did eventually put together both his concern for the poor and his belief that believers could prosper under God into one statement. It certainly has the ring of integrity about it. Entitled *Poverty or Prosperity: Why Some People are Rich* and *Others Poor*, it was published by Harvestime. There are virtually no echoes of Copeland in this, but there is a strong insistence that poverty is primarily caused by social systems of oppression, economic greed and tyranny.[39]

Personally, I do not think the doctrines of prosperity and social concern in this document logically cohere, and I would be more in favour of the rule of evangelical poverty embraced by many of the Desert Fathers, the Franciscans and Wycliffe, than Bryn appears to be. Nevertheless, I think it fairest to end this section with Bryn's favourite definition of prosperity and its relationship to generosity. He insists that this is his core concept of prosperity, and as he rightly surmised when I last interviewed him, only the churlish could object to it: 'God is able to bless you with ample means, so that you may always have quite enough for any emergency of your own and ample besides for any kind act to others' (2 Cor 9:8, Moffatt's translation).

Terry Virgo: from Coastlands to New Frontiers

Terry Virgo was not a member of the 'magnificent seven' (see chapter 3). Neither was he a major figure in the Restorationist split of 1976 (see chapter 4). Consequently, we have not focused on him as much as some of the other leaders in the house church movement. But this should not lead us to assume that Terry has been an insignificant figure in Restorationist circles.[40] On the contrary, Terry was an important leader from the beginning. Since the early 1970s in Seaford, East Sussex, Terry was a familiar landmark on the south coast charismatic landscape. In those early days he was much influenced not only by David Mansell, but also by Arthur Wallis, Edgar Trout, Denis Clarke and Campbell McAlpine. Before he became involved with Bryn Jones, *Restoration* magazine and the Dales Bible Week, he was already known at the earlier Capel Bible Week and later, in what was to be very much his own venture, Downs Bible Week.

Nevertheless, although Terry was a respected figure on the south coast – the so called British 'Bible-Belt' – and despite his recognition as an apostle within the wider structures of R1, he was almost unknown on the larger charismatic stage until after 1985. It is tempting to speculate that Terry began to shine when he stepped out from the shadow of Bryn Jones and became his own man. However, such a temptation should be resisted, for there is no evidence that Bryn kept Terry Virgo down in any way. Terry himself feels that his growing acceptability was due to the fact that he was the beneficiary of a decline in anti-Restorationist feeling. Certainly, by 1989 he was able to tell me:

> For the first time I was able to stand at the Brighton Centre last spring and preach to just over 5,000 people, the sort of thing that thrills my heart, instead of having to defend scare stories. Suddenly the door flew wide open because people said, 'Hey, he is saying these sort of things'. And I think going to Spring Harvest and doing the Bible studies there allowed people to say, 'I thought he was supposed to be into this heavy-handed thing. How come he just preaches the word?'[41]

Terry's success is perhaps the more remarkable because in fact after 1985 he did not radically change his controversial methods of recruitment or alter his paternalistic version of Restorationism. The same man who had enraged certain sections of the Baptist Union for what they saw as 'poaching' some of their congregations, was invited to conduct the morning devotions at Spurgeon's College. And the same man who collected strays and defectors from the Assemblies of God was invited to write a major article for *Redemption* magazine.[42] And despite the fact that his churches had made no concession to feminism or democratic principles, Terry Virgo and many of the fellowships in his network became voting members of the Evangelical Alliance.[43]

Before we look at Terry's churches and their practices, we must account for his personal success and as to how, in the words of a leading Renewalist, 'Terry came in from the cold'.

The rise and rise of Terry Virgo – I think Terry is right to stress that people became more interested in what he had to say than in hearing scare stories about his churches.[44] It was not that Terry ceased to be loyal to his Restorationist principles,[45] but that he had much to say that other evangelicals could relate to without feeling they were being taken over by an alien ideology. Unlike many Restorationist leaders – for example, Bryn Jones and Gerald Coates – Terry is Calvinist rather than Arminian. This is not the Calvinism of the mainline Reformed tradition, mediated through Karl Barth, in which we find theologians such as Professor T. F. Torrance and Bishop Lesslie Newbigin. Neither is it quite the principled Calvinism of John Stott (although Terry admires him). Terry's Calvinism is in the spirit of the great Puritan leader John Owen, mediated through the separatist tendencies of Martyn Lloyd-Jones and the earlier evangelicalism of C. H. Spurgeon.

No disrespect to Arminians is intended, but evangelical Calvinists have a long tradition of being Bible teachers and expositors in ways which sometimes give the impression of greater scholarship and weight than their Arminian counterparts. In this respect, Terry's Calvinist expository skills have earned him the role of a teacher of the Bible. Indeed, it might be said that this is his cherished charism, rather than the formal title of apostle or the quixotic role of the prophet. Terry's Calvinism has a sobering effect on his platform performances. Rather like a high Puritan – not unlike those other house church Calvinist leaders, Peter Fenwick of Sheffield and Brian Howell of Gateshead – Terry is measured in his approach and style. He is not flashy, and he is not the master of the *ad hoc* remark, or effortless in his delivery. Consequently he may not come over as a 'star', but he does come over as a man of authority.

Terry's Calvinism and biblicism shade into his personality. And here Terry could be said to score over Bryn Jones. Bryn is a very likeable person, but by his own admission, he is a very strong character. Nigel Wright put it bluntly: 'Bryn Jones is an admirable person, hugely able and attractive in many ways, but he will have his way or he will push you out.'[46] If this is too strong, shall we say that Bryn Jones, like fellow apostle Gerald Coates, evokes strong feelings of attraction or dislike.[47] Terry does not excite such extreme reactions. Nigel Wright can say: 'I do like Terry immensely: in spirit I feel that he is a man I can trust.'[48] Many people tell me the same thing.

Looking at the uniformity of belief and practice within Terry's churches prevents us from being lulled into a false sense that Terry is a soft man: he tends to get what he wants. But his public persona is courteous, friendly and open. I do not know if he is open to persuasion, but he is certainly a man of persuasion, open to dialogue and friendship. He has established good relationships with his fellow clergymen in Brighton, and in conversation with him he clearly honours them. Because he is not confrontational or aggressive, he wins a hearing for himself wherever he goes.

He is thoughtful, too. I took him out for lunch and he arranged a splendid meal, with excellent food and an intimate atmosphere, but it was very reasonably priced. He has also been quick to offer praise of my work in his letters to me,[49] and has never been defensive even when, as we will see shortly, I probed him on his controversial relationships with other churches. He also listens. Even when I took some time to explain to him why, sociologically speaking, I thought New Frontiers was a denomination in the making, he did not violently protest or vehemently deny the possibility.[50]

As important as Terry's Calvinism, expository skills and pleasant personality are in explaining how he emerged as a major evangelical leader from the mid-1980s, they are probably not so significant as his friendship with John Wimber. That the two of them forged a friendship and a working alliance is, on the surface, surprising. Wimber's background was Quakerism and the Californian pop scene. Terry is Calvinist Baptist, London Bible College and south coast Restorationism. Wimber's introduction to British churches was through the mainstream Renewal. Terry's experience was primarily house church. In meeting together, there was a crossing over of boundaries. John became more acceptable in house church circles, and indeed the establishment of Vineyard churches in Britain began to look like the beginnings of a new church denominationalism. Conversely, Terry greatly benefited through his relationship with Wimber and became more acceptable in broader circles.

Terry is quick to acknowledge the importance of John Wimber in his life. 'Our friendship with John Wimber – God brought us together – has proved strategically important.'[51] Not only did Wimber visit Brighton, but Terry Virgo went to California. Just as we earlier recalled (in chapter 12) that Aimée Semple McPherson's Hollywood style rubbed off on George Jeffreys in 1926 and gave Elim an unexpected boost, so did Wimber's friendship almost certainly help Terry's visibility and credibility outside Restorationist churches. Once Terry was seen as a national charismatic leader, his Restorationism was no longer a disadvantage. Indeed, he was even invited to Bognor Bible Week organized by the Elim Church. This was certainly not because of the Wimber connection (Wimber was not popular with the leadership in Elim and the Assemblies of God in those days), but because by then Pentecostals were prepared to accept Terry's own 'gifting' – to use a favourite term of Restorationist argot.

By 1988, Terry Virgo had become one of the most respected charismatic leaders in England. An article appeared in *Renewal* magazine in January 1988 entitled, 'Who is this Terry Virgo?' The article was remarkably free of rancour and the anti-Restorationist tone of a few years earlier. It was almost as if Terry, the former poacher, had turned gamekeeper and was now acknowledged as a supporter of the charismatic establishment.

The controversy surrounding Terry Virgo's *modus operandi* – In fact, there were still people who saw Terry as poacher. This was primarily due to Terry's involvement with other churches. Unlike Bryn Jones, who, after the Goos Vedder incident (see chapter 13), preferred to plant his own churches, Terry continued to oversee a number of churches within the Baptist Union. This is not as odd as it sounds and is certainly not illegal. The Baptist Union is a union of congregational churches which have considerable autonomy within the larger structure.

Furthermore, Terry pointed out, 'I am not conscious of bad vibes. They may be there – but they don't reach me.'[52] He also cited the time that he was present at the laying of the foundation stone for the Bracknell church (which was part of Terry's organization but still formally Baptist Union). 'I sat next to the superintendent at the meal and we chatted very warmly. There was no question of "what are you doing here?" or anything. He was just very warm and friendly.'[53]

Terry insisted that he never went knocking on Baptist doors asking if he could come in. He only responded if asked, and usually there was already a charismatic awakening before Restorationists came on the scene:

> The flow of the Baptism of the Spirit runs wild. It's in there and it's running, and usually leaders would not ask me in if they were frightened. When the pastor is established and he is quite happy with the state of affairs regarding the Spirit, he might then ask me in.[54]

Sometimes churches would stay in the Baptist Union but change their names. Queen's Road Baptist Church became plain Queen's Road, for example. Or South Lee Baptist became South Lee Christian Centre. In 1989, Nigel Wright said that he knew of at least a dozen churches that had remained in the Baptist Union but had become

Restorationist. He felt that the situation could be looked at in two ways. On the one hand you could say that the Restorationists 'wanted the benefits of the Baptist Union but they tend to give no loyalty to it. Logically they should opt out of it.' On the other hand, 'they genuinely see the value of being in Terry Virgo's world, but they know that is not everything. There are networks, particularly theological resources, available in the Baptist Union, which they would not have access to if they left.'[55]

It must be said that not all Baptists were as sanguine about the situation as Nigel Wright. At least one former General Secretary and a well-known metropolitan superintendent felt that the Restorationist *modus operandi* was ethically underhand. They felt, I think, that it was somewhat fortuitous that a theocratic structure under the direction of a charismatic apostle was able to take advantage of the democratic tradition of the Baptist Union in order to move in like the proverbial cuckoo and take over the nest.

Judging the merits of the case is difficult because of the unusual legal structure of the Baptist Union, but by 1989 the 'covering' of these denominational churches – which never anyhow amounted to more than a handful of Terry's churches – had slowed down. As Terry put it: 'As it happens, I cannot remember the last "new" one of those sort. We are much more involved in aiming to plant new churches rather than to adopt established ones.'[56]

Restructuring and new directions – Surely one of the best moves ever made by Terry Virgo was to change the name of his network from 'Coastlands' – with its 'hi-de-hi' feel – to the altogether more challenging legend, 'New Frontiers'. New Frontiers heralded the pioneering spirit of the Church – the radical Christianity which was supposed to be the hallmark of Restoration. By 1989, these churches had grown into a well-organized network with common doctrines and practices (women's hair covering seemed almost mandatory at one time) which did not deviate in any great detail from the earlier Restorationist vision.

There was a stability and a certain uniformity about these churches which suggested that by 1990 they were the most established, and the largest, Restorationist grouping in the country. By Terry's own account, there were some fifty-eight churches in the network at that time with some 10,000–12,000 members.[57] There is no evidence that the new-found interdenominational activity and the Wimber influence had radically altered the Restorationist principles of Ephesians chapter 4 or the commitment to shepherding. 'Filial, paternalistic and benign' would not be an unfair shorthand of New Frontiers at this time – although applying to local congregations the principles of obedience normally associated with monasteries and covenanted communities remained a controversial programme.

If, however, New Frontiers Restorationism remained undiluted, there were changes. Like Bryn Jones, Terry spent time in the United States (he was to live there for some time in the 1990s), and New Frontiers had considerable interest in missionary work outside Britain. But perhaps the biggest change of emphasis was the growing interest in establishing large churches as a Restorationist presence in Great Britain. This was itself part of the general trend in charismatic Christianity in the 1980s. Influenced by Pastor Cho in Seoul, South Korea, and Dr Kriangsak in Thailand (who had a personal influence on Terry), Western leaders began to abandon the 'small is beautiful' ideology in favour of the establishment of 'power centres'. John Wimber himself came to be in favour of the megachurch as a 'power line' to God.[58]

Bryn, as we have seen, had already built a large church in Bradford. Gerald Coates, for a while, was committed to buying an abandoned aircraft hanger in Surrey to turn into a large church. Tony Morton oversaw the large parent church in Cornerstone Ministries in Southampton; and Clarendon Villas itself could boast a church of 1,000 members by the late 1980s. (This trend towards the large church was to be a feature of charismatic activity in the 1990s – nowhere more so than the 5,000 membership of

Kensington City Temple in London.)

Terry's Clarendon premises were to prove too small in time for the burgeoning Hove and Brighton Restorationist population, but other large churches were to spring up in the South. I recall, for example, first driving through Bracknell in 1989 to see what one resident called 'a bloody great cathedral'. This was a spanking new, 1,000-seater, purpose-built church. Led by a powerful Welsh pastor, Ben Davies, Bracknell became one of the jewels in the Restorationist crown.

The move from the anti-denominational front room fellowship and then on to the larger church hall, and then further still to the mega-church, is, perhaps, self-consciously at least, more a change of scale than ideology. Terry saw the progression in terms of likening the Restorationist 'large centres' to the metropolitan churches of Christianity in Jerusalem, Antioch and Ephesus, which in turn reached out to the outlying churches. 'I feel that God has encouraged me to believe that in Brighton we have a large base from which we can send a team in and out (but not every church will have that).'[59] Economies of scale, however, do in the long run alter theological precepts. The progression from front rooms to mega-churches demands structures that eventually promote denominationalism. At the very least, we might posit, the move from flexible network to inflexible organization is the hardening of the new wineskin into the old one.

Terry, however, would resist this interpretation. Indeed, by 1989, at the very time that Bryn's proposed move to Nettle Hill suggested a greater concentration of power at the centre, Terry was telling me that his team had become more flexible and decentralized.

We have now developed a team basis, and we have regionalized. I no longer get involved in every church. We had a prophecy that we must give responsibility to men who were loyal and knew what our vision was. God said to us two things. One – give away administrative things, otherwise you will get clogged up with them; and two, give away other responsibilities as well.[60]

One example of this giving away was to appoint an overseer for Kent, and another was that the West and the North can be said to have come under Ben Davies of Bracknell. Other strong personalities at that time were Don Smith of the Hastings church and nearby John Houghton of Hailsham (who fell out with Don and went independent). Perhaps the most respected thinker in New Frontiers in the late 1980s – although he soon left – was Phil Rogers of South Lee.

The successful development and decentralization of Restorationist churches did not blind Terry to the failure of the early vision of becoming the mountain to fill the earth. 'I have been baptized in the Spirit since 1962, involved in the so-called Restorationist movement I guess for a couple of decades. At this pace, we are not going to impact our nation in any very great way. We have got to see something of another measure to fulfil my hopes.'[61]

Final Thoughts on R1

By the end of the 1980s, R1 had consolidated behind structures that had the makings of a denomination – though more so New Frontiers – but had still not hardened into formal sectarian enclaves. By 1990, however, R1 had solidified into the core Restorationist formation because, as we will shortly see, R2 had disintegrated as a working coalition of apostles and churches. In effect, therefore, my working rubric of R1 and R2 is no longer tenable after this time. With the absence of an R2, there is no longer any point in talking of an R1. R1, in the guise of Covenant Ministries and New Frontiers, is Restoration.[62]

Recommended Reading

Brian Hewitt, *Doing a New Thing? Seven Leaders Reflect on the Past, Present and Future of the House Church Movement* (London: Hodder & Stoughton, 1995).

Dan McConnell, *The Promise of Health and Wealth* (London: Hodder & Stoughton, 1990).

Restoration (January/February 1990).

Andrew Tyler, 'Prophet Margins', *Time Out* (16th December 1987).

Terry Virgo, *Restoration in the Church* (Eastbourne: Kingsway Publications, 1985).

Wendy Virgo, *Leading Ladies* (Eastbourne: Kingsway Publications, 1986).

Andrew Walker, 'Fundamentalism and Modernity: The Restoration Movement in Britain', in L. Caplan (ed.), *Studies in Religious Fundamentalism* (Macmillan, 1988).

16

DRIFTING APART AND BREAKING AWAY: LIFE IN R2

To trace the breakdown of R2 is to outline the end of the working relationship between John Noble, Gerald Coates and David Tomlinson. It is also to note the end of John Noble's networks and David Tomlinson's churches. This same period, however, also witnessed the rise of the new church concept and the great success of Gerald Coates and Pioneer. So while R2 fell apart, something dynamic and new came out of it which cannot any more, in my opinion, be called Restorationist. By 1989, Terry Virgo, after telling me of the excellent spirit of co-operation at the 1988 Sheffield Conference, 'Together for the Kingdom', which was organized by Gerald, admitted that he could no longer see the focus or direction of R2.[1]

By contrasting the different directions and style of Gerald Coates and David Tomlinson we will be able to see something of the measure of the changes in R2, but first we will concentrate on what happened to the working relationships between the R2 apostles.

The Contours, Networks and Relationships of R2

When David Tomlinson defected from R1 to R2 in 1983, he moved into a working and committed relationship with John Noble and Gerald Coates. The unity of this relationship was expressed at the annual Festival celebrations at the Staffordshire Showground, which lasted until 1987. This unity was further strengthened by the close association of the Sheffield House Church, and the return of two leaders from the original Restorationist membership of the 'magnificent seven'.[2] These men were Peter Lyne from the West Country, and Graham Perrins from South Wales. By the mid-1980s, David Tomlinson was also working closely with Philip Mohabir in the inner city of London. Philip had formerly worked with Bryn in his native Guyana, and he had become one of the most well-known West Indian speakers in Great Britain, not least through his leadership of the West Indian Evangelical Alliance.

The size of the R2 network – From the mid-1980s onwards, R2, like R1, began to slow down in terms of growth. Nevertheless, in 1987, the overall size of R2 could be said to be marginally larger than R1. What follows is a guesstimate of the churches and numbers in John's, Gerald's and David's churches at that time. The first thing to notice is that the number of churches was greater than R1, but that each church was smaller. David thought that he was connected with, but did not necessarily govern, fifty churches. John and Gerald talked more in the region of forty each. David thought there might be 7,000 members in his churches, Gerald talked more in terms of 4,000. John probably had less. He tended not to insist on holding on to everything, and it might be more accurate to speak of his influence rather than his control over a dwindling network of churches.

The 12,000–14,000 members of this axis were considerably boosted, however, if we remember that Peter Lyne had some six churches and Graham Perrins still had a handful in Wales and the West. If we were to add R2's closest associates, the Sheffield House Church, under Peter Fenwick's leadership, his network, at that time, extended to at least forty churches around the Midlands and North of England. For the sake of argument, we could also include Tony Morton in R2 (although outside the John–Gerald–David axis). He had in excess of thirty churches and over 3,500 people.[3] Altogether, therefore, we are probably talking in excess of 200 churches and 20,000 people.[4]

The John Noble, Gerald Coates and David Tomlinson axis – This axis was not based on identical interests and programmes, but it was a real unity for all that. There was a desire to remain Restorationist but not exclusivist. Increasingly, there was a concern for both evangelism and a greater involvement in social and political action. Women were becoming more involved in leadership, and there was a growing desire to debate both the apostolic ministries and Restorationist theology.

Nowhere were these changes more evident than at Festival 1986. On offer were seminar programmes on women and leadership, ethics and social responsibility, theological modernism and racism. To be sure, there were also seminars for the 'gifts'. A highlight of Festival was the charismatic singing ministry of the Slagels – billed as 'prophetic psalmists' from San Antonio, Texas.[5] And of course there were the evening charismatic celebrations.

Imagine my amazement, however, when I walked into the auditorium of the showground during an evening celebration and heard from the main platform an address given by Jonathan Porritt, perhaps the best-known leader of the Green movement![6] Not only is he not a charismatic, he is not known to be a Christian. This extraordinary turn of events – unthinkable at the Dales and unlikely even at Spring Harvest – was too much for some people. I could see the bewilderment, and in some cases resentment, of some of the people present. John Noble made a powerful prophetic intervention which assured the R2 faithful that God was in control.

The 'greening' of Festival was David Tomlinson's idea and indicated the sort of issues which occupied him over the next few years. It was also clear that while neither John nor Gerald openly disassociated themselves from David's green turn, it was not a direction they themselves took. Curiously, a number of people approached me at Festival after Porritt's (extremely good) speech, and asked me if I would now expose R2 as the new antichrist, or at the very least as a movement that had succumbed to the dark forces of paganism. Perhaps, some of them were saying, Restorationism was a form of New Age in disguise. (Some years later, not only was David continually accused of being a New Ager, but the same charge was once levelled at Gerald Coates!).[7]

Although the Porritt incident caused some dismay, if not disruption, at Festival 86, many of the people there were attentive and eager to learn. Everywhere I went, particularly among the young people, there was great interest in 'Band Aid', relief work in Africa, and a desire for greater debate and more interaction with other Christian confessions.

Throughout the period 1985–88 there was a considerable and noticeable softening of shepherding practices in R2. There was also a shift in understanding apostolic ministries – away from a governmental model and towards a servant ministry model. There was also an openness to criticism of the movement both from within and without. After the first edition of this book was published in 1985, many people in R2 not only read it but wrote to me about it (mostly in appreciation).[8] Steve Goddard, who was then editor of *Buzz* magazine, pointed out to me that many grass roots people who were in the movement were caught up in the euphoria but had little means of testing out their commitment against any objective, outside criteria. Material written on Restorationism was either in-house or anti. 'So what happened,' claimed Steve, 'was that a lot of people started to read that book and place themselves within an historic context for the first time. It had a sobering effect and in my opinion helped slow down the euphoric tendency of "kingdom come", which was very much part of early 80s Restorationism.'[9]

What all this demonstrates is not the importance of *Restoring the Kingdom* in changing the situation,[10] but the receptiveness of R2 to dialogue, outside criticism and self-reflection. Nowhere did I see this more clearly than in July 1987, when I was invited to Gerald Coates' home, Clive House, in Esher, Surrey.[11] Present there were Gerald,

David Tomlinson and John Noble. With them was Philip Mohabir, Peter Lyne, Peter Fenwick and someone who was new to me. This was David Matthews (not to be confused with the David Matthew of R1), a prophet in John Noble's team, although he now works with Tony Morton. David is an Irishman with considerable wit and incisiveness. As befits a prophet, he seemed to be the most critical of those present.

All the men agreed with Peter Lyne's comment that the whole concept of apostolic authority should be understood much more in terms of serving the body of Christ than exercising government over it. There was a consensus that they had become less sectarian, more inclusivist and less triumphalist. David Tomlinson, comparing his situation with other denominations, said:

> Speaking for myself, I would be far more sympathetic to some of the struggles that I have seen in the denominational churches in the past and the present than I might have been at one time. I can understand why problems exist, and why they have done certain things that they have done to try and preserve what they have got.[12]

Gerald felt that 'folk now looking in would say that our profile has changed from being elitist (which we don't think it ever was, but it might have been) and inward looking to outward looking – to asking ourselves now what contribution we can make to society'.[13]

Peter Lyne, speaking of some R1 groups, was afraid that the institutional was taking over from the relational. All the men present seemed to think of R1 in terms of creeping denominationalism. David Tomlinson felt that apostolic authority within R2 only had a future as a resource ministry for planting and establishing churches, not as the centre of an ecclesiastical hub. 'I parted ways with Bryn on issues of authority, hierarchy and that sort of thing.'[14]

All the leaders present were more concerned with continuing their work and getting things done than in bothering about the niceties and finer details of Restorationist theology. For David Tomlinson, at least, the question of restoring a New Testament pattern of Church government had become secondary to the business of building churches and being active in evangelism and social concern. He admitted:

> I personally find that I am less sure that I am doing things in the right way than I have ever been. You know, I find that I am questioning everything and I think gosh, you know, any idea I had of an ideal New Testament pattern to do things has long since evaporated.[15]

Philip Mohabir was of the opinion that the new collective mood of sobriety and reflection was all to the good:

> I think that from my observation, just being here, for four years now, I have noticed that the churches and groups linked directly (and somewhat indirectly) with us here, are showing us four things. One is a more balanced approach to the whole issue of authority and how it is exercised. Secondly, the enthusiasm and the passion for evangelizing Britain (if you like) is not just a parochial vision of building an empire, but is a growing concern for taking Britain back for God. The third thing is the resetting of agendas with the taking on of things like social concern, social justice – contemporary issues if you will. And fourthly, there is a willingness to get our hands dirty with people and reclaiming, as it were, things that were surrendered. The house church movement, so called, is beginning to think of issues like that. So they are not just, in quotes, 'kingdom people', 'relationship people', with an airy-fairy meaning.[16]

It was clear that neither Philip nor his fellow leaders had lost their visionary fire, but they had come to understand their part in restoring God's kingdom in a more modest way. John put it bluntly: 'The question the so-called house churches have to ask is whether we are part of the rocket, or whether we are a fuel tank. A fuel tank helps the rocket to get into orbit but then ceases to have any relevance.'[17]

Gerald also saw their fellowships as having an enabling role:

We were viewed when Spring Harvest started nine, ten years ago, with great suspicion, whereas now the ethos of their ministry – the ethos of the music, the ethos of everything they are communicating – is the ethos of what we were endeavouring to do in our very immature, imperfect, limited way. And, of course, in that sense we have been a fuel tank.[18]

David Matthews seemed to speak for most of those present when he insisted that there was a great deal more in God's mind than merely house churches and Restorationism:

We never set out to be a permanent feature of the landscape and we have no vested interest in maintaining the house church movement. If it has peaked – and I don't know that it has – and God is doing something fresh, our heart is, let's get into the fresh thing that God is doing. And if we need to give the house church thing a decent burial, let's do it. May it rest in peace.[19]

David Matthews' words were to be more prophetic than he could have known, for symbolically, I believe, R2 really did die with the literal burial of Arthur Wallis, whose funeral took place at Southampton in September 1988. This event, followed shortly by the Sheffield Conference, 'Together for the Kingdom', marked what David Matthews was also accurately to describe as 'the end of an era'.

Drifting Apart

When I left Clive House after interviewing the R2 leaders, I did not realize at the time that R2 was in the process of drifting apart. This growing fragmentation was not dramatic nor overtly divisive. It was just that the three apostles began to go in different directions. By 1989, David Tomlinson saw it in this way:

> John, Gerald and I have worked together on common projects in the past and we have enjoyed a fellowship and relationship which has been beneficial and gratifying to all. There is no doubt that at the moment it isn't the way it was. It is an interesting thing looking back over numerous circles that go beyond your own immediate operation of working, that it seems, that with all the high ideals you may hold, relationships work best if you have got common projects you are working on. And the fact is that with the demise of Festival we did not have the discipline of a framework of meeting together regularly to talk about that. Without anyone actually intending it to, the wheels have turned on that one and we have found ourselves spending less time together. I don't think that there is any secret about the fact that we recognize there are questions about whether, on certain issues, we are going in the same direction.[20]

Gerald's direction, as we will shortly see, was to lead the new churches into closer co-operation and emerge as a national figure through the Marches for Jesus. David Tomlinson clearly 'came out' as politically to the centre-left, and attempted to follow the path of Tony Campolo and Ron Sider in combining radical social action with the gifts of the Spirit. He also became involved in the arts and alternative approaches to 'happy-clappy' worship. Before we compare and contrast Gerald and David's paths, however, we must say something about John Noble.

John Noble – John's direction was really different to both David and Gerald. Until the 1990s, when he moved to Surrey, he continued to live in Romford and oversee his churches. He still led a team, 'Team Spirit', but they were an autonomous lot. So much so, that John's segment of R2 began to shrink. Gerald felt that John gave away too much power and permitted too much devolution.[21]

Anyone who knows John and his wife Christine (a formidable team in themselves) know that if John gives things away, it is not out of weakness of character, but because it is in character. John has been proud to be in the forefront of Restoration, but he has never felt particularly alienated from other denominational expressions of Pentecostal Christianity. Indeed, while Clive Calver has called Gerald the statesman of Restorationism, this is mainly true within the context of the new churches.[22] When it comes to co-operating with older denominations, including Catholicism, John Noble is probably the most respected and accepted Restorationist to come out of either R1 or R2.

During the late 1980s, John and Christine could be seen together at most of the charismatic jamborees in Great Britain. They somehow transcended the denominational/independent distinction. John, in particular, became involved in many international and interdenominational projects. He worked closely with Michael Harper, for example, in bringing together charismatics from all confessions to an international conference of charismatics in Brighton.

Like Arthur Wallis before him, John continued to look forward to a 'bigger wave coming', one that would overtake both Renewal and Restoration. In a sense, we might say, John Noble outgrew Restorationism. It is certainly the case that many mainstream evangelicals and Catholics whom I have talked to about John Noble have no reservations about him. There is no doubt that John is big-hearted – it is what people remember about him. By the late 1980s, however, he was getting a little long in the tooth – shall we say late-middle-aged, rather than old. His experience and maturity had become his badge of entry to all the houses of charismata, but as for his own house, he left the door open for those inside to drift away.

Very few charismatics, from any corner of the movement, have been able to transcend the narrow boundaries of their own sector. If Bryn Jones can be said to be the loyalist who stayed and held the fort for the kingdom, and Terry Virgo is Restoration's ambassador abroad, then John Noble can be said to have moved out altogether to become the senior statesman of the charismatic movement. This is no small achievement, but then, as we saw earlier in this chapter, John wondered if Restorationism was only the fuel tank that gets the rocket off the ground. He did not want to burn up clinging to the wreckage of a fuel booster – he wanted to be on the rocket heading for the stars.[23]

The contrast in style between David and Gerald – It will already be apparent from previous remarks that David Tomlinson's approach to things was markedly different from Gerald's. Steve Goddard, former editor of *Buzz* magazine, put it more directly: 'Gerald and David are from different planets: they look different; they think different; they are different.'[24]

They are certainly different to interview. Gerald always seems to have an answer to anything you ask him. David likes to take his time in replying, and he usually qualifies what he says. Gerald talks about his plans and aspirations with great enthusiasm. David mainly talks about his mistakes and how he is trying to come to terms with reality. Gerald is ebullient. David is reticent. Gerald the public speaker is much the same as the private interviewee. David the private man is far more introspective and tentative than David the public performer. Gerald talks like an activist, David like a commentator at other people's events.

Their differences in interview style were reflected in the way they dressed in the late 1980s. Gerald was smart and snappy, Tory blazer, conservative slacks. David either looked like a plumber (which he once was), with a Bob Dylan hat, or he looked rather arty in a non-contrived, slapdash sort of way. The two men's houses were radically different too. Gerald lived in a small, exquisite mansion with expensive drapes, carpets and furniture.[25] David's home was rough-and-ready comfort in terraced Clapham. It was – and remains – a fun place for dropping in and flopping down. You could take your children there and not worry that they would damage anything.

These differences were also reflected in the offices of their respective teams. Gerald's Pioneer offices were housed in the former stables of his mansion, Clive House. They were easy to find, clean, cheerful, friendly and functional. The inevitable word-processors and photocopying machines were evident but not obtrusive; the whole place had the air of an efficient cottage industry.

I had some difficulty in finding David's 'Team Work' office in Brixton. Eventually I stumbled across it right opposite the West Indian Bakery – 'The No. 1 for Jamaican Patties'. Squeezed between Region Wines and Help 71, it did not look out of place in the inner city (which, I suppose, was the idea). Inside, the front office reflected the cosy chaos of the sixties counter-culture. It was a bit like an artists' colony with prints and Team Work fliers scattered around like abandoned cushions. In order to get into the office you had to brave your way through the heavy smoke of Richard Nicholson, a Geordie sitting with giant boots on the table and puffing away on an enormous pipe.

David and the Direction of Team Work

In 1986, Team Work consisted of fourteen members, of whom David was the leader. Team Work was understood to be David (as apostle) and his team who ran the network of churches. David was still working with Gerald and John and planning ahead for another Festival along the lines of the previous ones. In partnership with Philip Mohabir (who was very much considered the prophetic voice of the group), David was committed to planting new churches in the inner city. Pete and Jess Gilgan, who had come down with David from Middlesbrough, were initially to play a major role in what was then called 'Operation London' (although their relationship with the Tomlinsons deteriorated soon afterwards).

Holy Joe's and Workshop – A major initiative of Team Work, which has actually survived its demise, was Holy Joe's. It was originally housed beneath the team office – although it later moved out to a pub – and was a church for the unchurched, designed more as a night club than a chapel. The club provided opportunities for open debate and for Christian singers and artists of various kinds to promote the gospel in alternative style. You might, from time to time, have caught the Hendersons there (Carol and Stewart), the Wobegone Brothers, or Oxford Circus. Team Work also for a time had a Christian roadshow, but its biggest venture was the alternative youth festival, Harry, which ran at the Great Yorkshire Showground in 1988 and 1989. Harry was not a financial success, nor was it attended by huge crowds. It was greatly appreciated by a significant minority of disaffected teenage charismatics, but disliked by many of their parents who rightly discerned that it was not really a Restorationist celebration at all (see the epilogue).

Another initiative of Team Work from the mid-1980s was Workshop. This was the brainchild of Noel Moules (son of famous missionary Len Moules). With virtually no money, Noel ran theological educational training programmes for leaders in the churches. Noel was of Anabaptist conviction, charismatic but not fundamentalist. He was very much his own man and not afraid to offer strong counsel. He has, to this day, a reputation for balance in both political and theological matters.[26]

He told me in interview that while he was committed to peace and green issues, he had no time for a gospel that was not rooted in the incarnation and the cross. If you had taken Noel out of Restorationist circles and dropped him into any mainstream church, no one would have found him strange. He avoided Restorationist jargon and argued his informed theological position with care and clarity. In fact, many of the people that Noel was teaching in those days were not Restorationists. By 1987, Noel did not want to call himself by that label anyway. I think 'mere Christian' would have been good enough for him.[27]

Scattered directions – Directions in Team Work, however, were somewhat scattered. Their apostle, who since 1985/86 had been well and truly bitten by the social justice bug, came to feel more at home with the likes of Tony Campolo, Ron Sider and Jim Wallis than, shall we say, the Wimber–Virgo kind of ministries. In fact, Tony Campolo and Ron Sider were to become friends of David. But it was not only the justice bug which had forced its attention on him. He was thinking through the whole history, theology and development of Restoration to such an extent that he began to talk himself out of it. This left the troops feeling somewhat jittery as they felt themselves pulled this way and then that way.

David has a tendency to think out loud, and not everybody liked what they were hearing from 1986 onwards. While there remained an intense personal loyalty to David as leader, many of the churches attached to Team Work would have preferred more 'signs and wonders' and less of the green and pink politics. Not everybody appreciated the alternative humour of the first Team Work celebration event, Harry in 1988, and when the satirical magazine *Nous* appeared at that time, many found it was too irreverent for their taste.

And it was not only David's followers who had trouble with his new directions. Philip Mohabir, one of David's greatest admirers, could not easily take to the artistic approach, the cigars and pipe tobacco that suddenly seemed to be in, and the close-to-the-knuckle humour. After all, Philip is from a traditional Holiness background and certain cultural and religious standards are expected. He and David ceased working together – as did old friends of many years standing, such as Derek Fields from Middlesbrough. Derek hung on until the end of the decade, but by 1988, Kit and Sue Mason had already pulled out of Team Work and moved to the West Country.

Strictly speaking, the new directions and the unguarded spoken thoughts of David Tomlinson become more obvious after the Sheffield Conference of 1988. From that time on, while Gerald was mobilizing the spiritual warriors to march the streets of Britain, David was planning a Christian counter-culture for the unchurched, and for those who were the children of committed charismatics but had become disenchanted with their own religion. When I interviewed David at Harry 89, he told me that he found the acceleration of change in himself and his churches, 'quite frightening', and admitted that there had been a 'sort of disintegrating influence'. This was reflected in the issues that were debated at that time. David's outspokenness on political and racial matters were matched by his changing views on Restoration, worship, the Christian family, the role of women, the desirability of women elders, the abolition of heavy shepherding and an attempt to introduce democratization from below.[28]

Some of David's team members were distraught that he was allowing dissent and encouraging criticism. Here was their strong leader saying that he wanted the freedom to go in his own direction and was encouraging others to go their way too as long as they did not crusade against him. It was all a bit like Gorbachev and glasnost. When it came to it, many Restorationists, like the workers in Soviet Russia, did not want the new freedom they were being offered. What they really wanted was to go back to the old certainties, where they all knew their place.

Many of David's people wanted their shepherd to lead from the front so that they could loyally, and unquestioningly, follow from behind. After 1986, David was leading from the front all right, but he was hurrying down the road so quickly that he was leaving them all behind, unable to catch up. As David Hall put it in the summer of 1989: 'David Tomlinson is changing fast. People are staying with him because they like him so much, but they haven't got a clue as to what he is going on about. There are some, and I am probably one of those, who wish David would carry a Wimber agenda.'[29]

Festival 1990: the last gasp – Clearly, David had been changing too fast for most of his followers, and by continuing down the Harry trail without reaching out to his broader constituency, he ran the risk of the total disintegration of his team and ending up as a shepherd without any sheep. Indeed, by the early 1990s, that is in effect what happened. One of the last things David was to do, before he broke away from Restoration altogether, was to hold a final Festival in May 1990 at Southport.

I had the opportunity to participate in this event, which did not include John and Gerald, but it was supported by Peter Fenwick, Brian Howell and other leaders sympathetic to David's work.[30] On the whole, I thought it was a great success, and I could hear fewer mutters of dissent than I had done at Harry 89. Ron Sider was over from America, and he and Philip Mohabir made a considerable impact on the 2,000 people at Southport. More importantly, however, Festival was an occasion for all the family, and it did not have the alternative flavour of Harry.

The seminars which I saw and participated in at Southport were far more academic and intense than any I had seen at previous Festivals or at Spring Harvest. For the first time, in Restorationist circles, I caught a glimpse of the young intellectuals trying to make their voice heard in dissent, without always having to kowtow to the official leadership. A number of them talked of their previous frustration of not being heard, despite the fact that many of them were far more theologically trained than some of their elders. There was a vigorous discussion on what some of them saw as the theological weakness of fundamentalism. Many of them were also convinced that demonology was out of hand in the charismatic movement and needed knocking on the head. Most of these young people were new to me, but it looked like strong evidence that a new and more critical leadership was coming through. An energetic woman, Vivien Culver, was there from Sheffield House Church. Although she was busy running errands, she could also run theological circles around most of the aspiring male leaders.

In the event, however, although Team Work was reorganized, streamlined and democratized before Festival 1990, it was not to survive. In retrospect, therefore, the new Festival, with all its promise, was a false dawn. David's churches had lost coherence and direction. In effect, as one Team Work member put it, 'the apostle took himself off' and left the network to unravel like a ball of twine.

It must be remembered, however, that while many Restorationists had been confused and alarmed by David's rapidly changing spots, others in and outside his network had been impressed by his theological and moral integrity. For a man who was unschooled – although he later earned an MA at London Bible College in the 1990s – he clearly had a first-class brain and was able to set things out far more clearly, rationally and doctrinally than many of his colleagues. So while it may be true that the new David Tomlinson turned many people off, he turned others on, especially those outside his circle. Nigel Wright of Spurgeons, for example, found David's version of Restorationism by far the most appealing.

In time, David found a new role as a leader among the 1990s Christian counter-culture, where he became the darling – if not the founder – of the postevangelical movement.[31] In 1996, he abandoned his sectarian past altogether, and with his wife Pat was received into the Anglican Church.

Gerald Coates and Pioneer

It is worth beginning with a parenthesis, which I do not think is a trivial point in relation to the emergence of Gerald Coates as a national leader of the charismatic movement. By 1988/89, Gerald was looking quite different from his earlier apostolic days. Gone were the yellow suits, punkish hairstyles and outrageous shoes. In had come the very smart suits and what I earlier called the Tory blazers. The new Gerald looked like someone who could be your friendly bank manager. In 1989, I asked him about the change in image and appearance. He responded:

> Well, I think it is ageing. I am 45 in a few weeks time. My wife prefers me in suits and jackets. But a strange thing happened two years ago when a girl had a vision of me. She saw me in a large room, sitting on a sofa in a suit with a black attaché case. Then she saw me in a suit with a regular hairstyle going through the doors of London Airport. Well, one morning, someone I knew was arriving in England, so I cancelled everything on the spot, made lots of phone calls, and just before rushing to the airport threw a suit on, put a brush through my hair, and jumped in the car. As I walked through the doors at Heathrow, I realized: I am in the vision. I am in a grey suit, with a regular hairstyle. Ever since that day, I have realized that my ministry is in terms of bridge-building, and I have tended to wear suits and ties – and a regular hairstyle.[32]

Before the bridge-builder emerged, Gerald underwent a period of transition from 1985 to 1987. He was still in those days a controversialist. His book in 1986, *Divided We Stand*, got him into hot water with some evangelicals for seeming to suggest that the inerrancy of Scripture was a misleading doctrine.[33] For a while, he tried a number of new directions. One remembers the Pioneer excursion into religious popular music with the singers Sheila Walsh and Alvin

Stardust. (Sheila was soon to leave England and move to America to co-host Pat Robertson's *700 Club* chat show).

Gerald forged links during this time with the South African evangelist Dudley Daniels, and he made several trips to South Africa. Gradually, the Pioneer team changed, and it continues to be streamlined to this day (although singer–songwriter Noel Richards seems to have been close at hand since those early days). Younger leaders were given their head, such as Martin Scott, who today has become a theologian and teacher of some weight. Another direction was the establishment of the Pioneer charitable trust, which goes back to the mid-1980s. The trust became involved in serious charity work (notably the Jubilee Campaign, under the directorship of Danny Smith). Meanwhile, Gerald continued to speak up and down the country, including appearances at Spring Harvest.

And then three things happened which showed that Gerald had found a clearer focus, as well as a need to change his wardrobe. The combination of these three things gave him a national visibility which he did not have before, and led him away from Restorationism *per se* to larger arenas.

Aids Care Education & Training – The first change in direction was the involvement of Pioneer trust in the founding of Aids Care Education & Training (ACET) in June 1988. This work was begun by Dr Patrick Dixon, but Pioneer was involved initially – indeed, the programme was originally called Pioneer for AIDS. The importance of this work lay in its sheer professionalism and its Christian ethical base (although it had some pro-gay support). ACET was not a shoestring operation, and Gerald told me that a major donation of £0.5 million went into its foundation.

A new trust was formed, and with major support from an existing trust, World in Need, offices were established in Ealing with a staff of fifteen. Staffing included home care help. Gerald described ACET as 'the largest independent agency caring for dying AIDS patients in their homes anywhere in the UK'. He became one of the members of the advisory council, but the importance of ACET in relation to Gerald are twofold. First, it gave Gerald, and Pioneer, a major foothold in mainstream counselling and welfare, complete with government grants and a board of distinguished people, including Alec Reed of Reed Accountancy, and Sir John Ford, the UN Ambassador. Secondly, it set a trend for Pioneer to become involved in partnerships with other enterprises, without necessarily having control or directing policy.[34]

The Sheffield Conference and the new churches – The second change of direction for Gerald was for him to become the spokesman for, and in many ways the initiator of, the concept of the 'new church'. This new idea stemmed from Gerald's own career as an anti-denominationalist on the one hand, and from his contact with other independent fellowships on the other hand. Several meetings were held and the new churches could be said to have gone public first through the Sheffield Conference, 'Together for the Kingdom' in 1988. Subsequently, a number of gatherings were held which were specifically for these new churches to discover more about themselves.

Clive Calver believes that Gerald's work, specifically at Sheffield and later with Roger Forster of Ichthus and Lynn Green of Youth With A Mission (YWAM), earned Gerald the right in the late 1980s to be called the Restorationist statesman:

> Gerald Coates has changed from being an angry young controversialist into being the nearest thing to a statesman that Restorationism has produced. Gerald is in fact a larger-than-life character, who has been able to bring most folk together. Looking at Sheffield is to see a classic illustration of what he has achieved.[35]

Here, I think, we have the key to Gerald's clearer focus. By

1988, he was working in close co-operation with Roger Forster. Both were Arminian in theology, and both were pragmatic and realistic about church co-operation.[36] Gerald was also closely in touch with people such as Roger Ellis of the Chichester fellowship, Revelation, and Stuart Bell from Lincoln. From that time, Gerald consistently championed the 'new church' concept.

In fact, the idea of 'new church' is more sociological than theological. These are independent networks, or one-off fellowships, that are outside the established denominational structures. But other than being evangelical and charismatic, there is little which binds them together. So, for example, some new churches are run by charismatic apostles, but most are not. Roger Forster does not claim to be an apostle, but some of the Pioneer churches have looked upon him as one.[37] Some people think of Gerald as an apostle, others as prophetic (a view that Gerald does not reject), but in the case of some people from R1, Gerald is viewed as a prophet so that they do not have to think of him as a rival apostle.

When the Sheffield Conference was over in 1988, no one was sure at that time whether there was to be another one. However, Gerald encouraged new church leaders (rather as Arthur Wallis had brought together the 'magnificent seven') to talk over issues such as prophecy. These church leaders met sometimes in Gerald's home and sometimes at Fairmile Court (a favourite spot, as we have seen, with earlier Restorationists). Leaders included David Tomlinson, John Noble and Graham Perrins from R2, but also present were Terry Virgo and Barney Coombs from R1. Roger Foster from Ichthus was a working member of the group, and so too were Stuart Bell, Derek Brown and other independent leaders. Bryn was invited, but he chose not to go.[38]

Gerald saw the meetings as working seminars, and not merely for re-establishing contact:

When the new church leaders met together it was in an attempt to really work at differences. The sort of things we have been doing, apart from fellowship, eating, drinking, worship, telling funny stories and so on. We have been discussing what are the distinctive features of so-called new churches. Do we see these churches as a movement? If they are a movement, what are the goals? What do we see as the role of apostles today? What is our attitude to spiritual authority? In what ways do we think we, as a church, are being prophetic? How should we involve ourselves in spiritual warfare? What does Reconstructionism mean, and are we committed to it?[39]

Did Gerald see himself as the new 'apostle of the apostles'? The answer to this must be no, for as he said to me, 'you can't have an "apostle of the apostles", and anyhow, in the new church coalition, many people did not recognize apostolic ministry at all.'[40]

But he did admit that his position was uncomfortable, because, he pointed out, he was more than the administrator, but he was not really the leader (a similar problem faced by Arthur Wallis in the 'magnificent seven' back in 1971). He did say, however, that these informal meetings with his colleagues were not about Sheffield and the end of the Restorationist era, but about new churches and their future. I have talked to two others present at these meetings. They neither saw them as an extension of either Restorationism or as an alliance of new churches. They saw them simply as a forum for discussion and fellowship. And certainly, hard issues came up – over apostles, differences in theories of the second coming, and women's ministry.

Following Roger's lead, and no doubt influenced by his theology, Gerald was about to launch out into women's ministry with a new elder, Linda Harding.[41] This in itself was a radical break with the old Restorationism, but it was a new direction supported both by David Tomlinson and John Noble. Brenda Robson, under John's support, was probably to emerge as the first Restorationist woman elder. Terry and others did not take too well to women elders, and this was not a question of R1 versus R2: Peter Fenwick did not much like the idea either. But these new church consultations, disputations and disagreements did not lead to 'dis-fellowshipping'. On the contrary, the meetings were conducted in warm regard for each other.

In March 1990, there was a second Sheffield Conference which if anything was even more successful than the first one (although it seems not to have led anywhere). By now, of course, there had been the national March for Jesus. Marching was to be the third and most successful way in which Gerald was to emerge as a national leader within the evangelical movement.

The big march – When I was visiting Gerald in 1989, we started our interview about the Marches for Jesus with Gerald quoting from a letter by Rodney Kingston (the elder of a fellowship at Broadwater, Worthing, and a former member of the Pioneer team).[42] The quote simply said: 'The day of the streams is over, the day of the river has begun.' Gerald took this to be a prophecy. It had in fact come as a response to the great national March for Jesus in September of that year, but Gerald had already been thinking about the idea of marching before Sheffield in 1988.

Many people who were involved in the City of London march in 1988, and the first national march on 16th September 1989, did not know that it was a new church initiative through and through. As Gerald put it:

> I don't think you will find, if you talked to the vast majority of people on the March for Jesus, that they would have ever heard about Pioneer or whatever. They knew that Roger, Lynn and I were involved because of our profile on the day, and particularly mine, because they asked me to do the land-line link which I hosted.[43]

The national march, which was supported by the

Evangelical Alliance and many other evangelical groups, was able to muster nearly 250,000 people on the streets of Britain's major cities. Gerald felt that in many ways he, Roger and Lynn were a bunch of nobodies, but their success was a vindication for the initiative of the new churches.[44]

I think there is no doubt that the ability to put nearly a quarter of a million people on the streets was a major triumph for Gerald and the new churches, and it would be churlish to suggest otherwise. A great deal of hard work and enterprise went into the event and much of the success was due to Graham Kendrick's imaginative processional liturgy – *Make Way*. I saw the draft proposals, which were perhaps overlong and elaborate, but the structure was ideal for street celebration, using a fairly traditional antiphonal structure in which the leader called out such phrases as: 'Make way, make way', and 'Prepare the way of the Lord', while the crowds responded accordingly.

This street liturgy was highly structured, and included traditional prayers and motifs interspersed with new church hymnody. The familiar echoes of tradition, entwined with new church hymnody, is surely the hallmark, and inspiration, of Graham Kendrick's approach.

Reaction around the country differed. Belfast and Newcastle were considered to be great successes (although people in Newcastle felt that it was a success because they had made it a regional rather than a national occasion). Perhaps the greatest problem was the land-link. There were numerous technical problems, and Gerald could not be heard too well. At Sheffield, for example, people became restless and bored. Curiously, for such a vast Christian event, the press gave it less than a comprehensive coverage. However, the Sunday broadsheets were quite impressive in their reports. The headline 'Catching sunbeams from the new disciples' was jolly, and Gerald could hardly have complained with the *Sunday Times* headline: 'Actress and the bishop upstaged'. Nevertheless, tabloid and television coverage was poor.

I believe there were two reasons for this. The first is the lack of interest that Fleet Street and the BBC have in evangelical religion. They tend to see it as marginal religiosity, and Establishment religion tends nearly always to catch their eye. I made some enquiries with former colleagues in the BBC and discovered that some of them chose not to cover it. One producer thought that it was a Gerald Coates publicity stunt and he did not want to advertise it – or give it a 'puff', in journalistic jargon.

But I think that there was a second, more basic reason. It was never really clear, despite all the advance literature, what the march was actually for. Why call 200,000 people out onto the streets? Was it a demonstration of power, of triumphalistic evangelism, of Christian solidarity? Many people were confused by this, including the *Christianity Today* editors, who were over from America to cover the resurgence of British evangelicalism.[45] I asked Gerald, after the event, to explain what it was all for. He responded:

> Well I think what has happened is this. We (the new churches) have been around for twenty years. Our accountability to Scripture and to one another has given us credibility, and this credibility now needs visibility. Because if folk want to go to church, they look in the local paper and they see the Church of England, or whatever, because they have visibility. But the new churches haven't got national visibility at all. So I think that the March for Jesus has given those of an orthodox faith a visibility in the country which has been seen and taken note of in various quarters and will continue to be.[46]

In fact, as Gerald has already pointed out in an earlier quotation, it was not the new churches that gained visibility, but personalities – and in particular himself. That very visibility was to extract a price. The *Mail on Sunday* carried a major feature on Gerald entitled 'Gerry and the Peacemakers'. The journalist, Val Hennessy, chose to write it tongue-in-cheek, and the pictures of Gerald, Bible in hand, standing in front of Clive House and sitting inside his elegant drawing-room with his wife Anona, gave the impression of opulence. The whole report had an American televangelist feel about it. It certainly was not a friendly piece, as the following quotation demonstrates:

> Forty-five-year-old Coates, short legs, low-slung bum, freshly blow-dried hair and oleaginous smile, clapped hands and shimmied up on the platform beside the band. Hallelujah. Ignore the basketball nets and the giant 'Milk for all' poster . . . and he looked like the compère of 'Sale of the Century'.[47]

In fact, although the report was cruel, I was reminded by a senior BBC reporter how lucky Gerald was that it was only the soft tabloids who had gone for him. 'If it had been the *Sun* or the *News of the World*,' he said, 'it would have been a lot worse.' There is another way of looking at it: to be the subject of a lampoon in a national newspaper is evidence that you have arrived.

There was another aspect of the March for Jesus which I found intriguing. I had heard it said that behind it was a theology of spiritual warfare. There was a video tape of Roger Forster's which I had seen which seemed to suggest that prayer and rebuking the devil could lead to changes in social and national behaviour. Gerald confirmed that there was a sense in which the March was intended to 'shift the atmosphere'. As he put it:

> We all give off the atmosphere that we live in, and though I can be speaking about peace and blessing and purity and cleanliness, if I am actually immoral you will say, 'Well, he is saying the right things, but there's something not right with the bloke', because I give off the atmosphere that I live in . . . I think that just as that is true of an individual, it is true of entire nations.[48]

I believe that Gerald thinks that the 1988 March in London helped cleanse the atmosphere of corrupt City practices (he had the insider trading scandal in mind). It was not so much a case of saying that there is a cause and effect relationship between Christian marching and changing social and political events, but, as Gerald put it: 'I think that when we go out on the streets and we are worshipping, there is a cleansing of the atmosphere which of course only those with a transcendental view of life can believe'.[49]

By 1990, Gerald believed that although Pioneer would continue to launch new initiatives and plant new churches, the next move, in conjunction with the other new churches, was to influence Europe:

In 1992, our thoughts are that there will be a major March for Jesus in the capital of every European nation, East and West – although the distinction might not exist then. It will be satellite-linked. Now if the police move in on one of those marches in what is now Eastern Europe, the whole of Europe will hear, because it will be satellite-linked.[50]

Of course, as the 1990s progressed, the Marches for Jesus did become a worldwide phenomenon, and the new churches did go on to become a significant player in the Revivalist game. Gerald emerged as the most visible and influential leader to come out of R2, citing among his friends charismatic leader John Wimber, singer Sir Cliff Richard, and Member of Parliament, David Alton. Gerald also, in a different way to David Tomlinson, unwittingly helped to dismantle the Restorationist movement. Essentially, Gerald is a pragmatist who is prepared to work with others outside his sphere.[51] But unlike Terry Virgo in R1, he has been happy to be influenced by others from outside Restoration to such an extent that the Pioneer network itself has changed from being distinctively house church to becoming the looser and more nebulous new church.

Recommended Reading

Rodney Clapp, 'Democracy as Heresy', *Christianity Today*, 20th February 1987.

Gerald Coates, *Divided We Stand* (Eastbourne: Kingsway Publications, 1986).

Gerald Coates, *An Intelligent Fire* (Eastbourne: Kingsway Publications, 1991) chapter 6.

Brian Hewitt, *Doing a New Thing? Seven Leaders Reflect on the Past, Present and Future of the House Church Movement* (London: Hodder & Stoughton, 1995).

Philip Mohabir, *Building Bridges* (London: Hodder & Stoughton, 1988).

James Martin Scott, 'The Theology of the So-Called "New Church" Movement' (unpublished MTh thesis, Brunel University, 1997).

CONCLUSION

THE END OF AN ERA

As the 1980s were drawing to a close, Gerald Coates, as we have already seen, was anxious to call together many of the streams of Restorationism in a show of reconciliation, solidarity and expectation of a great revival. Gerald had already been meeting with some of the early Restorationist leaders and other leading figures among the new churches. Remarkably, given the history of the split, he was able to win support from people in both R1 and R2 to come together for a major conference in Sheffield on the kingdom, in mid-September 1988.

Not since the schism of 1976 had there been such an effort to bring Restorationists together.[1] Arthur Wallis was a key figure in this reconciliation. He was the father of the movement and was still greatly respected among all the fellowships in R1 and R2. The Sheffield Conference also included Roger Forster of Ichthus, Clive Calver of the Evangelical Alliance, and leaders from the independent new churches such as Derek Brown of Aldershot and Stuart Bell of Lincoln. Terry Virgo agreed to come, and also Tony Morton and Barney Coombs. The controversial head of the 'Jesus Army', Noel Stanton, had also been invited. In fact, virtually everybody who was anybody in Restorationist and new church circles was to be there, except Bryn Jones.

The death and funeral of Arthur Wallis – A short while before the conference, Arthur visited Bryn and Keri in Yorkshire. Gerald was hoping that Arthur would persuade Bryn to come.[2] On 7th September, Arthur was playing croquet with Keri and others when he collapsed and died.

A thanksgiving service was held at Above Bar, the

famous independent Baptist church in Southampton. It was a very dignified occasion and was handled with great sensitivity and professionalism by Tony Morton. There was a solo, in silver tenor voice, by Ivor Hopkins – a member of Bryn's team. At one point, the whole congregation stood and applauded Arthur for his life and ministry. There were contributions from Arthur's family, Joe Tosini from Missouri, and others. Bryn Jones' remembrance was particularly apt. He mentioned Arthur's habit of always praising and encouraging before he offered criticism (a habit I can confirm from his correspondence with me).[3]

Arthur never became an apostle in the movement that he founded. Yet he was always the senior teacher and spokesman for the Restorationists. He more than anyone felt the pain of the 1976 division, and he never ceased to maintain personal relationships in both R1 and R2. Indeed, I think it was a measure of his authority that he never really ceased to influence both sides of the Restorationist divide.

Sheffield: from house church to new church – Paradoxically, Arthur's death was both a great loss to the Sheffield Conference and a spur to its success. The conference, as we have already seen, was really the brainchild of Gerald. He had become increasingly enamoured with the new church concept and was really looking to move beyond kingdom Christianity in its specifically Restorationist form to a more open alliance of independent churches.

Gerald spoke to me at some length about the beginnings of the Sheffield idea:

I had a burden for about four years to call the apostolic team leaders and the people they represented together, because I believed that the things that united us were of far more importance than those that divided us. It was absolutely absurd that brothers who were orthodox in their faith, who were baptized in the Spirit, who were church-planting with a great emphasis on team ministry, relationships, non-religious approach to church life, etc., never saw each other, except for an occasional meal.

I had hoped that somebody else would do the job, to be honest, but I eventually called the brothers together for a day of sharing and prayer, out of which I floated the conference. They were all for it to various degrees. Some came *en masse*, others showed up with a token force, partly because they had already arranged their future programmes, and partly because they were not sure what was going to be said.

A day or two before the conference we got the news that Arthur Wallis had died . . . Many have put it to me that I picked up the mantle. Actually, I picked it up before he died. It wasn't that he died and then I picked it up.[4]

To pick up Arthur's mantle was not without ambiguity. In the second book of Kings, when Elisha took upon his shoulders the cloak of Elijah, it symbolised the continuity of the prophetic office. Arthur, who was never recognized as an apostle, could be said to be a prophet, but in a loose, evangelical sense, rather than in a specifically Restorationist sense. It is difficult to know, therefore, what 'picking up the mantle' entailed. If, however, picking up the mantle meant continuing a ministry of reconciliation, than it can fairly be said that Gerald took on that role.

The absence of Bryn Jones from Sheffield was perhaps its greatest failure. Some of those present regretfully saw Sheffield as Hamlet without the prince. Others, more cynically, believed that Bryn stayed away precisely because he could not be the prince. His absence, however, should not be read as a slap in the face for Gerald Coates, for in fact relationships between them did improve. Bryn told me in 1989 the reason why he did not feel impelled to go to the conference:

My understanding of Sheffield initially was that it was 'house group leadership' and these things. Now call it the idealist in me if you like, but I am not prepared to meet my brothers on that basis of common agreement. I will meet with them if I think it is important on the basis of Christ. But I did not feel, for myself, that I wanted to meet under the auspices of 'house church', or what they call 'new churches', and things like that. I believe that I am part of the whole body of Christ and I want to keep it that way.[5]

In the event, notwithstanding Bryn's absence, most people believed Sheffield to be a great success. Participants thought that the worship was outstanding and the sense of togetherness was very strong. To quote Gerald again: 'Some of us thought that this was the end of an era. David Matthews said, as far as the conference was concerned, that Arthur's death was the end of an era, the end of a chapter, and God had given us a blank sheet of paper to start anew.'[6]

In reality, however, while Sheffield did herald a new sense of co-operation among many independent charismatics, Renewalists, and even some of the older-style Pentecostalists (which proved to be significant in the revivals of the 1990s), it really was the end of an era, if not the Restorationist movement.[7] Looking back with hindsight in 1997, Gerald was able to say of the 1988 Sheffield Conference: 'I think the conference itself was a defining moment in seeing the house church movement diversify. And therefore it became lost in the complex relationships represented by charismatic evangelicalism.[8]

Recommended Reading

'Arthur Wallis 1922–1988: A Tribute', *Restoration*,
   November/December 1988 (a 30-page supplement).

EPILOGUE

THE GREAT YORKSHIRE SHOWGROUND, AUGUST 1989

It was Thursday the 4th of August. The weather, as it had been for most of the summer of 1989, was as perfect as weather can be in England. I was back at the Great Yorkshire Showground, near Harrogate, almost seven years to the day after my last visit there, when I was covering the Dales Bible Week for BBC radio.

Any ghost that might have lingered from those heady, rousing days, when the great crowds of Restorationists were dancing and chanting, 'The church of God is moving, the church of God is moving . . .' were clearly in hiding; maybe they had even flown away. Certainly, 'Harry' (short for Harrogate), the event I had been invited to as a participant observer this time, and not as a journalist, bore no more resemblance to the Dales Bible Week than vegetarian burgers (on sale at Harry's alternative food stall) did to MacDonald's 'Big Macs'.

Dales was replete with massive crowds of some 8,000 or more; Harry attracted some 800 people, most of them young. The Dales was ordered with military precision; Harry was cosily shambolic and anarchic. Evening celebrations and apostolic ministry dominated the Dales Bible Weeks; at Harry, the worship services were morning events and distinctly low-key. David Tomlinson and his team – the organisers of Harry – were noticeably unobtrusive. Everything at the Dales reflected Restorationist teaching, from the seminars to children's fun-time. Harry did have seminars on the 'gifts of the Spirit', but these were tucked away between workshops on religion and science, sexual relationships, capitalism and the exploitation of the Third World.

Everything for sale and on display at the Dales reflect-

373

ed Restorationist concerns. At Harry, there were stalls representing Christian CND (complete with yellow frisbees), Amnesty International and environmental organizations. It could be said that Dales represented the arts in the sense that art was used for propaganda purposes, to extend the kingdom message. At Harry, the artists – whether Christian street poets or the sculptors and painters – seemed content to promote 'art for art's sake'.

The bands and artists at Harry, ranging from the country and western style 'Country Potatoes', to the avantgarde 'The Revolutionary Army of the Infant Jesus', seemed to be there primarily for fun and honest revelry, rather than for specifically religious reasons. It was difficult to imagine any of them 'doing a gig' at the Dales. The Dales bristled with kingdom directives and military metaphors. Harry was decidedly pacifistic and conciliatory in tone. 'It is better to light a candle than curse the darkness,' spluttered David Tomlinson, enigmatically, on numerous occasions.

The young of Harry, some with punk and gelled hairstyles, rocker or romantic clothes, seemed to be excited, yet relaxed. These teenagers were not, on the whole, the 'unsaved' or the waifs of inner cities – they were the second generation of Restorationists and their friends. No longer interested in the revivalist stories of their parents, they were bored or irritated with charismatic worship and wanted some hard answers to tough questions about love, life and, in Woody Allen's phrase, 'the whole damn thing'.

What has to be said, as a matter of fact, is that Harry's hard-working team diligently tried not to go for the easy-answers approach. This was probably just as well, for it was quite obvious that many of the teenagers were in no mood for answers that always fell into the category, 'the Bible says that . . .' Indeed, when Josh McDowell, one of the most polished performers on the American campus circuit, dropped in for a night and a day, he was, if not exactly heckled from the floor, given a run for his money.

On the whole, Harry was judged a great success by most of the participants. Complaints were of the order of 'more toilets', rather than criticism of the seminars and workshops. Certainly, the bands and speakers were thoroughly appreciated, and the intimate, almost club-like atmosphere created in the main auditorium was warm and friendly rather than intense or revivalistic. Swigging non-alcoholic lagers and wines, wolfing down traditional hot dogs and chips, or the far healthier vegetarian dishes, the ethos was more Student Christian Movement 'with signs following', than the yuppyish Christian Union of mainstream evangelicalism. Harry was still (just) recognizable as a charismatic gathering – tongues could be heard and the baptism of the Spirit was sought by a few – but it was an event that seemed to have swallowed a radical mixture of Tony Campolo, *Third Way* magazine, and the rock band U2.

If this was still Restoration, it was not the apostolic Restorationism of Bryn Jones. Neither did it look like the typical Cobham 'bashes' of Gerald Coates, with their more home counties Conservative flavour of cheerful charismata. Indeed, neither was Harry 89 a logical extension of the Festival jamborees, when David Tomlinson, John Noble and Gerald Coates worked together. It was radically different and daring; bold, to the brink of folly.

Intimation that not everyone at Harry would be totally happy with this novel Restorationist approach came to me as I arrived on the Thursday afternoon. Pausing at the entrance gate, I picked up a copy of the satirical magazine, *Nous*, which was on sale for £1. It is not my experience that Restorationists have been particularly adept at self-deprecation, especially during the early years of the movement, when they thought they were the last chapter in religious and world history.

But here, in this rather arty, student magazine, I was seeing not only written skits designed to convince charismatics not to take themselves so seriously, but cartoon strips which were intended to critique (as the Americans say) charismatic culture and theology. There was the barely disguised questioning of televangelism in the form of the 'eager evangelist, Oriel Robplops'. Then there were the 'zany adventures in cloud-cuckoo land with super-spiritual supremo, Danny the Dualist'. This story included a comic representation of God sitting on a chair in the clouds, feet in a bowl of water, puffing a pipe behind the *Brighton Morning Star*!

Stronger evidence that Harry would be too much for some people to take came during Friday evening's 'entertainment'. Some people arrived late, saw the CND posters, the nude picture on the wall, heard the Gregorian and Russian Orthodox chanting to the accompaniment of complex percussion rhythms, and demanded their money back, muttering words about 'demonic influences' and 'medieval music'. There were other participants too (mainly older people), who were not so much censorious of Harry as bemused by the whole proceedings.

Harry, for better or for worse, was a radical departure from the days of the Dales Bible Weeks. Not only did it not reflect the Restorationism of yesteryear, but it also did not resemble the clean-cut family ethos of Spring Harvest. Watching Stewart Henderson beating time with his foot to a snare drum, and listening to his stabbing delivery of 'My Heart Had a Riot on Waterloo Station', I felt that I might well have been at Greenbelt.

Harry, kingdom people might argue, was a rogue stream that broke the banks of the Restorationist river and went on its own brief and wild way. This may be true, but if it is, then it also holds that other streams burst the banks, some to meander to nowhere in particular, others to dry up, and still more to head back to the larger charismatic flow from which they originally came.

APPENDIX 1

Arthur Wallis kindly wrote an afterword for the second edition of this book in 1988. I though it improper to include it in this form, as Arthur has now died and has not seen this edition. So I thought it best to include it as an appendix.

The Final Word

O wad some Pow'r the giftie gie us
To see oursels as others see us!

Two years ago I scribbled these lines in the flyleaf of the first edition of *Restoring the Kingdom* as I put it back on its shelf, for it had, if nothing else, answered for me that prayer of Robbie Burns. I feel it is important that we as 'insiders' study the portrait, warts and all. But it is equally important that we don't equate the exercise with seeing ourselves as we really are – a view that only God can give us.

Andrew Walker has, in my judgment, striven to be as fair and as impartial in his reporting as one could expect from an outsider who is also an ex-Pentecostal. I don't endorse a number of his assessments and predictions, but then I don't even pretend to be impartial. It is a measure of his big-heartedness to have given me the opportunity of a final, unedited word.

Roots may claim to provide us with a natural explanation of why we are where we are. According to this critique, Restorationism has its theological roots in Brethrenism, classical Pentecostalism and Irvingism. I would discount the last named entirely. With the other two I believe we have welcomed all that seemed to us in those movements to be a genuine recovery of New Testament teaching and practice. But other things we have rejected, such as that eschatology of disaster called 'dispensationalism' – which the Brethren so warmly espoused, and which deeply influenced Pentecostals – in favour of an eschatology of victory, the triumph of the kingdom of God. I do believe it is important to have 'a sense of history', but even more important that in the end we are not governed by past roots but by present revelation, and in this we acknowledge how much we have still to learn.

'Radical', an unpopular word in many circles, has been frequently used in this book to describe us. If in addition to its theological connotation is meant also 'dedicated', 'committed', 'whole-hearted', we receive the compliment. I could wish that we were much more so. Since this vital commodity seems to be in such grievously short supply, perhaps our critics will acknowledge that, despite the warts, we have recovered something significant of New Testament Christianity.

As to our future, Andrew sees aggressive evangelism as the only prospect for our survival. We agree. Without that we don't deserve to survive. We are limbering up. No, we have not yet seen the harvest the Jeffreys brothers saw. I don't think this is to be explained by their greater evangelistic zeal or anointing, but that they were borne along on a revival wave. There is a bigger wave coming. God birthed us with the vision of it. Though it tarry, we wait for it – not just for the survival or enlargement of Restoration, but for the blessing of the whole Church and the bringing in of God's kingdom.

Arthur Wallis
1988

APPENDIX 2

MONEY, SEX AND POWER

Over the years I have received many letters, been engaged in copious conversations, and read numerous reviews of *Restoring the Kingdom*, which have suggested that I have been too soft on Restorationists. Apparently, I have pulled my punches, or, to change metaphors, failed to dish the dirt.

These criticisms, I believe, fail to distinguish between academic journalism and exposé journalism. Exposé journalism is a means of making a quick buck by using shock tactics. It is not particularly concerned with truth, it seems to me, but rather seeks to provide titillation. Academic journalism, on the other hand, is really an academic work of understanding, written in accessible language. Consequently, it does not centre on gossip or scandal in itself. This appendix covers three areas on which I chose not to over-concentrate.

Money

I did come across financial issues of some seriousness. For my money, 'heap offerings' are open to manipulation. Tithing (and I've come across double-tithing) can also be a means to feather the nests of leaders, or more typically, to help build up a small empire. In revivalistic or enthusiastic gatherings, the giving of rings, personal valuables, and so on, may often be regretted at a later and more sober date. These issues, however, while they are all too familiar in some charismatic circles, are not to be confused with legal matters, where money is acquired through deception, or downright crookedness is involved.

If there was financial looseness in the early days of the movement, this was more a reflection of the anarchic style. There might have been carelessness, but certainly not crookedness. As the Restorationist kingdom grew, so did the accountants.

Of course, some readers want to know how rich leaders are. Few are in fact wealthy, and those who have made money, such as Bryn Jones, did not make it through Restorationist churches, but through business or property ventures. (One of the curious memorabilia I have from this research is the asking price of Riddleston Hall from the local estate agent.)

Some Restorationists, including two elders, did come to see me about what they took to be short-hand accountancy procedures. My own view is that such people should deal with these matters themselves, or take legal advice, rather than seek redress through publication. This is a difficult area for an author. To say nothing of potential financial irregularities is to be dishonest. But to say something, without slander, is difficult, and comes over as innuendo without foundation.

Sex

This in my opinion was an easier area to deal with. I did come across various cases of adultery, most of which were being dealt with on a pastoral level by leaders. I could not see how it would be in the public interest to expose such matters because I take it that adultery occurs everywhere and is not a special feature of Restorationist churches. In the late 1980s, I was approached by a leading BBC political reporter who told me of an imminent exposé of a senior figure in the movement that was of a more exotic nature. Frankly, I did not believe the story and, as I was told that it was going to be splashed in a well-known tabloid, I thought I would let them get on with it. Nothing in fact came of the threatened exposure.

Power

Academic journalism obviously tries to avoid misinforming, and so naturally it follows that great care needs to be taken in accusing leaders of abusing others, or misusing their authority. This is a particular problem with the practice of shepherding. As I told Timothy Larsen of R1, I have large files of complaints, including one sent to me after the broadcast of the BBC documentary, *The Apostle and the Prophet*, some years ago. The trouble with such complaints is that many people, when contacted, do not wish to talk; and the complaints are often cries of disillusionment, rather than specific claims.

In 1988, I contacted Dr Paul Booth, who then worked for INFORM (Information Network Focus on Religious Movements). At that time, he told me, out of eighty different religious movements they were monitoring, house churches came second in the number of enquiries – just behind the Scientologists, but some way ahead of the Moonies. This sounds shocking, and it is certainly a matter of concern, but the figures have to be treated with care. Firstly, INFORM did not have a rubric, Dr Booth told me, which distinguished types of house churches from each other. Secondly, and of far greater importance, is the fact that the house church movement involves many thousands of members, whereas the average new religious movement is tiny. In fact, therefore, the large number of enquiries is relatively small if measured against house, or new, churches as a whole.

I remain convinced that shepherding still exists in some Restorationist churches, but, as it has always been, it is primarily paternalistic rather than despotic. However, it was shepherding that led to my interest, in the last few years, in what I call religious abuse – the misuse of power – which I see as a phenomenon in mainstream churches as well as in sects and cults – see Andrew Walker and Lawrence Osborn (eds), *Harmful Religion: An Exploration of Religious Abuse* (London: SPCK, 1997).

Last Words

Clearly, Restorationism is more casuistic than most Christian movements, and charismatic apostolates will always tend towards authoritarianism. Without doubt also, some leaders display authoritarian personalities. This does not, however, make them evil, any more than authoritarian leaders are evil in politics; neither is strong leadership bad in itself, if properly exercised. And this brings me to my final word.

I have been with Restorationists on and off now for fifteen years. Rather like Professor Eileen Barker, who is often accused of being too friendly with Moonies, and Dr Bryan Wilson, whom some say is too open-handed with Exclusive Brethren, I am accused of being too soft on Restorationists. This 'softness', I believe, comes naturally when you take the trouble to get to know people over the years. They turn out, in the end, to be just like people everywhere. Empirically, if you will, Restorationists are made up of good sorts, bad ones, and those in between. At the very least, if they did not change my beliefs, nor win my heart, they did gain my respect. I shall be content if I earned theirs.

Notes

Introduction to the Fourth Edition
Beyond the Kingdom

1. The words are mine, but the insight came from Bryan Wilson in conversation with him at All Souls Oxford in 1986. See A. Walker, *Restoring the Kingdom: The Radical Christianity of the House Church Movement*, revised and expanded edition (London: Hodder & Stoughton, 1989) p 333.

2. Interview with Nigel Wright at Spurgeon's College on 20th October 1989.

3. A spokesman from Clarendon Villas (telephone call, 28th May 1997) thought that New Frontiers may now be involved with (but not necessarily govern) 180 churches or more. On the other hand, he felt this probably amounted to no more than 12,000 members, a figure which is not substantially up on that from a few years back. On 4th July, however, Terry Virgo wrote to me saying that a recent survey shows that 'numbers have grown to 20,000 rather than 12,000'. If this is so, it means that New Frontiers is not only by far the largest Restorationist grouping, but is reaching the critical mass that might soon merit the title 'denomination'.

4. Keri Jones, Bryn's brother and fellow apostle, has recently moved to North America.

5. This judgment is not based on the number of churches or size – Terry Virgo is probably the most successful in that respect – but on Gerald's national profile and contribution to the charismatic evangelical scene as a whole.

6. I captured something of the new excitement in two articles for *The Tablet*. See 'Charismatics on the March', Part One, *The Tablet*, 20th October 1990, pp 1332–33; 'Charismatics on the March: a People's Army', Part Two, *The Tablet*, 27th October 1990, pp 1368–70.

7. Kensington City Temple has recently pulled out of the Evangelical Alliance over its continued support of Morris Cerullo. Cerullo is not supported by the Alliance and Gerald Coates is only one of many well-known evangelists who will not share a platform with him.

8. For an uncritical appraisal, see David Pytches, *Some Say it Thundered* (London: Hodder & Stoughton, 1990). For a more critical engagement, see M. G. Maudlin, 'Seers in the Heartland', *Christianity Today* (14th January 1991, pp 18–22).

9. Bryn did not approve of the animal noises at Toronto and had no interest in visiting there. He did, however, endorse the ministry of Rodney Howard Browne from South Africa as an expression of this 'move of God'.

10. Gerald mentions fifty or so churches in Pioneer with some 10,000

members or more. Interview with Gerald in his home in Esher, 5th February 1997.

11. Gerald does not object to the word 'discipling', or 'mentoring', but he sees 'heavy shepherding' as belonging more to the churches of Bryn Jones and Terry Virgo. He admits that some have found it very helpful, but others oppressive (ibid). It is only fair to say that Tim Larsen, who works closely with Bryn Jones, categorically denies that 'heavy shepherding' is a practice in their churches (letter dated 20th June 1997).

12. David Lillie, *Restoration: Is This Still on God's Programme?* (Kyrtonia Press, 1994) chapter 7. Most mainline churches have seen St Paul to be a foundational apostle along with the twelve.

13. Ibid., p 80.

14. Interview with Dave Tomlinson at King's College, 10th December 1996.

15. Ibid.

16. The fellowship was formerly in Pioneer, but it is now New Frontiers.

17. Interview with Rodney Kingston in his Worthing home, 16th June 1989.

18. Not many house church leaders can boast a good relationship with the former bishop of Durham, David Jenkins, as can Brian. I have made several visits to the north-east and it is clear that Brian Howell certainly is not treated like an apostle, but the Anglicans are quite happy with him as a kind of house church bishop.

19. Indeed, although 'shepherding' now seems to be a dead duck ideologically, many of the independent fellowships still show a considerable, and possibly growing interest, in the revival of apostolic ministries.

20. Interview with Tim Larsen at King's College on 13th March 1997. Tim also pointed out that their Bible College only catered for approximately twenty-five full-time students and that the fifty-five or so British churches probably housed some 7,000–8,000 members. These numbers are much the same as for 1989, so we are not seeing strong evidence of an expansionist movement in Britain. However, there are twenty-five or so churches in the United States, three in Canada, three in Norway and three in Asia, all of which have a strong affiliation; as well as a few in Namibia and South Africa. My own view is that Bryn's unique role is to carry the flag for an unflagging Restorationism when most other Restorationists have adapted or abandoned their former beliefs.

21. Interestingly, Gerald and I once debated the merits of old versus new churches at St Andrew's Chorleywood in the early 1990s. These days, Gerald sees the new church more in terms of ethos than confessional exactitude or denominational fixity. In this respect, he sees Holy Trinity Brompton as new church, while some new churches he finds to be old hat. Information in interview with Gerald Coates, op. cit.

22. I believe the 'new church' ethos will continue, and under this loos-

er rubric Restorantionism will play some significant role, but is unlikely to be the dominant partner.

Prologue The Great Yorkshire Showground, August 1982
1. I was also there the previous year with the BBC's Everyman team. Most of my brief stay was spent talking to leaders.
2. Songs 72 and 27 respectively, *All Hail King Jesus* (Harvestime Press, 1982).
3. Ibid., Song 63. These songs were heard by me on both Thursday and Friday night, but I have recorded my impressions of them, not a literal description of when exactly each song occurred.

Chapter 1 'House Churches? Never Heard of Them!'
1. This is the heading of an article I remember seeing from an old newsletter of David Tomlinson's house churches.
2. This was in October 1979, when I was a consultant observer at the British Council of Churches consultation on the Charismatic Renewal (organized jointly with the Fountain Trust). Tom Smail, former director of the Fountain Trust, and Dr David Russell, then General Secretary of the Baptist Union, introduced the church leaders to the House Church Movement.
3. In no sense, however, should Ichthus be confused with Restorationist churches.
4. These numbers of course refer to 1984/85.
5. The Charismatic Renewal is within the mainline churches, and the many West Indian Pentecostal churches were primarily started outside Britain. Those started here are very significant, in my opinion, but they are still small and fragmented on the whole.
6. Though in time Bryn was to own a Mercedes car and his house in Yorkshire was to be worth considerably more than £150,000 when he sold it.
7. 'The Dales Bible Week', report, 8th August 1982 (Radio 4's Sunday); *Front Room Gospel*, a 45-minute documentary on house churches, 23rd March 1984 – repeated in slightly changed form in 1985 (Radio 4). In 1981, 'Charismania' on *Credo* (LWT), 'Unearthly Powers' on *Everyman* and *Brass Tacks* (both BBC television), covered aspects of the house church movement. The year 1987 saw a major BBC documentary on Bradford.
8. This section contains the only substantial conceptual change from the original 1985 edition. By the second edition in 1988, I had already come clean and admitted that my historical categories and sociological ones were somewhat confused (op. cit. p 301). I believe that there is a tendency in the first edition to over-identify R1 with those who sided with Bryn Jones and Arthur Wallis after the 1976 split, and similarly to over-identify R2 with those who sided with Gerald Coates and John Noble. This leaves the impression that R1 and R2 are merely a shorthand rubric to describe specific historical entities. In this edition, by stressing R1 and R2 more in terms of a

sociological ideal type (see next note), I believe this to be not only conceptually more useful but also to allow us to deal with the considerable fluidity and complexity of the actual historical development of Restorationist Christianity. Indeed, as I argue in Part Three, by 1990 I believe that R2 had disappeared, leaving R1 as the only approximation to the ideal type I call Restorationism.

9. My use of ideal types is mainly influenced by Max Weber and Alfred Schutz. But for a useful understanding of how these constructs can be methodologically fruitful, I still think that Aaron Cicourel is hard to beat. See his *Method and Measurement in Sociology* (New York: Free Press, 1964). Following Cicourel, ideal types need to be understood as the distillation of the primary characteristics of the phenomenon under investigation. In short, ideal types are constructed after initial observation and familiarity with the field of study. They may not be empirical models, but neither are they arbitrary or a priori.

10. 'Apostles' here denotes a deliberate ambiguity – that is, to follow apostolic teaching is to follow the apostles of the New Testament and the modern apostles of Restorationism.

11. And David Tomlinson until 1983.

12. In interview with me on 23rd November 1983.

13. It seems to me no coincidence that in the late 1980s it was Gerald Coates of R2 who began to re-characterize house churches as 'new churches'.

14. For a time Gerald Coates and John Noble called their fellowships 'Fulness' after their short-lived magazine. In interview with me on 14th October 1983.

15. It might be argued that MacLauchlan is more R1 than R2, but I think in terms of his history and relationships he emerges in an R2 milieu. Suffice it to say that we should expect R2 – as the 'less pure' Restorationist movement – to be more mixed, or hybrid, than its R1 cousin.

16. See Michael Harper's important little booklet, *Charismatic Crisis: the Charismatic Renewal – Past, Present and Future* (Hounslow Printing Company, 1980).

17. Its strong emphasis on the supernatural and miraculous is still influential. Ian Andrews is widely recognized as a Chard evangelist with a healing charism.

18. Joyce V. Thurman, *New Wineskins: A Study of the House Church Movement* (Verlag Peter Lang, 1982) p 34. Thurman's work is the pioneering study of the House Church movement, and I will make considerable use of it throughout this book. However, all pioneering work soon becomes out of date and some of the material is no longer relevant. On a more problematic note: much of my historical material is ordered differently from Thurman's. I feel that she fails to recognize the historical linkage of 'Harvestime' with the London Brothers.

19. Ibid., p 26. Joyce Thurman refers here to Peter Paris, who was the first major leader to defect from R1. Bryn Jones does not accept

Joyce Thurman's version of this story.
20. Ibid., p 33.
21. Founded by the well-known evangelical, Norman Grubb, this movement sounds like an insurance company. 'Union' refers to the union of Christ with believers. Some charge it with antinomianism; a charge often levelled at John Noble and Gerald Coates by people in R1.
22. In the 1990s, however, Ichthus would certainly fit the looser rubric of 'new churches'.
23. After 1985, I conducted several more rounds of interviews, but much of my field-work, especially at celebrations, was conducted as a participant observer. My role was, appropriately enough, either as the author of *Restoring The Kingdom*, or as a Christian academic. For an understanding of participant observation, see Cicourel, op. cit., pp 46–49.
24. See Appendix 2.
25. Arthur Wallis, 'Focus', *Restoration* magazine (July/August 1980).

Chapter 2 The Origins of Restoration 1958–70
1. Editorial introduction to Arthur Wallis's 'Springs of Restoration', Part 1, *Restoration* (Harvestime Publications, July/August 1980).
2. I remember reading this book in the 1950s – many classical Pentecostals, at that time, believed it was a prophetic work. The book is now reissued (and partly rewritten) under the title *Rain from Heaven* (London: Hodder & Stoughton, 1980). Strangely, it has not had the impact of the earlier edition.
3. Op. cit., p 23.
4. P. J. Lineham, 'Tongues Must Cease: The Brethren and the Charismatic Movement in New Zealand', *Christian Brethren Review*, No. 34 (November 1983).
5. Wallis had originally intended to stay only for the Easter camp, but he found that Campbell had laid a foundation on which he felt compelled to build. See 'Springs of Restoration', op. cit.
6. P. J. Lineham, op. cit., p 40
7. Ibid., p 41.
8. Phone call to Gerald Coates, June 1984.
9. So I suggested in an Agenda article in the *Guardian* newspaper, 'A New Spirit to Light up the Church' (24th November 1980). However, I feel less sanguine about the Renewal now than I was then. See my 'Pentecostal Power: Charismatic Movements and the Politics of Pentecostal Experience', in *Of Gods and Men: New Religious Movements*, edited by E. Barker (United States: Mercer University Press, 1984).
10. W. T. H. Richards, Pentecost is Dynamite (London: Lakeland, 1972).
11. This was his view in conversation with me in June 1984. I now realize that Michael was right (see chapter 13, note 5).
12. Even in the late 1990s, I feel the jury is still out on this one.
13. Gerald Coates, *What on Earth is this Kingdom?* (Eastbourne: Kingsway, 1983) p 23.

14. The quotes from Maurice Smith in this book come from four hours of interview on 16th May 1984 (and/or numerous letters and phone calls).

Chapter 3 The Restored Kingdom Emerges 1970–75

1. Few leaders appear to have a firm grasp of the overall picture from those early days.
2. See Ián Bradley's excellent study, *The Call to Seriousness: the Evangelical Impact on the Victorians* (London: Jonathan Cape, 1976).
3. This is not proof that women were not more evident. Although she provides no specific instances, Eileen Vincent insists that women ministries were around (Jean Darnell certainly was active in those days both at Capel Bible Week and in London). See Vincent's exciting version of Restoration written from the inside: *Something's Happening* (London: Marshalls, 1984) p 21.
4. There are many wild rumours about George Tarleton. On investigation, however, they turn out to be extremely prejudicial. George is interested in alternative medicine and all kinds of related phenomena. He is a natural anarchist who simply prefers to plough his own furrow. It would seem that the Restoration kingdom is not designed to accommodate deviants like George.
5. This changed when Nick Butterworth joined the editorial staff; the improvement in presentation was quite dramatic.
6. Three-hour interview with John Noble and Gerald Coates on 10th March 1984.
7. See 'Springs of Restoration' op. cit. While he is writing for an R1 audience, Arthur sees Restoration as a worldwide movement of the Spirit of God.
8. Enigmatic, I know, but simple enough really. For example, total commitment/fanaticism; purity/exclusiveness; will power and determination/bullying; total conviction and certainty/inability to accept criticism. According to the Eastern tradition, only limitless love and holiness prevents the shadows from lengthening.
9. Joyce Thurman, op. cit., p 26.
10. Other people view his preaching differently. An old classical Pentecostal told me: 'Too little of Jesus, and too much of Bryn Jones.' Bryn is certainly a performance preacher, and it is in the nature of that style of preaching that you can never always be up to the mark.
11. See 'Springs of Restoration', Part 2, op. cit., p. 8.
12. Alan Halden, 'Barntalk' (undated), 27 Daggs Dell, Hemel Hempstead.
13. Not wishing to distort Bryn Jones's position, he did point out to me, on the phone, that he recognized John Noble and Gerald Coates's ministry as similar to, though more liberal than, his own. Gerald, on the other hand, thinks that the recognition amounts to admitting their existence, but not accepting them as equals. As evidence for this assertion, he points out that he and his associates have never been invited to participate in either Dales or Downs Weeks.

14. As remembered by Maurice Smith, see chapter 2, note 14.
15. Confirmed to me by the president of the Apostolic Church.
16. Now renamed Regent's College and relocated to Nantwich, Cheshire.
17. See 'Springs of Restoration', Part 2, op. cit.
18. Maurice Smith, op. cit.
19. The split was among the leadership. The rank and file did not notice much difference, as the leaders had already established separate spheres of influence.

Chapter 4 The Kingdom Established in Division 1974–76

1. Interview with Gerald Coates and John Noble, see chapter 3, note 6.
2. Ibid.
3. Remarks made to me by Bryn Jones in his office on 21st March 1984. As my tape recorder was not on at the time, I am relying on memory (David Matthew and Goos Vedder were also present at the meeting).
4. See Joyce Thurman, op. cit., p 98.
5. I have never met Ern Baxter, so I have nothing to go on but hearsay.
6. Professor Hollenweger was an Assemblies of God pastor as a young man, and was responsible for translating Branham's words for continental readers. He therefore speaks with more than just academic knowledge.
7. Michael Harper alludes to this in *Charismatic Crisis*. An early editorial in the May/June 1976 issue of Restoration comments on it.
8. Conversation with Bryn Jones, see note 3.
9. Taped conversations with David Tomlinson over the weekend of 16–17th March 1984.
10. Bryn Jones confirmed over the phone in June 1984 that this was a solution to the problem, but left unsaid what the alternatives might have been.
11. Interview with Maurice Smith, see chapter 2, note 13.
12. I have it on good authority that, radical though he might have been in his beliefs, Arthur Wallis had a good record for bringing together people who had fallen out.
13. See note 9.
14. Bryn Jones's enemies would obviously go for the first one, and his followers for the second one. I feel inclined to take his part in this matter. Arthur Wallis pointed out to me in January 1988 that it was in fact the case that the five were the ones who initially shut the door, and so 'we pulled back'.
15. This is not, of course, historically true, but I think that is how many of the leaders of R2 felt at that time.
16. They cannot all have been so furious, for I notice that Gerald Coates was on the editorial board of the new magazine until he was removed after the split.
17. Though there have been meetings since 1985 and greater co-operation in the 1990s.
18. Op. cit., p 98.

19. They are in good company here. Bawdiness, beer and tobacco were characteristic of C. S. Lewis's circle (tobacco seems to be universally decried in R1).
20. Though Mansell was removed from ministry from late 1984 or early 1985 until 1987; this was an internal sanction for personal problems. Mansell was restored to Bryn Jones's team in 1987 (though he maintained certain business interests). While David Mansell is seen as a prophet, I don't wish to give the impression that he is 'way-out' or an unruly person. He sees his prophetic task as intellectual as well as intuitive. A university graduate, he has knowledge of Classical Greek, and speaks modern Hebrew.
21. See note 1.

Chapter 5 Extending the Kingdom 1975–85
1. See chapter 1, note 2.
2. Taped conversations with David Tomlinson, 16–17th March, op.cit.
3. I am indebted to Joyce Thurman for this information. Op cit., pp 28–29.
4. Discussion with Bryn Jones at Church House, see chapter 4, note 3.
5. Ibid.
6. This was the thrust of my report on the Dales Bible Week for Radio 4's *Sunday* programme, 8th August 1982.
7. Information from Bryn Jones in a telephone conversation in June 1984. (A former member of R1 claims that many of the crowds at these evangelistic campaigns were Restorationists 'bussed in' from Bradford.)
8. David Pawson is recorded in the *Methodist Recorder* on 9th February 1984 as claiming that there are 100,000 fellowships meeting in homes. Taking all kinds of house churches, inside and outside the denominations, this figure is fairly accurate. Restoration per se is much smaller. None of the leaders of R1 and R2 have tried to augment their figures for media presentation, but I have overestimated the numbers myself in previous publications, including the first edition of this book. Not clearly making a distinction between those attending the Dales and Downs Weeks, those pro-Restorationist but not yet committed members, and the members themselves, I have tended to see the overall size of R1 and R2 as 70,000. Now I feel, with greater confidence, that 40,000 would be the maximum figure for both R1 and R2, and I suspect this number in the mid-1980s represents the peak of the movement. As I pointed out in 1985 to Peter Brierley, who edits the *UK Christian Handbook,* the handbook's figure of 180,000 house church members had to be inaccurate. He promised to look into the whole matter, and in fact halved the number the following year (1986).
9. According to sources in the London-based Church of the Latter Day Saints in Exhibition Road, by June 1997 they had approximately 165,000 members in Great Britain.
10. I say complaining, but few have been willing to talk in specifics. We could find nobody willing to talk for the programme *Front Room*

Gospel, broadcast on Radio 4 on 23rd March 1984. In researching this book, I have been presented with little firm evidence, and few people who were willing to give their names. My own view is that if such stories exist in any great numbers, it will be only a matter of time before they surface.

11. There is no formal constitution, or officially established leadership. What has emerged is a de facto leadership.

12. The *Havering Post* headlined on 14th July: 'Shock Report Slams School'. This is typical media hype. The report by H. M. Inspectors on 'Acorn Independent School, Romford, Essex' is available from the Department of Education and Science, Publications Despatch Centre, Honeypot Lane, Stanmore, Middlesex HA7 1AZ.

13. In interview on 11th May 1984.

14. I lost contact with Maurice until 1997 and have not seen him since 1989.

15. I said 12,000 in 1985, but I underestimated numbers in the R2 'hard core'.

Chapter 6 The Radical Principles of Restoration (Part One)

1. George Tarleton thinks that most leaders in R2 tend towards Conservatism politically. However, I met a number of people at Festival 84 who were Labour, Liberal or SDP supporters. Bryn Jones expressed admiration to me for Arthur Scargill's fight to save miners' jobs and communities (Bryn's father was a leading member of the Welsh Communist party).

2. Kingsway, 1981.

3. Ibid., pp 15–16.

4. It is not so much because it offends my Eastern Orthodox sensibilities, but more a question of scholarship. For example, Arthur Wallis's attempt to bring alive the New Testament Church in *The Radical Christian* looks, to me, not how I (imperfectly) understand the New Testament Church to be, but like the modern Restoration movement read back into the canons of scripture. Compare Wallis's version of the New Testament Church with Professor James Dunn's 'Models of Christian Community in the New Testament' in *Strange Gifts? A Guide to Charismatic Renewal*, edited by D. Martin and P. Mullen Oxford: (Blackwell, 1984).

5. The head of BBC religious broadcasting, David Winter, has recently spearheaded this distinction. See his *But This I Can Believe* (London: Hodder & Stoughton, 1980).

6. Wallis and E. Vincent, op. cit.

7. Ironically, one of the better ones comes from an old friend of Ern Baxter. See Larry Christenson, What About Baptism? (Minneapolis: Bethany Fellowship, 1973).

8. Though this is by no means de rigeur.

9. As they are often purportedly based on scholarship, then they can be called 'historicist'. See C. S. Lewis's scathing criticisms on 'Historicism' in *Fern Seeds and Elephants*, ed. Walter Hooper (London: Fontana, 1975).

10. Daniel 2:44 (KJV).
11. In conversation with me on 11th September 1984.
12. Song 63, *All Hail King Jesus* (Harvestime Press, 1982).
13. J. N. D. Kelly, *Early Christian Doctrines* (London: Adam & Charles Black, 1977).
14. David Matthew has written a very good article against purely intellectualist approaches. I am sure he feels it should have been read more carefully by me! See 'It's All In The Mind', *Restoration* (May/June 1983).
15. 'Church Adrift' series, Part 8, *Restoration* (March/April 1984).
16. Interview on 10th March 1984.
17. Pickering & Inglis, 1931.
18. D. J. Beattie, *Brethren: the Story of a Great Recovery* (Kilmarnock: John Ritchie Ltd., 1939).
19. 'Church Adrift' series, Part 6, *Restoration* (November/December 1983), p 40.

Chapter 7 The Radical Principles of Restoration (Part Two)

1. These are the words of Paul, but their meaning is expanded and put into apostolic context by Arthur Wallis in 'Apostles Today? Why Not!', *Restoration* (November/December 1981).
2. David Tomlinson, 'Some Burning Questions About Apostles', *Restoration* (November/December 1981).
3. Robert Brow, 'Voices', *Restoration* (November/December 1981).
4. Ern Baxter at the Lakes Bible Week, 1975.
5. Ibid.
6. In interview, 23rd November 1983.
7. Herbert Harrison, 'Voices', *Restoration* (Nov-ember/December 1981).
8. A collection of texts of the spiritual masters of the Orthodox Church. Volume one of the complete text is now available in English, translated and edited by G. E. H. Palmer, Philip Sherrard, and Kallistos Ware (London: Faber & Faber, 1979).
9. Derek Prince, Discipleship, Shepherding, Commitment (D. Prince Publishing, 1976) p 19.
10. See for example Ron Trudinger's *Built to Last* (Eastbourne: Kingsway Publications, 1982).
11. See chapter 4.
12. This does not hold for Bryn Jones (see chapter 15).
13. Spiritual Authority (Christian Fellowship Publishers, 1972).
14. David Lillie, a key figure in the early days as we have seen, has pointed this out in *Beyond Charisma* (Carlisle: Paternoster Press, 1981) pp 49–50. Lillie's book is both sensible and intelligent.
15. See also N.H. Cliff, *The Life and Theology of Watchman Nee, Including a Study of the Little Flock Movement Which he Founded* (unpublished MPhil thesis, Open University, 1983).
16. *Spiritual Authority*, op. cit., p 71.
17. Ibid., p 72.
18. Eileen Vincent, op. cit., p 166.

19. David Tomlinson, 'Is Discipling Biblical?' *Restoration* (July/ August 1980).
20. Meaning 'protecting', or 'watching over'. The origin of this term is the concern Japheth demonstrated in covering Noah's nakedness (Genesis 9:20–27). David Tomlinson of R2 hates this term because he thinks it smacks of animal husbandry (emasculation of rams in the north of England, for example).
21. Derek Prince, op. cit., p 23.
22. So Bryn Jones told me at Bradford.
23. Though I believe such doctrines are dangerously close to Bryn Jones's segment of R1.

Chapter 8 The Structure and Shape of Kingdom Life
1. Compare this chapter with part three.
2. In fact, teams started earlier in embryonic form. John Noble, for example, had a team in operation as early as 1975.
3. I have never managed to get any accurate figures, before 1985, of the number of churches under the leadership of the R2 apostles. David Tomlinson brought some twenty-seven churches with him. Both John and Gerald have less than that (though with influence inside a number of other churches). The typical R2 church is smaller than R1. The Cobham Fellowship is some 400, but it consists of smaller units.
4. He means in the sense that Bryn is formally under authority to someone; not whether Bryn ever accepts criticism.
5. Terry Virgo, in R1, is also involved with churches who are not directly under his control (particularly Baptist churches). I also know of at least one elder in his team who is actively involved in inter-denominational work.
6. I did in fact do that, although these were really issues of moral misconduct rather than the direct abuse of power. Bryn made no attempt to hide the issues. In fact, no one from R1 has tried to buy my silence, influence what I write or suggest that I keep names out of it. For my part, I feel that some of my telephone conversations with Bryn Jones were off the record.
7. Though in the 1990s, after he joined R1, he came to be seen by some as a prophet (see chapter 16).
8. 23rd March 1984.
9. Ibid.
10. The Catholic organization 'Housetops', which investigates new religious movements, has recently been looking at house churches. It is still my conviction, as I told the Catholic newspaper, *The Universe*, that the majority of Restorationist churches exhibit benign paternalism.
11. 'Shepherds or Sheep Stealers?', *Buzz* magazine.
12. Until 1985 at least, when they cease to work together (see chapter 15).
13. The 'miracle' has in fact happened several times since those days!
14. (And R2). See the first edition of *Restoring The Kingdom* (chapter 5).

Chapter 9 A Kingdom Tour

1. This slightly tongue in cheek chapter has been left much in its original form from the 1985 edition, and is offered here as a slight respite from the information overload. It can also be seen as the halfway staging post to what has now turned out to be a long journey to the final destination of this book.
2. Such an observation does not hold for the 1990s.
3. Bryn Jones has written a very sensitive piece called 'Is There Life After Divorce?', *Restoration* (March/April 1984). The Church of England evangelicals, who seem to find so much difficulty with this issue, could do worse than look into the Restoration approach to remarriage. Basically, Restoration does not take a liberal, secular approach. They see repentance as the core biblical doctrine in this matter.
4. Professor Walter Hollenweger and I once discussed the central importance of songs and choruses in the Pentecostal movement. We both agreed that if you were to take away the music, Pentecostalism might not survive.
5. Whereas the new *Methodist Hymnal* is totally barren. (The charismatic movement does not have the same foothold in Methodism that it does in the Anglican and Baptist churches.)
6. Donna Adkins, first verse (© Maranatha Music 1981).
7. If one wishes to attack the Restorationist movement on account of the nature of its charismatic activities, then one would need to see this in the context of Pentecostalism as a whole. I have seen things in the charismatic renewal per se that have been more 'way out' than Restorationism.
8. *Front Room Gospel*, Radio 4, 23rd March 1984.
9. Though there will be much more of this kind of co-operation in the 1990s (see chapter 14).
10. Many mainline evangelicals, however, doubt the house churches' real support and interest in such inter-church evangelism.
11. He told me on the telephone in July 1985.
12. Since I wrote this in 1985, I have raised some of these issues with Bryn Jones and Terry Virgo. Both of them seemed to have put in place sensible accountancy systems.
13. They are not, however, optional in the kingdom.
14. I confess to finding the heap offering distasteful. Both Peter Fenwick and Brian Howell from R2 regret a heap offering taken at Festival 1984 seeing it, in hindsight, as 'not honouring to the Lord'.
15. Under the auspices of the Dales Television Company, Bryn Jones began satellite television, speaking to Europe from Oslo, on Sunday 30th June 1985. See chapter 15.
16. Institutionalisation can occur in close-knit religious groups as well as formal institutions such as prisons and mental hospitals. See E. Goffman's chapter on 'Total Institutions', in *Asylums* (Bath: Anchor, 1961).

Chapter 10 Is the Restoration Movement a Denomination?

1. In *That We May Be One* (London: Hodder & Stoughton, 1983) chapter 12.
2. Not that everyone played ball: there is still a small Congregational Union.
3. Michael Hill, *A Sociology of Religion* (Oxford: Heinemann Educational Books, 1973) p 47.
4. Ibid., p 58.
5. Ibid., pp 76–77.
6. Whether Elim can make the leap from its sectarian past to a denominational future is doubtful in my opinion. To become integrated into the mainstream of religious life would be, for them, to risk apostasy.
7. Brethrenism has also over the years standardized many procedures and liturgical practices. These are not uniform, but Brethren can easily recognize each other and feel at home in each other's churches. Some Brethren have no difficulty in seeing themselves as a sect as long as this is understood sociologically (John Boyes, the editor of the *Christian Brethren Review*, for example).
8. Bryan Wilson, *Religious Sects* (London: Weidenfeld & Nicolson, 1970) p 207.
9. This is slowly changing with the realization that sociologists are not all Marxists and atheists! The work of Clifford Hill and Os Guinness has been much appreciated. Christians from an evangelical background could do worse than start with David Lyon's *Sociology and the Human Image* (Leicester: IVP, 1984). I think it not unfair to say that Christian sociology is often bad sociology. Os Guinness's work is important here, because he writes good sociology with Christian insight.
10. Some members of Restoration found my comments hurtful in 'The Theology of the Restoration Churches', because of my use of the word 'sect'. See D. Martin and P. Mullen (eds.), *Strange Gifts, A Guide to Charismatic Renewal* Oxford: (Blackwell, 1984).
11. What I like about David Matthew is his resistance to pessimism. I am sure that he will read my comments fairly and thoroughly, but I already know what his response will be: 'Scripture makes it plain . . . that sooner or later the pattern of history must be broken . . . One day there will be a generation of the church that makes it to God's ideal . . . Why should not that generation be your generation and mine?', *Restoration* (March/April 1984) p 22.

Chapter 11 Catholic Apostolics and Christian Brethren as the Forerunners of Restorationism

1. Irving and the movement which took his name should really be separated, as the latter group included views which were not his own. Catholic Apostolics, on the whole, object to the nickname 'Irvingites'.
2. Many mainline Christians were indifferent to the Second Advent. But the rector of Salisbury, Daniel Whitby (1673–1726) made a con-

siderable impact with his views.

3. I am indebted to Harold Rowdon's Prologue in his *The Origins of the Brethren* (London: Pickering & Inglis, 1967) for this information.

4. Though strictly speaking the notion of a 'secret rapture' is more likely to have emerged in the thinking of Irving. Darby certainly held such a view.

5. There is some uncertainty as to how long these conferences continued. There seems to have been a conference in 1838, but the earlier ones made the major impact.

6. I recall a lively discussion with Roger Forster and the family of Kenneth Frampton on this matter (it was a fine occasion of Brethren hospitality and open-mindedness).

7. F. D. Maurice, the great nineteenth-century churchman, also held Irving in high regard. He called the doctrines of the Scottish minister, 'the grounds of all theology'.

8. 'Irvingite Pentecostalism and the early Brethren', *CBRF*, No. 10, December 1965. (See also issue No. 12, May 1966.)

9. Darby's dispensationalism, for example, in which he distinguished the Jewish law and covenant from the covenant of grace (for the Church). Dispensationalism was a major contribution of Darby to Brethren thought. His views look very much like Irving's least satisfactory doctrines. The notion of dispensations took on extended meanings in both Brethrenism and other forms of evangelicalism. The New Testament canon, for example, was seen as a dispensation of miracles denied to the later and contemporary Church. Darby influenced Scofield, who in turn had a major effect on twentieth-century fundamentalism.

10. See Donald Tinder, 'The Brethren Movement In The World Today', *CBRF*, No 25.

11. These doctrines and their relationship to Pentecostalism have been admirably treated by Gordon Strachan in his *The Pentecostal Theology of Edward Irving* (London: Darton, Longman & Todd, 1976). It is to Gordon's credit that we can see the emergence of a new interest in Irving.

12. They expressed their views in my dramatized documentary on Edward Irving, *The Angel of Regent Square* (Radio 4, 1st December 1984).

13. *Religious Sects* (London: Weidenfeld & Nicolson, 1970)   p 207.

14. *Front Room Gospel*, op. cit.

15. They believed that the angels of the seven churches in the Apocalypse were not heavenly beings, but bishops or chief pastors.

16. Revd W. J. E. Bennet, *The Church's Broken Unity* (J. T. Hayes, Lyall, undated but approximately 1867) p 148.

17. Harold Rowdon, op. cit., p 260.

18. Although I believe that they are growing again in the 1990s.

19. Pickering & Inglis (second edition, undated).

20. I do not mean by this that Restorationism has self-consciously adopted Irvingism and Brethrenism. On the contrary, they have either ignored or eschewed Irving and the Catholic Apostolic

Church. Sociologically and historically speaking, however, I believe that the Catholic Apostolic Church was a forerunner – a prefigurement – of modern Restorationism.

Chapter 12 Classical Pentecostalism and Restorationism

1. I have heard 1885/86 quoted by some Church of God Holiness groups.
2. It seems to me that Pentecostalism can take root in a Reformed Calvinist soil, but it is likely to be a different flower from the Pentecostalist plant that we are used to. I think that Dr Gordon Strachan and Tom Smail would prefer to bypass the holiness route.
3. Though they are all members of the British Pentecostalist Fellowship.
4. Unfortunately for me, plausible though such a hypothesis may be, it is empirically false according to David Lillie, who told me by phone that he and Arthur were not directly influenced by Apostolic teaching.
5. I owe this information to Philip W. Cawthorne, who complained to me – in the most gentlemanly way – after the broadcast of Front Room Gospel. In the first edition, I quoted 10,000 members, but there has been a rapid decline in the last five years. The Apostolics are optimistic that they will grow again.
6. Hollenweger, op. cit., p 193.
7. Ibid., p 199.
8. Desmond Cartwright's article on early Pentecostalism, 'Echoes from the Past', *Elim Evangel* (5th February 1983) p 6. Pastor Cartwright's series in the *Elim Evangel*, phone conversations, letters and a copy of an academic paper have been invaluable sources for this section.
9. After Aimée's infamous disappearance, George Jeffreys was asked to go to Los Angeles and take over her Metropolitan Temple. It is difficult to imagine a more opposite pair in the whole history of Pentecostalism. (George's refusal was Elim's gain.)
10. 'The Elim Foursquare Gospel Church' in *Sects and Society* (London: Greenwood Press, 1978). Hollenweger's criticisms of Wilson are themselves now out of date.
11. Desmond Cartwright, *The Beloved Evangelists: the Lives of Stephen and George Jeffreys* (London: Marshalls, 1986).
12. Notably Pastor Edsor, who worked with Jeffreys before and after the Elim split. See his private booklet, 'In Defence of a Man of God Falsely Portrayed' (1986).
13. By the 1940s, Pastor Cartwright reports, nobody knew where they were with George. He was uncertain and constantly changing his mind.
14. The 1996 *UK Christian Handbook* puts the 1985 figures as 40,000.
15. Evan Roberts may be able to claim a great success as an evangelist per se; but he was no healer.
16. Though both denominations have achieved sustained growth in the 1990s.

17. It seemed too complicated to outline this in Figure 2, but the Restorationist membership from the renewal has tended to come from its periphery (and, of course, other Independent Churches).
18. Though this observation does not hold for the 1990s.
19. See my article, 'Pentecostal Power', in *Of Gods and Men*, ed. E. Barker (Macon: Mercer University Press, 1983).

Chapter 13 The Kingdom Under Attack

1. A number of parents contacted me after the first broadcasting of *Front Room Gospel*. Two of them were desperately worried about their teenage children and felt that house churches were manipulative and dangerous. I was visited by three parents, and spent an afternoon with two sixth-formers from the west country.
2. *Front Room Gospel*.
3. Report on Dales Bible Week, for *Sunday*, Radio 4, 8th August 1982.
4. Both involved conversations for BBC programmes that were, in the event, not used. Subsequently, I talked to Michael on the telephone and came across Douglas McBain's article in the August/September 1984 edition of *Renewal* magazine, 'Emptiness at the Centre'.
5. This information from the Church of England Board of Mission and Unity is the first strong evidence that Michael Harper's assertion that the renewal is quietly but surely expanding may be correct after all. It looks as if I will have to revise my view that the renewal has entered decline – 'eating humble pie' is part of the social scientist's stock in trade! Furthermore, since the death of Canon David Watson, the influence of John Wimber untilo his death in 1997 was considerable.
6. *Buzz* magazine, August 1984.
7. Dales Bible Week, see note 3.
8. For his most stringent criticism, see 'The Curse of the Hallelujah Chorus', *The Guardian*, 28th July 1984.
9. *Front Room Gospel*.
10. Ibid.
11. This case study is from Joyce Thurman's book, op. cit. However, Bryn Jones pointed out to me on the telephone in July 1985 that he and Goos were already in a covenanted relationship before Goos became pastor of Hoole Baptist church. The experience at Hoole, says Bryn, led him to build up his own churches and not work inside existing denominations. (This whole story is really, then, a major factor in the direction of the Bradford-based R1 churches.)
12. From my dramatized documentary on the fall and restoration of Edward Irving, *The Angel of Regent Square*, Radio 4, 1st December 1984.
13. From John Miller's article, 'Tongues Drove Him from Regent Square's Pulpit', *Reform*, December 1984.
14. I was very impressed with John Race's intelligence and thoughtfulness. We had many long conversations on the phone, and he sent me a fourteen-side statement, and a number of further letters (all

quotes are from John's statement). Since this story appeared in the first edition of 1985, John Singleton's church has itself split!

15. I think it fair to say that while John and Liz did not like the implications of Restorationism, their beef is really with the leadership of Emmanuel Community Church.

16. Gene Edwards, *A Tale of Three Kings* (California: Christian Books, 1980).

17. *Front Room Gospel.*

18. E. Barker, *The Making of a Moonie* (Oxford: Blackwell, 1984).

19. Certainly Maurice Smith says so. David Tomlinson is worried that they have a disproportionately high number of mentally-ill and unstable people. I have made similar observations about my own confession! A more worrying aspect of this question would be whether such people are in positions of leadership.

20. Tom Smail, for example, thinks that Paul can legitimately claim to have been a witness of the risen Christ. There is certainly no doubt that tradition has accorded St Paul a unique status (after the twelve).

21. Though when I eventually got to see George face to face at his home in 1989, he told me that he had become convinced of the truth of gnosticism – a truth which Maurice Smith, who was also present, had come to share. I do not know if they would hold this position today.

22. A statement used by Pastor George Canty of Elim on *Front Room Gospel.*

23. The *Gazette*, 8th October 1982.

24. John MacLauchlan's groups are from my extended use of R2, and I thought it only fair to give John the chance to present his work and commitments in his way.

25. Subsequent to the events described here in Yeovil, John MacLauchlan's groups have ceased to operate under his leadership and have virtually ceased to function.

Chapter 14 The Beginning of Restorationist Decline

1. The demographic portion of this chapter reveals little different from information in chapter 5, which was written in 1984.

2. Notably the New Frontier churches of Terry Virgo.

3. More disturbing are the reports I get from former members who have abandoned Christianity altogether.

4. Though after 1990, whole sections of the movement disappear, and before that time, John Noble's network dwindled away.

5. There have of course been far more people involved in new churches of broadly charismatic evangelical hue, but these have been independent of the apostolic streams of Restorationism. A simple rule of thumb in judging Restorationist numbers at their height is to recognize that no stream in R1 or R2 could be said to have more than 10,000 members, and many influential groups, such as Pioneer, for example, had half that number (see chapter 5).

6. I happened to be at Sheffield House Church (Central) in the autumn

of 1989 when they were completing their forms for Marc Europe's English Church census. Here is a breakdown of the figures. Present on that occasion were 9 males and 4 females under the age of 14. There were 13 males and 10 females between the ages of 15 and 19. The young adults (20–29) comprised 17 men and 12 women. Adults (30–44) totalled 11 males and 13 females. Adults (45–64) consisted of 8 men and 12 women. Over the age of 65 there was only one person (a male) present.

7. A number of people criticized me for not including Ichthus in my first edition of this book. I believe that I was right not to do so, because their history is different, as is their understanding of restored New Testament ministries. Strictly speaking, it is not correct either to talk of Roger and Faith Forster as if they were synonymous with Ichthus.

8. Interview with Clive Calver at the Evangelical Alliance, Kennington, 8th September 1989.

9. Of course, the EA is responsible for and supports far more organizations and events than I can mention here.

10. Pioneer bulletin (volume 7, issue 4, p 3.)

11. Against the possible charge that I am being mischievous here, I must point out that this view has been put to me by a number of senior evangelical academics in this country and in North America. It is my opinion that if they feel so strongly about this matter, as some seem to do, then they should speak out.

12. Of Bridgehead Communications at the end of the 1980s, but earlier with *Buzz* magazine.

13. Of course I am not for a moment suggesting that Clive and Pete were responsible on their own for the phenomenal success of Spring Harvest. Rob White of BYFC was very involved too and so were hundreds of other leaders. But it remains true that Clive and Pete were responsible for the early vision.

14. Spring Harvest is so closely associated with the EA that it is often not realized that they are entirely separate organisations.

15. Interview with Clive Calver, op cit.

16. Pete Meadows, for example, wrote to me that there was very little overlap with the development of Spring Harvest and R1 and R2 (letter dated 25th September 1989).

17. Interview with Clive Calver. op.cit.

18. Though Clive Calver told me that people were asked to rate their favourite activity and the teaching came out top with 52 per cent, compared to worship which attracted 16 per cent. Ibid.

19. Clive Calver was able to give me a breakdown of the personnel from the 1989 Spring Harvest. A third present were Anglican, a third were Baptist, and the other third were made up of classic Pentecostalists, new churches, and other denominations. Ibid.

20. I saw many of them at Spring Harvest in 1988, and particularly remember sitting behind John and Christine Noble, who were waving a flag together like a couple at a political rally.

21. See chapter 6.

22. With Kevin Springer (London: Hodder & Stoughton,1985).
23. Though I believe the Renewal to be more fragmented than it was in the 1970s.
24. Though to remind readers, I am talking about the period before Cain and Toronto.
25. It would be unfair to say that Wimber encouraged more phenomena, but there does seem to be, in practice, more emphasis on miraculous ministry.
26. See David Pytches, *Some Say It Thundered* (London: Hodder & Stoughton, 1990).
27. Though I have seen his temper flare. Wimber also had a habit of falling out with colleagues over the years, which suggests that he liked to be in control. One Renewalist, formerly connected to Wimber, told me that 'John is like a cuddly teddy bear – but bears bite.'
28. For my own part, I have close friends of great theological sophistication who are very pro-Wimber, and so I do not feel inclined to dismiss him as yet another American Shamanite in Pentecostal clothing. However, as much as I liked the man, I did find his methodology hard to take and somewhat gnostic in flavour.
29. For Prince's part in the Restorationist story, see chapter 4.
30. Interestingly, I wrote this section in 1989, before the 1990s witnessed the fruit of this co-operation in terms of charismatic revival.
31. Many churches in the Baptist Union are in fact now charismatic; the same is true – though on a smaller scale – in the Brethren movement.
32. See Walker, 'Charismatic and Pentecostal Religion', ed. A. McGrath, **Blackwell Encyclopaedia of Contemporary** *Christian Thought* (Oxford: Blackwell, 1993) pp 110–14.
33. Ironically, I also think Toronto brought it to an end. It was so iconoclastic that it is difficult to see how the charismatics can move on together into the future.
34. Though Sunderland came into its own post-Toronto in 1995.
35 Strategic churches can also be producers themselves. Witness the success of Holy Trinity Brompton in the 1990s with its Alpha programme.
36. Too many entrepreneurs with their books, video and audio tapes for that to be possible.

Chapter 15 The Changing Character of R1

1. Letter to me from Terry Virgo, 1st October 1987.
2. Interview with Terry at Clarendon Villas, Hove, 16th June 1989.
3. Op.cit.
4. I consider the flag of Restorationism mainly now to be flown by Bryn and Terry – and perhaps Barney Coombs and Derek Brown.
5. See 'Tony Morton: Thinker and Theologian', in Brian Hewitt, *Doing a New Thing?* (London: Hodder & Stoughton, 1995).
6. These elders and their fellowship in a northern city asked not to be identified. Interview on 11th March 1989. I subsequently raised

some of these issues with Bryn Jones later in the year.

7. Gerald Coates and Pioneer would be another contender, but I shall later argue that Gerald is not really Restorationist any more.

8. This is an ad hominem remark anyway. Rodney Howard Browne, who makes Bryn Jones look as thin as a whippet, is hardly short of charisma.

9. The figure is not official, it comes from the northern elders, op. cit.

10. Information from elders in a northern city, ibid. However, I know of no churches that specifically left over this issue, although Bryn Jones did inform me that in the late 1980s, some churches had left the network. In particular, I know of fellowships in Barnsley, Bolton and Castleford, a portion of Dewsbury's fellowship, and a church on the east coast at Norwich.

11. From a letter to me by David Matthew on 5th October 1987.

12. Interview with Bryn Jones in the presence of Roger Day on 28th June 1989, Bradford.

13. David Matthew, op.cit.

14. Ibid. Norway does in fact have a number of strong churches in the Restorationist orbit.

15. In fact, Dales TV still exists under Julian Boden, its managing director, and is used for a number of purposes, ranging from providing editing suites to crewing packages.

16. 'Prophet Margins', *Time Out* (9th–16th December 1987) p 21. Tyler also, quite wrongly, imagined that Bradford's relocation to the Midlands was to set up something like Bakker's Heritage USA, the failed Christian theme park.

17. Bryn Jones, op. cit.

18. See D. McConnell's treatment of the Faith Movement in *The Promise of Health and Wealth* (London: Hodder & Stoughton, 1989), and Andrew Walker with Tom Smail and Nigel Wright, 'Revelation Knowledge and Knowledge of Revelation: the Faith Movement and the Question of Heresy', *Journal of Pentecostal Theology*, Vol. 5 (Sheffield Academic Press, 1994) pp 57–77.

19. In an interview with Tim Larsen, op. cit., he admitted that although he was not there personally, this story was well known and acknowledged in Covenant Ministries' circles.

20. Interview at Oxford, where I was teaching a summer school, with a marginal insider who went on to write a doctoral thesis on the house church movement (25th July 1989).

21. Roger Day, in his letter to David Wavre (16th February 1989), claims that in no way was the Bradford operation based on American experience as quoted in the 1988 edition, p 311. I accept what he says, but I did not mean that Bryn borrowed the structure from America (though he may have been influenced by his stay there) – rather I mean simply that the operation had the hallmarks of American south-west approaches. I have been a visiting professor in Dallas since 1987 and have first-hand experience of such structures in Texas and Oklahoma.

22. Northern elders, op. cit.

23. In 1987, an administrative officer at Bradford told me that the returns for Church House for that year were 7,700, including children.

24. I believe that there were supportive words of prophecy about the move to Nettle Hill, and certainly Bryn wanted to influence people in 'other parts of Great Britain outside of the North of England, South Wales, North Wales, the Midlands region.' According to Tim Larsen, the move to the Midlands was simply a question of its centrality (letter in June 1997, op. cit.).

25. See Rodney Clapp, 'Democracy as Heresy', in *Christianity Today* (20th February 1987) p19.

26. Barney Coombs, for example, but others were to attend seminars given by R. J. Rushdoony, its founder, and the popular economic spokesman, Gary North. Reconstructionism, it seems to me, is the kind of programme that could appeal to Restorationists who have given up on revival.

27. M. Scott, 'The Theology of the So-Called "New Church" Movement: An Analysis of the Eschatology.' Unpublished MTh thesis, Brunel University 1997, pp 48–54. This historical insight is reinforced by a more recent pro post-millennial document supporting the views of Bryn Jones, David Matthew, and Hugh Thompson. These views are refreshingly free of dogma. See David Matthew (ed.), 'The Return of Jesus. A Theology of Hope or a Hopeless Theology?' Covenant Ministries International, 1993.

28. Bryn's father was a leading member of the Welsh Communist Party.

29. Interview with Bryn Jones, 1989, op. cit.

30. For non-evangelical readers, this might not seem so radical, but within the evangelical camp there is a tendency to take Israel's side politically and also to assume that Jews have a special place in God's dispensation. Bryn's views on these issues demonstrates his independence of mind, which separates him totally from former 'Fort Lauderdale Five' leader Derek Prince, and even, less dramatically, from Terry Virgo and New Frontiers. It would be misleading, however, to think of Bradford and Nettle Hill as liberationist through and through. Neither the rhetoric of South American Catholic liberationists or feminist theologians tend to be heard.

31. Bryn prefers anti-militarism to the term pacifism, for he admitted that he might have to defend his wife if under attack (1989 interview, op. cit.).

32. I have been most impressed with the academic and pastoral seriousness of this organization. See AIDS and Your Response, the proceedings of the International Conference at Eskom, Midrand, South Africa (Institute of World Concerns, Nettle Hill, 1992).

33. Bryn Jones interview, op.cit.

34. According to Andrew Tyler, op. cit.

35. Though less so in the early 1990s and the later magazine, Restore.

36. When I was at Bradford in 1989, Bryn showed me a quotation that he liked from Abraham Lincoln which was in favour of a principled self-help programme.

37. Interview with Bryn at Bradford in 1989, op. cit.
38. However, such a criticism is not really about prosperity teaching per se, but about the built-in dangers of tithing.
39. There are, however, echoes of Copeland's and Oral Roberts's seed faith theology in Paul Scanlon's booklet, *Your Financial Prosperity* (Nettle Hill: CMI Publishing, 1995).
40. I am already on record as admitting that his lack of profile in the original edition of *Restoring the Kingdom* is a serious omission on my part. See the second edition, op. cit., p 329.
41. Interview with Terry Virgo at Clarendon Villas, Hove, 16th June 1989.
42. 'You Can Reign in Life', *Redemption*, January 1988.
43. In interview, Terry told me that local churches made up their own mind as to whether they joined the EA or not.
44. And in fact although I have a large file of alleged shepherding abuse said to have occurred in many house churches, I have scant material on New Frontiers.
45. As can be seen by his book *Restoration in the Church* (Eastbourne: Kingsway, 1985).
46. Interview in Spurgeon's College, 1989, op.cit.
47. Though the older Gerald Coates seems to be far more accepted than the younger one.
48. Nigel Wright, op. cit.
49. On 18th April 1989, for example, he told me that Arthur Wallis had written to him saying that he was encouraged by what I had written about New Frontiers in the second edition of this book. Terry said that he had been encouraged by the references too.
50. Conversation, ibid. Though while he said without protest – 'I understand what you are saying' – he did go on to say subsequently – 'It is almost as if our thrust would be a mission agency rather than a denomination.'
51. Ibid.
52. Ibid.
53. Ibid.
54. Ibid.
55. Interview with Nigel Wright, op.cit.
56. Terry, op.cit.
57. Ibid. Terry admitted that he did not really know exact numbers and thought that it might be better to count things in the future. Compare this with the Introduction, note 3.
58. Although this is not how Wimber used the phrase.
59. Terry, op.cit.
60. Ibid.
61. Ibid.
62. Although, as already stated, perhaps we could augment Restorationism with the churches of Derek Brown and Barney Coombs. If I had to hedge my bets, I would be tempted to add Tony Morton's churches to that list from the late 1990s onwards. Certainly, Graham Cooke left Pioneer to be the prophet under the

apostolic authority of Tony Morton (information from Revd Stephen Latham, who has interviewed both Cooke and Morton for his PhD at King's College, London). My notion that Restorationist sectarian formations may end up in the classical Pentecostal camp (see chapter 12) must be one of my more silly ideas. It has been my conviction, however, that it would be Bryn's and Terry Virgo's churches that would have the staying power as a distinctively Restorationist movement. I shared these thoughts with Bryn in 1989 as he drove me to the station through the rain.

Chapter 16 Drifting Apart and Breaking Away: Life in R2

1. Terry, 1989, op. cit. There was nothing judgmental nor triumphalist in Terry's remarks.
2. See chapter 3.
3. Information from Tony Morton in a letter to me on 7th November 1989.
4. Though to be frank, my estimate could be several thousand out in either direction.
5. Though their ministry might be called 'words of knowledge in song', they were a very professional couple. I visited them when I was in San Antonio in 1989 and found them very engaging.
6. Author of *Seeing Green: the Politics of Ecology Explained* (Oxford: Basil Blackwell, 1985).
7. This really quite weird charge was made against Gerald by S. Bartlett in a newsletter entitled, *Evangelisation 2000: Which Gospel?* (British Beacon, Exeter, Devon).
8. Indeed, that is how I came to be at Festival 86: to face up to my critics. I defended myself in front of some 600 or 700 people. It seemed as if I had more friends than enemies. I was certainly treated with the greatest of courtesy.
9. Interview at Harry, 4th August 1989.
10. I agree with David Hall's observation at Harry 89, that the book had no long-term effect at all.
11. All quotations in the rest of this section are taken from a recorded interview at Gerald's house.
12. Ibid.
13. Ibid.
14. Ibid.
15. Ibid.
16. Ibid.
17. Ibid.
18. Ibid.
19. Ibid.
20. Interview with David Tomlinson at Harry 89, 3rd August 1989.
21. Interview with Gerald at Clive House, 2nd October 1989.
22. Interview with Clive Calver at the Evangelical Alliance, 8th September 1989.
23. In the 1990s it might be thought that John went into semi-retirement with his move to the Leatherhead area, but Gerald Coates insists

that as senior adviser, he maintains considerable influence on Pioneer.

24. Interview with Steve Goddard at Harry 89, 4th August 1989.
25. This was Clive (of India's) House in Esher. Gerald never owned it outright but he and his family shared it for a while with Shelia Walsh and her former husband. Gerald moved to a modern and far more modest house in the 1990s.
26. Workshop has continued to operate since the demise of Team Work
27. I managed a good interview with Noel, but lost the transcribed tape en route to North America.
28. Interview with David Tomlinson at Harry 89, 4th August 1989. I have never published the interview in full, but it was clear to me then that mentally and spiritually, though not yet organizationally, David Tomlinson had already abandoned Restorationism.
29. Interview with David Hall, Harry 89, 4th August 1989.
30. I shared a seminar with Graham Cray on fundamentalism, and I also remember listening to a talk on Christian feminism by Elaine Storkey of Christian Impact.
31. See his book, *The Postevangelical* (London: Triangle, SPCK, 1995).
32. Gerald, op. cit.
33. (Eastbourne: Kingsway, 1986). Actually, the book was more a warning against biblical idolatry. The theme was strong and the thesis defendable, but a book of this kind demands a level of scholarship not suited to the popular paperback.
34. In *Pioneer* bulletin, (Volume 7, issue 2) considerable space is given to the restructuring and streamlining of Gerald's many activities. In order not to give undue space to Gerald, I have had to limit my coverage of Pioneer's activity. Perhaps mention should be mentioned of Tie Teams (Training In Evangelism). These short and long term training programmes is yet another example of an independent organization in partnership with, rather than under, Pioneer.
35. Interview with Clive Calver on 8th September 1989.
36. Roger Forster did not worry about denominationalism – in the sense that it frightened him – and despite his new church and Anabaptist leanings, he was eager to work with fellow Christians wherever they could be found.
37. Interview with Gerald Coates at Clive House, 2nd October 1989. Though by the 1990s, I think Gerald was quite happy with a looser and more interchangeable role of apostle/prophet.
38. See chapter 17, note 5.
39. Interview with Gerald at Clive House. op. cit.
40. Ibid.
41. I interviewed Linda Harding who came to see me in Teddington. She was very articulate and enthusiastic about her new role. Unfortunately, the tape was ruined, including the verbal information on the tape as to date and time of interview.
42. Now seen as a senior prophet in New Frontiers. Coincidentally, Rodney and I were old friends and colleagues back in my Pentecostal days in the early 1960s.

43. Gerald, op. cit.
44. 'The last think we want is to have all sorts of people who don't share our philosophy, who will then slow us down . . . We just can't afford to do that. So Roger Lynn and I want to keep it a new church theology while being broad in our churchmanship.' Ibid.
45. See David Neff and George K. Brushaber, 'The Remaking of English Evangelicalism', *Christianity Today* (5th February 1990).
46. Interview with Gerald at Clive House. op. cit.
47. Gerald Coates deals with this incident and many of the larger issues raised in this section in his autobiography, *An Intelligent Fire* (Eastbourne: Kingsway, 1991) pp 182–83.
48. Interview with Gerald, op. cit.
49. Ibid.
50. Ibid.
51. Although Gerald was anxious to tell me that he was fussy with whom he worked, and cited Morris Cerullo as one man with whom he would not share a platform. Interview in 1997, op. cit.

Conclusion The End of an Era
1. For details of the schism, see chapter 4.
2. In fact, Gerald is of the opinion that Arthur did try to persuade Bryn 'to stand with us at the Sheffield conference' – although he admits that while he heard this from 'fairly senior sources', he is not sure if that is what actually happened. From an interview with Gerald Coates at Clive House, 2nd October 1989.
3. I am grateful to Tony Morton for sending me a tape of Arthur's funeral. A fitting tribute to Arthur can be found (among others) in Insight, issue 4.
4. From an interview with Gerald at Clive House, op. cit.
5. Interview with Bryn Jones at Church House, Bradford, 28th June 1989.
6. Interview with Gerald Coates at Clive House, op. cit.
7. Not, of course, the end of Restorationism as a distinctive Christian enclave, and we certainly cannot say that 'new churches' – in all their diversity – have entered decline. Indeed, as this book goes to press, Gerald is at the centre of yet another 'revival' at Marsham Street in Westminster.
8. Interview with Gerald Coates, 5th February 1997.

INDEX

Aberdare, 252
Abinger Bible Week, 84
Adventism, 134, 141-142, 219, 228-229
Albury, 230-233, 240
All Soul's, 61, 68, 304
Alton, David, 366
Anabaptist(s), 144, 146, 213, 352,
Anarchic, 35, 62, 70, 72, 78, 86, 89, 120, 178, 286, 373
Andrews, Ian, 386
Anglican(s), 19, 27, 35-36, 54, 57-59, 62, 64, 94, 112, 131, 135, 207, 215, 217, 231, 233, 249-250, 255, 264, 266, 269, 274, 311-312, 356
Anti-denominationalism, 225, 247, 338, 359
Anti-intellectualism, 257
Anti-restorationist, 331, 334
Antichrist, 137, 140, 229-230, 343
Apocalypse, 396
Apostasy, 131, 139, 143-144, 156, 230, 232, 243, 395
Apostate, 72, 169, 225, 243, 277
Apostle(ship), 14, 22-23, 25, 40-41, 44, 46, 53, 56, 61, 64, 66-67, 71, 75-79, 81-82, 86, 90-91, 94-97, 99, 102, 108, 111, 114-116, 120-122, 132, 144, 147, 149, 151-158, 161, 164-166, 168-169, 171, 174-178, 179-183, 185, 187-188, 192, 194, 197-198, 200, 204, 207, 211, 224, 231-233, 237- 241, 252, 258, 251-252, 254-255, 274, 285-286, 289-291, 303, 318, 322, 324-325, 331-333, 336, 339, 341, 348, 351, 353, 356, 360-361, 369-370
Apostolate(s), 151, 158, 161, 181, 192, 238, 252, 254-255, 285, 382
Apostolic(s), 18, 21-22, 34, 37, 41-42, 55-56, 73, 76, 78, 81-82, 84, 91, 93, 96, 107, 111, 116, 144, 147, 151, 155-158, 161, 173-174, 176-177, 180-181, 187, 192, 194-195, 207, 218, 222, 225, 239, 241, 252, 254,
271-272, 274, 285, 291, 309, 319, 343-345, 357, 361, 369, 373, 375
Apostolic Church, 250-255, 263
see also Catholic Apostolic Church
Arminian(ism), 135, 236, 332, 352, 360
Armstrong, Rev, 231-232
Arnott, John, 20
Assemblies of God, 19, 36, 51, 52, 53, 75, 91, 107, 115, 133, 136, 175, 218, 230, 250, 253, 255, 256, 257, 258, 260, 261, 262, 263, 264, 266, 274, 285, 306, 313, 331, 334,
Augustine, 235
Austin Sparks, T., 63
Authoritarian(ism), 36, 49, 74, 89, 122, 125, 162, 187, 189-190, 246, 251, 253-254, 257, 260, 280-281, 309, 382
Authority, 24, 44, 59, 74, 78, 93, 98, 101, 107, 120, 140, 151-153, 155-165, 169, 175-180, 182-183, 185, 187, 190, 192, 197, 199, 206, 210, 217, 233, 239, 241, 252, 255, 259, 261, 271, 279, 281, 286-287, 289, 291-292, 294-295, 309, 318-319, 332, 345-346, 361, 369
Azusa Street Mission, 249

Baigent, John, 10
Bakker, Jimmy, 321, 328
Baptism(s), 43, 44, 52, 55, 59, 63, 133, 135-136, 140, 144, 146-147, 156, 189, 198, 219, 233, 238, 246-247, 249, 258, 273, 335, 375
Baptist Union, 10, 63, 135, 198, 264, 272, 274, 275, 331, 335, 336,
Baptists, 49, 52, 54, 111, 115, 131, 135, 193, 213, 217, 233, 274-275, 278, 283, 286, 314, 335, 369,
Baptized, 27, 43-44, 52-53, 61-62, 190, 259, 309, 339, 369
Barker, Prof Eileen, 284, 382
Barrat, T. B., 250
Barth, Karl, 332

Bartrop, Richard, 325
Basham, 93
Basingstoke Fellowships, 41, 56, 161, 188, 270, 288-289
Bassett, Michael, 328
Baxter, Ern, 83-85, 92-97, 99-101, 103, 107, 118, 157, 159, 163, 166, 191, 234, 258, 276, 321, 329, 389, 391-392
Bell, Stuart, 360, 368
Bennet, Dennis, 83
Berger, Peter, 227
Bethany Community, 266
Bethesda Chapel, 244
Bethshan Tabernacle, 194
Birchinall, Peter, 278-279, 281
Boddy, Alexander A., 250, 255
Bognor Bible Week, 334
Bonnke, Reinhard, 19
Booth, Dr Paul, 381
Boyes, John, 10
Bracknell Church, 335, 338-339
Bradford, 34, 37, 44, 46, 56, 72-74, 111-115, 118, 135, 174, 176, 195, 200, 206, 263-264, 266, 270, 318-321, 323-324, 326-327, 337
Branham, William, 20, 93
Brethren, 10, 39, 43, 47, 49, 51-56, 59, 61, 63-64, 72, 88-90, 104, 111, 135, 137, 144, 147, 157, 218, 223-225, 228-248, 251, 254, 264, 274, 282-283, 285, 304, 314, 378,
Brethrenism, 55, 133, 135, 144, 162, 224-225, 228, 231-232, 236, 238, 242, 245, 247, 258, 263-264, 285, 377
Brewster, Pastor, 260
Bridge, Donald, 317
Brighton Centre, 331, 334, 349
Brighton Restorationsts, 338
Broadbent, E. H. ,147, 149
Broadwater Fellowship, 23, 362
Brother Andrew, 275
Brow, Robert, 156
Brown, Derek, 306, 360, 368
Bruce, F. F. 247
Bulteel, 232
Burning Bush Assembly, 251
Butterworth, Nick, 91, 120-121,

125, 206

Cain, Paul, 20, 312
Calver, Clive, 13, 304-307, 309, 349, 359, 368
Calvinism, 160, 235, 332-333
Calvinist(ic), 135, 143, 236, 250, 332, 334, 397
Cambridge Seven, 256
Campolo, Tony, 308, 348, 353, 375
Canty, Pastor George, 275
Capel Bible Week, 66, 83-86, 92, 166, 330
Cardale, Mr, 233, 239
Carlyle, Thomas, 228
Cartwright, Rev Desmond, 10, 267
Catholic(ism), 7, 10, 34, 36, 47, 49, 51, 54, 57-59, 64, 67-68, 87-88, 94, 111, 123, 135, 143, 151, 158-160, 164, 181, 184, 188, 209, 213, 215, 218-219, 224-225, 228-229, 231-233, 235-243, 245-248, 251, 254, 264, 271, 273-274, 285, 289, 312, 314, 327, 349
Catholic Apostolic Church, 8, 10, 51, 53, 84, 158, 171, 175, 181, 218-219, 224-225, 228, 231-233, 235-245, 247-248, 251, 285
Catholicity, 238, 246, 251, 285
Cessationist, 14
Chalmers, Dr, 261
Chard, 53, 57, 67-68, 73, 136, 264
Charismata, 154, 285, 350
Charismatic(s), 13-14, 18-19, 21, 23, 26, 34, 39, 43-44, 49, 51-62, 64-65, 67-70, 75, 83, 90, 93-94, 106, 110-111, 115-116, 123, 132, 135-136, 138, 144, 151, 154-155, 158-159, 161, 188, 192-193, 198, 204-205, 212, 215, 223, 227, 233, 238, 247, 252-255, 259, 261, 263, 268-269, 272-273, 275-277, 281, 285, 303, 305, 307-317, 330-331, 334-337, 343, 349-350, 352, 354, 356-357, 360, 366, 371, 374-376, 379, 382
Charismatically (ordained), 40, 55, 78, 96, 102, 143, 149, 156
Christadelphians, 137, 219-220

Christology, 234-235, 240
Church-planting, 370
Clapp, Rodney, 367
Clarke, Denis, 54, 57, 64, 77-78, 330
Cliff, Norman, 10
Coates, Gerald, 9, 18-21, 23, 25, 34, 38, 42, 56, 61, 66-67, 70-71, 77, 84-85, 88, 90-91, 100, 102-107, 120-124, 126, 160, 166, 176, 180-181, 195, 205, 210, 270, 282, 290-292, 309-310, 312, 319, 332-333, 337, 341-345, 347-351, 354-355, 357-371, 375
Cobham Fellowship, 38, 61-62, 120-121, 200, 303, 375
Collier Row, 86, 120, 124-125
Congleton, Lord, 246
Congregationalism, 260-261
Congregationalists, 213, 304
Coombs, Barney, 25, 41, 56, 64, 77, 84, 360, 368
Coomes, David, 10
Copeland, Kenneth, 323, 328-329
Cornwall, 44, 46, 53, 73, 85
Cotton, Ian, 25
Cousen, Cecil, 53, 64
Covenant College, 325
Covenant Ministries, 9, 18, 24, 324, 325, 327, 328, 339,
Cox, Harvey, 25
Craik, 244
Culver, Vivien, 9, 356
Cuninghame, W. 229
Cuthbert, Nick, 313

Daniel, Gwyn, 325
Darby, John Nelson, 137, 230-235, 237, 243-246, 277
Darbyism, 162, 245
Darbyite(s), 235, 245
Davies, Ben, 338-339
Day, Roger, 9, 325
Denominationalism, 22, 51-52, 71, 78, 125, 130, 136, 148-149, 173-174, 212, 215-216, 224-227, 245, 247, 250, 324, 334, 338, 345
Divorcees, 201
Dixon, Dr Patrick, 358
Docklands Arena, 20

Drain, Wayne, 83, 122
Drummond, Henry, 231, 239
Duffy, Gareth, 325
Dunsford, Martyn, 9
Dye, Colin, 19

Ecclesiology, 22, 24, 40, 151, 171, 173, 177-178, 183, 212, 231, 237, 247, 252, 254, 257
Ecumenical, 24, 255, 263, 314
Ecumenism, 59, 72, 270, 283
Edwards, Gene, 282, 297
Elim, 10, 19, 36, 51-52, 84, 107, 115, 117, 133, 135-136, 175, 194, 218-219, 221, 230, 250, 253, 255-265, 266, 274-275, 285, 306, 313, 334
Elim Bible College, 84
Elim Pentecostal Alliance, 260,
Ellis, Roger, 360
Enlightenment, 221, 236
Eschatological(ly), 37-38, 40, 70, 75, 134, 137, 142, 168-169, 194, 228
Eschatology, 24, 75, 107, 133, 137-138, 141-142, 149, 230, 326, 377-378
Eucharist, 35, 58, 88, 238
Evangelical(s), 13, 17, 19, 24, 32, 36, 40, 45, 47, 54, 59, 68-69, 85, 88, 104, 110, 117, 121, 123, 131, 133-134, 137, 141, 163, 191-192, 201, 215, 218, 226, 229-231, 234-236, 238, 243, 246-247, 268, 274, 277, 284, 304-311, 313-314, 317, 320, 327, 330-333, 342, 349, 357, 360, 362-364, 368, 370
Evangelical Alliance, 11, 13, 47, 123, 304-306, 310-311, 331, 342, 363, 368-369,
Evangelical Free Baptists, 59, 274
Evangelicalism, 23, 45, 63, 130, 137, 144, 160, 219, 225, 232, 236, 246-247, 249, 268, 305, 332, 364, 371, 375
Evangelism, 18, 22, 47, 63, 77, 117, 179-181, 236, 287, 311, 317, 343, 346, 364, 378,
Evangelist(s), 40, 52-55, 68, 74, 77, 116, 153-154, 169, 174, 178-180, 239, 246, 250-251, 256, 258-262, 267, 275, 304, 328, 358, 376

Evangelistic, 18, 34, 73, 116-117, 124, 144, 179, 181, 198, 208, 254-258, 260, 262-264, 266, 305, 322, 324, 378
Exorcism, 28

Fairmile Court, 90, 103-104, 360
Fenwick, Peter, 9, 14, 42, 124, 126, 309, 312, 332, 342-343, 345, 355, 362
Fenwick, Rita, 9
Festival of Light, 67-69, 76
Fields, Derek, 354
Finney, C. G. 250
Flegg, Columba, 248
Forster, Roger, 10, 19, 47, 64, 305, 309, 312, 359-363, 365, 368
Forster, Faith, 309
Fort Lauderdale Five, 14, 83, 93, 95, 97, 101, 114, 165-166, 252, 271, 350
Fountain Trust, 57, 60-61, 255, 273, 309
Fundamentalism, 131, 340, 396, 406
Fundamentalist(s), 132, 134, 203, 219, 230, 352

Gee, Donald, 250, 253, 262, 267
Gilgan, Pete and Jess, 352
Gnostic, 235, 329
Goddard, Steve, 328-329, 344, 350
Gordon Square, 242
Graham, Billy, 117, 132, 144, 202, 314
Green, Rev Bernard, 10, 274-275, 282-283
Green, Lynn, 19, 359, 362,-263
Greening, 343
Greenwood, Harry, 63, 267
Grubb, Norman, 125
Gunton, Prof Colin, 235

Hagin, Kenneth, 323, 328-329
Hall, David, 280
Hall, Captain Percy, 233, 246
Harding, Linda, 361
Hare, Richard, 58
Harper, Michael, 10, 58, 60-61, 64, 85, 212, 255, 270, 273, 285, 298, 349

Harrison, Mrs Buddy, 323
Harry (Youth Festival), 352-355, 373-376
Hartill, Rosemary, 10, 283, 288
Henderson, Stewart and Carol, 352, 376
Hennessy, Val, 364
Henry's Revival, 43
Heresy, 45, 58, 148, 234-235, 243, 367
Heretic(s), 220, 235
Heretical, 220, 234, 240, 242, 277
Hermeneutics, 95, 134, 161
Hermits, 160
Heterodox, 243
Hewitt, Brian, 340, 367
Hierarchy, 68, 96, 132, 153, 166, 181-182, 222, 251, 345
Hill, Peter, 68
Hocken, Peter, 58
Holiness Assembly, 111
Hollenweger, Prof Walter, 93, 253, 256, 267
Holy Joe's, 352
Holy Trinity, Brompton, 315
Honor Oak Fellowship, 63
Honor Oak Baptist Church, 63
Hoole Baptsit Church, 275
Hopkins, Ivor, 325, 369
Houghton, John, 339
Howell, Brian, 9, 24, 332, 355
Howell, Irene, 9
Hutchings, Eric, 246

Ichthus Fellowship, 19, 33, 47, 64, 286, 305, 315, 359-360, 368,
Impey, Keith, 293, 295-296
Irving, Edward, 10, 137, 140, 217, 225, 228-240, 244, 248-249, 251, 258, 260-262, 276
Irvingism, 234, 236-239, 247, 258, 264, 377
Irvingite(s), 51, 231-232, 234, 236, 248,
Israelism, British, 260-261

Jeffreys, George, 52, 117, 175, 250, 256-262, 266-267, 334, 378
Jeffreys, Stephen, 175, 250, 256-

411

257, 259, 267, 378
Jesuit(s), 229-230
JIM (Jesus in Me), 18, 19
Jones, Keri, 44, 73, 90,174-175, 179, 195, 252, 276, 323, 325, 328, 368
Jones, Bob, 312,
Jones, Bryn, 7, 18, 20-21, 23-24, 28,32, 34, 37-38, 41, 44, 46, 48, 49, 53, 56, 67, 72-73, 75-76, 78, 81-82, 84-85, 87-89, 91, 92, 93, 94, 95, 96, 99, 100, 101, 102, 103, 104, 105, 106, 107, 112, 115, 116, 117, 118, 119, 120, 155, 170, 174,175, 176, 177, 178, 179, 180, 181,192, 194, 195, 200, 205, 207, 208, 209, 226, 252, 264, 271, 272, 275, 276, 278, 282, 289, 302, 303, 304, 310, 318, 320, 321, 323, 324, 325, 328, 329, 330, 331, 332, 333, 335, 337, 350, 368, 369, 370, 375, 380

Kansas City Prophets, 20, 312
Kelvin Grove Christian Fellowship, 24
Kendrick, Graham, 19, 308-309, 363
Keswick Conventions, 236, 249, 307
Kingston, Rodney, 9, 23, 179, 362
Kinnear, Angus, 162, 171

Lambert, Lance, 67
Landreth, Gordon, 304
Larsen, Timothy, 9, 381
Lawson, Dominique, 289
Lewis, Wyn, 19
Lillie, David, 21-23, 25, 52-53, 56-57, 64, 71, 84, 162, 252
Little Flock, 162,
Ling, Tony, 90, 175, 325
Liturgy, 42, 49, 57, 60, 62, 66, 82, 133, 194, 203, 218, 223, 238-241, 243, 363
Lloyd-Jones, Dr Martyn, 304, 307, 332
London Brothers, 67-68, 72-73, 78, 82-87, 89, 91, 95, 104, 106-107, 120-123
Long, Brian, 10

Longcroft, 44-45
Lucunza, Manuel de, 229-230
Los Angeles Revival, 250
Luther, Martin, 231
Luther King, Martin, Jnr. 327
Lyne, Peter, 9, 42, 64, 71, 76, 85, 87, 89, 91, 99, 106, 121, 123, 342-343, 345
Lytham fellowship, 10

MacLauchlan, John, 9, 42, 77, 79, 83, 90-91, 121-123, 142, 290-291, 293-297
Mansell, David, 9, 67, 71, 76-77, 86, 89-90, 92, 97, 99, 107, 111-112, 120, 122, 155, 179, 203, 278, 319, 325, 327, 330
Mamhead Park, 53
Martin, Prof David, 10, 217, 227
Marx, Karl, 328
Mason, Sue, 354
Mattersey Hall, 262
Matthew, David, 9, 119, 140, 146, 148-149, 179, 192, 205-206, 215, 225-226, 301, 322, 325, 345, 347, 371
McAlpine, Campbell, 53-57, 61, 64, 77, 87, 90, 330
McBain, Douglas, 10, 270
McCullogh, Ian, 64, 77, 121-122
McDowell, Josh, 374
McPherson, Amee Semple, 258-259, 334
Meadows, Pete, 307-308
Methodism, 213-214, 216-217, 220, 236, 271
Methodist(s) , 52, 63, 126, 135, 144, 213, 249, 264, 283
Methodology, 47, 95, 208, 311-312,
Millerites, 137, 219
Modernism, 58, 220, 343
Modernity, 23, 309, 340
Mohabir, Philip, 9, 73, 309, 342, 345-346, 351, 353, 355
Montanist(s), 143, 146
Moonies, 17, 192, 381-382
Mormons, 118, 137, 219
Morton, Tony, 9, 21, 37, 41, 81, 90, 155, 175-176, 195, 205, 264, 278, 282, 318-319, 337, 342, 345, 368-369

Moules, Len, 352
Movement(s), 17, 20, 29, 33-36, 38-39, 41, 43-44, 46, 48, 51, 63, 67, 83, 89, 94, 108, 110, 126, 129, 133, 137, 144, 146, 173, 175, 194, 210, 212-213, 218, 220, 223-226, 228, 232-233, 236, 239, 242, 247, 249, 251-252, 264, 285, 305-306, 312-313, 326, 377, 381-382
Mullen, Rev Peter, 273, 284
Müller, 244
Mumford, Bob, 14, 97-98, 100, 161
Mystic of Maesteg, 259

Neo-brethren, 61
Neo-fascist, 260
Neo-pentecostal(s), 49, 235, 258, 271, 284
Neo-pentecostalism, 51, 57, 123, 133, 264
Nettle Hill, 320-321, 325-326, 338
Newbigin, Lesslie, 332
New Covenant Church, 46
Newton, Benjamin, 231-235, 243-244, 246
Nicholson, Richard, 351
Niebuhr, H. Richard, 216
Noble, Christine, 190, 309, 349
Noble, John, 9, 14, 34, 42, 60-61, 66-67, 70-72, 76-77, 81-82, 84, 88-89, 91, 96-97, 99-104, 106, 108, 118, 120-126, 146, 168, 176, 179-180, 190-191, 199, 205, 211, 215, 225, 238, 252, 270, 277, 282, 309, 313, 319, 341, 343, 345, 348-350, 360-361, 375
Norris Groves, Anthony, 246
North, Pastor G. W. (Wally), 33, 42-46, 56, 64, 67, 118, 264

Okehampton, 53
Orthodox, 47, 49, 54, 143, 151, 215, 238, 240, 242-243, 285, 289, 376
Ortiz, Juan Carlos, 14, 69, 83, 85, 93, 252
Osborn, Lawrence, 381
Owen, Harold, 84

Paganism, 229, 344

Palau, Luis, 302, 309
Paris, Peter, 112, 118, 124, 276
Parkyns, Edgar, 53
Parr, Nelson, J. 256, 261
Paternalism, 182, 185, 192, 254, 268, 288, 331, 337, 381
Pendine summer camp, 74
Pentecostal(s), 19-20, 34, 36, 40, 43-46, 49, 51-59, 61, 65, 69, 72, 74-75, 83, 85, 93-94, 95, 97, 105-106, 111, 115-117, 131, 133-138, 142, 144, 146-147, 154, 156, 160, 162, 193-194, 198, 202-203, 207, 210, 218-219, 222-223, 226, 232-235, 242, 249-253, 255-257, 259-264, 267-268, 270, 273, 283-284, 286, 306-307, 312-313, 317, 334, 349, 371, 378
Pentecostalism, 7, 43, 45, 47, 51, 54, 58-60, 62-63, 70, 75, 78, 85-86, 130, 133-136, 138, 166, 168, 175, 219, 225-226, 234-238, 240, 247-251, 253, 255-259, 261-264, 266-267, 273, 285, 310, 377
Perrins, Graham, 42, 53, 64, 71, 76-77, 79, 81-83, 87, 90-91, 97, 99-100, 102, 106-107, 121-123, 138, 142, 291, 342, 360
Phillips, E. J. 257
Pluralism, 26, 309
Plurality, 13, 279
Polhill, Cecil, 256
Porritt, Johnny, 343-344
Post-millennial, 24, 141, 326
Postevangelical, 356
Postmodernity, 13
Powerscourt Conferences, 230-233, 243
Powerscourt, Lady, 232
Presbyterian(s), 135, 151, 213, 231, 238, 257
Presbyterianism, 231, 237, 240
Presbytery, 152, 234, 276
Prince, Derek, 14, 93, 166, 171, 313
Prophecy, 53, 62, 70, 75-77, 79, 90, 97, 122-123, 142, 165, 178-179, 204, 208, 229, 234, 239-240, 251-253, 261, 293, 338, 360, 362
Prophesy, 76, 178-179, 190, 323
Prophet(s), 20, 40, 76, 77, 79, 81,

413

91, 116, 121, 142, 152-156, 166, 169, 174, 178-179, 181-182, 188, 220, 224, 234, 239, 251-252, 254, 285, 287, 290-291, 294, 312, 322, 332, 340, 345, 360, 370, 381

Prophetic, 18, 55, 67, 72, 75-76, 79, 81, 90, 101, 138, 142-143, 147-148, 178-179, 229-230, 240, 252, 254, 293, 325, 343, 347, 351, 360-361, 370

Protestant(s), 34, 58, 83, 94, 111, 131-132, 143-144, 159, 164, 228-229, 235, 240, 283, 289, 303, 314

Protestantism, 133-134, 144, 151, 237

Puritan(s), 57, 69, 160, 276, 332

Puritanism, 69, 88, 106, 144, 160

Purse, Sidney, 43

Pusey, Edward, 240

Pusey, Mike, 84

Pytches, David, 311

Quaker movement, 213, 218-219, 237, 334

Quicke, Rev Stephen, 10

Race, John & Liz, 277-281

Reconstructionism, 326, 361

Reed, Alec, 359

Reformation, 58, 143-144, 283

Reformism, 270

Renewalism, 75, 85, 133

Renewalist(s), 47, 59-60, 84, 135, 138, 269-273, 284, 312-314, 332, 371

Restorationism, 7, 10, 13-14, 18-25, 38-43, 46-49, 51-52 56-57, 62, 66, 71-72, 79, 81, 83-84, 87, 94-95, 100, 103, 110-111, 115-116, 118, 123, 126-127, 129-144, 146-149, 151-174, 177-183, 185, 188-189, 191-194, 198-199, 203-205, 208-212, 215, 217, 220-221, 223-228, 236-240, 243, 247, 249, 251-255, 257-259, 261-264, 266-273, 276-277, 279, 281-286, 288, 291, 297, 301-315, 317-321, 323-326, 330-332, 334-339, 341, 343-344, 346-347, 349-350, 352-356, 358-361, 366-371, 373-377, 379-382

Revival(s), 20-21, 43, 52, 58, 69, 133, 136, 138, 147, 194, 213, 218, 226-227, 242, 250, 255, 258, 260, 263, 304, 307, 310, 312-313, 368, 371, 378

Revivalism, 57, 85, 213, 253, 263, 266

Revivalist, 17, 136, 226, 366, 374

Richard, Sir Cliff, 366

Richards, Noel, 358

Riddleston College, 114, 323, 328, 380

Roberts, Evan, 250

Robertson, Pat, 358

Robson, Brenda, 361

Rogers, Phil, 339

Romford Baptist Church, 14, 67, 86, 120, 199, 277-279, 281, 349

Rotherham, Ted, 9, 191, 290-291, 295, 297

Rowden, Harold, 244, 248

Russell, Dr David, 10, 274

Sacramentalism, 156, 238

St Thomas Crookes, 315

Schmitt, Charles, 83

Schuller, Robert, 14

Scotland, Alan, 325

Seventh Day Adventists, 137

Shepton Mallet, 278

Sider, Ron, 348, 353, 355

Simms, Dick, 9

Simpson, Charles, 14, 93

Singleton, John, 278-281

Smail, Tom, 10, 58, 285

Smith, Danny, 358

Smith, Don, 339

Smith, Brian, 277-280, 282

Smith-Cameron, Canon Ivor, 34-35, 211

Smith, Maurice, 10, 61-64, 66-68, 70-71, 77, 89, 91, 97-100, 102, 104, 118, 124-125, 161, 179, 191, 206, 282, 286, 294

South Chard, 42-44, 46, 53, 58, 63, 67- 68, 136, 264

South Lee Baptist, 335, 339

South Lee Christian Centre, 355

Spurgeon's College, 17, 331

Spurgeon, C. H. 332

Stanton, Noel, 368

Stardust, Alvin, 357
Stoneleigh Bible Week, 18
Stott, Rev Dr John, 304, 332
Strachan, Dr Gordon, 10
Stunt, Timothy, 232
Suenens, Cardinal, 58
Sullivan, Emmanuel, 58
Sunderland Christian Fellowship, 315
Sussex Downs Week, 116
Swaggert, 321
Swindoll, Orvil, 83, 112

Tarleton, George, 10, 66-67, 77-78, 84, 86, 89-91,102, 108, 121-122, 125, 179, 182, 187-188, 201, 207, 210, 286, 288, 297
Taylor dynasty, 245
Tempest, Ron, 325
Theocracy, 132, 151, 157, 168, 173, 182, 281
Thompson, Hugh, 56, 64, 71, 76, 89-90, 112, 179
Thurman, Joyce, 9, 45-46, 86, 104, 109, 188, 298
Tinder, Donald, 242
Tomlinson, David, 9, 14, 22-23, 34, 38, 42, 46, 90, 95, 99, 101, 103, 111-112, 118-119, 123-124, 126, 142, 165, 171, 175-176, 179-180, 186-187, 191, 200-201, 203-204, 227, 269-270, 282, 303, 309, 312, 318-319, 341-346, 348-356, 360-361, 366, 373-375
Tomlinson, Pat, 9, 352, 356
Toronto Blessing, 14, 20, 313-315
Torrance, Prof Thomas, 235, 332
Tosini, Joe, 369
Totalitarian, 187, 192, 221-222
Tractarian(ism), 238, 240
Trinitarian, 136, 231, 233
Troeltsch, 214, 216, 218
Trout, Edgar, 63-64, 330
Trudinger, Ron, 189, 279-280
Turner's Hall, 67, 179
Tyler, Andrew 323, 340, 402-403

Universalist, 214, 216-217, 252
Urquhart, Colin, 58, 138, 242, 266, 313

Vedder, Goos, 9, 275-277, 335
Vincent, Alan, 112
Vincent, Eileen, 109, 126, 164, 196
Vineyard, churches, 20, 311, 334
Virgo, Terry, 9, 18-21, 23-24, 26, 34, 37, 41, 64, 67, 71, 85, 90, 99, 111-113, 122, 135, 158, 171, 175-176, 179, 188, 195, 205, 207, 237, 264, 272, 282, 306, 309-311, 318-320, 330-341, 350, 353, 360, 362, 366, 368

Wagner, Peter, 310
Walker, Andrew, 11, 26, 227, 248, 377, 381
Walker, Rev Tom, 269-270, 273
Wallis, Arthur, 9, 14, 20-21, 49, 52-59, 61-62, 64-65, 72-73, 75-76, 78, 81, 84-90, 92, 96-98, 100, 102-110, 112, 120, 130, 138, 142, 148-149, 158, 166, 171, 179-180, 185, 226, 239, 252, 271-272, 276, 278, 330, 347, 349, 360-361, 368, 370, 372, 377-378,
Wallis, Jim, 353
Wallis, Capt Reginald, 52
Walsh, Sheila, 357-358
Watchman Nee, 10, 61, 63, 144, 162, 177, 235
Watson, David, 58, 311
Weber, Max, 214, 216-217, 224, 261
Welsh Bible Week, 116, 174, 203, 208, 323
Welsh Revival, 242, 250, 255, 313
Wesley, Charles, 143
Wesley, John, 44
Wesleyan(s), 146, 250
White, Richard, 9
Wigglesworth, Smith, 52, 256, 259
Williams, D. P. 175, 250, 251, 252
Williams, W. J. 175, 251
Wilson, Dr Bryan, 10, 47, 219-221, 224-225, 227, 236, 245, 259-261, 267
Wimber, John, 15, 19-20, 205, 273, 310-313, 317, 333-334, 337, 353, 355, 366
Wittgenstein, Ludwig, 129
Women, 47, 89, 98, 124, 152, 161, 184, 188-190, 200, 287, 303, 336, 343, 354, 361-362

Woodfalls Brothers, 244
Worship, 35, 69, 70, 74-75, 85, 114,
120, 148, 168, 182, 202, 203, 222,
277, 280, 309, 371
Wright, Dr Nigel, 10, 17, 18, 21,
333, 335,-336, 356
Wright, Norman, 278